CANADA

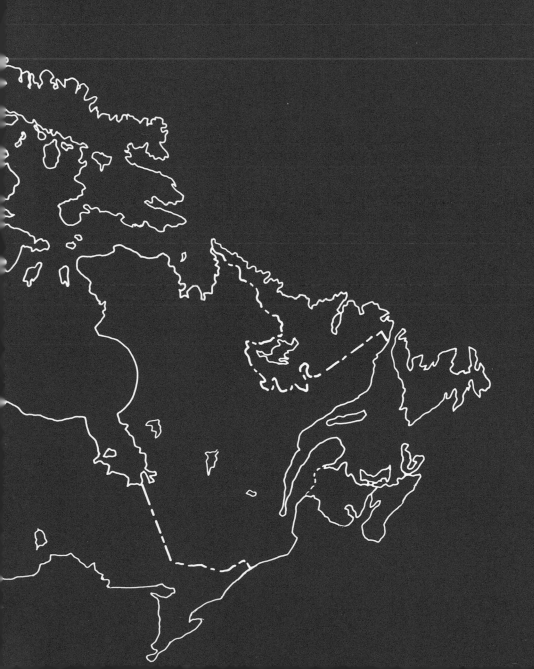

Contemporary Canadian

Theatre

T·H·E·A·T·R·E

NEW WORLD VISIONS

D avid Ferry, Martha Henry, Donna Goodhand and Susan Wright in the 1985 National Arts Centre-CentreStage co-production of John Murrell's *New World*, directed by Robin Phillips. Photo: Robert C. Ragsdale.

Contemporary Canadian

THEATRE

NEW WORLD VISIONS

A Collection of Essays
prepared by
The Canadian Theatre Critics Association/
Association des Critiques de Théâtre du Canada.

ANTON WAGNER, EDITOR

Simon & Pierre
Toronto, Canada

We would like to express our gratitude to The Canada Council and the Ontario Arts Council for their support.

Marian M. Wilson, Publisher

ISBN 0-88924-152-X

1 2 3 4 5 • 9 8 7 6 5

Canadian Cataloguing in Publication Data

Main entry under title:
Contemporary Canadian theatre: new world visions

Bibliography: p.
Includes index.
ISBN 0-88924-152-X

1. Theater — Canada — Addresses, essays, lectures. 2. Performing arts — Canada – dresses, essays, lectures. 3. Performing arts — Government policy — Canada — Addr essays, lectures.
I. Wagner, Anton, 1949-

PN2304.C66   1985   792'.0971   C85-098634-6

General Editor: Marian M. Wilson
Copy Editor: Jean Paton
Indexer: Sarah Robertson and Christopher Redmond
Typesetting & Design: Cundari Group Ltd.
Printer: Imprimerie Gagné Ltée
Printed and Bound in Canada

Order From
Simon & Pierre Publishing Company Limited
P.O. Box 280 Adelaide Street Postal Station
Toronto, Ontario, Canada M5C 2J4

Canadian Theatre Critics Association/Association des critiques de théâtre du Canada

The Canadian Theatre Critics Association/Association des critiques de théâtre du Canada was founded in 1980 with the assistance of the Toronto Drama Bench. Under its founding Chairman Herbert Whittaker and President Jeniva Berger, the Association has attracted a national membership of more than sixty critics writing for the print and electronic media across the country.

The objectives of the Association are to promote excellence in theatre criticism, to improve training opportunities and working conditions for critics, to disseminate information on theatre at a national level, and to promote the development and awareness of Canadian theatre nationally and internationally.

The Association has organized annual conferences in Toronto, Quebec City and Montreal.

Editorial Advisory Committee
Herbert Whittaker, Jeniva Berger, Don Rubin,
Mira Friedlander, Renate Usmiani

Publication of *Contemporary Canadian Theatre: New World Visions* was made possible through the generous financial support from the Ontario Ministry of Citizenship and Culture, the Honorable Susan Fish, Minister, and the Samuel and Saidye Bronfman Family Foundation/Fondation de la Famille Samuel et Saidye Bronfman, Montreal.

Contents

PART III The Electronic Media

PART IV The Canadian Performing Arts Mosaic

PART V The Emergence of the Theatre Professional

APPENDICES

Illustrations

Illustrations

CANADIAN
Illustrated News

ol. XII.—No. 23.   MONTREAL, SATURDAY, DECEMBER 4, 1875.   } SINGLE COPIES, TEN CENT } $4 PER YEAR IN ADVANC

The opening of Montreal's 2,000-seat Academy of Music on November 15, 1875 starring E.A. McDowell and Fanny Reeves in Lester Wallack's drama *Rosedale*.

MONTREAL: INTERIOR VIEW OF THE NEW ACADEMY OF MUSIC

Contemporary Canadian Theatre: New World Visions

This collection of essays on contemporary Canadian theatre was prepared for the XXIst World Congress of the International Theatre Institute held in Montreal and Toronto June 1-8, 1985. In order to introduce foreign theatre artists to the performing arts in Canada, the Canadian Theatre Critics Association/Association des critiques de théâtre du Canada, one of the national member organizations of the Canadian Centre of the ITI,[1] initiated a detailed assessment of theatre, playwriting, opera and dance in Canada since the Second World War. Such a comprehensive examination of the unprecedented growth of the performing arts in this country would also provide an opportunity for Canadian theatre artists and their public to take pride in the accomplishments of their profession, as well as recognize past achievements and present challenges facing the arts in Canada.

Since the dissolution of the Canadian Theatre Centre (which also acted as the Canadian national ITI Centre) in 1972, the International Theatre Institute has not had a high public profile in this country.[2] Yet Canada's connection with the ITI can be traced to the United Nations Charter, established in San Francisco in the spring of 1945, whose Article 55 called on signatory countries to promote "international cultural and educational cooperation." Vincent Massey headed the Canadian delegation to the November 1945 conference in London at which representatives from forty-four countries approved the charter for an United Nations Educational, Scientific and Cultural Organization.

At the first UNESCO conference, Paris, November 20–December 10, 1946, Canada was officially represented by the director and playwright Herman Voaden, President of the Canadian Arts Council (the forerunner of the Canadian Conference of the Arts), and the sculptor Elizabeth Wyn Wood, chairman of the CAC's Foreign Relations Committee.[3] Voaden and Wood were active participants in the deliberations of the UNESCO Subcommission on Arts and Letters and in discussions on the creation of an International Theatre Institute.[4]

The purpose of the International Theatre Institute, as stated in its founding charter, is "to promote international exchange of knowledge and practice in theatre arts." The ITI would attempt to implement this objective through the international exchange of literary and artistic leaders, theatre productions and exhibits; the translation of classic authors and modern works and the circulation of books, musical scores and playscripts (while at the same time improving copyright protection); by promoting closer contact between theatre and education; improving the quality of theatre for young people and amateur theatre; by diffusing technical information on developments in the visual arts for the stage; establishing an Information Service on all matters concerning international theatre; and by promoting international understanding "through its obvious ability to forge cultural, educational and technical (professional) links between the peoples and artists of all nations."[5]

From its inception, the ITI attracted the support of leading literary and artistic figures. The Subcommission on Arts and Letters at UNESCO's first General Conference in 1946 included such distinguished writers and dramatists as François Mauriac, J.B. Priestley, and Archibald MacLeish. An international committee of theatre experts, chaired by Priestley in Paris in June of 1947 to adopt the charter of the ITI and plan its future work, included Jean-Louis Barrault, Tyrone Guthrie and Lillian Hellman. Priestley became the ITI's founding chairman.

The Canadian Opera Company's 1983 production of Monteverdi's *The Coronation of Poppea,* directed by Lotfi Mansouri, set and costume design by Ita Maximowna. Photo: Robert C. Ragsdale.

In Canada, too, leading theatre artists supported the establishment of the International Theatre Institute and the creation of a Canadian national ITI Centre. Jean Gascon represented Canada as an observer at the first ITI Congress in Prague, June 28-July 3, 1948. The attempt to create a Canadian ITI Centre from 1948 to 1950 involved such leading theatre figures as Andrew Allan, supervisor of drama for the CBC; Earle Grey, director of the Earle Grey Players and President of the Toronto Branch, Association of Canadian Radio Artists (then the only national organization of professional theatre artists in Canada); Mavor Moore, production manager of the New Play Society; Ernest Rawley, manager of the Royal Alexandra Theatre; Father Emile Legault, director of Les Compagnons de Saint-Laurent in Montreal; and Park Jamieson and Charles Rittenhouse of the Dominion Drama Festival.

At the second ITI Congress in Zurich June 27-July 2, 1949, Father Legault and Guy Beaulne represented Canada as observers. Summarizing the leading issues of international concern addressed during the Congress, Beaulne reported that "it seems the general problem is that of theatre architecture. Nearly all countries lack suitable houses for theatrical productions or, at least, lack enough of them to stimulate a popular theatre and to permit young and new authors to experiment [with] new formulae."[6]

Though Canada had escaped the physical destruction caused by World War II, theatre across the country faced a much more difficult struggle for survival than in Europe. Already in the 1930s, the Depression brought to an end the numerous tours by American, British and French companies which had provided much of Canada with most of its professional theatre for half a century. Theatre buildings fell into disuse or were converted into movie houses by companies like Famous Players.[7] While the Little Theatre movement of the 1920s and the Dominion Drama Festival of the 1930s had begun to train Canadians in the technical aspects of theatre production and playwriting, these theatre movements lacked sufficient time and resources to develop fully into a popular indigenous professional theatre. Such an evolution from amateur to professional status did not occur until after World War II.

Canada had, of course, a long history of indigenous playwriting and amateur and professional stage production before the 1920s and 1930s. The scope of this dramatic activity over the past three and a half centuries has been analyzed in detail in a number of theatre history studies.[8] Canadian theatre historians have not yet reached a firm consensus, however, at what period theatrical activity began to coalesce into a genuinely creative indigenous *tradition* of theatre production and dramatic writing.[9] The beginnings of such a tradition can be seen in English Canada in the 1920s and 1930s. Many theatre historians date such a comparable transformation in French Canada to Gratien Gélinas' work in the 1940s.

Artistic Obstacles

In the 1980s, the obstacles confronting Canadian theatre professionals still parallel those facing artists since the settlement of the country beginning in the 1600s. Prominent among these is Canada's immense 5,187 kilometer-wide landmass (the second largest continent after the Soviet Union) in which a relatively sparse population of 25 million is concentrated in two dozen large urban centres. In terms of audience support, wide-spread acceptance and the popularization of cultural activity among the general public has only occurred over the last two decades. Until the 1960s, federal, provincial and civic governments similarly were often only reluctant supporters of the arts.

Faced with these obstacles, as Jack Gray observes in his analysis of government policy and the performing arts, "the essential problem to be tackled by any federal cultural policy in Canada is how to make it possible for Canadians to create, distribute, use and enjoy Canadian materials of all kinds." The thirty-four essays which follow attempt to analyze the cultural environment in which Canadians have created theatre, drama, opera and dance in various regions of the country and how their art has been disseminated to the public.

The six essays in "Government and Cultural Expression" focus on the primary cultural institutions and organizations creating and distributing theatre and other artistic forms of expression to the Canadian public. In his essay, Jack Gray concludes that federal government policy has been characterized by a general *absence* of a coherently articulated and implemented philosophy towards the arts. One of the few consistent federal government policies has been the support of Canada's large regional theatres, through subsidies from the Canada Council, analyzed by Mark Czarnecki.

While large-scale government funding of regional theatres has undoubtedly built audiences and established the economic basis of the profession, the attempt to create a truly national theatre and drama through the regionals has so far had limited success. Creative indigenous theatrical and dramatic activity did burst into life in the "alternate" theatre movement, beginning in Quebec and English Canada in the mid and late-1960s, described by Renate Usmiani. The most important development of that movement, the emergence and public recognition of the Canadian playwright, is discussed in Paul Lefebvre's and Robert Wallace's essays on playwriting in French and English Canada. Brian Arnott's survey of performing arts buildings concludes this initial overview of the interaction between government funding, the artist, and his audience.

Ten essays in "Theatre and Drama Across Canada" provide the historical background to current theatre activity and note the most significant achievements in play production and dramatic writing on a provincial level. The Stratford and Shaw Festivals, respectively the largest and seventh-largest of all performing arts organizations in Canada, are discussed in detail.

Three essays in "The Electronic Media" analyze the relationship between radio and television drama and indigenous dramatic writing and stage production. Radio played a particularly vital role in the 1930s and 1940s through its dissemination and popularization of Canadian cultural expression. By providing extensive work opportunities for actors, playwrights, directors and technicians, radio created Canada's first national "theatre on the air" in the 1940s. Through their programming mixture of classic, contemporary international and indigenous dramatic writing, radio and television in fact played a cultural function similar to that of the regional theatres which emerged in the late 1950s and 1960s.

Following these discussions of what kind of work is being produced by theatre artists, and how this work is disseminated to audiences on stage and in the electronic media, the eight essays in "The Canadian Performing Arts Mosaic" examine further the wide creative variety of the performing arts in Canada. Richard Courtney analyzes our first genuinely indigenous form of theatre in his discussion of native Indian and Eskimo ritual drama. Only a leap of the imagination is required to move from Indian and Inuit rituals and ceremonies to dance in Canada, as described by Jillian Officer. The world view expressed by classical and modern dancers is no longer a religious one, though many choreographers of modern dance do rely on ritualistic forms.

Because of high production costs, Canadian opera and musical theatre have not grown as rapidly as dance since the Second World War, though their achievements, as William Littler points out in his essay, have also been noteworthy. In contrast, because of substantial government subsidies, quality theatre for the young has proliferated across the country since the 1970s. Critical recognition has been slower to follow, though a separate annual Chalmers Children's Play Award, administered by the Ontario Arts Council, was established in 1982 to encourage original dramatic writing for young audiences. (The 1984 first-prize winner was Colin Thomas' *One Thousand Cranes,* produced by Vancouver's Green Thumb Theatre.) Yet both Dennis Foon and Hélène Beauchamp, in their surveys of theatre for the young in English Canada and Quebec, still lament a general critical neglect of "our distinctively invisible genre" and of "cet autre théâtre."

"That other theatre" also aptly describes the largely amateur multicultural and community theatre movements and theatre and drama in education summarized by Jeniva Berger, Mira Friedlander and Wayne Fairhead, respectively. Like theatre for the young, these companies and theatre animateurs annually reach audiences numbering in the hundreds of thousands, yet receive only limited recognition by critics and the professional theatre community.

The steadily increasing exposure to live theatre from childhood on has led many young Canadians into a great variety of university theatre programs, theatre schools and performance studios, as Don Rubin describes in his article on theatre training. The seven essays of this concluding section, "The Emergence of the Theatre Professional," point out the still precarious financial status of the theatre profession. R.H. Thomson, Diane Cotnoir, Ray Conlogue and Tom Doherty analyze the strengths and weaknesses of acting, directing and theatre design in Canada. Discussion, by Herbert Whittaker and Jean-Marc Larrue, of the objectives of the Canadian Theatre Critics Association, theatre journals, and the encouragement of artistic excellence points to the important role of theatre criticism in the development of contemporary professional Canadian theatre.

Artistic Self-Creation

R.H. Thomson's conviction that acting constitutes "an expression of your own people" and that "making it" in Canada means not primarily reaping financial rewards, but actually helping to "make the culture," points to the subtitle of this collection, "New World Visions."

For despite its several centuries-long history, Canada is still a nation in the process of social and artistic self-creation. As late as 1929, the writer, painter and critic Bertram Brooker appealed to Canadians to shake off their colonial mentality and to embark on a journey of national and imaginative self-discovery. In his introduction to the *Yearbook of the Arts in Canada 1928-1929,* Brooker called on his fellow countrymen to "awake and *see* this country as ours instead of merely calling it ours....This is *our* homeland, and some of us can see it so with *our* eyes and not with the eyes we brought across the Atlantic, still hazy with Scottish mists and rose-tinted by English blossoms."[10]

A year later, in his introduction to *Six Canadian Plays,* Herman Voaden similarly called for "a new theatre art and drama here that will be an effective revelation of our own vision and character as a people....the vision and beauty of a new people in a new land."[11] Over the last four decades, several million immigrants from all corners of the globe have contributed not only their varied cultural backgrounds but also their own vision and belief in what is no longer perceived as an American but as a distinct Canadian "dream." For new and old Canadians alike, Canada is no longer a cultural backwater, a second-choice economic limbo to be endured while awaiting the greater economic haven of the United States.

The increased economic prosperity of the country since World War II has enabled a growing number of Canadians to participate actively in cultural self-expression and self-discovery. Fear of, and the struggle against, an indomitable, hostile physical environment has been transformed into a greater appreciation of the beauty of nature and a celebration of "place."[12]

This process of collective self-discovery has also been an interior discovery of self in what the poet and playwright James Reaney has referred to as a frequently unchartered "iconography of the imagination." For the past two decades, theatre and drama have played as important a role in the creation of a Canadian self-perception and identity as the novel and poetry. The essays which follow trace the efforts of our theatre artists to create a distinctive Canadian dramatic speech, characters, themes and a unifying historical-mythic background in place of the former European and American literary forms and dramatic styles which dominated our stages and our playwrights' consciousness.

This liberation of our stages and dramatic imaginations, significantly assisted by government subsidies to performing organizations and individual artists, has resulted in the development of our own production styles and literary dramatic forms, as well as a rediscovery of the inherent values of the classics. No longer perceived as the *only* valid artistic representation of a recognized international culture, classics are appreciated, as in Jean-Pierre Ronfard's experimental directorial work, Michel Garneau's adaptation of *Macbeth* and Toronto Free Theatre's popular 1985 success, *The Changeling,* for their challenges in dramatic form and their poetic content. Thus audiences and playwrights alike are discovering similar themes in a great variety of dramatic styles. Human passion, the descent into crime, and the power of evil were not only effectively dramatized in Middleton and Rowley's 1622 *The Changeling* but in two other 1984-85 Toronto box office hits: the award-winning comedy *Criminals in Love* by George Walker at Factory Theatre and Richard Rose's expressionist *Mein,* produced by the Necessary Angel Theatre Company at Theatre Passe Muraille and Toronto Free Theatre.

Government Retrenchment

It is ironic that just as the performing arts in Canada are reaching a new level of maturity, and a vitality and sense of excitement not seen since the early 1970s, government cutbacks in the arts are threatening the very existence of what has been achieved culturally over the past generation. In a June 21, 1944 "March on Ottawa," artists appeared before a committee of the House of Commons to lobby for government assistance to the arts since "millions of persons living in Canada have never seen an original work of art, nor attended a symphony concert or a professionally produced play. Millions have opportunities neither for realizing their own talents nor for achievement in post-educational fields."[13] In 1985 artists again gathered in cities across the country, culminating in another "The Arts Go to Ottawa" rally on March 20, to protest cuts of over $100 million in federal government expenditures for the arts. (Presumably half of this amount has been allocated for the $50 million required to restore distinctive navy, army and air force uniforms for Canada's Armed Forces, a Conservative government election promise.)

The fact that artists today have greater political influence than ever before is a direct result of the substantial increase in audiences over the past decade. A public survey commissioned by the Ontario government in 1983 concluded that "the attendance base for the performing arts has broadened since 1974, with a significantly higher proportion of Ontarians now attending live plays/musicals in the theatre (55% versus 42%), dance performances (23% versus 13%) and concerts of classical music (33% versus 26%)."[14]

It must be acknowledged that this growth in the audience for the performing arts would not have occurred without the extensive financial assistance provided by federal, provincial, municipal and corporate funding sources. The budget of the Ontario Arts Council, for example, increased from $300,000 in 1963 to $21 million in 1985. The Ontario government's overall spending on culture now exceeds $300 million annually. Collectively, the ten provinces allocate approximately $975 million to culture. The federal government's annual cultural budget exceeds $1.5 billion, over half of which is allocated to operate the Canadian Broadcasting Corporation.[15]

The total economic impact of all cultural industries in Canada has been estimated as high as $16 billion, or 4% of the Gross National Product. It is clearly this profound economic impact of the arts, plus broad public support, which has delayed still further cuts in government subsidies for culture. Yet as Tom Hendry emphasized in a 1985 cultural policy report commissioned by the Toronto Arts Council for the City of Toronto, "one can endlessly cite statistics to prove employment, economic impact and tourist magnetism. What the arts—given a chance—bring to a city is something in addition to all these material rewards. They give a city an image of its soul."[16]

Cats Meets *The Blue Snake*

The hundreds of millions of dollars in government subsidies spent on the performing arts over the past two decades have resulted not only in more adequate performing spaces but also in the highly trained creative artists who can attract audiences in large numbers. In a 1983 essay entitled "A Circle Without a Centre: The Predicament of Toronto's Theatre Space," Ross Stuart suggested that the renovation of the Elgin and Winter Garden theatres would result in "what is probably essential for a world-class theatre community—a theatre district [which] may indeed become the heart of Toronto theatre."[17]

The two 1,600 and 1,100-seat Elgin/Winter Garden theatre complex opened in 1913 and 1914 as part of the Marcus Loew vaudeville circuit. In 1981 it was purchased by the Ontario government for $4.5 million from Famous Players which had operated the Elgin as a movie house. The Winter Garden, located on top of the Elgin, has been in disuse since 1927 and still requires approximately $19 million in renovations to transform it into a much-needed transfer house for commercially successful productions. The refurbished Elgin Theatre reopened in March of 1985 with a visually stunning production of Andrew Lloyd Webber's musical *Cats* that heralded a new phase in the development of Canadian theatre.

By the show's opening, its producers, Marlene Smith and Tina VanderHeyden, had already recouped their production costs with the highest pre-opening sale (nearly $4 million) for any show in Canadian history. More importantly, the all-Canadian 35-member cast (a number of them veterans of the Charlottetown Festival and Canada's numerous cabaret theatres) were favorably compared with the performers of the musical's London and New York productions.

And *Cats* was not the only production of international calibre in 1985. Richard Rose's production of John Krizanc's *Tamara*, a major critical and public success at the 1981 Toronto International Theatre Festival, swept the Los Angeles Drama Critics Circle Awards in April of 1985. Interest in Canadian work abroad was also indicated by the revival of R. Murray Schafer's eleven-hour epic opera *Ra*, premièred by Comus Music Theatre in 1983, at the 1985 Holland Festival. Thom Sokoloski again directed the ancient Egyptian sun god's journey through the Netherworld to repeat what William Littler, in the *Toronto Star*, called "one of the most extraordinary events in the history of Canadian musical theatre."[18]

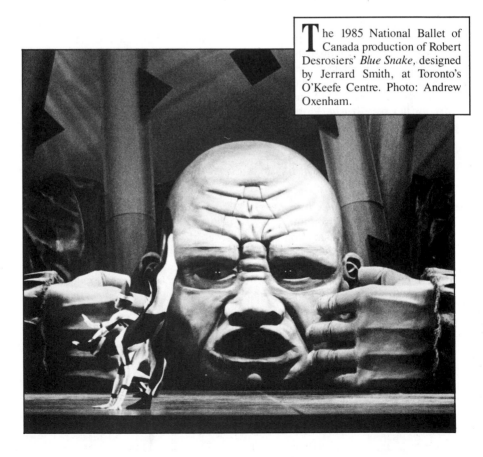

The 1985 National Ballet of Canada production of Robert Desrosiers' *Blue Snake*, designed by Jerrard Smith, at Toronto's O'Keefe Centre. Photo: Andrew Oxenham.

In the field of dance, Robert Desrosiers' surrealist *Blue Snake*, produced by the National Ballet in February of 1985, is surely the equal of the best the contemporary dance world has to offer. Desrosiers, in *Ultracity* (premièred by his own Desrosiers Dance Theatre in December of 1984) had already transformed an urban metropolitan landscape into a startling series of dream images and visions whose phantasmagoric juxtapositions of real and surreal ran the gamut from Hieronymus Bosch to Salvador Dali. In *Blue Snake* he elevated his "futurist" style, a hypnotic mixture of pulsating electronic music, vibrant primary colours, fantastic sculptural shapes and Eastern mysticism, to the level of religious ritual and myth. A golem-like giant crushed dance-figures in his enormous fists and swept them into his mouth. Dancers emerged from the head of a gigantic reptile which gave birth to a smaller blue snake that seemed to float effortlessly high above the stage.

Desrosiers' collaboration with the National Ballet exemplifies the greater artistic possibilities today for Canadian artists whose imagination and self-expression is less confined by economic restrictions. Only a decade ago, the playwright and director Hrant Alianak engaged in a series of similarly startling experiments with music, mime and dramatic action culminating in major dramas such as *Night* (1975), *Passion and Sin* and *The Blues* (1976), and *Lucky Strike* (1978). Though he developed a strong cult following with Toronto's "alternate" theatre audiences, Alianak never received the opportunity of establishing himself in the mainstream of Canadian theatre production.

Calgary playwright John Murrell, by contrast, has greatly benefitted from productions at major regional theatres such as the National Arts Centre, Theatre Calgary, the Grand Theatre and from directors such as Robin Phillips. The care with which new Canadian plays are beginning to be treated on our major stages was suggested by the 1985 National Arts Centre-Toronto CentreStage co-production of Murrell's *New World*. Phillips' sensitive direction and the uniformly high ensemble acting of the cast immeasurably enhanced Murrell's dramatic text and theme of the search for spiritual and physical renewal. Murrell's drama about the final summer of Sarah Bernhardt, *Memoir* (1977), has already been translated into more than fifteen languages and produced in over twenty-five countries.

Cultural Take-Off

Enriched by multi-disciplinary experimentation, high artistic standards, co-productions, and increasing contact between various disciplines, the performing arts in Canada have reached a cultural critical momentum which augurs a new phase in Canada's artistic history. Canada is poised on a phase of "cultural take-off" in which regional artistic reflection and expression has attained national and international standards of significance.

Government cutbacks in arts subsidies could easily abort this new phase of cultural expansion. (Even at present funding levels, the average income for Canadian artists is only $9,000 a year.) Besides such economic considerations, vital artistic questions must also be answered. After half a century of indigenous dramatic development, Canadian theatre has come full circle. Toronto cinemas such as the Elgin and the Crest have been reconverted into playhouses. The all-Canadian *Cats* parallels the professional production work of Toronto stock companies producing British and American musicals and drama in the first three decades of the century. The London West End has been brought to Toronto in a former New York vaudeville house through an English musical based on the work of an American-born English poet.

Paradoxically, just when Canadian theatre has freed itself from the domination of foreign stylistic models, we are again facing the danger of a new form of "franchise" theatre. *Hair,* which ran for a year at the Royal Alexandra Theatre in 1970, spoke to its own time and expressed the anguish of a young generation in revolt against the repressive, war-torn world of their elders. Its cultural-political rebellion was strongly echoed in the work of Toronto's emerging "alternate" theatres. *Cats,* despite a plethora of lighting and special effects and the whimsy of T.S. Eliot's verse, like the Emperor's new clothes, could not hide the spiritual nakedness beneath. *Cats* was devoid of reality, its theme of the pathos of human mortality overwhelmed by the vaudeville garishness, artificial sentimentality and false, pump-and-grind sexuality of the Broadway musical.

Now that Canadians have proven they can sing and dance as well as London and New York, Canada must continue its own self-discovery and create its own artistic visions of the world which can attract sufficient audiences for large-scale commercial productions. Marianne Ackerman suggests that New York and London are "poor stops on the journey to the self" and, pointing to creative artistic activity in Quebec, proposes that "now is the time to rediscover *le nouveau monde* here at home....The mid-1980s could be a turning point in Canadian cultural history, the moment when English and French cultures may finally establish some kind of ongoing conversation, and in that exchange, find new solutions to our problems, new inspiration for artistic projects."

Problems, both artistic and economic, certainly are plentiful. Several contributors warn that, despite the appointment of a number of "alternate" theatre directors to artistic leadership in the major regional theatres, the danger exists of creating a predominantly middle-class theatre and repertoire. This trend will accelerate as government subsidies decline, inflation and production costs increase, and ticket prices for some performances top the $40 range. The transformation over the past half-century of an elite cultural consciousness into a more wide-spread culture of the people will be retarded. The goal of providing a life in the arts not merely for a privileged number of creative professionals, but creating art as a living experience, will become more difficult to attain. Toronto, whose cultural facilities are almost exclusively concentrated in a small area of its downtown core, has not yet achieved the kind of proliferation of performance groups, a movement from "poor" theatre to "*théâtre pour,*" Michel Vaïs describes occurring in metropolitan Montreal.

Yet these concerns will undoubtedly be addressed as Canadian theatre continues its creative evolution. The essays which follow in part consist of such a collective self-examination of the role of the arts and the artist in contemporary society. Like Canadian theatre itself, not one central homogeneous viewpoint, but many critical perspectives, are presented. Despite its extensive coverage, *Contemporary Canadian Theatre: New World Visions* cannot attempt to be a definitive history of the performing arts. Important companies, individuals and issues have had to be omitted. Further research is facilitated by the Selected Bibliography which concludes this collection.

Collectively the essays in *Contemporary Canadian Theatre* suggest that any theatre which speaks to its own immediate community and society and there finds its own reality can discover and dramatize universal truths and values. Theatre will retain its vitality as long as it continues to explore the violent impulses hidden beneath the veneer of human civilization and protests man's inhumanity towards his fellow man and the destruction of the order within nature. If theatre in Canada remains true to itself, whatever the economic restraints and artistic challenges, it will continue to be reborn, like Desrosiers' *Blue Snake,* in still more dynamic and vibrant manifestations.

Anton Wagner

Notes

[1] The member associations of the Canadian Centre of the ITI (English-language) are the Professional Association of Canadian Theatres, Canadian Actors' Equity Association, the Playwrights Union of Canada, the Dance in Canada Association, Canadian Association of Professional Dance Organizations, ASSITEJ-Canadian Centre, Associated Designers of Canada, Canadian Theatre Critics Association, *Canadian Theatre Review,* and the Association for Canadian Theatre History. The member associations of the Centre québécois de l'IIT are the Union des artistes, Association des directeurs de théâtre, Association québécoise du jeune théâtre, Centre d'essai des auteurs dramatiques, Maison québécoise du théâtre pour l'enfance et la jeunesse, the Association des professionnels des arts de la scène, and the Association québécoise des marionnettistes. Canada is the only ITI member with two autonomous language centres. However, the two centres have only one vote at meetings of the ITI world body. Curtis Barlow, Executive Director of the Professional Association of Canadian Theatres, has been President of the Canadian Centre of the ITI since 1979. Hélène Dumas, directrice of the Centre d'essai des auteurs dramatiques, is the President of the Centre québécois de l'IIT.

[2] The Canadian Theatre Centre was founded in 1956. Until its dissolution in 1972, it was headed by such prominent theatre artists as Gratien Gélinas, Guy Beaulne, Norma Springford, Jean-Louis Roux, Tom Hendry, Jean Roberts and Jack Gray. Canada became the 40th member of the ITI in 1959. In May of 1969, Herbert Whittaker and Martial Dassylva represented Canada at the UNESCO conference in Paris at which the International Association of Theatre Critics became independent of UNESCO.

[3] The Canadian Arts Council in 1946 consisted of sixteen national arts organizations with a total membership of nearly ten thousand.

[4] See "Canadians Win Point At Unesco Conference", *London Free Press,* December 20, 1946 and Herman Voaden, "The Arts and Unesco", *University of Toronto Quarterly,* Vol. 17, No. 2, January 1948.

[5] United Nations Educational, Scientific and Cultural Organization Preparatory Commission, "The Need for Unesco to Promote the Creation of an International Theatre Organization". UNESCO/C/12. Paris, November 13th, 1946. p. 2. See also *International Theatre Institute: Formation 1947-1948.* Paris, United Nations Educational, Scientific and Cultural Organization, 1948.

[6] Guy Beaulne to Herman Voaden, Past-President, Canadian Arts Council, Paris, August 27, 1949. Correspondence in the Herman Voaden Papers, York University Archives.

[7] See John C. Lindsay, *"Turn Out the Stars Before Leaving": The Story of Canada's Theatres.* Erin, Ontario, Boston Mills Press, 1983.

[8] For histories of Canadian theatre, see the publications listed in "General Surveys" of the Selected Bibliography.

[9]For histories and anthologies of indigenous dramatic writing in English Canada and Quebec see Anton Wagner, ed. *Colonial Quebec: French-Canadian Drama, 1606-1966; Canada's Lost Plays: The Nineteenth Century* (Richard Plant, co-editor); *Women Pioneers* and *The Developing Mosaic: English-Canadian Drama to Mid-Century.* Toronto, CTR Publications, 1982, 1978, 1979, 1980. Rolf Kalman, ed. *A Collection of Canadian Plays.* 5 vols. Toronto, Simon & Pierre, 1972-1979; Richard Perkyns, ed. *Major Plays of the Canadian Theatre 1934-1984.* Toronto, Irwin Publishing, 1984; Richard Plant, ed. *Modern Canadian Drama.* Markham, Ont., Penguin Books Canada, 1984; Jan Doat, *Anthologie du théâtre québécois 1606-1970.* Québec, Editions la liberté, 1973; Étienne-F. Duval, *Anthologie thématique du théâtre québécois au XIXe siècle.* Montreal, Leméac, 1978 and Jean-Cleo Godin and Laurent Mailhot, *Le Théâtre québécois* and *Théâtre québécois II: Nouveaux auteurs, autres spectacles.* Montreal, Hurtubise HMH, 1970, 1980.

[10]"When We Awake!" in *Yearbook of the Arts in Canada 1928-1929,* ed. Bertram Brooker. Toronto, Macmillan, 1929. p. 7.

[11]"Introduction", *Six Canadian Plays,* ed. Herman Voaden. Toronto, Copp Clark, 1930. pp. xxi, xxiv.

[12]See Ann Saddlemyer, "Thoughts on National Drama and the Founding of Theatres" in *Theatrical Touring and Founding in North America,* ed. L.W. Conolly. Westport, Connecticut, Greenwood Press, 1982. p. 193.

[13]See Session 1944 House of Commons Special Committee on Reconstruction and Reestablishment, Wednesday, June 21, 1944. *Minutes of Proceedings and Evidence No. 10.* Ottawa, Edmond Cloutier, 1944. p. 332. The Committee received briefs from sixteen cultural societies representing the visual and performing arts, authors and other artists.

[14]Access Survey Research Corporation, *The Perceptions, Attitudes and Behaviour of Ontario Residents Toward the Arts in the Province: 1983.* Toronto, Special Committee for the Arts, Ministry of Citizenship and Culture, Government of Ontario, 1983. p. 39. Also cited in The Special Committee for the Arts, *Report to the Honourable Susan Fish, The Minister of Citizenship and Culture* (The Macaulay Report). Toronto, Ministry of Citizenship and Culture, Government of Ontario, 1984. p. 3/4.

[15]See Mathew Fraser, "Who's Who in the Culture Clan?", Toronto *Globe and Mail,* February 23, 1985. p. E5 and Curtis Barlow, "Ottawa Deals Arts 'Devastating' Blow", *Toronto Star,* February 17, 1985. p. H4.

[16]Tom Hendry, *Cultural Capital: The Care and Feeding of Toronto's Artistic Assets.* Toronto, Toronto Arts Council, 1985. Cited in "The Arts Pay Off", *Toronto Star,* February 22, 1985. p. A16.

[17]Ross Stuart, "A Circle Without a Centre: The Predicament of Toronto's Theatre Space", *Canadian Theatre Review,* No. 38, Fall 1983. pp. 23, 24.

[18]William Littler, "Ra Knows We Tried to Take It all Seriously", *Toronto Star,* May 6, 1983. p. D9. For the June 17-29, 1985 Lieden revival, the production was condensed to 7½ hours.

PART ONE

Government and Cultural Expression

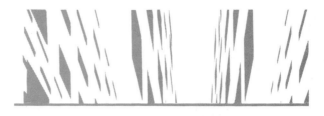

The Performing Arts and Government Policy

These notes explore the proposition that while Canada has a flourishing culture, it does not have a cultural policy. Or perhaps more precisely, that Canada's cultural policy is not to have a cultural policy.

There is no question that culture in Canada is flourishing. Between 1973 and 1983 companies presenting full seasons grew from 40 to about 200. These groups sold $50 million worth of tickets, about half of their $100 million in operating budgets. In 1983 there were 60 symphony orchestras, and 120 professional theatre companies (only four professional theatres were operating when the Canada Council was formed in 1957). At a conservative estimate the cultural sector in Canada in 1980 was the country's eleventh largest manufacturing industry with revenues of $7 billion. It employed 234,000 persons with salaries and wages of $2.3 billion. There were over 15,000 art galleries, museums, orchestras, theatres, dance and other performing groups, choirs, cinemas, libraries, bookstores, radio and television stations, publishers and other cultural establishments.[1]

And all of that activity was developed without recourse to any consistent or coherent guiding principles, and without any real understanding of the role of culture and the arts in society.

Basically, culture is what makes human beings human. It is what people do, and how they do it. It is rooted in the particular characteristics of mankind, in the capacity for language, for example, with the consequent ability to store and transmit knowledge, a trait that allows us to manage and adapt to the environments in which we live.

At the heart of this extraordinary achievement is a set of processes that depend on man's ability to use his imagination, processes that in their more developed forms are called science and art. Art and culture are processes all human beings are capable of employing. They are not something peripheral to our existence, they are its centre, its core, quite as important to us as those activities that ensure mere survival.

This is what most governments have never understood, and one explanation of why, though they try consistently to ignore culture, culture continues to exist, and even to flourish.

The Canadian Approach

Canada's approach to culture and the arts has, from the beginning, been suspicious, reactionary and pragmatic. This was perhaps inevitable in a group of colonies that imported their culture and many of their basic attitudes from their home countries. "God help the minister who meddles with art," said Lord Melbourne in 1835, a point of view Canadian governments subscribed to for a hundred years, and still honour to a large degree.

To these inherited traits were added harsh environmental and geographical factors. The first stages of cultural development in Canada, for example, produced what Northrop Frye has described as garrison cultures, which were spawned in isolation and terror.

Canadian attitudes to culture were certainly intensified by the fierce isolation bred by Canada's vast space. While the sense of isolation has been tempered in recent decades by the marvels of communications technology, by radio, the airplane, television and so on, to the point where we have become blasé at the ease with which we can transport our bodies, our images, our "messages" across wide spaces, the truth is that our awareness of isolation has not disappeared. It has to some degree been transformed into a regionalism that—though it continues to feed on the suspicion, paranoia and insecurity engendered by isolation—is nevertheless a fundamental strength of the country.

Accompanying the paranoia, perhaps a main constituent of it, is a feeling possessed by each region that it, and perhaps it alone, possesses that genuine creative flair without which the entire Canadian experiment would long since have gone down in flames or up in smoke. Francophone Quebec, for instance, rightly considers that it has a distinct and unique culture. But then so does francophone Acadia—and Newfoundland, the various regions of the Maritimes, those subtle variations on common themes that make up the regions of the west, to say nothing of Ontario, the large central province which is traditionally and rather uncharitably viewed by *everyone else* as centralist, power-mad, and greedy. Ontario is actually itself a loose federation of a number of particular and particularly interesting regions. And all these divisions ignore the "original" cultures of Canada, the Inuit and Indian, who continue to feel left out of things.

When the old colonies were merged in 1867 in Confederation, a major role for the new federal government was to work in various ways to mitigate the divisive aspects of the regions. The concern, as one commentator puts it, was for national unity as opposed to national identity. Typically, this took the form of nation-building through the improvement of communications (railways, broadcasting, airlines), and through a general fostering of the means to achieve "national unity." The emphasis throughout was on economics and industry, on business and enterprise, rather than on culture, although as an aspect of the drive for unity, culture did gradually attract various kinds of federal support.

Culture has never had an easy time of it, however. In addition to the points noted above, there were other daunting hazards to be overcome. Canada has from the beginning had to recognize and rationalize the fact that it is home to two major "cultures," French and English. Neither of these is homogeneous. Successive governments have faced great pressure from waves of immigrants from other cultures not to come down on the side of any single "cultural" approach, which has led to the policy of "multiculturalism," an emphasis on keeping all cultures alive.

S panning the continent through railroads and radio: the Canadian National Railway and its 1929 coast-to-coast CNR radio network.

Another fact of life for Canada is that it shares the longest undefended border in the world with one of the most powerful nations in history. There has been continuous and relentless pressure exerted on Canada by its big, friendly, relatively benign neighbour, the United States of America. In one sense Canada can be considered an enormous "No," a group of disparate entities that were forced to come together so that they would not become a part of the emerging American Union. This factor has always played a major role in Canadian development, attitudes and actions, as it does today. Cultural nationalists in Canada traditionally appeal to the bogeyman of domination by a rapacious, culturally imperialistic United States, when they seek to awaken governments (and others) to the need to support Canadian culture, art, and expression of every kind.

"The state or the United States!" cried Graham Spry in the 1930s when fighting through the Canadian Radio League for a publicly owned Canadian broadcasting system. A document distributed in 1984 by ACTRA, the writers and performers union, as part of their fight against massive cuts in federal funding for the Canadian Broadcasting Corporation, stridently suggests that "Canada is a culturally-occupied country." In 1978 when artists from coast to coast banded together to fight a previous massive cut in federal cultural funding, they organized themselves into a brilliantly named "1812 Committee." (The War of 1812 was fought between a number of protagonists, but for Canadians it marks the last *armed* struggle with the United States, the first significant cooperation between English and French Canadians in a common cause, as well as an early concrete manifestation of that ever elusive sense of identity.)

In spite of frequent government neglect, culture did inch its way onto the national agenda in various ways. Yet federal cultural initiatives have consistently tended to be specific responses to specific problems.

Canadian Federal Cultural Policies

For a long time there was no conscious attempt to even consider such a thing as a cultural policy in Canada. Soon after Confederation in 1867, Canadians were provided with a Public Archives, a National Gallery (both 1880), while the Library of Parliament served as a national library until that institution was formally established in 1953. Copyright has been the responsibility of the federal government since 1867, though until a Canadian Act was passed in 1921, coming into force on January 1, 1924, Canada followed the old Imperial copyright acts. New copyright acts have been under review for the past half-century.

The performing arts received no formal attention from the federal government until it had to face the specific problems raised by the development of radio broadcasting in the 1920s. The coming of radio raised urgent problems that have become the classic items in Canadian discussions of culture: how much Canadian programming is needed, or wanted by the Canadian public; how great is the danger of cultural domination by the United States; who will pay?

The government's approach to the radio problem was itself classically Canadian: a three man Royal Commission under the Chairmanship of Sir John Aird, the President of the Bank of Commerce, was appointed in 1928 "to examine into the broadcasting situation in the Dominion of Canada and to make recommendations to the Government as to the future administration, management, control and financing thereof." Aird's elegant *Report*, delivered in 1929, is one of the shortest Royal Commission reports ever produced in Canada—13 pages, 29 if the four appendices are included. It was also one of the most important in cultural terms.

First, it established the principle of federal government intervention in cultural matters. Second, it resulted in the setting up in 1932 of the Canadian Radio Broadcasting Commission, which in 1936 became the Canadian Broadcasting Corporation, whose effects on the performing arts and the cultural life of Canada are literally incalculable.

Third, it established a pattern for federal involvement in culture which has, with variations, been more or less followed ever since. This is characterized by action being taken only in respect to a specific problem as opposed to an overall policy that establishes objectives, for which appropriate action is then developed. Action, when taken, is invariably at arm's length, ordinarily through an organization or institution which, once its mandate is established, is given almost complete autonomy. Control is exercised mainly through a rein on funding, which typically is insufficient to genuinely deal with the problem.

In the case of radio broadcasting, a public corporation was formed, authorized by an Act of Parliament. This corporation was charged with producing and distributing programming to all Canadians, in both official languages. But in typical Canadian fashion the corporation was required to act in a semi-commercial manner, so that the public funds required for its support, insufficient by themselves to do the job required, would not be too great.

This is a pattern that has been followed to a greater or lesser degree in supporting activity in the mass-media cultural industries of television and feature films. Other, usually indirect, ways have been developed to support publishing, and the recording industries. The traditional arts have received direct funding through an agency, the Canada Council, especially set up for that purpose.

From the beginning of the modern period that started with Aird, the basic problem has been, simply, the need to provide a minimum, stable source of Canadian materials that will reflect Canadian interests and serve Canadian audiences.

The National Film Board (NFB) was set up in 1939. Though its original purpose was essentially the production of propaganda, it ultimately developed into something better and more important than that.

The most significant of the cultural initiatives taken so far by the federal government came in 1949 when it appointed another Royal Commission, this time on the Arts, Letters and Sciences, chaired by one of the most established cultural leaders in Canada, Vincent Massey. The Massey Commission was established partly as a result of sustained pressure from the then very active voluntary associations at that time. Its *Report*, delivered in 1951, was patrician, comprehensive and full of recommendations. Almost all of these were acted on by the federal government over the next decade. The most important recommendation implemented was the creation of the Canada Council, modeled on the British Arts Council, in 1957, with funding drawn from death duties on the estates of two multi-millionaires who had had the good taste to die in a timely manner. This rationale was very Canadian, suggesting that it was all right to fund culture with a windfall from the rich rather than use tax revenues contributed equally by all citizens—another variation on the luxury and frills motif.

In due course, the Canada Council was maintained and developed from general tax revenues. This and other actions resulting from the Massey Commission marked the beginning of an increasingly active phase of federal intervention and support for the arts. Several major national institutions followed in the wake of the Massey Commission. In 1969 the National Arts Centre was completed in Ottawa at a cost of over $46 million. This was shepherded through its many development stages by retired diplomat Hamilton Southam (another rich man with impeccable cultural credentials).

Active lobbying and a sense of opportunities that could be realized, resulted in the creation of the Canadian Film Development Corporation (CFDC) in 1967. Now Telefilm Canada, this agency was put in place to attempt to build a new Canadian feature film industry. Regulation of broadcasting was also revised. The CBC had originally been given the job of overseeing the national broadcasting picture. But pressure from the private sector managed to have this changed; first to a Board of Broadcast Governors in 1958, and later to a stronger Canadian Radio Television Commission (CRTC) in 1968. The latter group, under the initial chairmanship of Pierre Juneau, and later Harry Boyle, pursued a vigorous policy of both encouraging and, when that proved inadequate, of forcing Canadian broadcasters to make and use more Canadian material on both radio and television. These regulations had substantial effects on the growth of the Canadian performing arts community and ancilliary industries.

The euphoria produced by the preparations for and the celebrations that marked Canada's Centennial in 1967 obviously had an effect on the federal government's efforts, contributing to the founding of the National Arts Centre in 1966, the formation of the CFDC, the establishment of the National Museums of Canada (also in 1967), and the revision of the Broadcasting Act with the newly established CRTC in 1968. Some of this impetus also came from the reorganization of the federal agencies under one Minister, the Secretary of State, which occured in 1963.

By the late 60s the government was discussing actually developing a cultural policy. In 1965 the Secretary of State had commissioned a study on the need for such a comprehensive policy. In 1968 Gérard Pelletier, now himself Secretary of State, announced a federal cultural policy would in fact be implemented.

> We need only reflect for a moment to see that any country which wants to attain humane, balanced and harmonious growth is compelled to establish a cultural policy and follow it through...The government I represent is aware of this truth...from now on it intends to co-ordinate...under a true cultural policy. It will not be content to follow different objectives more or less at random.[2]

But progress was fitful, slow, and ultimately little happened. Pelletier did indeed, in 1970, propose a global cultural policy that stressed five elements: pluralism, democratization, decentralization, federal-provincial cooperation, and international cooperation. But seven years and two Secretaries of State later, John Roberts (then Secretary of State) could say, "If there's any kind of generally agreed-on government policy or overall strategy, I don't know what it is."

By the beginning of the 1980s it was obvious a new look at the whole question of culture and the arts in Canada was needed. Finally, in 1981 a Federal Cultural Policy Review Committee, chaired by Louis Applebaum and Jacques Hébert, was set up. "Applebert," as it came to be called, reported in 1982 in a long, rambling document which basically satisfied no one, including the federal government. "Applebert" is likely to have a long-term effect, however, hopefully in its basic stance and assertion that "the role of creative artists should be given special priority in consideration of cultural policies."[3]

Parallel Movements

The federal government has never lacked for advice on what it should be doing about culture and the arts. We have already noted the powerful lobbying that could be organized by voluntary groups like the Canadian Radio League (later the Canadian Broadcasting League) which originated in the 1930s, and was instrumental in the establishment of the CBC.

Two other movements are worth noting. The first centres on what is today the Canadian Conference of the Arts (CCA), an apparently unique national arts lobby and advocacy group. The CCA had its beginnings in the mid-1940s when the agitation for government support by national cultural organizations resulted in the Massey Commission. Today the CCA has about seven hundred organizational and almost as many individual members, drawn from all walks of cultural life in Canada. While the CCA began as a voluntary organization, it is today substantially funded by the federal government, currently to the tune of about $550,000 of its annual $750,000 budget. (At arm's length, of course).

The second movement is even more interesting, and not well documented. This has been the gradual development of a widely varied group of unions and professional associations that represent artists of all kinds. Most of them, for example, are members of the CCA.

The unions in Canada began in two ways, either as off-shoots of powerful American organizations, or as small, often locally organized craft groups that evolved in an effort to negotiate and manage basic minimum rates and working conditions in the performing arts. The American Federation of Musicians (AFM) is an example of the first type, The Alliance of Canadian Cinema, Television and Radio Artists (ACTRA) of the second.

ACTRA had its origins in a number of local groups including the Radio Artists of Toronto Society (RATS), which later became the Association of Canadian Radio Artists (ACRA). ACRA teamed up with a number of French groups in a Canadian Council of Authors and Artists/Conseil canadien des auteurs et artistes (CCAA), but this coalition dissolved when the English language group refused to support their French colleagues in the 1953 producers strike in Montreal, an early manifestation of the kinds of troubles that were coming as Quebec prepared to enter its Quiet Revolution in the 1960s.

With the coming of television, ACRA became ACTRA. But internal confusion in the mass-media union during the movement to organize stage actors following the founding of the Stratford Festival in 1953 finally led the stage actors' (most of whom were already members of ACTRA) to invite American Actors' Equity to form a Canadian branch. In due course this group became the autonomous Canadian Actors' Equity Association. While English Canada ended up with two unions handling performers' affairs, French Canada has managed to combine these interests in a single group, the Union des artistes. On the other hand, English Canada has one union representing writers and performers in the mass-media (ACTRA), while French Canada has a separate group that takes care of writers, originally Société des auteurs (SAC), now Société des auteurs, recherchistes, documentalistes et compositeurs (SARDEC).

All these groups, ACTRA, Equity, U de A, SARDEC, are unions, in the sense that they have written negotiated agreements with their major contractors.

There are numbers of other groups, many of them very effective, which are active in the cultural life of the country. They include the Writers Union of Canada, the Playwrights Union of Canada, CARFAC (which represents visual artists), the Canadian Association of Professional Dance Organizations and the Dance in Canada Association, the Canadian League of Composers and the Professional Association of Canadian Theatres, to name only a few of those in English Canada.[4]

The development of these groups has been critical, not only to the well-being of their own members, but also to cultural policy and initiatives generally, because it is these organized groups that have been among the strongest and most insistent advocates for cultural policies and action that will work for the benefit of Canadian expression generally.

This returns us to the main problem.

The Problem

The essential problem to be tackled by any federal cultural policy in Canada is how to make it possible for Canadians to create, distribute, use and enjoy Canadian materials of all kinds.

Strangely, after a hundred and twenty years of "ad hockery," this seems to be generally agreed. In 1981 the Canadian Conference of the Arts, after wide consultation in the cultural community, enunciated in *A Strategy for Culture* the following basic objectives for cultural policy in Canada:

— The creation and production, by Canadians, of Canadian materials primarily for the use of the Canadian public.

— The development of the individuals, institutions, corporations and the legislative and economic framework that will make possible the creation, production, distribution and preservation of Canadian materials.

— The long-term commitment and organization of the public and private resources necessary to permit the orderly, continuing creation, production, distribution, use and preservation of Canadian materials.[5]

Donald Davis, Robert Goodier, Douglas Campbell and the 1955 Stratford Festival cast in the 1956 film of *Oedipus Rex*, directed by Tyrone Guthrie.

By 1983 even the Minister of Communications — who is responsible for culture at the federal level in Canada—was backing these objectives. Speaking to the annual meeting of the CCA in May of that year, Francis Fox stated:

> We have discovered that we do agree. We agree fundamentally. The objectives you described for cultural policy are the objectives we subscribe to. Decisions affecting the cultural life of Canadians will be tested against the following principles:
>
> New initiatives must
> — recognize and enhance the contribution of culture to the quality of life of Canadians, through the promotion of Canadian-inspired cultural activities;
> — help to create conditions conducive to the development and growth of Canadian cultural expression, both nationally and internationally;
> — ensure the accessibility of Canadians to culture, wherever created.[6]

The Results

While cultural policy in Canada is characterized by inconsistency, a tendency to state fine principles and then to ignore these in practical programs, and by consistent under-funding—sometimes to the point of cynicism—there has nevertheless been a very extensive range of cultural activities put in place. Not all of this is due to the federal government of course: provincial and municipal governments, the private sector, and the public are all major contributors.

But whether guided by overall principles or not, the spark for most activity has come from the federal level, and its cumulative effects have been a gradual strengthening of the arts generally, and the performing arts in particular.

The existence of the various institutions and programs set up federally provides a sensitive, interdependent network of activity and support. The mere existence of the CBC, for example, is critical to the maintenance of the entire talent pool in Canada, a pool that serves not just broadcasting but also the music world, theatres, the film industry, design, writing, and creative work generally. An active theatre activity in Toronto and Vancouver in the 1940s and 1950s depended to a large degree on an equally active program of dramatic production by CBC radio—one enterprise feeding the other. There was a close connection between the development of television writers and stage writers in Quebec in the years following the introduction of television in Canada. The situation in Quebec was that there was simply no repertoire of existing programming to draw on (English Canada was able to import American programs), with the result that a number of writers had to be developed almost overnight.

The function of the major institutions in training talent of all kinds has been critical. Both the NFB and the CBC have trained several generations of writers, performers, directors, as well as the broad range of technical personnel needed. These talented people have been the mainstay of both the television and the film industry. It took public money to develop them, and it takes public money to keep them at work. The training of performing talent received special recognition with the establishment of schools like the National Theatre School, and the ballet training schools in various centres.

The music business in Canada has been substantially assisted by federal cultural initiatives. There is direct support of performing artists through engagements with the CBC, the NFB, and through the extensive funding given by the Canada Council to particular orchestras and music groups. Less direct, but equally important, was the boost given the Canadian recording industry by CRTC regulations in 1971 that require a minimum percentage of all music played on AM radio stations to be "Canadian" as defined.

It would be safe to say that there would be substantially less professional theatre in Canada had it not been for the interference of the federal government, some of which has been quite inadvertent. While the Canada Council is the more direct instrument in the development of the regional theatre network in Canada, the quite phenomenal growth of smaller theatres that has taken place was to a large degree sparked by two emergency work programs of the federal government: Opportunities For Youth (OFY), and the later Local Initiatives Program (LIP), were extensively and imaginatively used by young people (and some not so young) to start theatres of every kind. Many of them continue to flourish today. The problem with such government programs, of course, as with so much of the ad hoc cultural activity in which Canada has engaged, is that projects are started but the resources to develop and maintain activities are not provided in later years.

The Future
The main task of those concerned with the future of cultural development in Canada (and in most countries) is to gradually convince the public, and following that the politicians and the bureaucrats, that the processes and activities we group under the name of culture and the arts are not luxuries or frills in any sense of those words, but critical activities that are at the centre of every individual life and at the core of our social and communal existence. As such, these activities have a value far beyond any material assessment that can be placed on them, on their capacity to earn revenues, or to attract tourists. It is true they do these things, that the whole sector is labour intensive, and so on and so on, but its importance goes far beyond that.

A main task for artists, whether they recognize it or not, is not so much to provide solutions to the problems society faces as to identify those problems, to do this accurately, sensitively, credibly, in terms of an overall objective to improve the quality of life of all human beings.

Solutions will follow only if this process is fully developed, a task for which the arts and culture are ideally suited. Any cure depends on the accuracy of the diagnosis. It is dangerous, misleading, and could be fatal, for example, to base our future projections for humane societies on the present frenetic state of the current technologies and the myriad problems they have brought forth. The problems do not rest in the technologies, but in man. And who better to deal with human problems than our artists?

Once governments, and we ourselves, recognize that the problems with which we must deal are basically human problems, long-term, recurring, perhaps even ineradicable, then we will begin to understand that the role of the artist in our society is critical, central and continuous.

Jack Gray

Notes

[1] "The Arts in Canada." Notes for remarks by Andrew Lipchak, Director, Arts Branch, Ministry of Citizenship and Culture, Province of Ontario, to the Canadian Studies Seminar for European Educators, Toronto, July 14, 1983 and The Special Committee for the Arts. *Report to the Honourable Susan Fish, The Minister of Citizenship and Culture* (The Macaulay Report). Toronto, Special Committee for the Arts, Ministry of Citizenship and Culture, Government of Ontario, Spring 1984. p. 4/3.

[2] Gérard Pelletier, Address to the Board of Trade of Montreal, October 28, 1968.

[3] *Report of the Federal Cultural Policy Review Committee*. Ottawa, Information Services, Department of Communications, Government of Canada, 1982. p. 4.

[4] For a complete listing of national arts organizations in Canada, see the CCA's annual *Who Does What* (in French, *Les Services*): A Guide to National Art Associations, Service Organizations and Unions. Ottawa, Canadian Conference of the Arts. See also the annual *Who's Who* (in English and French): A Guide to Federal and Provincial Departments and Agencies, Their Funding Programs and the People Who Head Them. Ottawa, Canadian Conference of the Arts.

[5] *A Strategy for Culture*: Proposals for a Federal Policy for the Arts and the Cultural Industries in Canada. Ottawa, Canadian Conference of the Arts, 1980. p. 25.

[6] Notes for an address by the Honorable Francis Fox, Minister of Communications, at the Annual General Meeting, Canadian Conference of the Arts, Ottawa, May 5, 1983.

The Regional
Theatre System

Understanding the concept of a regional theatre in Canada is difficult, and in the mid-1980s possibly irrelevant. Despite the idealized portrait of a regional theatre in the 1961-62 annual report of the Canada Council, no formal or legal definition of the term exists—and the distinction between regionals and several other large theatres has become increasingly blurred. By common consent, however, by 1974 a baker's dozen of the largest subsidized theatres across Canada (exclusive of festival theatres such as Stratford and Shaw) were called "regionals." Attempts to assess their common characteristics have foundered, but the history of Canadian theatre since 1945 is largely the story of their ongoing evolution.[1]

From Regional Theatres: A National Audience
Looking back over the decade since the Massey Commission on the arts, the Canada Council in its 1961-62 annual report concluded that huge strides in theatre had been taken, among them the founding of the Stratford Festival in 1953 and the establishment of Winnipeg's Manitoba Theatre Centre (MTC) in 1958—the model for what were later termed regional theatres. But the gains were insufficient. Particularly elusive was the holy grail of a national theatre accessible to audiences across the country. In this regard the report noted drily, "Stratford reaches that part of a national audience which can pay to get there."[2]

The Council's further thoughts merit quoting at length:

> In a country with the configuration and population of Canada, a truly national theatre is not likely to be created in any one city—however much money might go into a building. Stone walls do not a theatre make nor licensed bars a stage. The essential of a *national* theatre, as we see it, is that it should reach a *national* audience—even if this audience must for convenience be broken down into regional audiences....
>
> A regional theatre must first be situated in a city with a population capable of giving it support and bearing the brunt of its expenses.... In addition to a regular

season of plays, the company would have to provide productions designed to be taken to small centres within its general area, or to plan one or two regular periods of touring each year with a small repertoire of plays. It would also have to provide theatre for children and, if possible, should organize a school for training embryo actors....

In a decade or so, a fairly close working relationship might develop among them and with Toronto and Montreal. It has been suggested that it might not be impossible with careful planning at the beginning of the season for at least one or two productions a year to be interchanged between two theatres....

If we strain our eyes a little further down the road in this hazy light, we still cannot see in any numbers those essential figures in the theatre landscape—the playwrights of great talent. We can only hope that they are lurking round the corner.[3]

The Council punctuated this general outline with two concrete conditions—strong local support and professional, inspired direction.

In 1985, over two decades later, we can conclude that many facets of that regional vision did materialize: each regional did incorporate some, if not all, of the functions outlined by the Council. Others did not, for complex but definable reasons. Among these, two predominate: an overall cultural bias, in the period under discussion, towards institutions (necessary in themselves but potentially limiting to creativity), and the absence of specific provisions for regionals to encourage the creation and development of new plays.

The first issue is general, applicable to all the arts in Canada, and was addressed by the report of the Federal Cultural Policy Review Committee in 1982 in terms demonstrating that the Council's warnings in 1962 had gone mostly unheeded:

Federal cultural policy has largely favoured physical plant and organizational development over artistic creativity and achievement....

What they add up to is more an industrial and employment policy than a cultural policy, properly understood. The bricks and mortar are necessary, but they are not the end product, the purpose of it all.[4]

The issue of playwriting also has a more general context. Obviously, problems facing Canadian playwrights as writers—poor distribution, massive U.S. and British or French competition, unconsciously colonized audiences—are shared by non-dramatic writers as well. More specifically, however, playwrights cannot survive without theatres, as an earlier Council report made clear: "The Council is of the opinion that living theatre demands living playwrights and that the Canadian theatre demands Canadian playwrights."[5] It is curious, therefore, that the Canada Council's statement of specific aims for regional theatres, apart from encouraging them to commission plays, does not explore in any detail the organic relationship between playwrights and theatres. Presumably the Council, by stating that the regionals must have strong local roots, might have felt it redundant to spell out that those roots would naturally sprout playwrights.

Initially, the regionals did nurture playwrights. MTC under John Hirsch and Tom Hendry produced their own plays as well as work by Ann Henry and James Reaney, then resident in Winnipeg. In Vancouver, the Playhouse under Malcolm Black had great success introducing the plays of Eric Nicol and George Ryga. No new works by those playwrights, and relatively few by other Canadian playwrights, have been premièred at the regionals since 1971 (the notable exceptions are Montreal's Centaur, Regina's Globe and, since the late 1970s, Theatre Calgary).

The Regional Ideal: Manitoba Theatre Centre and Theatre New Brunswick

Much of the Council's thinking on regional theatre was derived from observing the growth of MTC, which also became the ideal for the regional theatre system in the United States. Having garnered support in Winnipeg for children's and amateur theatre in the early 1950s, Hirsch and Hendry amalgamated two semi-pro companies to produce MTC in 1958. Young people's theatre remained an essential program, and a young company working out of its theatre school also developed. MTC toured shows around its region, and became a winter home for many Stratford actors, as well as National Theatre School graduates. As for programming, Hirsch stressed the need to educate audiences unused to theatre, gently alternating light comedy with the occasional classic and always encouraging local playwrights to develop their art within the practical confines of the theatre.

MTC's shining ideals have never been duplicated. In practice, from the particular viewpoint of regionality, a more influential model for regional theatres was Theatre New Brunswick (TNB), founded by Walter Learning in 1968. Both in that capacity, and later as theatre officer for the Canada Council from 1978 to 1983, Learning has been the most authoritative spokesman for the generally understood notion of regional theatre (in 1983, he resumed a direct association with the regionals when he became artistic director of the Vancouver Playhouse). Learning started TNB by persuading towns outside Fredericton to sign up for a tour of the theatre's mainstage productions. This all-encompassing embrace of its region constituted a definition of "regional" more in keeping with the name itself, and one which became more accepted than the far-flung "national audience" concept envisioned earlier by the Canada Council.

TNB's regionality also had significant implications for programming. According to Learning,

> There was no doubt that the organization had to be play-of-the-month. We were the only English-language game in the province. We had to work within the widest possible spectrum, and we had an obligation to the school curriculum. The audience wasn't sophisticated, but it had insight and we couldn't be condescending.[6]

What that meant in programming terms was initially two of the so-called "three C's"—contemporary plays with an occasional classic. Learning did not at first consider the third "C" (Canadian plays) necessary until the late New Brunswick poet Alden Nowlan prodded him into co-writing plays which Learning then produced at TNB. "Three C" programming evolved at other regionals as well and became an accepted rule, one that acquired further official sanction during Learning's tenure at the Canada Council. "If you have theatres operating on $2-2.5 million budgets," said Learning, "part of their function is a lending library—you have to pull out the classics once or twice a year."[7]

Several regionals diverge substantially from that norm. Montreal's Centaur Theatre, for example, produced nothing earlier than Ibsen from the time Maurice Podbrey founded it in 1969 to 1984. The Globe Theatre in Regina, founded by Ken Kramer and his late wife Sue in 1966, began as a community-oriented children's

Centaur Theatre in the remodeled old Montreal Stock Exchange. Photo: Basil Zarov.

theatre, quickly developing into a populist adult theatre with strong roots in Saskatchewan's past and present. Only since 1980 have classics appeared with any regularity in its programs. Significantly, the Globe and the Centaur are among the most successful regional theatres in terms of attendance and critical reception. And not by chance, both have had long associations with playwrights of stature resident in their respective cities—Rex Deverell at the Globe and, until 1984, David Fennario at the Centaur.

Subscription

In its 1966-67 report, the Canada Council was already asking fundamental questions about the regionals and their audiences. Having noted with approval that a co-production between MTC and the Shaw Festival would "provide larger audiences for not greatly increased production costs," it asked with some concern:

> The question still remains as to whether the regional audiences have been able to broaden in any fundamental way the outlook of their audiences. If the interest of the audience has developed, can plays and productions meet their rising expectations? Can the theatre reach beyond the habitués to an audience as yet almost untouched? Can they find the artists and technicians to carry out their aspirations and meet the demands made upon them? Can they uncover new playwrights of quality and thus provide a social commentary on our own society?[8]

Certainly, the regionals helped develop excellent actors and technicians, but thanks to certain aspects of their infrastructure, the answer to the report's other questions is a resounding no.

First, and most important in that regard, is the subscription season, a concept which came to Ottawa from the Chicago Lyric Opera in 1965 in the person of marketing consultant Danny Newman. Newman is the apostle of subscription—the pre-sale of an entire season, usually with a discount, in order to provide operating capital for a performing arts organization before its season starts. Since the Council was and remains chronically underfunded, it welcomed Newman's ideas and eagerly passed them on to the boards of the new regionals.

Although subscription undeniably works as an economic measure, it can also be detrimental from an artistic viewpoint, especially in theatre. Initially implemented with a conservative opera audience, subscription ignores the basic distinction between theatre—essentially a local, political (in the broadest sense) endeavour—and the other performing arts. By locking theatres into fixed time slots for productions, subscription does cut losses on unsuccessful works—but it also prevents capitalizing on hits, unless a transfer house is readily available. In such cases, the loss is not just economic, since both theatre artists and their audiences are also denied the opportunity to support and applaud a successful cultural endeavour. The result is that economic hedging curtails a community's potential to take pride in and enjoy its own work. Discounting plays has a similar effect: inevitably, an audience urged to buy six plays for the price of five will unconsciously depreciate the value of those works. And although the subscription philosophy calls for one risk—usually a new, i.e. Canadian, play—out of five or six to balance the "safer" classics and contemporary works, many artistic directors do not bother with the risk, and end up downplaying their wild card.

Subscription's shortsighted approach, based on erroneous assumptions, invites long-term programming disasters. The ideal subscription season in theory includes a judicious mix of the three C's. But such a division only raises artistically irrelevant questions of nationality. The basic premise underlying the three C's is a sliding scale of demonstrated worth: the classics by definition have proven themselves over the centuries; contemporary (usually taken to mean "foreign") works have only recently achieved prominence, but sufficiently so to allow them to travel from their countries of origin. That is a sign of universal appeal, perhaps indicating eventual status as a classic, but not necessarily an indication of quality. The epithet "Canadian" is misplaced—the category which should logically follow the previous two is in fact *new* work. In practice, if new work is lucky enough to be produced, it will most likely be produced in its country of origin; hence in Canada such work will be Canadian. But because cultural nationalism is such a contentious issue in Canada, the focus on new work has shifted from its innovative to its political aspect.

The result is that, far too often, *any* work by a Canadian playwright has been bundled into the new or risk category for the purposes of regional programming. That tendency disregards the fact that playwrights such as David French, George Ryga, Michel Tremblay and George Walker should clearly have "contemporary" status since their established work is frequently produced outside Canada. Even though their audience appeal and worth has been verified, remounts of Canadian plays in theatres on subscription are slotted into a category which should include only new work—with the result that their status is downgraded and new work does not appear at all. In short, the belief that balanced subscription seasons give regionals the opportunity to develop new work and take risks is in practice an illusion.

New work undeniably involves risk, whether the work is Canadian or not, but new plays are the lifeblood of theatre—without accepting their challenge, theatre artists wither and die, and so will their audiences. Safe commercial programming on subscription aimed at safe returns does not attract new audiences and kills the interest of established patrons. But given their need to generate box office income, some regionals understandably do not want to take the risk of new work. The problem could be solved if a certain portion of government subsidy were earmarked not for work by Canadian playwrights but specifically for *new* work, irrespective of origin. In practice, as noted, that work will invariably be Canadian. But such a stipulation would also encourage the regionals to break free from subscription blinkers and view established Canadian work in the same perspective as they do proven dramatic literature from abroad.

Boards and Buildings

Several economic developments in the late 1960s resulted in a hardening of fiscal arteries on the boards of regional theatres. That change had its origins in the Canada Council's basic funding philosophy, "partnership in the arts" — the concept that cultural funding should not be dependent on any one source: "The Council believes that the arts community will do best when there are a number of benefactors to which it can turn for help. A monopoly of subsidy from any single source would, in our opinion, tend to squelch the freeness and unpredictability characteristic of the arts."[9]

Such a statement reflects the thinking of governments which do not believe that culture is an absolute good in itself. If arts patronage overall is viewed as an informal consensus among competing vested interests, the inevitable conclusion is that the government is merely a broker for the consumer demands of the public. On the other hand, since the government is itself one of those vested interests, it could naturally expect stronger representation in proportion to its increased public funding. In the early and mid-1960s, at the height of government enthusiasm for arts funding, the federal government clearly identified itself with the artists. The Council even went so far as to withhold funding from Toronto's premier theatre, the Crest, on the grounds that its artistic standards were slackening. In a time of decreased government funding, however, the "vested interest" concept of arts funding would have different practical results.

To the extent that a theatre is funded by individuals or corporations, it might be reasonable to expect that its board members, as in any business, would proportionately represent those social or economic interests—not the wider interest of the community or public at large. Just how those interests would be manifested culturally is easy to define. In its 1967-68 report, the Council noted ingenuously:

> [Music] enjoys a much higher percentage of subsidy from the private sector than any other kind of performing art....Most theatre by tradition is an intimate form of art which must establish a close contact between the actor and his public which it can best do in small houses. It might therefore be thought that private donations to the theatre would be high, but on the contrary we are faced with the paradox that this most intimate of the performing arts obtains, as a percentage of expenditures, by far the lowest level of financial assistance from the private sector.[10]

That has always been true in Canada, and it is also true that the larger the theatre, the more likely it is to receive private subsidy.[11] But the Council saw a paradox where in fact there is none. What the Council does not say is that intimacy—sexual or political—is often socially unacceptable. A non-verbal art like music, which does not potentially deal in ideas, or any vision which might challenge the social or economic status quo, is obviously going to draw funding from organizations with a vested interest in maintaining that status quo.

Yet another trend contributed to the same result. 1967 had been Canada's centennial year, and a favoured centennial project across the country was constructing a performing arts complex. Previously, the Council had made it clear that plays and players came first, buildings later. But after 1967, the success of the arts was increasingly evaluated in terms of their economic impact: "Construction of cultural facilities across Canada during the last decade [the 1970s] partially reflects the perceived need to increase cultural amenities to compete for the industrial location of new companies...The arts also play a significant role in urban renewal, particularly in revitalizing the downtown core."[12]

Buildings and institutions represented visible and quantifiable capital investments which created jobs in construction, administration, technical production, even theatre acting—everything necessary for a vital theatre except the playwrights to create the works and directors of vision to interpret them. With significantly larger capital investments and operating budgets, the perceived wisdom was that such theatres required board members with fiscal acumen. This tendency dovetailed with the Council's promotion of private participation once its own role in the partnership of the arts had diminished.

Crisis and Resolution

In retrospect, it is clear that the general direction of the regional theatres was set in the late 1960s and early 1970s. In its 1969-70 annual report, the Canada Council notified its clients that a time of austerity was at hand. The predicted dark age in fact lasted more than a decade: from 1971 to 1980, federal grants to large theatre companies (budgets over $400,000) declined from $1,964,000 to $1,428,000 in constant 1971 dollars—while the number of companies sharing those grants increased from 8 to 13.[13]

One immediate result was a withdrawal of government from its previously perceived role as a patron of culture to a more functional broker role governed by undefined criteria of public taste. The Council likewise shifted responsibility for funding the arts onto the box office and corporate donation: "The idea 'partnership in the arts' can be converted into hard economic facts. It has become clear that unless much more support is forthcoming from private donors, many arts activities will simply not survive at anything like their current levels."[14] The Council's professed "good reason for optimism" in this regard was severely undercut by a statistic in its discussion that "between 1962 and 1971, business contributions dropped from 16% to 7% of total performing arts subsidy."[15] Taking into account just large theatres (over $400,000 budgets in 1971), that figure rose to only 9% by 1980.[16]

As a further austerity measure, the Theatre Arts Development Program, a major incentive for regionals to train theatre professionals, was discontinued in 1969. The Council also announced its intention to crack down on arts organizations with considerable deficits; while acknowledging that they "often attain their standards of excellence by taking severe risks," the Council nevertheless actively encouraged boards to choose financial stability over artistic creativity. At the same time, the federal government refused—and continues to refuse—to allow three- or five-year budgeting for arts organizations to help eliminate crisis financing.[17]

The threat of reduced funding and increased reliance on box office only strengthened the intrinsic conservatism of the regionals' boards. In 1971, an inevitable confrontation between boards and artists insured that most regionals never again mounted provocative theatre.

Throughout the 1960s, the Vancouver Playhouse had led the way in encouraging playwrights, notably Eric Nicol and George Ryga. (Ryga's *The Ecstasy of Rita Joe* and *Grass and Wild Strawberries*, along with Nicol's *The Fourth Monkey*, remain among the Playhouse's most popular productions.) But Ryga's next play, commissioned by the Playhouse, dealt with the most traumatic political crisis in Canada's history—the murder of Quebec minister Pierre Laporte by FLQ terrorists in 1970 and the subsequent imposition of the War Measures Act on Quebec by the Prime Minister at the time, Pierre Trudeau.

The perspective in Ryga's *Captives of the Faceless Drummer* was decidedly anti-Trudeau, and the board refused to allow production of the play, forcing the resignation of its artistic director, David Gardner. Since then, no new work of Ryga's has premièred in a regional theatre, even though Ryga is one of the most frequently produced Canadian playwrights outside of Canada. Ryga concluded in 1974, "A priority in the future development of theatre in Canada is for the theatrical artists of this country to insist on direct control of theatre institutions subsidized by the state."[18]

Just about the time ossification set into the regionals, a generation of young, innovative Canadian theatre artists, realizing that the established theatres were not sympathetic to their cause, began to create their own theatres. Ken Gass, who founded Factory Theatre Lab in 1970, said:

> [Establishing Factory Lab] was a simple and arbitrary way of escaping the theatrical rut of following fashion. Regional playhouses were (and largely still are) shaping their seasons to reflect fashions of Broadway and the West End…By limiting the Factory to only new Canadian plays, we were forced to abandon the security blanket of our colonial upbringing. We found ourselves in a vacuum without roots and, indeed, without playwrights. The plays soon surfaced.[19]

Aided in many cases by federal make-work grants from non-cultural ministries, these artists founded the so-called "alternate" theatre movement which has produced most of the noteworthy Canadian plays since 1970. This new reality was quickly rationalized into an ad hoc production hierarchy: smaller theatres would take the risks on new work, develop them and, if proven successful, the regionals would incorporate them into their Canadian play slot.

The fact was, however, that the regionals were not just reluctant to try new work on their own: a new work premièred elsewhere had to be complete and guaranteed at the box office before they would venture even a remount. Few regionals were interested in using their stages for the essential tasks of rewriting and improving new work—and the smaller theatres were not funded to do it either. The Lennoxville Festival in Quebec did perform this function during its decade of existence from 1972 to 1982, alleviating the pressure on the regionals to do so. But Lennoxville was a country festival, completely isolated from any community support since it did not reflect any of the life around it. When the festival folded in 1982, none of the regionals publicly accepted its developmental role. The result has been, as John Gray commented after *Billy Bishop*'s brief run in New York, a hit or miss mentality even more detrimental to the evolution of a play than the commercial jungle of Broadway:

> Canadian plays are a minority art form here, a kind of underground process. Tarragon: what's one hundred and fifty seats? Give me a break! If they'd make room for us at the regionals, we could probably become more structured, more formalistic, cleaner. But they don't. Too often, when we do move to the States, we go directly from an underground situation to a tremendously uptown, international one. It's small wonder we have a tough time.[20]

By 1978, the failure of the regional system to incarnate "Canadian" theatre had become so apparent that the Council issued policy statements assigning "priority to Canadian plays, Canadian artists, and the employment of Canadians for senior artistic and administrative positions with publicly funded theatres."[21] The policy was misguided since it addressed the irrelevant problem of nationality, not the crying need for innovative work. And since these guidelines were reinforced only by implicit financial censure rather than specific sanctions, many of the regionals obeyed their letter and not their spirit. In the same report, the Council also announced tighter austerity measures. Little incentive was therefore provided the regionals to change programming which, whatever its artistic merit, rocked no boats and kept their financial gunwales above water. In the same year, a playwright-in-residence program was funded by the theatre office, but few regionals took advantage of it.

T he new Citadel Theatre complex in Edmonton. Photo: Ed Ellis.

Until the mid-1980s, little changed in the regional system. With the exception of the Centaur, the Globe, and Theatre Calgary under the artistic direction of Rick McNair, seasons at each regional were virtually indistinguishable. Walter Learning commented: "A strange paradox arose. The more similar the programming became, the greater the isolation of the individual theatres despite umbrella organizations such as the Professional Association of Canadian Theatres. The artistic directors rarely talked to each other."[22] In fact, this paradox is not surprising—with similar programming and constant economic anxiety, mistrust is natural. Formal links with the major festivals (Stratford, Shaw and Charlottetown) had been dropped, insuring tighter competition over personnel and properties.

As the regionals became more institutionalized and socially acceptable, membership on their boards increasingly acquired the cachet of opera, ballet and the symphony. Certainly the appearance of conservative elitist theatre with essentially social functions is a fact of cultural evolution anywhere. The most successful example of that process is Edmonton's Citadel, founded in 1965 and still dominated by executive producer Joseph Shoctor. A millionaire impresario, Shoctor is a cultural czar with immense public, private and corporate funds at his disposal. His new, glittering three-stage theatre complex is the envy of regionals everywhere. Shoctor has at least one innovation to his credit—from 1980 to 1984 he dispensed with an artistic director, selecting plays and personnel on an individual basis in his capacity as producer. This role was a natural outgrowth of the tendency at his theatre—and to some extent at most other regionals—towards socially approved entertainment which would increase fundraising and audiences at the expense of artistic vision.

Signs of Change

In 1983 and 1984, the artistic directorships of every regional except the Centaur and the Globe changed hands. But an equally significant development was a revival of touring in unexpected formats.

A key player in this regard was Shoctor. His flamboyant approach to theatre—marked by repeated efforts to mount productions intended for Broadway—is shared by Richard Ouzounian, who became artistic director of MTC in 1980. Together they revived the Canada Council's long-dormant notion of co-producing shows and touring them. Although the Council had hoped that co-production would be put to best advantage with plays of merit that might not otherwise be produced, Shoctor and Ouzounian collaborated on the rock musical *Grease* in 1982 and set up a tour which ended disastrously in Toronto, having barely broken even.

In the spring of 1984, Shoctor took the idea of co-production and touring one step further when he and Montreal impresario Sam Gesser planned a tour for *Duddy*, a musical based on Mordecai Richler's novel, *The Apprenticeship of Duddy Kravitz*. *Duddy* marked the first time a regional had co-produced with private funds: the musical was aimed at Broadway but died in Ottawa. And, in the fall of 1984, Ouzounian—by that time producer at Toronto's CentreStage—co-produced the world première of Bernard Slade's *Fatal Attraction* with private producers Toby Tarnow and J.P. Linton on a tryout basis for Broadway.

Yet another variant on touring took place in 1984 with a tour of A.R. Gurney's off-Broadway comedy *The Dining Room*, privately produced by Gemstone Productions (Joseph Green, Gordon Hinch, Leon Major). In the spring and summer of that year it was shown as part of the regular season at MTC and Theatre Calgary, and later at Ottawa's National Arts Centre (NAC) and Toronto's St. Lawrence Centre. *The Dining Room* was another milestone: regionals had included in their seasons a production exclusively funded by private money—in other words, the theatres were leasing out their stages and sharing the profits. Some board members at MTC, however, felt such a production had nothing to do with what a regional theatre was about, and publicly expressed concern that it contradicted the mandate of the theatre.

While these innovations were taking place, the English-language section of the NAC—after a decade of performing the role of de facto regional theatre in the Ottawa area—also acquired a producer, Andis Celms. His producing role was part of a new mandate for the NAC, which included devoting most of its time to "showcasing" or co-producing works from Canada's regional theatres. To the extent that the NAC uses its vast resources to encourage the regionals to send successful Canadian dramas or innovative works which they might not otherwise attempt, the change in mandate should be beneficial to Canadian theatre as a whole.

There were other tremors witnessed in 1984 in the regional landscape, among them the demise of a grandiose experiment at London's Grand Theatre. There, Robin Phillips, former artistic director of the Stratford Festival, took over a large regional theatre with traditional three C programming and transformed it into a top-quality classical repertory company. The type of programming remained much the same but the individual plays were more challenging: *Timon of Athens* instead of *The Taming of the Shrew, The Doctor's Dilemma* instead of *Arms and the Man*. After opening in the fall of 1983, the season faltered at the box office and the board got cold feet, sabotaging the project before it had a chance to prove itself.

Placed at a disadvantage by a looming deficit, Phillips could not fight his board and win. At Theatre Calgary, however, playwright Sharon Pollock won a Pyrrhic victory in a similar confrontation. Pollock had worked closely with outgoing artistic director Rick McNair on her own and other plays. In the spring of 1984, she became the first Canadian playwright of note to be named artistic director of a regional theatre. Then, in a sudden *volte-face,* Pollock resigned, stating that the board had not taken seriously her reservations about the theatre's standards of management. Her resignation did make an impression on the board, however. While searching for a new artistic director, they stated publicly that the appointee would have full power over administrative as well as artistic matters. In January of 1985, Martin Kinch, a playwright and director who had co-founded Toronto Free Theatre in 1972, accepted the post at Theatre Calgary.

Other bright spots appeared on the regional horizon in 1984. MTC and TNB were taken over by James Roy and Janet Amos respectively, both former artistic directors of the Blyth Festival in southern Ontario. Blyth, an extremely successful community-oriented theatre with an all-Canadian mandate, has a strong commitment to new work. Amos has also written plays, and she and Roy are married to playwrights (Ted Johns and Anne Chislett) who both mined the region around Blyth for their best work.

As important as Amos' and Roy's commitment to community and new work is the fact that they will encourage Canadian playwrights to write plays for larger stages. Because the regionals have traditionally thought of Canadian work as risky, playwrights working on new plays were encouraged to minimize the number of characters and limit the physical settings. This gave audiences and critics the impression that their vision was limited—Canadian dramatists, it was commonly felt, were only capable of two-man chamber pieces. However, Theatre Calgary under McNair had gone a long way towards demolishing that myth by providing funds for Pollock, John Murrell and W.O. Mitchell to write large-cast, epic plays if they wished. Amos and Roy also undertook to present large-scale works by their respective spouses which had already proven themselves on the limited Blyth stage. Even in a confined Toronto production, the epic canvas of Chislett's *Quiet in the Land* won it the Chalmers Award for best Canadian play of 1982.

Further good news in 1984 came from an unexpected source when Shoctor re-established the position of artistic director by appointing the British director Gordon McDougall to the post. Among McDougall's 1984-85 offerings were four world premières, three of them Canadian. And in March 1985, Bill Glassco, former artistic director of Tarragon Theatre where he nurtured many Canadian playwrights, was named director of theatre at Toronto's CentreStage.

Conclusion

Placed in the 20-year historical perspective of regional theatre, the changes apparent in 1984 were decidedly beneficial to the growth of Canadian theatre. Out of 13 theatres, at least four—the Centaur, the Globe, MTC and TNB—had become committed to rooting themselves in local soil and growing theatre from the playwright up. At Halifax's Neptune, Tom Kerr, formerly of Kelowna, B.C., was gradually shifting his theatre in that direction, while Gordon McDougall at the Citadel promised to continue innovative programming.

These successes occurred relatively late in the regionals' history. The discussion in this essay of how such changes came about has stressed their importance at the expense of the regionals' obvious success in other areas. Thanks to the institutional intent of government funding, for example, most possess a more than adequate physical plant. Although the process of building theatres first and hoping theatrical talent will fill it later is patently cart before horse, it does not condemn the horse to follow the cart forever: the presence of an excellent facility should not be a necessary impediment to the growth of drama. And, simply in terms of statistics, such institutions have enormously enlarged the audience for theatre, just as the Canada Council intended in 1961. At the board and government levels, however, there is cause for concern. Subscription remains the *sine qua non* of marketing. Government and corporate funding continues to flow at an accelerating rate towards the largest institutions and the most conservative programming.

Official disinterest in new work that speaks directly to its audience is a symptom of a national malaise—a lack of confidence in one's own culture, whatever the city, province or region. No matter what the people think, most politicians in Canada do not view culture as an integral part of daily life. Concessions are made to the arts as if artists and their supporters were only an annoying lobby which unfortunately cannot be ignored because of its demonstrable economic clout. As long as regional theatres are funded—whether by government, business or the public via the box office—on other grounds than the necessity for cultural self-expression, their function will remain compromised and their achievements questionable.

Mark Czarnecki

Notes

[1] The following is a list of the regionals, with information about stages, touring, young companies, theatre schools, miscellaneous information and projected revenue for 1984-85. Revenue figures are taken from the 1984 *Survey of Performing Arts Organisations* conducted by the Council for Business and the Arts in Canada.

Bastion Theatre, Victoria, B.C.: McPherson Playhouse, proscenium, 657 seats; Youth Touring Company to schools; Bastion Theatre School; $979,560.

Vancouver Playhouse, Vancouver, B.C.: Queen Elizabeth Playhouse, proscenium, 647; Waterfront Theatre, flexible, 240; Playhouse Acting School; $2,079,750.

Citadel Theatre, Edmonton, Alberta: Shoctor Theatre, proscenium, 685; Rice, thrust, 217; Maclab, thrust, 700; Wheels/Wings touring to schools; Citadel Young Company in Edmonton; Citadel Theatre School; $3,991,290.

Theatre Calgary, Calgary, Alberta: Max Bell Theatre, flexible proscenium, 750; Stage-Coach company to schools; children's acting classes; Extensions Department—play readings, workshops; playwright-in-residence; $2,188,895.

Globe Theatre, Regina, Saskatchewan: Globe Theatre, in the round, 400; all mainstage shows tour to Moose Jaw and Yorkton; Theatre School touring to schools; Globe Theatre School; Alternate Catalogue experimental company; playwright-in-residence; $1,001,755.

Manitoba Theatre Centre, Winnipeg, Manitoba: Mainstage, proscenium, 785; Warehouse, flexible, 230; one Warehouse production tours rural areas; $2,746,200.

Grand Theatre, London, Ontario: Grand Theatre, proscenium, 800; McManus, flexible, 150; $2,543,000.

CentreStage, Toronto, Ontario: Bluma Appel Theatre, proscenium, 894; Hour Company tours to high schools; $3,280,300.

Théâtre du Nouveau Monde, Montreal, Quebec: mainstage proscenium, 850; Inactive.

Centaur Theatre, Montreal, Quebec: Centaur 1, flexible, 255; Centaur 2, proscenium, 440; playwright-in-residence; $1,500,104.

Théâtre du Trident, Quebec City, Quebec: mainstage flexible, 653; $1,275,400.

Theatre New Brunswick, Fredericton, N.B.: Beaverbrook Playhouse, proscenium, 763; all productions tour to 8 towns; Young Company tours to schools; summer company; $1,025,600.

Neptune Theatre, Halifax, Nova Scotia; mainstage proscenium, 521; one production tours province; Young Neptune to schools; Neptune Theatre School; $1,537,904.

[2] Canada Council. *Annual Report 1961-62.* p. 4.

[3] Ibid. pp. 4-8.

[4] *Report of the Federal Cultural Policy Review Committee* (the Applebaum-Hébert Report). Ottawa, Information Services, Department of Communications, Government of Canada, 1982. p. 6.

[5] C.C.A.R., 1960-61. p. 33.

[6] Walter Learning, private interview, September 24, 1984.

[7]Ibid.

[8]C.C.A.R., 1966-67. p. 22.

[9]C.C.A.R., 1973-74. p. 17.

[10]C.C.A.R., 1967-68. p. 11.

[11]Regional theatres are financed by box office receipts and other earned revenue, private and corporate donations and subsidy from the federal, provincial and municipal governments. In 1983-84, the largest regional theatre in terms of revenue, Edmonton's Citadel, earned 40% from box office, 24% from other earned revenue, 6% from private and corporate donations and 30% from government. The smallest regional, Regina's Globe, earned 35% from box office, 9% from other earned revenue, 8% from private and corporate donations and 48% from government. (Source: CBAC survey).

[12]"An Economic Impact Assessment of the Fine Arts", Canada Council, 1983. p. 48.

[13]Canada Council. *Selected Arts Research Statistics*. 3rd ed., 1983. p. 54.

[14]C.C.A.R., 1973-74. p. 18.

[15]Idem.

[16]*Selected Arts Research Statistics*. p. 54.

[17]C.C.A.R., 1969-70. pp. 57-58.

[18]George Ryga, "Theatre in Canada: A Viewpoint On Its Development and Future", *Canadian Theatre Review*, No. 1, Winter 1974. p. 32.

[19]Quoted in Renate Usmiani, *Second Stage: The Alternative Theatre Movement in Canada*. Vancouver, University of British Columbia Press, 1983. pp. 32-33.

[20]John Gray in *The Work: Conversations with English-Canadian Playwrights*, eds. Robert Wallace and Cynthia Zimmerman. Toronto, Coach House Press, 1982. p. 55.

[21]C.C.A.R., 1978-79. p. 15.

[22]Learning, private interview, September 24, 1984.

The Alternate
Theatre Movement

In societies with a well-established theatrical tradition, the alternate or radical movement of the 1960s and 1970s means no more than yet another ripple in an ever-changing pattern; in Canada, it constitutes a major phenomenon of cultural history. The emergence of a genuinely "Canadian" theatre is so new that the very existence of such a theatre has been questioned until quite recently. It was precisely through the rise of an "alternate" theatre, setting itself up in conscious opposition to the theatre establishment, that a full awareness of the existence of a theatrical tradition in Canada finally came about; for such strong opposition to arise, there must be *something* to oppose!

The Canadian alternative theatre movement shared with its American and European counterparts a strong political orientation; rejection of the traditional author-actor-director triangle; the use of non-traditional space; a new approach to the audience; improvisation and collective creation; "poor theatre" techniques; and an emphasis on "process," rather than "product." What distinguished it from parallel movements in other countries, however, is a passionate and militant nationalism.

In Canada, alternate companies set themselves up in protest against the "colonial" attitudes of the directors of regional theatres; it was felt the regionals offered no scope for growth or development to Canadian playwrights, and were unwilling to risk any departure from forms of production tried and tested elsewhere. Another target of the alternate companies' attacks was traditional theatre training in the universities and, in the case of Quebec, at the Ecole Nationale du Théâtre, with its heavy reliance on the classics in the curriculum, and its emphasis on the use of proper Parisian French—a "foreign language!" Finally, the young theatre enthusiasts who created the movement rebelled against the fact that the nation's showcase theatre should be located in Stratford and feature Shakespearian productions rather than Canadian plays. The promotion of young playwrights and original productions constituted a focal point, much as the Vietnam war provided a rallying point for the American radical theatre. The creed of the Canadian movement was summed up by playwright/director John Palmer: "We have embarked on nothing less than a fight for our own culture. I can think of nothing sadder than inaction...We will produce well and badly, but we must produce."[1]

As in other countries, alternative theatre in Canada reflects the aesthetics of Artaud (total theatre) and the ideology of Brecht/Piscator (theatre as a moral institution; epic theatre). The American radical theatre, of course, was a major influence, especially The Living Theatre and the environmental experiments of Richard Schechner. Canadian theatre history itself offers evidence of antecedents, both in the area of political theatre and aesthetic experimentation: Workers' Theatre in both English and French, Herman Voaden's "Symphonic Expressionism," the theories of Roy Mitchell.[2] However, there is no evidence of a direct link between these phenomena, which occurred mostly in the 1930s, and the alternative theatre movement of the 70s.

English Canada

In English Canada, the movement began in Toronto, with the First Underground Theatre Festival of 1970, when the term "alternate theatre" first appeared (coined by Tom Hendry); other significant dates are the founding of Toronto Workshop Productions by George Luscombe, 1959, and the Gaspé-Niagara Playwrights' Conference of 1971, with its reiterated demands for greater support to Canadian dramatists, e.g., the institution of a 50% Canadian content quota for all regional theatres. The decade which followed saw the rise of literally innumerable small, alternate companies across the country, most of them patterned after Toronto models, especially Toronto Workshop Productions and Theatre Passe Muraille.

Toronto Workshop Productions came about from the amalgamation of two groups, the Arts Theatre Club, founded by Basya Hunter, 1959, and Luscombe's Workshop Productions. In 1961, Luscombe was appointed permanent director of the combined operation. Although still on the amateur level, Toronto Workshop Productions' first show, *Hey, Rube!*, a collective creation, proved a great success. Since 1963, TWP has been a professional company, working in three genres: collective creation, free adaptation of classics and scripted plays. For the first eight years, the company performed in the basement of an old factory in Toronto's West End, with seating capacity for one hundred on bleachers around an open stage. In 1967, it moved to its present theatre facilities in downtown Toronto where the new house seats three hundred in an open stage arrangement.

A disciple of Brecht who has worked with Joan Littlewood in England, Luscombe feels the theatre's main function is to make a social statement. He defines his work as "popular theatre:" "Popular theatre means bypassing existing audiences, going into areas where people are totally unconverted and thereby creating new awareness."[3] He also insists on an extremely high standard of performance. To achieve this, Luscombe emphasizes actor training and the ensemble idea.

TWP pioneered the use of collective creation in English Canada; these productions were usually built around a current social or political problem. The company also first introduced the concept of "free adaptation," using classics for their *Materialwert* (as raw material—Brecht's term), in combination with original material, or in montage. Original scripts came from writer-in-residence Jack Winter (1961-1976), and other Canadian playwrights such as Len Peterson and Rick Salutin.

While TWP set the pattern for much subsequent development, Theatre Passe

Muraille evolved into the most successful and influential alternative theatre operation in Canada. From a humble start in the basement of Rochdale College, itself an "alternate" institution of higher education, it eventually acquired a more spacious, 250-seat home on Ryerson Avenue in Toronto. Within ten years of its founding in 1969, Passe Muraille had produced twenty-two collective creations, a large number of scripted plays by new Canadian authors, and had also developed a distinctive style of its own. Throughout this period, the company engaged in a nationwide "seeding" program, which led to the launching of alternative theatres from coast to coast: Codco in St. John's, Newfoundland; 25th Street House, in Saskatoon, Saskatchewan; and Theatre Network, in Edmonton, Alberta.

In Toronto, Passe Muraille provided young theatre hopefuls with a "New Works Program," offering expert advice and the use of its facilities. The dynamism, vision and energy of the company is due to a large extent to the two men who created Passe Muraille, Jim Garrard and Paul Thompson. Garrard founded the company and gave it its initial direction; Thompson created the special Passe Muraille style. Both men come from academic backgrounds and studied theatre in Europe— Garrard at the London Academy of Music and Art, Thompson with Roger Planchon at the Théâtre de la Cité at Villeurbanne. Garrard returned to Canada in 1968, and quickly became a part of the growing cultural and nationalistic protest movement. He briefly joined the Rochdale Theatre Project, then founded his own company, "Passe Muraille." Like Brecht, he had dreams of a theatre for the masses: "I'd like to make theatre as popular as bowling," he once said.[4]

Thompson's work was oriented towards two major goals: actor development and the invention of new, more effective methods of collective creation. Although he frequently called on the services of writers, his shows were always conceived with the actor foremost in mind. He felt that collective creation provides the best instrument to bring out an actor's potential. Building on the foundation laid by Luscombe, Thompson went a good deal further. His original contribution to the technique of collective creation was to put the onus for research and documentation entirely on the actors themselves. Critics often point out the strong sense of authenticity of Passe Muraille shows; it is a result of the actors' direct involvement with their material.

Passe Muraille pursued two major lines of investigation; sociological and historical. The sociological shows attempted to create authentic mirror images of a specific community: *The Farm Show*, *The Immigrant Show*, *The West Show*. To produce these, the director and the actors moved into the community themselves. Through personal contact, shared experience and observation, the actors assembled the necessary documentation to serve as a basis for the show. Improvisations followed, and gradually, with the addition of mime, song and poetry, a cohesive image of the community emerged. The most successful production in this genre was *The Farm Show*, first produced in a barn in the farming community of Clinton, Ontario, in 1972. There followed a successful tour of major centres, a radio version, a film of the production process, and finally, publication.[5]

Passe Muraille's historical shows are more complex, since they try to demonstrate the political significance of past events in relation to the present, and above all, to discover a national mythology within the material provided by Canadian history. The creation of myths which can be shared by all and provide a sense of national identity had long been the aim of poets and novelists; Thompson set a similar

Anne Anglin, Miles Potter, Paul Thompson and Fina MacDonnell in the "Man on a Tractor" scene from Theatre Passe Muraille's 1972 *The Farm Show,* directed by Paul Thompson.

goal for his theatre. Because of the complexity of the material, writers were usually called in to assist the company. Their main task was to help with the structuring of scenes as the play developed, and to give final shape to the actors' work. Passe Muraille's greatest success in the historical genre was *1837: The Farmer's Revolt*, produced in cooperation with Rick Salutin in 1972, and published in 1976.[6] The Passe Muraille approach to both sociological and historical shows set the pattern for alternate theatres across the country.

After TWP and Theatre Passe Muraille, Factory Theatre Lab was probably the third most influential institution on the Toronto alternate theatre scene of the 70s. From its inception, it was dedicated to supporting new Canadian playwrights. Founded in 1970 by Ken Gass, Factory Theatre Lab provided a training ground for young actors, directors, and especially writers who had no way of gaining access to the "establishment." It first opened in a makeshift complex on top of a garage, but eventually found more suitable quarters in downtown Toronto. Operations began with a series of playwriting contests, followed by a workshop program. Gass' policy proved highly successful: within a year, eight full-length plays and nine one-acters had been produced; within four years, an anthology of representative Factory Lab productions was in print;[7] within ten years, Factory Theatre had premièred fifty new Canadian plays, and many other small theatres were following its lead. Some of the new authors discovered at FTL "graduated" to the regional theatres: David Freeman, George Walker and others.

To illustrate the full range of alternative theatre in Toronto, three more companies should be mentioned: Toronto Free Theatre, which started out literally "free," i.e., not charging admission, but soon had to adopt a more realistic policy; Black Theatre Canada, an example of ethnic theatre; and the defunct Redlight Theatre, dedicated to the feminist cause.

Not all alternative theatre in English Canada, however, followed models developed in Toronto. In Vancouver, the movement took on a very different aspect, due to the influence of the counterculture of the American west coast. While alternative theatre in the rest of Canada was mainly concerned with making social and political statements, the most interesting work done in Vancouver was introspective, reflecting the west coast interest in the drug culture, Freudian psychology, Gestalt and other therapies. Theatre is seen, not as a tool for social action, nor as a comment on or interpretation of life, but rather as an integral and enriching part of life itself.

Underground theatre in Vancouver started early and developed vigorously: between 1965 and 1975, some forty small companies were active in the city. However, most of these were short-lived and had little impact. Tamahnous Theatre is the only company representative of the period which has survived into the 80s. It was founded in 1971 by John Gray, now the well-known author of popular musicals,[8] then a recent graduate of the University of British Columbia. With a group of other young idealists, he set up a small company dedicated to "poor" theatre; the name they chose was "Tamahnous," Chilcotin Indian for "magic." The undertaking proved highly successful. Within ten years, Tamahnous had produced thirty-eight plays, of which twenty-one were original works, either collective creations or collectives produced in association with house writer Jeremy Long. Their first shows were done at the Vancouver Arts Club. In 1974, they acquired a home of their own; since 1977, they have been operating as the resident company at the Vancouver East Cultural Centre.

Members of the company attribute their success to a strong ensemble feeling, heightened through a period of communal living in the early stages. Tamahnous' special interest lay in expressing inner reality: dreams, fantasies, memories. Visual images thus became more important than verbal expression. The most interesting production along those lines was *Vertical Dreams*, 1979, a collective creation developed with the help of two professional therapists and based entirely on dream and fantasy material.[9] It is interesting to note that alternative theatres in other areas of the west followed the pattern of Passe Muraille, rather than that of Tamahnous. This was especially true of 25th Street House in Saskatoon, but also, if to a lesser extent, of Theatre Network, Catalyst Theatre, and Theatre Three in Edmonton, and Alberta Theatre Projects in Calgary.

Across the continent in the Atlantic Provinces, a large number of short-lived alternate theatre companies also made their appearance during the 1970s (e.g. Pier

One, Seaweed Theatre, Theatre 1770 in Halifax). The most interesting and long-lived ventures, however, can be found in Newfoundland, with Codco and especially the Mummers' Troupe. The Mummers, founded in 1971, were active for over a decade; some of their productions toured across the country. Their work reflects the particular situation of Newfoundland within the Canadian confederation, which somewhat resembles that of Quebec. By the late 1960s, Newfoundlanders also were suffering from a severe identity crisis. Just as the Quiet Revolution followed the Duplessis rule in Quebec, an outburst of nationalistic cultural activity took place in Newfoundland after the end of the Smallwood era. Its thrust was to render the native culture, including the Newfoundland dialect, "respectable," and to agitate for social and economic justice.

Chris Brookes, founder of the Mummers' Troupe, formulated the company's goals: 1., to create a sense of identity through a restoration of the heritage of the past, and 2., to battle for social justice through a theatre of political agitation, using collective creation techniques. The revival of the medieval Mummers' Play proved an instant success and became an annual tradition. In their political shows, the Mummers followed the example of Passe Muraille; however, their actors were chosen on the basis of their political conviction, rather than their professional skills. As a result, the Mummers' "documentary community drama" often lacked polish and sophistication. On the other hand, they were able to achieve a strong sense of urgency and immediacy. Their production of *Gros Mourn*, e.g., was put together on the spur of the moment, in ten days of frenzied creativity, to assist a small community in its protest against eviction to make way for a national park. Most productions, of course, were more carefully prepared; some, like *They Club Seals, Don't They?*, raised issues of national relevance. Newfoundland playwright Michael Cook has summed up the importance of the Mummers' work to the people of their province: "The Mummers' Troupe...use their resources and their skill to help us share in our common heritage. Theirs is a living theatre, rich, functional, and vitally necessary to us in Newfoundland."[10]

Quebec

In French Canada, alternative theatre also represents the second wave in the evolution of an original dramaturgy; as in English Canada, it originated in protest against established forms of theatrical expression, against the theatre "establishment," against traditional training methods. But there are essential differences. Because of the existence of the Centre d'essai des auteurs dramatiques founded in Montreal in 1965, the alternative, or "jeune théâtre," movement here did not need to concern itself with supporting young playwrights. In fact, companies of the jeune théâtre set themselves up in deliberate antithesis to the more literary "nouveau théâtre québécois" (Michel Tremblay, Robert Gurik, Jean Barbeau, etc.), whose authors, they felt, sought success only to defect to the "bourgeois" mainstream. In general, the Quebec movement tended towards greater radicalism than its English counterpart, both in its political orientation and in its aesthetic creed. Collective creation here was seen as a political act: a demonstration of the need for action based on democratic, collective effort.

A further difference lies in the fact that in Quebec, alternative companies actually formed an organization, AQJT (Association québécoise du jeune théâtre), 1972, an outgrowth of ACTA, Association canadienne du théâtre d'amateurs, founded in 1958. The term "jeune théâtre," then, stands for the movement in general and for a specific organization (from which some of the member companies have since seceded), a great part of which is now professional, not amateur. It is also the title of the Association journal.

Although the main thrust of the "jeune théâtre" was political and social activism, a small number of companies carried on highly sophisticated experimentation and research, e.g., L'Eskabel, Les Pichous and La Grande Réplique. Of the other companies, Le Grand Cirque Ordinaire (1969-1978) probably provides the most representative example. It began as a gesture of protest, when the entire graduating class (seven students) of the Ecole Nationale du Théâtre withdrew and set up a collective creation group of their own under the leadership of Raymond Cloutier, who had just returned from a number of years with avant-garde companies in Europe. Members of Le Grand Cirque Ordinaire called themselves "comédiens-créateurs." Improvisation was to liberate them from the "foreign" language and culture they had been imbued with at the School, and to bring them back to their Quebec roots. Their approach to improvisation was almost mystical; at the same time, they never lost sight of social concerns and the need for consciousness-raising. Their *T'es pas tannée, Jeanne d'Arc*, 1969, reflected the strong nationalism of the time; it earned much critical acclaim. Other shows dealt with the family and consumerism (*la Famille transparente*), social problems (*T'en rappelles-tu, Pibrac, ou le Québecoi?*), and exploration of the collective subconscious (*la Tragédie américaine de l'Enfant Prodigue*).

At the other end of the spectrum are those companies which aligned themselves squarely with an agitprop approach, theatre seen as a tool in the fight for proletarian revolution: Le Théâtre d'la Shop, with a history of moving in on strike situations, Théâtre Parminou, which creates productions on commission, and, most representative, Le Théâtre Euh! (1969-1978). Le Théâtre Euh! was founded by Clément Cazelais, who had been in Europe with Raymond Cloutier. It started out as a fully democratic working commune of six. They worked exclusively in improvisation and collective creation; used only non-traditional theatre spaces; and made a conscious effort to bring their theatre to the people, rather than have the people come to them. The company engaged in a wide variety of activities: street theatre, commissioned plays, support of strike action, theatre for children, public demonstrations. They also produced a number of major shows, such as *Quand le Matriarcat fait des petits*, a vitriolic view of the position of women in Quebec society, *Cré Antigone*, an examination of the relationship between economic and political power, and *l'Histoire du Québec*, a look at Quebec history from a nationalist/marxist perspective.

Women's theatre, another aspect of the alternative theatre movement, became a much more visible phenomenon in Quebec than in English Canada. Two companies must be mentioned: the Théâtre expérimental des femmes, set up by a group of dissident women members of the Théâtre expérimental de Montréal, in protest against male domination of the theatre; and the Théâtre des Cuisines, a highly political group which has produced collective creations on key feminist issues such as abortion (*Nous aurons les enfants que nous voudrons*), and the demeaning character of housework (*Moman travaille pas, a trop d'ouvrage*).[11]

Finally, Jean-Claude Germain, critic, director, actor, producer and prolific playwright, must be included as a unique and original phenomenon on the Quebec

The Théâtre des Cuisines in the 1975 *Moman travaille pas, a trop d'ouvrage*. Photo: Murièle Villeneuve.

alternative theatre scene. From his headquarters at the tiny (114-seat) Théâtre d'Aujourd'hui in East Montreal, he has been battling since 1969 for a "liquidation" of the classics, the establishment of a genuinely Québécois stage idiom, and the advancement of Quebec from its present "folkloric" stage of development to the stage of true "culture." Starting out with improvisation (he pioneered verbal improvisation in Quebec) and collective creation, he soon moved on to create his own, albeit actor-oriented, scripts. By the end of the 1970s, Germain and his theatre had become an institution on the Montreal theatre scene.

The Alternative Theatre Scene Today

Although the movement of the 1970s has largely run its course, there remains a varied and active "alternate" to the establishment theatre scene; but the picture has changed considerably. Those alternate theatres of the earlier period which still operate are by now considered "mainstream," although the original concerns are still pursued. The new alternates have shifted their interest from political theatre and the promotion of new Canadian plays to experimentation with style and technique, and often return to the classics as a base.

In Toronto, Passe Muraille, now under Clarke Rogers, and Toronto Workshop Productions, still under George Luscombe, boast faithful audiences. Toronto Free Theatre and Factory Theatre continue to produce new Canadian plays, though Guy Sprung's recent successful productions of *Waiting for Godot* and *In the Jungle of the Cities* at Toronto Free Theatre exemplify the trend away from exclusively Canadian programming over the last few years.[12]

In Vancouver, Tamahnous Theatre continues to be the leading alternative company. Touchstone Theatre, in the Gastown section of the city, primarily performs Canadian scripts premièred elsewhere. Among Prairie companies, 25th Street Theatre has reached audiences which outnumber those of the regional theatres, due to its touring program. *Paper Wheat*, e.g., played in thirty-two centres to more than 14,000 people. However, the theatre is bent on retaining its "popular" and "populist" orientation: "For us, Shakespeare, Shaw and other classical writers will always be secondary."[13]

In the Maritimes, the tradition of the 70s remains alive with the work of the Mulgrave Road Coop, a Nova Scotia touring company, whose interest centers around regional and social concerns. Their major medium of expression is still collective creation.

In the province of Quebec, at least fourteen companies from the 70s are still in operation, four of them independent (Le Théâtre d'Aujourd'hui, La Grande Réplique, Le Théâtre sans fil and Les Pichous), the others belonging to AQJT (Le Théâtre de carton; La Grosse Valise; Le Parminou; Le Théâtre de quartier; Les Enfants du Paradis—now called Carbone 14; L'Eskabel; Le Groupe de la Veillée, Le Théâtre expérimental des femmes).

The two major original concerns of the alternative theatre movement are now dealt with by a number of new companies. Political theatre has appeared in Ottawa, where the Great Canadian Theatre Company (founded 1975) runs a regular series of agitprop productions, such as *Antinuclear Play, World Disarmament Play, Public Service Strike Support Play,* and *Yes, Pierre, There Really Is A Canada.* In the North, Magnus Theatre and Kam Theatre Lab of Thunder Bay tour Canadian plays to remote Northern communities, besides producing their own collective creations. In French Canada, Le Parminou remains the only politically militant group to follow the pattern set by the now defunct Théâtre Euh!

The major new phenomenon on the scene today is the shift to research and experimentation with the aesthetics of theatre. In Toronto, the focus of this new trend has been on several smaller companies: Buddies in Bad Times, under artistic director Sky Gilbert, explores the relationships between theatre and the printed word and sees theatre moving towards a "poet-playwright." Gilbert has also written and produced a number of plays exploring homosexual themes. Nightwood, under artistic director Cynthia Grant produces a "theatre of images" which takes its inspiration from other art forms, such as painting, sculpture, the novel; Necessary Angel, under artistic director Richard Rose, and Thom Sokoloski's Theatre Autumn Leaf try to establish new habits of perception by creating unusual challenges, such as masked actors, and produce avant-garde environmental, epic and political theatre. A.K.A. Performance Interfaces experiments with the integration of technological elements (video, audiotape, film) with live performance.[14]

In the same vein, Toronto's Video Cabaret creates a synthesis of rock music, video and live performance (*1984; Last Man on Earth*). Its founder and director, playwright Michael Hollingsworth, claims only such a blending of genres can reflect contemporary life, where "people are used to doing several things at the same time."[15]

Calgary now figures on the alternate theatre scene with Arete, which offers new Canadian plays, often based on multiple authorship; Sun Ergos experiments with adaptations, collage, music and choreography.

In Quebec, the orientation of the jeune théâtre has changed. It now defines itself as "théâtre de création, de recherche."[16] Gilbert David sums up the general trend, in and beyond Quebec: "Le jeune théâtre a...moins et moins le coeur militant....dans les années soixante-dix... plusieurs ont cru changer le monde; depuis quelque temps, c'est plutôt le théâtre qu'on veut changer."[17]

This change of direction notwithstanding, the phenomenon of the late 1960s and 70s has left a strong mark on every level of the subsequent theatrical evolution. It has changed audience expectations, widened audience horizons and created a new awareness for the audience of the importance of its own role in the production. To the actor, improvisation and collective creation have given a heightened sense of his own creativity and a new approach to the scripted text. On the level of the director, the new techniques have opened up a variety of new relationships— between actors and director, director and playwright, director and audience. Finally, the movement has had considerable influence on playwriting itself. Playwrights, who have seen their role questioned, now tend to work with much greater awareness of the actors and the practicalities of the stage. In the wake of collective creation, they are also more willing to write in cooperation with a company or with one or more other playwrights, instead of in their former "splendid isolation." Under the impact of the alternative theatre movement, literature has come to serve the theatre, rather than theatre serving literature.

Renate Usmiani

Notes

[1] In John Palmer, *Henrik Ibsen On the Necessity of Producing Norwegian Theatre*. Toronto, Playwrights' Co-op, 1976. p. 13.

[2] Roy Mitchell, *Creative Theatre*. 1929. New York, Kindle Press, 1969.

[3] George Luscombe, Toronto Workshop Productions European Tour Folder; (quoted in Renate Usmiani, *Second Stage: The Alternative Theatre Movement in Canada*. Vancouver, U.B.C. Press, 1983. p. 30.)

[4] Jim Garrard, quoted in Usmiani. p. 44.

[5] Theatre Passe Muraille, *The Farm Show*. Toronto, Coachhouse Press, 1976.

[6] Rick Salutin and Theatre Passe Muraille, *1837: The Farmers' Revolt*. Toronto, Lorimer, 1976.

[7] Connie Brissenden, ed., *The Factory Lab Anthology*. Vancouver, Talonbooks, 1974.

[8] *Billy Bishop Goes to War; Eighteen Wheels; Rock and Roll*.

[9]Unpublished; videotape at Tamahnous Theatre.

[10]Michael Cook, "Buchans—A Mining Town", *St. John's Evening Telegraph*, September 16, 1974.

[11]Théâtre des Cuisines, *Moman travaille pas, a trop d'ouvrage*. Montreal, Editions remue-ménage, 1975.

[12]See Boyd Neil, "Toronto Free Theatre: Guy Sprung Keeps Those Theatrical Bangs Coming", *Avenue*, November 1984, pp. 44-46.

[13]Andy Tahn, artistic director, 25th Street House, quoted in *Canadian Theatre Review*, No. 21, Winter 1979. p. 48.

[14]See Patricia Keeney Smith, "Living With Risk: Toronto's New Alternate Theatre", *Canadian Theatre Review*, No. 38, Fall 1983.

[15]Michael Hollingsworth, interviewed in *Canadian Theatre Review*, No. 25, Winter, 1980. p. 20.

[16]Michel Breton, quoted in *Jeu,* No. 29, 1983.4. p. 61.

[17]Gilbert David, ibid., pp. 51, 52. "The jeune théâtre has become less and less militant...In the 1960s, many people thought they could change the world; for some time now, it is the theatre one wants to transform."

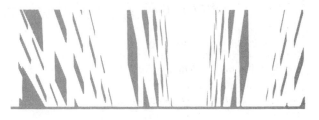

Playwrighting
in Quebec

With Gratien Gélinas' *Tit-Coq* (1948), a new and original undercurrent became apparent in indigenous dramatic writing which would lead to the flowering of the "new Quebec theatre" at the end of the 1960s. Gélinas rejected the desire for universality first and foremost (this usually took the form of a denial of external reality) which characterized a good part of the theatrical and literary community, in favour of plays that were firmly rooted in the everyday concerns of ordinary people and set in a universe they could recognize. This is the view expressed in his 1949 essay, "Pour un théâtre national et populaire," and enlarged upon in his lecture, "Jeune Auteur, mon camarade" (1960):

> And if you are to remain unknown to future generations or in faraway countries, that's too bad, or all to the good. Write for your own kind, and your life will not have been wasted. Write for the people in your country, in your city or on your street. . . . If you write for them, these forgotten people on your street will come and see your work.[1]

Gélinas was not in fact a very prolific dramatist. In 1959, while the whole theatrical scene was being markedly changed by the advent of Marcel Dubé and the establishment of the large professional institutions, Gélinas wrote *Bousille et les Justes,* a biting satire about a society which hides behind the mask of hypocrisy in order to maintain its images of power. Not surprisingly, this play has been produced in Czechoslovakia. His last drama, *Hier, les enfants dansaient* (1966), used the all-too familiar conflict between father and son to illustrate the problem of Quebec nationalism. As an answer to the well-worn question, "What does Quebec want?", this play was performed frequently in English Canada.

At the beginning of the 1950s, after only two years as a writer and with three plays to his credit, Marcel Dubé found himself entrusted with an overwhelming task by the theatre community. Being a prolific dramatist with something to say, it would be up to him to build a repertory of Quebec plays. And that is exactly what he did. Constantly moving back and forth between television (which was in its infancy) and the stage, he wrote almost uninterruptedly until the early 1970s, when his output gradually decreased. His achievements include more than twenty-five plays, twenty television dramas, twelve translations and four television serials. Although Dubé "looks for tragedy in his characters," he rarely finds it, and his plays are usually closer to psychological and social drama. His work seems to fall into two main divisions. His first period, in the 1950s, with such plays as *Zone* (1953), *Un simple soldat* (1956) and *le Temps des Lilas* (1958), is an exploration of working-class characters, using dialogue that reflects the way they talk, in dramas that clearly convey the author's real compassion for his characters. These first plays are "slices of life" focussing on the aspirations of the younger generation, even though it is the adults' conflicts that constantly come to the surface. Failure is the common denominator.

Dubé's second period, beginning with *Bilan* (1960) is quite different. To begin with, there is a definite change in setting, as seen in *Bilan, Les Beaux Dimanches* (1965) and *le Retour des oies blanches* (1966). From a working-class setting we move up into the upper-class. Dubé's reason for this is, to say the least, odd. He began to think that his plays should provide a good linguistic example (in the sense of setting *standards*), while at the same time wanting to maintain their realism. This led him to set the action of his plays in a social class where the language was more refined. These plays deal with young men (almost all of them rather spineless) trying to escape from the oppressive atmosphere of their families, and their middle-aged fathers who come to realize that they have made a mess of their lives despite their social and financial success. At the beginning of the 1970s, the public began to turn away from Dubé, after having remained faithful to him for twenty years. It is true that his writing has become outmoded. His omniscient characters often reveal too much and leave little subtext to be discovered by the audience.

Those who were writing plays at the same time as Dubé, in the 1950s and 60s, were primarily novelists or poets and wrote for the stage without managing to produce plays that were completely convincing. Their writing was far too literary and either undramatic or based on French plays. Paul Toupin, who wrote *Brutus* (1952), is a neo-classicist influenced by Montherlant, just as Jacques Languirand (*les Insolites*, 1956; *les Violons de l'automne,* 1960) followed in the footsteps of the French dramatists of the 1950s. The plays of poet and novelist Anne Hébert (*le Temps sauvage,* 1963), with their conflicts between noble and tormented souls, leave insufficient room for characters to carry the dialogue. The versatile and prolific writer Jacques Ferron wrote plays that are strongly marked by fantasy (*l'Ogre,* 1950; *le Cheval de Don Juan,* 1957) or resemble political allegory (*la Tête du Roi,* 1963), but never managed to win recognition, except for *les Grands Soleils* (1958, revised in 1968), an original treatment of certain national myths surrounding the 1837 rebellion of the "Patriotes."

By the beginning of the 1960s, conditions were ripe for the explosion of what the critic Michel Bélair has called the "nouveau théâtre québécois." It was among the theatre companies—both amateur and professional—and the collectives that the changes were more obvious. But they can also be seen in the career of a dramatist like Françoise Loranger, whose work ranges from middle-class drama

(*Une maison, un jour*, 1965 and *Encore cinq minutes*, 1967), through Pirandellian contrivances (*Double jeu*, 1969) to political plays (*Chemin du Roi*, 1968, a hilarious treatment of General de Gaulle's visit, and *Medium saignant*, 1970, a somewhat demagogic play about the future of French in Quebec).

The first plays of Robert Gurik also date from the mid-60s. The plots of his plays are a little too obvious because they are too contrived. They deal with the plight of individuals in conflict with the various authorities that compose modern society. Gurik is a playwright who uses every means at his disposal, including basing his plays on current political happenings, as in *Hamlet, prince du Québec* (1968) and *le Tabernacle à trois étages* (1973), or on a news item such as the murder of three bosses by one of their employees in *le Procès de Jean-Baptiste M.* (1972). This is probably his best play, about a man with a stronger belief in the socio-economic system than those who control it.

By 1968, the series of social upheavals which had wracked Quebec society since the beginning of the 60s and had already left its mark on poetry and the novel, had visible repercussions in the theatre. Within two years, Quebec plays, which had represented only a small percentage of those produced, accounted for more than half of the plays that were staged. The "nouveau théâtre québécois" would be kicked off by the production of *les Belles-Soeurs* by Michel Tremblay. Plays by Jean-Claude Germain, Jean Barbeau, Yves Sauvageau, Serge Sirois, Michel Garneau, Roland Lepage and other dramatists—not to mention the many collectively-written plays—would make up Quebec theatre until the second half of the 70s. This theatre worked at developing forms of dramatic language capable of transposing Quebec popular speech to the stage. The characters mostly depicted, more or less directly, aspects of the alienation felt by Quebeckers as a whole, which stemmed from the historical situation. The plays inevitably raised the question of nationalism at the centre of the problems and conflicts besetting Quebec society.

Although these were prevailing tendencies, they did not represent the totality of playwriting, and some important dramatists did not share these characteristics. This applies particularly to Claude Gauvreau, a *poète maudit* with all the mythical qualities the term implies. In the 1940s he wrote *les Entrailles*, a series of dramatic texts bordering on surrealism. His fame rests more on such plays as *la Charge de l'orignal épormyable* (1956) and *Les oranges sont vertes* (1970), "melodramas" which are written in flamboyant language and depict the torture and death of poets who are clearly the playwright's *alter ego*. Réjean Ducharme is another of these dramatists. He is a novelist, who, like Gauvreau, loves to play with language. He began to write for the theatre in 1968, with an attack on the classics and the values they stood for (in *le Cid maghané*) and a play about lost children and their quest for love (*Inès Pérée et Inat Tendu*, revised in 1975). In 1978 he produced *Haha!...*, one of the major works of Quebec drama, which constituted an abusive demolition of social facades and a desperate attempt to divest language of its powers.

The most striking thing about Tremblay's plays was the language. He completed what had been taking shape in the plays of Gélinas and in Dubé's earlier work, never allowing popular speech to be watered down for use on the stage. He practiced it like a song, bringing out its own sounds and rhythms, seeking out its special expressiveness, speaking a reality which could be spoken in no other way. And Tremblay used this language that the theatre had inhibited to bring out the inhibitions of Quebeckers, everything that was never talked about: economic, sexual

and intellectual privation, the necessity for self-disguise, and widespread powerlessness. Tremblay's plays are not easy to pin down with simple generalizations; his work is constantly shifting and evolving. Its interest, which has long been attributed to its appropriateness to the world he describes and to its expression of certain consequences of the national problem, goes beyond these interpretations. The large number of foreign productions of Tremblay's plays (particularly in the U.S.) proves this. The questions he raises about identity, or the family unit—which he smashed to smithereens in *En pièces détachées* (1972) and *À toi, pour toujours, ta Marie-Lou* (1972) before suggesting new solutions in *Bonjour là, bonjour* (1974)—and about the relation between mysticism and sexuality (*Damnée Manon, sacrée Sandra,* 1977) are not merely confined to Quebec itself, but have an impact far beyond its borders. After having practically abandoned playwriting in favour of novels, Tremblay has returned to the stage with *Albertine en cinq temps* (1984), in which he raises questions about human life and the different ways in which an individual can view her existence at different ages.

At the same time that Tremblay was beginning to write, Jean-Claude Germain was setting about the task of radically changing the relationship between Quebec audiences and the theatre. In plays that were therapeutic in intent, Germain led an uproarious investigation of the greater and lesser myths surrounding both the theatre and society in Quebec. These are episodic plays in which the characters play at acting and the playwright points out family flaws (as in *Diguidi, diguidi, ha! ha! ha!,* 1969), puts his finger on our cultural accretions (*Les hauts et les bas de la vie d'une diva: Sarah Ménard par eux-mêmes,* 1979), or conducts a dazzling mythological tour of Quebec in *Un pays dont la devise est je m'oublie* (1976). Germain, who is a direct heir of the pre-war revue artists and a formidable polemicist who knows his Quebec hagiography better than anyone else, has voiced most clearly and urgently the essential questions about our national history and culture and their relation to politics. He still teaches playwriting, although in the last few years he has done less writing himself.

Jean Barbeau's themes are similar to those in Germain's plays but his work does not have the same unity of vision, subtlety or formal experimentation. Barbeau deals with questions connected with the concerns of the moment, which is why several of his plays (such as *le Chant du sink,* 1973, on the language question) have quickly become dated. We should nevertheless mention *Ben-Ur* (1971), about the spread of American ideology through comic strips, and *Solange* (1974), perhaps the only play by Barbeau that cannot be reduced to a simple thematic reading, and portrays a lonely woman who combines her mysticism with dreams of political revolution.

Anouk Simard, Andrée Boucher, Ginette Morin and Louise Saint-Pierre as the Witches in Michel Garneau's 1978 *Macbeth,* directed by Roger Blay at the Théâtre de la Manufacture. Photo: Anne de Guise.

Michel Garneau, who is primarily a poet, mainly looked on his work as a dramatist as the work of a "wordsmith." Since he generally considered himself to be the *écrivain public* for the collectives he joined, his work presents many disparate themes which are nonetheless guided by a desire for liberation on every level and a spirit of conviviality. Garneau has developed a stage language that is dense, bold, consciously archaic and completely attuned to the beauty of popular speech. The finest example of his mastery of language is provided by his 1978 translation of Shakespeare's *Macbeth* into the French of early Quebec, perhaps the finest Shakespearian translation in the French-speaking world. Among his many plays, the following deserve particular mention: *Quatre à quatre* (1973), a striking simultaneous portrait of four generations of women; *Adidou, adidouce* (1977), dealing with the rites of passage in human life; and *Emilie ne sera plus jamais cueillie par l'anémone* (1981), a sensitive evocation of the American poet, Emily Dickinson, which never lapses into biography.

In keeping with the revival of interest in the traditional language and life of Quebec, the work of Roland Lepage has had great popular success. In *le Temps d'une vie* (1974) he tells the story of a woman from a rural background, from her birth to her death. (An adaptation of this play in Walloon had a long and successful run in Europe.) *La Complainte des hivers rouges* (1974) presented scenes of daily life during the rebellion of 1837. The renewal of interest in speech that is rooted in a particular region and its history was also reflected by the work of Antonine Maillet, who revealed in *la Sagouine* (1971) the world of Acadian culture and tradition with a remarkable portrayal of humble dignity in the face of oppression.

At the end of the 1970s (and some people see a direct connection with the 1976 election of the Parti Québécois, which was dedicated to the achievement of Quebec independence), playwrights gradually abandoned a nationalistic interpretation of Quebec reality and frequently turned to expressing concerns of an individual nature. This tendency, coupled with the strained relations between large theatrical institutions and young playwrights, led to the creation of "intimate" plays, intended to be performed in limited theatrical spaces. While most of these dramatists continued the trend to linguistic realism, other dramatists re-endowed their work with a self-conscious literariness. The concept of collective identity, which was clearly a national identity, began to take on other meanings: class identity, North American identity, generational identity, feminist identity, etc. This transition is clearly expressed in the work of Serge Sirois. In 1972 he wrote *Aujourd'hui, peut-être*, a captivating play about dreams, impotence and indecisiveness, which was obviously a metaphor for the situation in Quebec. His 1980 play, *les Pommiers en fleurs,* was set in Chicago and was based on a news item about a man who hid the bodies of his teen-aged murder victims inside the walls of his house. Sirois gave a taut and lucid treatment of the contradictory nature of the North American male.

One of the offshoots of the trend to realism was the "mirror play," which in a way was initiated in 1977 by *Une amie d'enfance* by Louise Roy and Louis Saia. This kind of theatre (which has been reinforced by many American plays transposed to a Quebec setting) is based on (even if all the plays do not fit this formula) a fanatical fidelity to the language, gestures, behaviour and clothing styles typical of the various sectors of Quebec society, but especially among the middle-class. Such plays depend on a photographic accuracy reminiscent of home movies. These are plays that the audience sees and hears, yet refuses to absorb, being completely captivated by the pleasure of becoming reacquainted with the surface of its own image. This phenomenon is comprehensible only because of the short history of theatre in Quebec and because it is still possible to derive tangible enjoyment from the mere fact of seeing oneself represented.

Louise Roy, who has always worked with co-authors (in addition to Saia, Michel Chevrier, Marie Perreault and Yves Desgagnés), has gradually managed to relegate the mirror aspect of her work to the background. In *Bachelor* (1979, in collaboration with Saia), the pathetic nature of the character managed to come across, and in *Je ne t'aime pas* (1984, in collaboration with Desgagnés) the playwright produced a disturbing portrayal of passion.

Danièle Panneton, Michèle Barrette, Jacques L'Heureux and Jean-Guy Viau in Elizabeth Bourget's 1979 *Bernadette et Juliette*, directed by Gilbert Lepage at the Théâtre d'Aujourd'hui.

Elizabeth Bourget is a playwright who pays attention to the questions implicit in the everyday life of individuals and is concerned with writing plays that are accessible and quietly challenge prevailing opinions. She won immediate recognition in 1978 for her first play *Bernadette et Juliette ou La vie, c'est comme la vaisselle, c'est toujours à recommencer,* a hilarious comedy (Bourget, who studied with Jean-Claude Germain, has a rare mastery of dialogue) about the new sexual confusion of the baby-boom generation. Drawing her material from everyday life, Bourget tries to avoid stereotypes which limit the lives of characters who resemble the audience watching them. Thus, *Bonne fête Maman!* (1980) is the de-dramatization of an affair that a 50-year-old woman imperturbably carries on with a young man at work.

The question of generations brings us to Claude Poissant, whose work is marked by the social and economic crisis of the 1980s, which prolongs adolescence into adulthood. Fascinated by outward appearances, he deals with poverty as a game of signs in *Tournez la plage* (1981) and in *Passer la nuit* (1983) sets the action in an imaginary bar where six people, on the verge of turning thirty, come night after night to play the same roles and bring about the actual failure of their dreams.

Marie Laberge has written both historical plays and modern psychological drama. *C'était avant la guerre à l'anse à Gilles* (1981) was in its way a revolutionary treatment of Quebec history, since it completely excluded the national question from the causes of the characters' problems, showing the traditional rural family as a source of oppression, depicting the class divisions within the francophone community itself, and presenting a certain concept of nationalism as being plainly advantageous to the French-Canadian upper-class. But the majority of Marie Laberge's plays are concerned with psychological analysis: the terrible inhibitions of quiet men (in *Avec l'hiver qui s'en vient*, 1980 and *l'Homme gris*, 1984); the reasons behind a young woman's suicide (*Jocelyne Trudelle, trouvée morte dans ses larmes*, 1981). By means of an intensified realism, her plays reveal the dark truths hidden behind the unspoken words of "ordinary people." Another play in a similar vein, although much more brutal is *Un reel ben beau, ben triste* (1977) by Jeanne-Mance Delisle, eight jolting tableaux that tell a story of madness, incest and murder, set in the Abitibi mining region.

Although, as we have seen, women dramatists are fairly numerous, there are fewer more radically feminist plays, despite considerable feminist involvement in literature and theatre. In this field the work of Jovette Marchessault commands attention. She has dramatized the connection between women and artistic creation, particularly writing, in *la Saga des poules mouillées* (1980), an imaginary meeting of four Quebec women writers; in *La terre est trop courte, Violette Leduc* (1982), scenes from the life of the French writer Violette Leduc dealing with the problems of achieving public recognition for her writing; and in *Alice et Gertrude, Nathalie et Renée, et ce cher Ernest* (1984), a dialogue on writing and exile among Alice B. Toklas, Gertrude Stein, Natalie Barney, Renée Vivien and Ernest Hemingway.

Jovette Marchessault's dramatic writing also partakes of another movement which has clearly emerged since the beginning of the 1980s, the return of consciously literary plays. But perhaps it would be more accurate to talk about the first appearance of this literary character, since the literary dramas that preceded the explosion of playwriting based on language, were either not very effective dramatically or were based on French plays. The new literary drama of the 1980s has digested and absorbed the dramaturgy of speech, and is in fact a direct result of it. The most spectacular example of this kind of dramatic writing was probably the presentation of *Vie et mort du Roi Boiteux* (1981) by Jean-Paul Ronfard, an epic dramatic cycle which linked Quebec speech with the whole gamut of Western literature including the Greco-Roman and Judeo-Christian traditions.

Several other dramatists who write in this vein should be mentioned, for example, Normand Chaurette, René-Daniel Dubois and Jean-Marie Lelièvre. Using elegant and somewhat dreamlike language, Chaurette formulates in very exalted terms (which does not preclude a strange humour, a very gentle sort of irony) the relationship of art, the artist and immortality. His plays include *Provincetown Playhouse, juillet 1919, j'avais 19 ans* (1981), which combines a detective story plot, the psychoanalytical process and the definition of a theory of drama, and *la Société de Métis* (1983), about the inevitable ordeal of death (in this case, painting) that must be gone through in order to attain immortality.

The work of René-Daniel Dubois is flamboyant, excessive and utterly brilliant. The text is generated by ready-made scraps of writing (taken from dictionaries, encyclopedias and psychoanalytical texts) juxtaposing shrieks of anguish and moments of introspection. The audience is pulled in all directions before they are aware of the individual and private suffering which gives meaning to what is happening on stage. In *Panique à Longueil* (1980), the seven floors of an apartment building are transformed into the seven circles of Hell. *Ne blâmez jamais les Bédouins* is set in the Australian desert and brings together a German mountain-climber, an Italian soprano, a Quebec student transformed into a monster and two army trains hurtling straight towards each other. In his last play, *26 bis, impasse du Colonel Foisy,* Dubois uses the conflict between the dramatist and his character, an old Russian Princess, to deliver a manifesto on the connection between dramatic art and private life. Similar themes are also found in the work of Jean-Marie Lelièvre whose play *Meurtre pour la joie* (1979) was about a woman who replays the murder of her husband at the same time as the playwright seeks release from his character.

The birth of Quebec theatre resulted from its encounter with speech, after its futile attempts to be sired by literature. In the words of Laurent Mailhot, "Drama entered literature the moment it left it."[2] Like every recent historical development, the course of Quebec theatre changes very rapidly, as various new approaches to playwriting are added on, layer by layer, in a collage of co-existence. This constantly shifting plurality creates a dynamic situation with constantly renewed tensions which will help the theatre maintain its vitality.

Paul Lefebvre
Translated by Barbara A. Kerslake

Notes

[1]See "Pour un théâtre national et populaire", *Amérique française,* Vol. 7, No. 3, March 1949 and "Jeune auteur, mon camarade", *Revue dominicaine,* Vol. 65, No. 2, November 1960. Gélinas' 1949 address is translated as "A National and Popular Theatre" in Renate Usmiani, *Gratien Gélinas.* Toronto, Gage Educational Publishing, 1977. pp. 77-84.

[2]Laurent Mailhot, "Prolégomènes à une histoire du théâtre québécois", "Le Théâtre", No. 5 of the *Revue d'histoire littéraire du Québec et du Canada français.* Editions de l'Université d'Ottawa, Hiver/Printemps, 1983. p. 15.

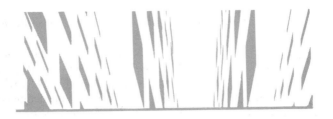

Writing the Land Alive: The Playwrights' Vision in English Canada

With the return to sources and regions, the dramatist discovers...the effect of climate and atmosphere on movement in Canadian plays. The way we dress—the dimensions and style of our clothing—the pace at which we must work to survive—all these things condition the internal person.

— George Ryga

With the exception of Diane Bessai's excellent essay "The Regionalism of Canadian Drama," published in *Canadian Literature* (Summer 1980), little critical attention has been given to Canadian drama's essential regionality nor to what this communicates about our playwrights' vision. This is ironic, in that the most obvious characteristic of Canadian theatre is its regional structure which, by the early 1970s, was firmly institutionalized in the ad hoc network of regional theatres that spans the land.

The oversight is astonishing in that the regional nature of Canadian literture is now generally accepted as one of its strengths. Rosemary Sullivan, in an article in *Canadian Forum* (March 1978), pointed out that "...much of the best contemporary writing is coming out of what one might call cultures in peripheral situations, [cultures] in the midst of a process of national articulation...dealing with the impact of bigger countries on their own." In Canada, she explains, the quest to define a national identity emerges most clearly in the assertion of indigenous writing that reveals a "heterogeneous complex of disparate identities...We can speak of a prairie identity, a West Coast, or Ontario or Maritime identity, and each of these can be broken into smaller units: Ukrainian prairie, Cape Dorset and so on, all under the loose umbrella of the Canadian complex."[1]

No doubt one of the reasons for this lack of attention is our playwrights' discomfort with the regional label. Margaret Hollingsworth speaks for many when she says "I think regionalism is a very confining term, particularly in Canada. Plays which are labelled regional tend not to be done in other parts of Canada."[2] Although this is much less true than it was five years ago, the notion persists that regional equals parochial, and that the parochial play doesn't "travel." While the positive potential of asserting regional identities to defend against the homogenizing influence of (American) cultural hegemony is increasingly acknowledged in Canadian studies, the strategy is viewed suspiciously by Canadian playwrights interested in national exposure and/or international success.

John Gray, winner of the 1982 Governor General's Award for best Canadian play in English for *Billy Bishop Goes to War*, said in an interview "You have to have recognition from the world, and the world, for us, is the English-speaking world. We have a longing for validation elsewhere because we feel a sense of continuity in our history with other countries." Yet, in the same interview, Gray railed against "a lot of people directing here, particularly in the regional theatres, who still identify with Britain and America and who would rather be working there, who look upon being there as the highest goal in their lives."[3]

Gray's desire to export Canadian plays and at the same time protect Canadian theatres from the importation of foreign talent is typical of the contradictory positions in which many Canadian playwrights find themselves in the mid-1980s, positions that inevitably vacillate between a desire for international approval and a rejection of international authority. By now, however, it is generally accepted that a play that succeeds in Canada will not necessarily interest audiences outside the country—a fact that Gray learned personally when *Billy Bishop Goes to War* played in New York and London.

As a consequence, Canadian playwrights interested in expanding their audience (and who isn't?) must question the commercial efficacy of addressing regional concerns. And while this doesn't lead them to avoid things regional in their work— I'll argue that it couldn't—it usually results in their discrediting the term. Sharon Pollock, the first Canadian playwright to win the Governor General's Award for playwriting with *Blood Relations and Other Plays* in 1981, sums this up when she says:

> Regional, national, universal: all of those words are used to confuse us, to give legitimacy to what one person believes is a good play and what somebody else will say won't travel....If you get done outside of this country you have a certain element of financial security which is nice, not having to worry about what you're going to pay your rent with next year. But there's nothing that makes an audience in Toronto more valuable than the audience in Calgary. And there's nothing that makes 300 people sitting in New York City more valuable. They're just people you're communicating to.[4]

Pollock's comment is doubly useful for it reminds us that the economic reality of Canadian playwrights affects their vision as much as their need for international recognition. The larger a playwright's audience, the greater his or her financial security. In Canada where the finite size of the theatre audience is relatively small, it is understandable that a playwright must consider subjects and styles that might have international appeal. But, as Mavor Moore noted in an address to the International Federation for Theatre Research in 1979, "while nothing can excuse the meretricious hoax that *because* a work of art is regional or parochial (Canadian, Québécois, Swiss, whatever) it is thereby as 'good' as anything produced elsewhere, this should not blind us to virtues and values *other* than comparability or compatibility with prevailing fashions—even those with impressive pedigrees."

Earlier in the same address Moore championed the artist's right to "see life through his own eyes and to express what he sees in his own way; to reflect his own reality, his dreams and his nightmares, instead of copying the empty shells of forms found suitable by others." Not coincidentally, this led Moore to consider that

> it may very well be that in time to come, the most valuable aspect of the Canadian theatre will turn out to be its difference from that of others; that it will offer the world not only an alternative North American art, but a model for greater diversity in general—because we are a pluralistic society in which no really 'national' theatre can exist nor should be expected to.[5]

Accepting that Canadian drama, like Canadian theatre, is essentially regional, it is important to consider not only how but why this is so. What constitutes the "regional" in Canadian plays and how does it shape and reveal our playwrights' vision?

To answer these questions, we'd do well to remember the definition of regional literature offered by Edward McCourt in his seminal discussion of Canadian regionalism, *The Canadian West in Fiction*:

> True regional literature is above all distinctive in that it illustrates the effect of particular, rather than general, physical, economic and racial features upon the lives of ordinary men and women.[6]

Diane Bessai, in the article cited at the beginning of this essay, echoes McCourt when she writes: "In its positive sense regionalism means rooted, indigenous, shaped by a specific social, cultural and physical milieu."[7] The emphasis on physical realities in both these definitions is particularly appropriate for, in Canada, geography continues to influence all aspects of cultural organization and expression even in this age of instant communications. In fact, the one persistent and obsessive concern of Canadian literature from its beginnings to the present is the land—specifically, the wilderness and its border on civilization, the frontier.

In his book, *The Canadian Identity*, W.L. Morton suggests that the alternate penetration of the wilderness and return to civilization is the basic rhythm of Canadian life, and he notes that the typical Canadian holiday is still "a wilderness holiday, whether among the lakes of the Shield or the peaks of the Rockies."[8] Northrop Frye in his celebrated "Conclusion" to *A Literary History of Canada*, expands this idea in his attempt to characterize the Canadian imagination through an analysis of our literature. He argues that our obsession with the land has had psychological effects which are most evident in the way we have developed our communities.

> Small and isolated communities surrounded with a physical or psychological 'frontier,' separated from one another and from their American and British cultural sources: communities that provide all that their members have in the way of distinctively human values, and that are compelled to feel a great respect for the law and order that holds them together, yet confronted with a huge, unthinking, menac-

ing, and formidable physical setting—such communities are bound to develop what we may provisionally call a garrison mentality.[9]

Later in the same essay, Frye moves the set of attitudes that he calls the garrison mentality into the twentieth century, explaining one way in which regional and local identities develop:

> As the centre of Canadian life moves from the fortress to the metropolis, the garrison mentality changes correspondingly. It begins as an expression of the moral values generally accepted in the group as a whole, and then, as society gets more complicated and more in control of its environment, it becomes more of a revolutionary garrison within a metropolitan society.[10]

Even if we reject the mythopoeic analysis that Frye constructs, we must recognize the truth of his initial observation that landscape in Canada is as much psychological as physical. As playwright David French puts it: "All art is set in specific localities." To this I would add, all localities are specific to individuals. While these statements apply to art created anywhere, they have important implications in Canada where the differences between our many localities (communities) affect the form and content of our drama.

Kay Hawtrey and Dan Mac-Donald in the 1982 Toronto Free Theatre production of Anne Chislett's *Quiet in the Land*, directed by Guy Sprung. Photo: Andrew Oxenham.

Much of the conflict in Canadian plays, for example, expresses our internal cultural differences. This is obvious in a play like *Balconville* by Quebec playwright David Fennario in which the tension between French and English people living in a small Montreal neighbourhood is expressed in both their languages. But it also is evident in a wealth of other plays less linguistically conspicuous. Anne Chislett's *Quiet in the Land*, for which she won the Governor General's Award in 1983, is a useful example here for it illustrates the way in which many of our playwrights transform what are basically sociological conflicts into personal actions. In her play, Yock, the son of an Amish farmer, rejects the doctrines of his pacifist community by enlisting as a soldier in World War I. The conflicts between the isolated Amish "garrison" and the society that surrounds it are thus dramatized in the rebellion of a son against his father: the differences that define the community become the disagreements that divide the family.

This transformational pattern is consistent to a long list of Canadian plays in which the conflict of a community and the larger culture to which it is peripheral is particularized as a generational battle. Plays dealing with the plight of Canada's native peoples provide primary example of this pattern, but others such as Sharon Pollock's *Generations*, David French's Mercer trilogy and Michel Tremblay's "family" plays illustrate it equally well. All demonstrate the way in which specific localities influence psychological development and, thus, reinforce the link between geography and individual outlook.

These dramas also suggest the continuing relevance of an essay by George Ryga—whose play *The Ecstasy of Rita Joe* is perhaps the classic example of this pattern—that has greatly influenced my thinking on this subject. Central to Ryga's argument is the idea that our playwrights are concerned not just with geographic regions or locales, but with "regions of social anxiety" that these often represent. Ryga writes:

> Today's drama to a large extent concerns itself with a vanishing landscape. The fisherman working depleted waters...the Nova Scotian family leaving its ancestral fields...the Indian torn between two worlds—these seem to be paramount sources of concern, and content matter of contemporary plays. Certainly these are critical regions of social anxiety. But what is the larger contribution we are instinctively making? Perhaps we are defining the more visible details of a canvas on which our national hopes and frustrations are enacted. Perhaps we are doing what our earlier theatre should have done but failed in undertaking—recording in a human way the agonies and triumphs of yet another transition when nature or economics beat us back and alter the course of our destiny as a people.[11]

When we recognize that Canadian regionalism refers not only to the physical and social specifics of a locality and culture but also to the psychological condition of its inhabitants, we begin to understand how it must contribute to our playwrights' vision. As prairie playwright Ken Mitchell puts it:

> ...where you live has a much stronger influence than most people understand or believe. I think that growing up in the prairies and gaining a perception of the world through this particular landscape has been very important to my development as a writer for the stage. In a general way, I think that prairie people and prairie writers and artists take a vaster view of things. I mean that's natural. If you grow up in a small neighbourhood of a large city and you don't go beyond

that, or if you don't have a sense of there really being much of a world beyond
that, in other words, if you're a city person, you write what we'll call city plays
or urban plays which tend to be about social mannerisms, about social intercourse,
that intensity of living in an electrical, highly charged atmosphere in which you
aren't really aware of the world outside....what I'm trying to do is convey a sense
of a man working alone and very much isolated from the rest of the people in
the middle of an empty space....[12]

But the sense of isolation that Mitchell attempts to convey in plays like *The Shipbuilder* is not just unique to the Canadian prairie; it emerges in all our regions—
and, in this regard, even (particularly?) our cities are regions of social anxiety.
The moral and spiritual isolation of Judith Thompson's characters in her gritty
drama of urban blight, *The Crackwalker*, is just as stark as that of Betty Lambert's
prairie housewife in *Jenny's Story*. The buoyant wit of Erika Ritter's stand-up comic
in her urban comedy, *Automatic Pilot*, is finally revealed as hollow: Charlie is
as alienated from herself and others as the repressed characters of Joanna Glass'
portrait of prairie drought, *Canadian Gothic*. Trying to pin-point the reasons for
the prevalence of this vision—and of its opposite, the sense of community that
many of our plays also present—George Ryga looks to our language; again, he
uncovers the shaping influence of the land.

> The language took the form of the land—uncompromising, hard, defiant—for three
> seasons of the year. The long months of winter isolation made the desire for human
> contact a constant ache. When you met another person, the meeting times were
> short and infrequent—there was much to say—the thoughts were no longer leisurely.
> You found the collective speech patterns becoming more rapid the further north
> you went—the consonants dropping or muted. This is a phenomenon which
> likewise developed in a parallel form in the outbacks of Australia.[13]

Whether or not Australian playwrights demonstrate a vision similar to their Canadian counterparts is not the question here. But it is reasonable to assume that as
a transitional culture in peripheral relation to larger countries, the Australian out-
back exists in a psychological space similar to that of Canada. Our ancillary relation to the United States informs much of our cultural activity: whether it be in
football games or television shows, we assert that we are *like* Americans yet
qualitatively different from them. That the assertion of regionalism is one of the
few viable strategies for resisting the homogenizing impact of technological culture
is a fact better understood in Canada than in most countries; and it feeds our continuing excitement about Canadian literature. As Rosemary Sullivan explains:

> ...[our] literature is coming to maturity against the pressures of mass culture in
> what may prove to be a post-national age, and in what many have defined as a
> post-verbal culture. It is seeking definition in the face of its own disintegration.
> The struggle is deadly, but it is clear that Canada, as a culture rejecting spiritual
> colonialism and exploring the meaning of indigenous identity in its physical,
> cultural and spiritual dimensions in a modern context, may be responding to one
> of the most pressing questions of contemporary culture.[14]

Nowhere in Canada is this situation more pronounced than in Newfoundland,
a province separated from the rest of the country not only by water but by values

and traditions that, like those of Quebec, manifest themselves in regional dialects and activities. Michael Cook, arriving in Newfoundland from England in 1965, "became aware that it was a culture that was not only threatened, but doomed;" and he "became a chronicler of that—what I consider to be the destruction of a spirit, language, culture and people."[15]

Cook's concern with Newfoundland has led him to write some of the most regional plays in the Canadian repertoire and to align himself with Ryga and others who see regionalism not as reactionary but radical—an essential and creative force in Canada's quest to survive as a country of creative distinction. Central to Cook's "record" of Newfoundland is an imaginative reproduction of regional speech that reflects his belief in the power of indigenous language to unite and stabilize endangered communities.

For Ryga, Cook's focus on language places him in the forefront of a development in Canadian drama that Ryga views as crucial to its maturation, a development evident not only in the work of individual playwrights but also in the group creations of collectives associated with theatres such as Theatre Passe Muraille in Toronto, The Mummers' Troupe in St. John's, 25th Street Theatre in Saskatoon and Tamahnous Theatre in Vancouver. Ryga writes:

> A qualitiative change is taking place in the language of our theatre. The common speech of people, carefully studied and reproduced, is now being elevated into theatrical poetry. Regional speech mannerisms are no longer treated as aberrations—they are examined and integrated into emotional lines not previously explored. For indeed, without the language differences, some emotional lines were not attainable....there will not...must not be, a return to one acceptable accent or language for this country.[16]

It is important to emphasize that Ryga does not say that our common speech is merely being reproduced in our plays; he states that it is being elevated into theatrical poetry. Probably one of the reasons that our playwrights are uncomfortable with the regional label is that it often has been used mistakenly to refer to plays from "the threshing machine period"[17] of Canadian playwriting—a term used by John Gray to describe a phase of Canadian playwriting which, if it existed at all, was typified by the prairie farm drama in which the representation of regional speech and concerns was considered dull or pedestrian.

The idea that Canadian plays are boringly naturalistic in their slavish attention to regional details still persists despite the fact that this has rarely been true. Discussing the 1972 Toronto season of plays, Urjo Kareda, then drama critic for the *Toronto Star*, suggested that "the most finished new plays of the season were all naturalistic in technique." But in the same essay he also suggested that "perhaps the poetic quality of naturalism has been underrated." He went on to argue that "far from being duplication, naturalism is an impressionistic method with strict and fascinating formal controls."[18] Writing a decade later in *Letters in Canada*, John Astington addressed the continuing fallacy of Canadian drama's naturalism:

> The fact is that naturalism *tout court* is not and has not been a particularly favoured style in Canadian dramatic writing, whether one looks at literary history or current writing. There isn't one among the plays published in 1982 that I would comfortably characterize as naturalistic. Far more frequent are stylization, selection,

or exaggeration; the common domestic theme or that of settlement on the land more often than not reveals a symbolic or mythological intention. Simplification and theatrical naiveté are apparent in the musical play or ballad legend, a tradition rather older than the collective documentaries of the last fifteen years, and there is a constant concern with the story, or with the yarn, on another level, which reveals a taste for shaping even and especially for closing the action, all quite out of key with naturalism.[19]

Both these critics acknowledge a fact which our playwrights and collectives instinctively understand. As Paul Thompson puts it: "characters have a capacity to go beyond themselves to say a large thing at the same time they say a small thing." As a director who has collaborated on over forty collective creations, Thompson knows what he's talking about. Taking his actors into rural communities like Cobalt and Clinton, Ontario, he popularized the process of "recording" regional speech and anecdote as the basis for constructing plays about living Canadians and our traditions. But he points out that the aim of this process is much more than mere reproduction or documentation, a term he, in fact, dislikes.

Toronto Workshop Productions' 1975 *Ten Lost Years,* adapted by Cedric Smith and Jack Winter from the book by Barry Broadfoot, directed by George Luscombe.

In *The Farm Show* and *Under the Greywacke*, for example, we didn't just talk with the people we ended up portraying, we listened to their speech patterns trying to understand them through a kind of verbal interplay. The actors' *ear* for detail was a very strong point. They were not just recording cameras. In the midst of talking and listening they were already imbuing the experience with a mythic dimension. They were already conscious of how the person they were talking to represented more than himself.[20]

"To make the living community yield its own material and to proffer a theatrical interpretation and analysis of this material has been the intent of a number of small theatre groups which came into existence in various regions during the 1970s,"[21] states Diane Bessai in her discussion of collective creation. But while her statement offers a pithy summation of the activities of many Canadian theatres in the last fifteen years, it does more: it provides an overview of the work of all those Canadian playwrights who realize the important connection between interprettion and documentation. No matter what subject or style a playwright chooses to utilize, he automatically involves himself in the process of interpreting life for his audience. Our best playwrights are those who recognize this fact and consciously seek to find in everyday language and events the distinctive qualities that make life special.

Inevitably, the language a playwright writes reveals as much about himself as the region he represents on stage. The regions of social anxiety that he depicts, in other words, are his own regions of personal concern. Usually it is the playwright's personal perspective that gives his material the ring of truth: and it is this that allows a play to travel effectively to a variety of people in different locales. Any arguments that regional diversity mitigates against national acceptance fail to take this into account. And in Canada where a number of regional plays have successfully toured the country—*Paper Wheat, Hosanna, Cruel Tears, Rock and Roll, They Club Seals, Don't They?* immediately come to mind—such arguments now are redundant.

In this regard, it is useful to consider Michael Cook's 1973 *Head, Guts and Sound Bone Dance*—arguably his most regional play—which was successfully restaged at Regina's Globe Theatre in 1980. I asked Michael Cook what allows his and other regional plays to travel across the country appealing to farmers, fishermen and city dwellers. He replied,

Well, certainly, both farmers and fishermen work in lethal landscapes. I mean, even in Regina you can't avoid the landscape. You go up five stories and it looks the same as it does in Newfoundland. I find it very significant that perhaps the best writing comes out of the prairies. When you are confronted with the enormity of the landscape, two things generally develop: personal relationships become of paramount importance, but at the same time, the environment makes them almost impossible. Sentiment, emotion, sensitivity, imagination are all put in peril from a very early age, because in order to survive they have to be compartmentalized. It's an awful irony: you are pushed inward to create incredibly tight family structures that can unitedly confront the universe; yet because of this position you have to take, all the tender things get lost.[22]

Cook is providing, of course, an illustration of Frye's "garrison mentality" at work. And in so doing, he offers Margaret Atwood—a disciple of Frye's critical theories—another example of the immigrant who views the Canadian landscape as a "violent duality," a term she explains in her "Afterword" to *The Journals of Susanna Moodie* where she uses one of Canada's pioneers to comment on the Canadian psyche:

> If the national mental illness of the United States is megalomania, that of Canada is paranoid schizophrenia. Mrs. Moodie is divided down the middle: she praises the Canadian landscape but accuses it of destroying her; she dislikes the people already in Canada but finds in people her only refuge from the land itself; she preaches progress and the march of civilization while brooding elegiacally upon the destruction of the wilderness.... She claims to be an ardent patriot while all the time she is standing back from the country and criticizing it as though she were a detached observer.... This country is something that must be chosen—it is so easy to leave—and if we do choose it we are still choosing a violent duality.[23]

The Canadian playwright's awareness of place often is heightened by a sense of discomfort or unease that results from his being in a *new* place. As Margaret Hollingsworth says: "Feeling out of context, out of place, motivates me and informs my work."[24] While she, like Michael Cook or Vancouver's Tom Grainger, is legitimately a landed immigrant, there is a sense in which all Canadians are immigrants, either because we have travelled from one region of the country to another—as is the case of Sharon Pollock, Carol Bolt and John Gray—or because the experience of immigration is common in our collective history: many of our parents and grandparents came from somewhere else. Rex Deverell, playwright-in-residence at the Globe Theatre, moved to Regina after living in central Ontario. Talking about living in the west, he says, "there's a sense of dislocation because I haven't grown up here.... But being uncomfortable is sometimes a necessary part of being a writer."[25] No doubt it is the prevalence of this sense of discomfort that leads Atwood to suggest, "We are all immigrants to this place even if we were born here: the country is too big for anyone to inhabit completely, and in the parts unknown to us we move in fear, exiles and invaders."[26]

While it is not my purpose to present thematic connections in Canadian drama such as Atwood develops in *Survival: A Thematic Guide to Canadian Literature* (Anansi, 1972), the images of isolation, entrapment and exile that appear so frequently in our plays culminate in a vision of dislocation as strong as any of harmonious relationship with locale. A comment by Canadian poet Eli Mandel, a westerner moved east, suggests that this vision is general to Canadians writing in all genres:

> ...it is not place but attitude, state of mind, that defines the western writer—and that state of mind, I want to suggest, has a good deal to do with a tension between place and culture, a doubleness or duplicity, that makes the writer a man not so much in place, as out of place and so one endlessly trying to get back, to find his way home, to return, to write himself into existence....[27]

But while this state of mind is not unique to our playwrights, they, more than other contemporary Canadian writers, feel it in their art as well as their lives for they, in a very real sense, must write themselves into existence. Canadian theatre is still in its infancy even though Canadian plays date from the seventeenth century. This often contributes to the Canadian playwright's sense of artistic as well as geographic isolation. "Often I've felt I was writing in limbo," says George F. Walker, a Toronto playwright, several of whose plays have been produced outside the country more often than at home. He continues:

Starting to write plays in Canada, as you know, was starting from nowhere, really. We had no tradition that we could hold fast to. Certainly I wasn't aware of any tradition. The second live play I saw was one of mine. So out of ignorance

Stephen Markle, Maury Chaykin and David Bolt in George Walker's 1977 urban comedy *Gossip,* directed by John Palmer at Toronto Free Theatre. Photo: Ellen Tolmie.

more than anything, I just started to write. And theatre for me was, literally, an empty room; you filled it up with what you thought and did. How is something I'm still arriving at. I'm not conscious of working in any particular way. When I have tried to, my experiments have been in Realism which for me is an unnatural writing style. It's not how I see the world. How so-called realistic or naturalistic writers portray the world is false to me. Their work never acknowledges that fact that you are in a theatre; it always requires you pretend.[28]

In Canada where our dramatic traditions are only now beginning to surface, it's hard to pretend that theatre is "real;" for many of our playwrights it still is too new to be viewed as ordinary. As a group, our playwrights demonstrate a self-consciousness about their art, if only because they still must fight to get it produced, published and recognized as worthy of attention. Writing themselves into existence, they provide the country with a paradigm of its tenuous position in international art and politics. Canada is still in the process of creating itself as a character in the play of world events. Seeking their place in world theatre, Canadian playwrights give a voice to those who assert the necessity of regional responses to global issues. Sifting through the layers of international influence to uncover the seed-bed of their art, our playwrights offer a vision of culture that nurtures the land, not flattens it.

"For the longest time I felt that being a playwright in Canada was really an illegitimate thing to be,"[29] says George Walker. This need not be. For so long as the country exists, to be a Canadian playwright is to write the land alive.

Robert Wallace

Notes

[1] Rosemary Sullivan, "Beyond Survival", *Canadian Forum*, March 1978. p. 7.

[2] Robert Wallace and Cynthia Zimmerman, *The Work: Conversations with English-Canadian Playwrights*. Toronto, Coach House Press, 1982. p. 91.

[3] Ibid., pp. 56, 58.

[4] Ibid., pp. 124-125.

[5] Mavor Moore, "An Approach to Our Beginnings: Transplant, Native Plant or Mutation?", *Canadian Theatre Review*, No. 25, Winter 1980. p. 15.

[6] Edward A. McCourt, *The Canadian West in Fiction*. Toronto, Ryerson Press, 1949. p. 56.

[7] Diane Bessai, "The Regionalism of Canadian Drama", *Canadian Literature*, No. 85, Summer 1980. p. 7.

[8] W.L. Morton, *The Canadian Identity*. Madison, University of Wisconsin, 1961. p. 5.

[9] Northrop Frye, "Conclusion to *A Literary History of Canada*" in *The Bush Garden: Essays on the Canadian Imagination*. Toronto, Anansi, 1971. p. 225.

[10] Ibid., p. 231.

[11] George Ryga, "Contemporary Theatre and Its Language", *Canadian Theatre Review*, No. 14, Spring 1977. p. 9.

[12] Wallace and Zimmerman, pp. 144-145.

[13] Ryga, p. 6.

[14]Sullivan, p. 7.

[15]Wallace and Zimmerman, p. 157.

[16]Ryga, p. 6.

[17]Wallace and Zimmerman, p. 48.

[18]Urjo Kareda, "Introduction" to *Leaving Home* by David French. Toronto, New Press, 1972. p. viii.

[19]John M. Astington, "Drama", "Letters in Canada 1982", *University of Toronto Quarterly*, Vol. 52, No. 4, Summer 1983. pp. 370-371.

[20]Wallace and Zimmerman, p. 240.

[21]Bessai, p. 13.

[22]Wallace and Zimmerman, p. 160.

[23]Margaret Atwood, "Afterword" to *The Journals of Susanna Moodie*. Toronto, Oxford University Press, 1970. p. 62.

[24]Wallace and Zimmerman, p. 91.

[25]Ibid., p. 139.

[26]Atwood, p. 62.

[27]Eli Mandel, "Writing West: On the Road to Wood Mountain", *Another Time*. Erin, Ontario, Press Porcepic, 1977, p. 69.

[28]Wallace and Zimmerman, pp. 221-222.

[29]Ibid., p. 221.

Performing Arts Buildings in Canada

The history of Canada's performing arts buildings is a subject which has received little critical attention. This is regrettable because the number, style, conditions and geographic distribution of these buildings affect the life of every performing artist, every theatrical worker and every audience member in the country.

A discussion of Canadian theatre architecture is best begun with a few words about the principal distinguishing features of performing arts buildings which, as everyone knows, have highly variant individual manifestations. Theatres belong to a building type which has its distant origins in people's instinctive gathering around a storyteller. This gathering around instinct was formalized by the Greeks whose "seeing-place," (*theatron*), while not technically a building, did give us the word "theatre." The form of building which we are accustomed to call a theatre today did not really emerge until the Renaissance. In the ensuing period, the theatre building has manifested itself in three identifiable sub-types: the lyric theatre; the concert hall; and the playhouse.

The form of the lyric theatre is distinguished primarily by its size and by the two separate structural elements which house, on the one hand, the audience and, on the other, the players and their scenery. The lyric theatre is the largest of the theatres because of the acoustic, economic and technical needs associated with ballet and opera—the art forms for which this type of theatre was created. The concert hall, alternatively, is distinguished from the lyric theatre principally by having only a single structural volume to enclose both the audience and the performers. This single volume best meets the needs of the art form—music—which this theatre type was created to serve. Traditionally, there has also been a direct relationship between the size of a concert hall and the type of music which it was meant to accommodate. Accordingly, concert halls can be either quite big or rather small. The smaller rooms are usually known as recital halls.

The playhouse is a less easy building to characterize than the other two. It tends to be a much smaller building than either the lyric theatre or the concert hall because of the need for every member of the audience to be close enough to see the actor's face clearly. But it can also vary in its form from the single space of the concert hall (the open or apron stage) to the two volume arrangement of the lyric theatre (the proscenium stage). All three of the building sub-types exist in Canada and within each group there are many variations.

These variations may be related, in part, to the very nature of Canada's history and geography. In comparison to the development of theatre buildings in Europe, Canada did not even begin to build theatres widely until the 1870s, well after the last major European theatre style—the "fan-shaped" auditorium—had been established; like most building styles, it took decades to reach this country. When Canada did begin to build, our settlement pattern, which largely occurred as an east-to-west movement, meant that there were vastly differing needs and styles in virtually every decade until quite recently. Also, because so much of our country was frontier until well into this century and the population so sparse, we were never able to capitalize on the railways as a delivery system for our own commercial entertainments to the same extent as the U.S.

Then again, our urban centres were just becoming large enough to support commercial theatre about the time that commercial theatre began to die in the late 1920s. The architectural legacy of this period, scant though it was, eventually fell victim to the rising price of downtown land in the post World War II period. This loss of performing arts housing stock was offset in the initial post-war decade by well-meaning civic and provincial governments who were fixated by the idea of large-capacity, cavernous "multi-purpose" auditoria. Still later, when the baby boom collided with the educational system, school boards and post-secondary institutions madly built gymnatoria, cafetoria and varied mutant forms of lecture halls intended as adequate places for performance.

Two other building trends helped redress the early post-war imbalance in the later period. The first of these was the rise of festivals and regional theatres which were largely controlled and run by professionals. The second, and somewhat less propitious, was the movement to renovate and retrofit extant purpose-built theatres and to convert into theatres other buildings which had been originally constructed for non-performance purposes.

To say, therefore, that Canada has no identifiable style of performing arts buildings is simply to state an obvious and superficial truth. Less obvious is the fact that performing arts building design throughout the western world has been in a state of flux for the last hundred years—coincidentally, the period in which Canada built virtually all of its buildings. Our bad luck was that we had no buildings from the previous tradition when this period began. If we separate the evolutionary waves of theatre building in Canada, it is possible to see that we are not without a sense of direction and, indeed, a sense of destiny.

Our first phase of theatre building can be characterized as the frontier era. It occurred anywhere up to World War I, depending upon location. In this phase, theatre was accorded its first permanent place in our settlements. The second phase is the commercial era which extended primarily from the 1880s through the 1920s. This phase brought building design influences from the U.S. and the U.K. and a much higher level of expectations of theatre buildings on the part of performers and audiences alike. The third phase was the movie era which occurred between the two world wars and which put large and extravagantly decorated auditoria in the centre of every major urban area. Next came the early post-war boom which lasted until the early 1960s. In this phase, governments began to take part in arts management at the point where they perceived the now-defunct commercial managements had left off. The second post-war phase occurred between the early 1960s and the late 1970s and was characterized by two highly divergent trends. On the one hand, professional performing arts managements built well designed and well equipped facilities for their own specific and exclusive purposes. On the other hand, educational institutions were constructing a host of poorly designed and poorly equipped facilities which were individually an embarassment and collectively an opportunity squandered. In the most recent phase, which began in the 1970s, there was an attempt to re-use existing buildings for reasons of cost, location and symbolism—and these mixed motives have produced mixed blessings.

While the results have been a polygot, the pattern, however, is clear. Performing arts buildings are now accepted in Canada as an integral part of a complete community. People also understand that different performing arts disciplines have differing needs and that there is no one building which will satisfy all. Furthermore, demand is increasing at the rate where most communities need more than one building. And finally, we have had enough successes and enough failures that we know the difference.

Theatre Architecture

The Frontier Era "Opera House." Victoria Hall, Petrolia, Ontario (1889).

Commercial Theatre in Toronto. Royal Alexandra Theatre, (1907).

Movie Era Theatres in Toronto. Yonge/Winter Garden Theatres, (1913).

Commercial Theatre in Halifax. Strand Theatre, Halifax, Nova Scotia (1915).

Early Post-War Multi-Purpose Theatres in Edmonton/Calgary. Jubilee Auditorium, Edmonton, Alberta (1955).

Festival Theatre, Stratford. The Festival Theatre, Stratford, Ontario (1957).

Educational Theatre, Vancouver. Frederic Wood Theatre, Vancouver, British Columbia (1964).

Regional Theatre, Winnipeg. Manitoba Theatre Centre, Winnipeg, Manitoba (1970).

Black Box in Quebec City. Salle Octave Crémazie, Québec, P.Q. (1971).

Adaptive Re-Use in Vancouver. Vancouver East Cultural Centre, Vancouver, British Columbia (1973).

Retrofit of Existing Theatre in London. Grand Theatre, London, Ontario (1978).

Later Post-War Multi-Purpose in Kitchener. Theatre, Centre in the Square, Kitchener, Ontario (1980).

Legend
1. Stage
2. Auditorium
3. Public Lobby

The Frontier Era "Opera House"

Generally speaking, our building tradition begins with a simple flat-floored room. In these buildings there is a small arch which opens into an equally small stage with no fly loft. The auditorium is sparsely decorated and often contains vestigal boxes and a pit. The entire complex was frequently part of another building. Often it was the entire second floor. Though modest in dimension and appointments, the facility was usually called an "opera house." A building which is typical of many in central and eastern Canada is found in Petrolia, Ontario, the once wealthy capital of Canada's early oil industry. It is an example of an early civic theatre built in 1889 as part of a municipal building which also housed police, fire departments, court, council chambers and town offices. The 50 feet auditorium is a wide rectangular flat-floored room about 70 feet long which originally sat 500-600 on loose chairs with a balcony which sits an additional 150-200. The narrow proscenium is flanked by boxes which are actually part of the stage which is narrower than the auditorium. There were originally virtually no public or backstage spaces.

Victoria Hall, Petrolia, Ontario (1889)

Commercial Theatre in Toronto

The Royal Alcxandra Theatre, built in 1907, is important for a variety of reasons. It is an early example of a commercial theatre and it is in a particularly good state of repair due to the complete restoration by new owner Ed Mirvish in 1963. It is also undoubtedly our strongest link to the buildings designed for the great era of New York commercial theatre pre-World War I. It has a distinguished facade and an equally distinguished interior. Its plan also reflects a spatial sophistication and generosity not usually seen in theatres of this era. The Royal Alex is also notable for the compactness of its auditorium which manages to house 1,497 spectators in a room which is 66 feet deep on a gently sloping main floor and two balconies. The 75 feet full-width stage is comparatively deep and has a full height fly loft. It has well developed areas for both audience and performers and uses its tight urban site very efficiently.

Royal Alexandra Theatre, Toronto, Ontario (1907)

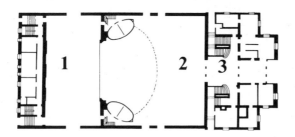

Legend
1. Stage
2. Auditorium
3. Public Lobby

Movie Era Theatres in Toronto

In 1913, the Loew's theatre chain opened a major building in downtown Toronto which consisted of an 1,800-seat "continuous run" vaudeville house called the Yonge Theatre, on top of which was the 800-seat Wintergarden Theatre decorated to simulate a romantic garden setting. Both auditoria had a single balcony. These theatres which alternated between live entertainment and movies, together represent two halves of the bridge between buildings designed for live performance and cinemas—the Yonge being superficially reminiscent of past lyric theatres and prophetic of "movie palaces" to come; the Wintergarden clinging desperately to the threatened traditions of the playhouse. Like The Strand in Halifax, the complex is sited mid-block and public access is provided through a long narrow lobby corridor which serves both auditoria. Audience circulation space is minimal. Both theatres have generous prosceniums which open into shallow stages with lofts that are less than full height. A series of small dressing rooms which serve both theatres is stacked on one side of the complex.

Yonge/Winter Garden Theatres, Toronto, Ontario (1913)
(upper plan is the Winter Garden)

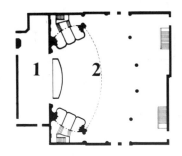

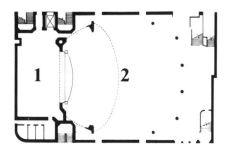

Commercial Theatre in Halifax

A slightly later and differently styled commercial theatre exists in Halifax within the complex currently occupied by the Neptune Theatre company. The Neptune's auditorium was originally constructed in 1915 as The Strand Theatre although subsequent interior alterations have destroyed the decor. Unlike Victoria Hall which is sited in a park setting, or the Royal Alexandra which has a full-width facade on the street, The Strand's presence on the street consisted solely of its marquee. The auditorium itself is located mid-block in order to make the best use of the less expensive downtown land without sacrificing the benefits of a downtown location. While reports indicate that The Strand's auditorium was handsomely appointed, complete with boxes, there is no evidence remaining of these features. Though lacking in decorative appeal, the 521-seat auditorium is charmingly intimate and nearly square in plan at 50 feet deep by 45 feet wide. A narrow proscenium opens into a shallow full-width stage. Accommodation for the public or for the performers is minimal.

Strand Theatre, Halifax, Nova Scotia (1915)

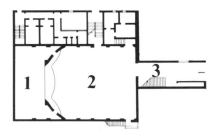

Legend
1. Stage
2. Auditorium
3. Public Lobby

Early Post-War Multi-Purpose Theatres in Edmonton/Calgary

The multi-purpose auditorium is a North American creation. Its invention challenged the long-standing European tradition of building distinctly different facilities for the performance of opera, symphonic music, chamber music, and plays. Its well-intentioned promoters expected that it would serve all these disciplines and serve them equally well. The Jubilee Auditoriums which seat 2,700 were built in 1955 to celebrate the fiftieth anniversary of the province of Alberta. They are the earliest Canadian examples of this form of building and are a testament to the belief that a very large seating capacity was the paramount design consideration. To their credit, this type of facility did have a larger stage house, large lobbies, better ancilliary spaces and was more fully equipped than any of its predecessors.

Jubilee Auditorium, Edmonton, Alberta (1955)

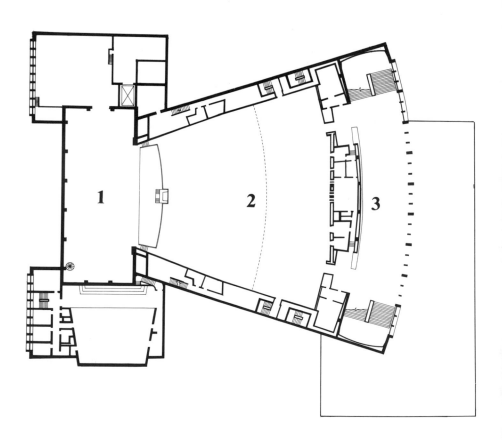

Festival Theatre in Stratford

Stratford is the patriarch of Canadian theatre festivals and the Festival Theatre is perhaps Canada's best known performing arts building. It is also the most successful open stage facility. Though built in 1957 to serve a repertory of Shakespearean plays, the theatre is designed on a Greek model with the addition of a balcony which the Greeks might have included had they had the technology. The Festival Theatre is most notable for the fact that it is able to place many spectators (2,262) close to the centre of the stage. The stage itself occupies a small portion within the semi-circular auditorium which has a radius of roughly 55 feet. Amenities for the audience and performers were only tolerable in the original building, which gained much of its efficiency in the unique circular form of its plan. This plan was made possible by the size and relatively unencumbered nature of the park setting in which the building is placed. Enlarged production facilities, rehearsal and office space were added in 1985.

The Festival Theatre, Stratford, Ontario (1957)

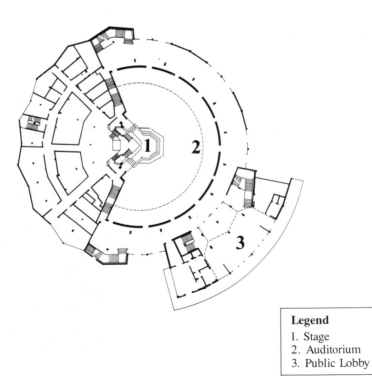

Legend
1. Stage
2. Auditorium
3. Public Lobby

Educational Theatre in Vancouver

Collectively, educational institutions have run neck-and-neck with governments as the owners of the majority of our performing arts buildings. The educational institutions are, however, winners by a long shot in the race to build the highest number of poor buildings. One of the few exceptions is the Frederic Wood Theatre located on the University of British Columbia campus in Vancouver. Built in 1964 with the addition of a large scene shop and studio wing in 1968, the Freddy Wood closely resembles a professional resident theatre facility in every respect save its modest 420 seats. The auditorium is a moderately raked single tier sparsely decorated fan-shaped room 40 feet deep and 80 feet wide at its widest point. A 36 feet proscenium opens into a deep, full-width stage with a full-height loft. The stage floor has a built-in revolve. The production capability and practice of the facility is reflected in the large two-storey height shop. Facilities for the audience and performers are only adequate by comparison.

Frederic Wood Theatre, Vancouver, British Columbia (1964)

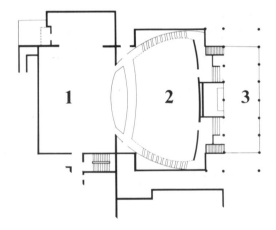

Regional Theatre in Winnipeg

By and large, North America is a land of cities which exist in relative physical isolation from one another. The realities of this regional settlement pattern has had its effects on the performing arts: in a word, cities which are isolated have to be self-sufficient. Founded in 1958, the Manitoba Theatre Centre is acknowledged to be Canada's first regional theatre company. In 1970, MTC built a playhouse facility which reflects the needs of a resident producing company for administrative, shop and rehearsal space within the same building as the performance space. The auditorium which seats 531 on the main floor is 60 feet wide by 65 feet deep. There is a single asymmetrical balcony which seats 298. The auditorium opens into a fully equipped stage house.

Manitoba Theatre Centre, Winnipeg, Manitoba (1970)

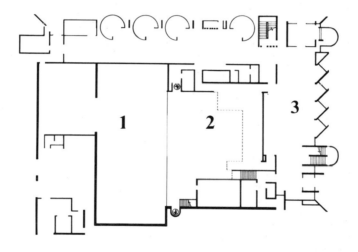

Legend
1. Stage
2. Auditorium
3. Public Lobby

Black Box in Quebec City

The Salle Octave Crémazie, which was built in 1971, represents a type of small playhouse whose fashion came in and went out again in about a decade. The style of this facility had two manifestations: the first was an informal version which adopted any large existing space—most often a warehouse—as a theatre; the second was a purposefully built room of three thousand to four thousand square feet, more or less square in plan, having at least two storeys of height, a flat floor, a gallery running around all four walls and a grid over the entire area. Both versions were founded on the belief that drama needed a "neutral space" which can be shaped into any playing form (arena, thrust, end stage) simply by re-arranging the seating. These rooms were comparatively cheap to build and were often constructed as part of a complex of larger spaces, as if admitting a need for intimacy which the accompanying spaces could not fulfill. This type of room eventually fell out of favour with producers because of its basic inefficiency. Compromises in seating, sightlines and general ambience similarly seemed to turn audiences away.

Salle Octave Crémazie, Québec, PQ (1971)

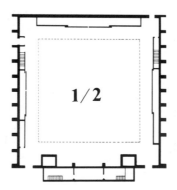

Adaptive Re-use in Vancouver

Re-use of buildings for performing arts purposes makes two essential demands on existing structures: capability of creating free span space; and capability of conforming to public safety standards. Most buildings constructed for other purposes have difficulty in meeting these two demands. One building type which has little difficulty in adapting is a church. The 325-seat theatre in the Vancouver East Cultural Centre was created in 1973 in the nave of a 1909 congregationalist style church to serve as a multi-purpose performing arts and community centre. The auditorium which is roughly 60 feet wide by 40 feet deep contains a small open stage. A single balcony extends around three sides of the room. Production space is minimal. The audience is served by a comparatively large lounge/lobby.

Vancouver East Cultural Centre, Vancouver, British Columbia (1973)

Retrofit of Existing Theatre in London

The Grand Theatre, London, opened in 1901, was the flagship of a group of theatres built by impresario Ambrose J. Small. The theatre had a downtown location and a typically modest street-front presence while the auditorium was located in the centre of the block. After the London Little Theatre, which acquired the building, turned professional in 1971, the decision was made to renovate the existing structure and supplement it with new space to accommodate the offices, shops, rehearsal space and studio theatre required by a professional production organization. The 76 feet x 40 feet stage house was left intact; the auditorium which is 76 feet x 53 feet was re-built within its original volume; the property between the auditorium and the street was developed to include the studio theatre, greatly expanded lobbies and administration areas; shop and rehearsal space was provided in a new wing attached to the side of the stage tower. Seating capacity in the main auditorium is now 800. The McManus studio theatre seats 150.

Grand Theatre, London, Ontario (1978)

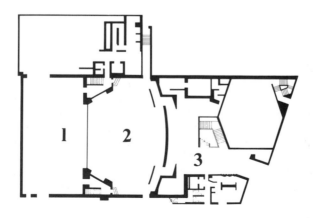

> **Legend**
> 1. Stage
> 2. Auditorium
> 3. Public Lobby

Later Post-War Multi-Purpose Theatre in Kitchener

The Centre in the Square which was opened in 1980 belongs to the generation of buildings whose design criteria were developed to meet strict professional standards. It is a building which successfully combines the needs of opera and ballet performance with the needs of concert music. This achievement is the product of having included two large pit lifts which rise to form a concert platform downstage of the curtain line. This playing position places the orchestra in the same acoustic space as the audience. For lyric theatre production, there is a large (85 feet x 115 feet) fully equipped stage house with an off-stage area upstage as well as in the wings. Centre in the Square also differs from earlier multi-purpose houses because of its smaller seating capacity, 1,900 to a maximum of 2,016 seats, and its efficient and generous ancillary spaces.

Theatre, Centre in the Square, Kitchener, Ontario (1980)

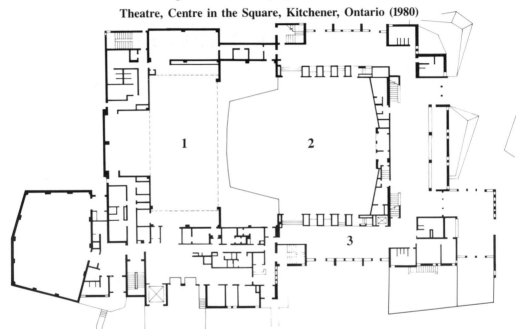

Conclusion

These twelve performing arts buildings which have been built over the last ninety years together represent virtually all there is by way of a tradition of such structures in Canada. Their annoying disparity of purpose, placement and style is more a product of our social and economic growth than a reflection of the state of our artistic achievements. But the presence of these buildings and many more like them in cities and towns all across the country is nevertheless cause for hope and a symbol that Canada has come of age culturally. Accordingly, our next goal will be to recognize and understand the forces which have shaped this legacy of performing arts buildings, to accept the failures among them and to resolve to create a national network of facilities which will be worthy of our artists and a source of pride for our citizens.

Brian Arnott

PART TWO

Theatre and Drama Across Canada

Newfoundland

Although Newfoundland only entered the Canadian Confederation in 1949, it was one of the earliest colonies established in British North America in the sixteenth century, with all the cultural influences that the term implies. In a period when British theatre tours of North America began by ship, St. John's was a logical starting point, contributing to Newfoundland's extreme colonial experience in the post-World War II professional theatre.

The Alexandra Players from Birmingham, England, arrived in 1947, metamorphosing in 1951 into the London Theatre Company, which lasted until 1955. British by origin, scripts and most of its personnel, the two companies contributed some continuing faces to the Canadian theatrical scene, such as Leslie Yeo, Gillie Fenwick, and Moya Fenwick. As noted in Paul O'Neill's history of St. John's, *The Oldest City*, the Alexandra and London are now best remembered as way-stations for future stars, particularly Alex McCowan and Hal Holbrook, the latter having begun his theatrical career while part of a different colonizing force, the overwhelming American military presence in Newfoundland during and immediately after the Second World War.

The long hiatus which followed the demise of the London Theatre Company was somewhat filled by Dudley Cox and his Newfoundland Travelling Theatre Company, which had a short life in the mid-70s. It provided a starting point for a number of young actors who went on to form the Mummers' Troupe, Codco and Rising Tide Theatre, and also some professional experience for one of Newfoundland's two reasonably established playwrights. The modifier is necessary because there are many quite prominent amateur playwrights and the poet Al Pittman has had some success with his plays *A Rope Against the Sun* (1970) and *West Moon* (1980). David French is certainly an established playwright but a Newfoundlander only by birth, and, to an extent, by the subject matter of many of his dramatic works.

But Tom Cahill is of a different order. A writer/producer/director with the CBC, he is known nationally for his drama-documentaries and for his television adaptations of short stories by Ted Russell. For the stage he has adapted Harold Horwood's novel, *Tomorrow Will Be Sunday* (1967), and has written his own pieces on Newfoundland history, *Beaumont Hamel* (with Dudley Cox, 1975) about the First World War, *As Loved Our Fathers* (1974), on Confederation, and his most recent, commissioned in 1984 by Rising Tide Theatre, *So Oft It Chances*, a portrait of Newfoundland politics at the turn of the century.

Newfoundland's one claim to a major playwright is Michael Cook. Originally Irish, he has been a Newfoundland resident for some twenty years, much of that as a professor at Memorial University. His major beginnings as a playwright came in the 70s, but for the most part in amateur productions by other university faculty. Most of his early plays were intensely concerned with Newfoundland traditions, although seldom traditional in form. Today Cook spends much of his time on the mainland of Canada and his success is more national or even international. It is some time since Newfoundland saw a new script by Cook and, in fact, a revival of his one-woman play, *Therese's Creed*, is the only professional production of a Cook play in Newfoundland in many years. Still, Donna Butt, Rising Tide's artistic director and star of *Therese's Creed*, constantly hints that a commissioned work by Cook is in the offing.

Rising Tide is the "child" of the Mummers' Troupe, which must be seen as the real beginning of indigenous professional theatre in Newfoundland. It was the first company to devote itself to providing professional productions on Newfoundland subjects, performed by Newfoundlanders. Founded by Chris Brookes, a Newfoundlander with extensive theatrical experience in Canada and the United States, the name reflects his original interest in the indigenous theatre, the Newfoundland Mummers' Play. This collective reworking of traditional material in a form responsive to the community provided the model for all future activity.

The Mummers are at least partially the "Passe Muraille system" functioning in Newfoundland, a place particularly suited to it. The first major example of this was *Gros Mourn* in 1974. While touring the west coast of Newfoundland, the Mummers discovered the communities around Gros Morne mountain up in arms over being forced to give up their homes and businesses in order to provide a suitable environment for Gros Morne National Park, something which held little interest for them. The Mummers went to work and the resulting show, some ten days later, had elements of Passe Muraille's *Farm Show* but with an added agit-prop thrust, something which defined the Mummers and made an indelible mark on Newfoundland culture.

Almost all of the Mummers' productions were collective creations under the careful (some have said autocratic) direction of Chris Brookes. As a rule, they were left-wing interpretations of Newfoundland situations, as was one of the best, *Weather Permitting* (1977), a very sensitive view of Labrador. But the Mummers could also go beyond political rhetoric, as in *The Bard of Prescott Street* (1977), a musical biography of Johnny Burke, writer of many of the best-known Newfoundland folksongs. Their first major show seen on the mainland was an impressionistic view of Newfoundland under capitalism called *What's That Got To Do With the Price of Fish?* (1976).

In the spring of 1978 they toured *They Club Seals, Don't They?*, a tough defence of the seal fishery. The *Toronto Star*'s review seemed Greenpeace-inspired but

David Ross, Rhonda Payne and Jeff Pitcher in the Mummers' Troupe's 1978 *They Club Seals, Don't They?*, directed by Chris Brookes. Photo: Kent Barrett.

even those who disagreed with the message tended to see it as accomplished propaganda. Their version of what Newfoundlanders call "the silly season," with clowns and actresses on the ice and a seal who hopes the television cameras will get his best side, was the Mummers at their best, politics as theatrical metaphor. A year later they did much the same with Newfoundland's burgeoning oil industry in a rock cabaret called *Some Slick*. Someone in the audience might have felt the Mummers were as strong as ever but in fact productions were becoming few and far between.

To most mainlanders, Newfoundland theatre at that time consisted of only the Mummers and Codco. And the latter was winding down as well. Codco also had Passe Muraille roots but their approach was not ardent agitprop but collective insanity. Their anarchic madness appeared under a variety of names but always came back to one thing, inconoclastic satire, with Newfoundland's most sacred cows as the targets. Today Codco has momentary regroupings but in essence it exists only in the talents of those who participated. Robert Joy is a film and stage star in the United States, Andy Jones and Mary Walsh are heavily involved with St. John's Resource Centre for the Arts, while Greg Malone and Tommy Sexton continue the Codco style, both on their own and in stage shows with the rock group, the Wonderful Grand Band.

Codco's demise is probably just natural diffusion but the cause of the end of the Mummers was more specific. They ran on the energies of Chris Brookes and, as has been proven again and again, any artistic director has a limited life, especially in a collective theatre. Brookes passed control on but without success, perhaps partly because of his own previous accomplishments. A number of Mummers performers had become disenchanted with Brookes' methods, and particularly his control over the LSPU Hall, built in 1926 as a meeting place for the Longshoremen's Protective Union, which had become the major theatre space in St. John's. One might expect that pride of place should be held by the Arts and Culture Centre, the largest of five such theatres in the province, created as Centennial projects. The fact is, however, that the only theatre usually seen in these culture barns, besides a few amateur productions, was British or mainland touring companies doing stereotypical comic-mystery drivel. As a result, power over the Hall was a major issue.

Two disaffected Mummers, David Ross and Donna Butt, formed a new company, Rising Tide Theatre, to present a Mummers-like collective, *Daddy What's a Train?* (1978), a very popular portrait of the death of the Newfoundland narrow gauge railway, to which American servicemen gave the decidedly ironic name of The Newfie Bullet. Even at this point, Rising Tide were clearly a coming force, as seen in their ability to eventually get the *Train* show into the Arts and Culture Centres. Their success, since then, is reflected in the many productions which have been seen in the St. John's Centre, national tours, a national radio show spin-off from the *Train* show, and the national telecast of *Joey* (1983). Such collectives have been their greatest success. But the present director, Donna Butt, states that Rising Tide will emphasize Newfoundland material while also providing as much variety as possible, as seen in the production of scripted plays ranging from Arthur Miller to Sharon Pollock. A symbol of the theatre's achievement is their new position as resident company at the St. John's Arts and Culture Centre with a subscription season in 1984-85 which included *Amadeus, Children of a Lesser God*, two Newfoundland collectives and a children's show.

The other major professional company is the Resource Centre for the Arts (RCA), the production arm of the group which now administers the LSPU Hall. Unlike Rising Tide, they are ardently democratic, with no artistic director but Andy Jones as chairman of the board and Mary Walsh as program animateur. But they are also ardently poor, consistently refusing to bend their principles in order to acquire sustaining funding. Also unlike Rising Tide, they see no reason to look too far outside Newfoundland or too far beyond the collective. Most of their productions bear at least some similarity to the Mummers, as in their show about the American military in Newfoundland, *Making Time With the Yanks* (1981) and in *The Last Resort* (1984), an account of politics in Newfoundland immediately before responsible government was suspended in 1934. The argument might be made, however, that their shows have thus far lacked both the political thrust and the artistic inspiration of the Mummers. Perhaps the Mummers, in their apparent sacrifice of democracy offstage, in order to do a better job of presenting it onstage, had the right idea regardless of how bad it seemed to many of the participants.

At this point it is difficult to see where Newfoundland theatre is heading. There is little reason to assume that Theatre Newfoundland and Labrador, a small company now based in Corner Brook, or the Stephenville Festival, both founded by the flamboyant Anglo-Indian actor, Maxim Mazumdar, will become much more than the essentially local operations they are at present. The Stephenville Festival's theatre workshops are a positive educational component and it has been able to attract some significant performers, such as Gordon Pinsent. But a few weeks of productions in the summer, brief tours, and a dependence on typical warhorses such as *Godspell* and *Jesus Christ Superstar* have limited its impact.

There is a possibility that the combination of Rising Tide and the Arts and Culture Centre might lead to something like the regional theatres so well-known in the rest of Canada. This could also have the effect of strengthening the Resource Centre's position as alternative theatre by giving it something to be alternative to. In 1984, a group of St. John's actors, partially under the sponsorship of the RCA, went to the small south coast community of Burin at the request of the Burin Action Group, to create a show about the closure of their fish plant. The result, *Between a Rock and a Hard Place*, collectively written by the cast, which consisted of the St. John's actors and an equal number of amateur performers from Burin, had many rough edges but also the political bite and theatrical spark the old Mummers had. It has generally been assumed in Canada that the collective is dying, but many in Newfoundland, most particularly Andy Jones and Mary Walsh, have been raging against the dying of the light. The Mummers are dead, long live the Mummers.

Terry Goldie

Prince Edward Island

Professional theatre in Prince Edward Island is centered largely around the Charlottetown Summer Festival whose annual production of *Anne of Green Gables* has received international recognition. Based upon Island author Lucy Maud Montgomery's novel of the same name, this poignant musical depicts the joys and sorrows of the freckle-faced, red-haired orphan Anne. A Donald Harron-Norman Campbell musical, it is everything the Montgomery story has been to millions since its publication in 1908.

During the summer of 1984—the Charlottetown Festival's twentieth anniversary season—*Anne of Green Gables* celebrated its one thousandth performance. As the longest running Canadian musical, *Anne* has been the mainstay of the Festival, enjoying national tours in 1967, 1974 and 1981. The third tour exceeded all expectations of attendance and revenue, marking the first time a Canadian touring production, without government subsidy and without corporate support, sustained a profit.[1]

Anne represented Canada at Expo '70 in Osaka, Japan. It played New York in 1972, receiving perhaps the least favourable notices in its history. What New Yorkers dismissed as old-fashioned sentimentality, London's West End whole-heartedly embraced in an earlier independent production in 1969. *Anne* was voted Musical of the Year in the United Kingdom. Although the London production was not sponsored by the Charlottetown Festival, it remained under the direction of Alan Lund, the Festival's artistic director. A second independent production was mounted at the O'Keefe Centre, Toronto, in 1979. *Anne of Green Gables* continues to draw capacity houses each season. It has become a major tourist attraction, drawing many of the Island's two hundred and fifty thousand annual visitors to its home in the Confederation Centre of the Arts.

The Confederation Centre dominates the heart of Charlottetown, the provincial capital of 18,000 and a bustling tourist city. Officially opened on October 6, 1964 by Her Majesty Queen Elizabeth, the Centre was built to commemorate the one hundredth anniversary of the Charlottetown meeting of the Fathers of Confederation. The historic meeting led, three years later, to the birth of Canada as a nation.

The Confederation Centre is the brainchild of Dr. Frank MacKinnon, a former principal of Prince of Wales College, Charlottetown, and an original member of the Canada Council. MacKinnon first proposed the idea of a national memorial in 1950, in a brief to the Massey Commission. By 1956, armed with preliminary drawings for the Centre, MacKinnon was granted permission to proceed by provincial authorities. The following year he visited cultural facilities in England as a guest of the British Arts Council. Before the next decade a powerful sixteen member board of directors, representing each province, existed with MacKinnon as president and a fellow Canada Council member, Eric Harvie, a Calgary lawyer and oil man, as chairman.

By 1960 the ten provincial governments all agreed to share half the $5.6 million cost of construction. Prime Minister John Diefenbaker promised the remaining $2.8 million in federal money. An architectural competition selected, out of forty-seven entries, the design by the Montreal firm Affleck, Debarts, Dimikopolus, Lebensold and Sise. Dr. Frank MacKinnon's dream finally materialized during the Centennial year, providing Prince Edward Island and Canada with a modern 1,000-seat theatre, a library, an art gallery and an archives.

The first artistic director of the theatre was Mavor Moore, noted actor, director, playwright and critic, whose career has placed him in the forefront of Canadian theatre, radio and television. At the time that he was the Festival's artistic director, Moore owned the rights to the musical revue *Spring Thaw*. An already proven success mounted annually in Toronto, *Spring Thaw* joined *Anne* in the Festival's first repertoire in 1965. Also on the boards was the non-musical *Laugh with Leacock*. Before an all-musical policy was instituted in 1968, two other non-musicals were mounted on the Festival stage, Moore's *The Ottawa Man* (1966) and Gratien Gélinas' *Yesterday the Children Were Dancing* (1967).

One mandate firmly adhered to since the curtain first rose on the stage is the commitment to an all-Canadian repertoire. The Charlottetown Summer Festival has become this country's National Musical Theatre. It is the leading producer of original Canadian musicals, of which it has staged more than forty.

After the first season Alan Lund replaced Mavor Moore as artistic director and has continued to direct and choreograph all but a few of the Festival shows. Lund's career goes back to the World War II entertainment revue *Meet the Navy*. He and his wife Blanche were a top Canadian dance team of the late 1940s and 50s. Directing and choreographing large-scale musicals for nineteen consecutive seasons has not been intimidating to Lund who has also choreographed grandstand shows at the Canadian National Exhibition, CBC superspecials and the closing ceremonies of the 1978 Commonwealth Games.

Although Mavor Moore's term as artistic director was brief, he continued his creative input. His name remains linked with a number of Festival shows. He is co-lyricist of *Anne of Green Gables*. He wrote the book, lyrics and music for *Sunshine Town*, the 1968 musical adaptation of Stephen Leacock's stories, *Sunshine Sketches of a Little Town*. Moore also wrote the book and lyrics for a second show that season, the adaptation of Elmer Harris' play *Johnny Belinda*. Most recently, Moore's contribution to the Festival stage has been the book for *Fauntleroy*.

This musical, based on Frances Hodgson Burnett's novel *Little Lord Fauntleroy*, drew crowded houses for two seasons, 1980 and 1981.

Over the years the Festival has produced musicals of widely varying themes. Some are dressed in the familiar flashy Broadway style, complete with an abundance of glitter and lavish production numbers. The best of these pure musical extravaganzas is *By George!* (a pastiche of Gershwin songs) costumed in black and silver, with a stage setting dominated by the classic illuminated staircase of the Hollywood musical. The more gaudy and less successful in its use of cohesive, memorable material is the recent Alan Lund creation *Singin' & Dancin' TONIGHT* which, nonetheless, entered its third season in 1984. Although *TONIGHT* got off to a slow beginning, it grew to a box office success, selling 85% capacity.

The trend for the Broadway style musical was first set in 1974 with Cliff Jones' *Kronborg. 1582*. This contemporary pop/rock musical, based on Shakespeare's *Hamlet*, represented a bold departure for the Festival on the eve of its first decade. *Variety* distinguished it from the ephemeral quality of the more familiar pastoral musicals aimed at the tourist audiences:

> This *Hamlet* is something special. Lacking dialogue, it rolls with ease from ballads to boogie woogie, blues, country and western and campy musical style and yet maintains the basic tragic plotline right to the bloody finale.[2]

After two seasons in Charlottetown, *Kronborg* was picked up by American producers and headed off to New York. Paradoxically, the rock opera began with all the earmarks of a Broadway hit yet became doomed to failure after a total revamping in American hands. It became so thoroughly transformed that it was unrecognizable beneath the vulgar, grotesque guise of *Rock-A-Bye Hamlet*.

A previous success for the Festival was again a Harron/Campbell/Lund creation. *The Adventures of Private Turvey* (1966), based on Earle Birney's award winning novel *Turvey*, is the story of Private Turvey's recruitment and service in World War II. Eager to serve overseas, Turvey finds himself, instead, guarding the Welland Canal. This promising version received a major overhauling and revival as *Private Turvey's War* (1970). Now more than just an evening of nostalgia, the revue became a contemporary criticism of war.

A far more successful musical on a war theme is the 1977 *The Legend of the Dumbells*. It featured original Dumbell sketches by Jack McLaren and a host of popular songs from the World War I era. This lively revue was based on Merton Plunkett's group that entertained Canadian troops overseas during World War I. The original Dumbells continued to perform after the war, becoming a smash hit in London (1918), on Broadway (1921) and enjoying continued success across Canada until 1929.

A style of musical frequently associated with the Charlottetown Summer Festival is the wholesome, pastoral musical, epitomized by *Anne of Green Gables*. It is good summer fare for the tourist family. One such musical, second only to *Anne*, is *Johnny Belinda*. Originally mounted in 1968, *Belinda* has since added four seasons and three tours to its stage history.

The original play was inspired by the people and locale near Elmer Harris' Prince Edward Island home. It had a Broadway run of over three hundred performances and became particularly well known as a film for which Jane Wyman won an Academy Award. Set at the turn of the century in Souris, a small fishing village,

S usan Cuthbert as Anne Shirley and Douglas Chamberlain as Mathew in the 1980 Charlottetown Festival production of *Anne of Green Gables*. Photo: George Zimbel.

it is the story of Black MacDonald's deaf-mute daughter. What is unique to this Festival musical drama is that the central character neither speaks nor sings. Rather, Belinda speaks through sign language, dance and the richly interpretive score by composer John Fenwick.

In 1977 the Festival opened a second stage, offering its audiences cabaret fare, in the small 180-seat David MacKenzie Theatre. Camoe Cabaret has presented such hits as *The Road to Charlottetown*, the ever popular *Eight to the Bar*, and *My Many Husbands* featuring the husband and wife team of Don Harron and Catherine McKinnon.

The end of a summer season and the close of the Charlottetown Festival does not leave the stage in darkness until the next year. It is used by road shows and local entertainments. The theatre department of the Confederation Centre gives assistance to community theatre and co-sponsors local groups, such as the Island Theatre Guild, in productions mounted in the MacKenzie Theatre. The formation of Island Community Theatre by the provincial government and the University of Prince Edward Island, has brought many productions to both the MacKenzie Theatre and the main stage. Nor is the Charlottetown Festival the only summer theatrical activity in Prince Edward Island. Noteworthy are two summer stock theatres that, for the most part, have been created and maintained by local theatre enthusiasts.

Victoria Playhouse, located in the picturesque seaside village of Victoria, is a half hour drive from Charlottetown and Summerside. After a few years developing, Victoria Playhouse now advertises itself as a professional repertory theatre. A combination package of a lobster supper and an evening at the Playhouse makes this an appealing alternative to musical theatre.

At the far eastern end of the Island, in the once vital, nineteenth century shipbuilding community of Georgetown, is King's Playhouse. The original theatre, named the Town Hall, was designed by Island architect William C. Harris. Built in 1897, the Town Hall housed local and touring companies until it fell into disuse at the end of the touring era. In 1966 it was reopened as King's Theatre. Since the mid-60s, companies struggled for survival until the formation of King's Theatre Foundation in 1981. The Foundation and the town of Georgetown took over the responsibility of maintaining the theatre from the individuals who had previously leased the facilities from the town. The Foundation aimed at maintaining the theatre as a Victorian heritage building in which a summer stock and community theatre could make a permanent home.

This once elegant 200-seat Victorian theatre was destroyed by fire while under renovation in March 1983. The same need and determination to survive that returned theatre to Georgetown in the 60s, was a force behind the immediate rebuilding of a theatre. It opened its doors in time for its 1984 season. In keeping with the original architectural style, the new and more spacious King's Playhouse, designed by Oliver Foster, is faithful to the Harris building in its exterior design—complete with buttresses and hipped gables.

The Victoria and King's Playhouses, in their modest efforts, attempt to provide good quality shows for the pleasure of local and tourist theatregoers alike. King's Playhouse, in maintaining the original architectural style of the Town Hall, keeps theatre in an historical perspective. Though it recently has been criticized for some bland programming and direction,[3] the Charlottetown Summer Festival's twenty years as the leading Canadian musical theatre has helped it to make its mark in what has hitherto been a predominantly American genre. Theatrical activity in Prince Edward Island is indeed both a national and community venture.

Linda M. Peake

Notes

[1]"Confederation Centre of the Arts, 20th Anniversary 1964-1984." Supplement to *The Guardian-Patriot*, Saturday, June 16, 1984. n.p.

[2]J. Frederick Brown, "The Charlottetown Festival in Review", *Canadian Drama*, Vol. 9, No. 2, 1983. p. 312.

[3]See for example Sid Adilman, "Festival's Anniversary is a time for mourning", *Toronto Star*, August 18, 1984. p. F3.

Nova Scotia

Nova Scotia's theatre is rooted in the many communities, often in remote parts of the province, which have practiced creative performing arts over many decades. The chief catalyst in the development of community theatre has been the Nova Scotia Drama League (NSDL). Founded in 1949 by Don Wetmore, Dramatics Advisor for the province's Adult Education Division, it has grown into a major resource centre for encouraging and promoting amateur theatre arts, acting as an information and communications centre for the province's theatre activity, promoting training in all aspects of theatre through workshops, encouraging writing and production of new plays, and continuing to organize provincial drama festivals even after the demise of Theatre Canada in March 1978.

NSDL foundered only in the early 70s, at a time when professional theatre became most active in the province. A 1974 public theatre conference, sponsored by the provincial Department of Culture, Recreation and Fitness, looked to the NSDL for leadership in drama training and communication. Under the expert guidance of President Gerry Gordon, the League was totally reorganized with the establishment of a central office in Halifax with two staff members, funded by the Recreation Department. For the first time an Executive Director, Pat Griffiths, was appointed, and through her and successors Jody Briggs, Susan Renouf, Penelope Harwood and Eva Moore, this educational and resource service has been fully developed.

By the early 80s about seventy amateur theatre groups and several small professional companies were benefiting from NSDL membership, which has helped to raise the standard of their performances through workshops and professional adjudication at festivals. Older theatres, such as the Savoy at Glace Bay, the Bridgewater Playhouse and the King's at Annapolis Royal have been refurbished for community performances. The Bayside Players are active in Glace Bay, while the Hubtown Players of Truro, the Maple Players of Oxford and the Amherst Drama Group have made their mark in the central mainland. Notable on the south shore

106

are the Yarmouth Performing Arts Group, which since 1980 has enjoyed its new facility Th'Yarc (Yarmouth Arts Regional Centre), the Winds of Change company at Liverpool, the Playhouse Theatre company in Bridgewater and the Parkview Players from Lunenburg County.

In the Annapolis Valley the Greenwood Players, the Bridgetown Players and the Annapolis District Drama Group have achieved much success over the years. One of the most colourful amateur groups in the province is the Kipawo Showboat Company, named by founder Jack Sheriff from a ferryboat that served Kingsport, Parrsboro and Wolfville before World War II. Sheriff has refurbished the original boat for performances, the first of which was staged at Parrsboro in 1984. If quantity of productions has at times overshadowed attention to artistic quality, Sheriff's energetic leadership has built an enthusiastic company, performing in Halifax and even in Ontario as well as at its home base of Wolfville.

Colleges and universities have been frequent leaders in the field of community drama. The very active Cape Breton (formerly Xavier) College, which stages a major theatre festival every year, has created the highly successful satirical review *The Rise and Follies of Cape Breton* among its many original productions. Like the Winds of Change group, Theatre Antigonish celebrates its tenth anniversary in the 1984/85 season. Formed as a community theatre with the blessing of St. Francis Xavier University when its own prestigious performing group collapsed, it has achieved a major artistic and popular success with several large-scale productions each season. Truro's Cobequid Educational Centre has pioneered the staging of original musicals, and university drama societies at Acadia, Mount Saint Vincent, Saint Mary's and Dalhousie have long traditions of play production. The Dalhousie University Theatre Department has been more successful in its design department, boosted by such names as Robert Doyle and Peter Perina, than in the general standard of its performances, though some of its former students have passed successfully into professional companies. Several of its graduates, for example, formed Another Theatre Company, which after some outstanding productions in Halifax ran a successful repertory season at Annapolis Royal in 1984. The annual N.S. High Schools Drama Festival, skillfully co-ordinated by David Renton, continues to aid younger students with the expertise of many theatre professionals.

Renton was a member of the first Neptune Theatre company in Halifax, for which he has played over a hundred roles. The founding of Neptune in 1963 was a major step in the development of the province's professional theatre. Subsidized by the Canada Council, it was established by its first artistic director, Leon Major, as one of Canada's most important companies. Its first president, Dr. Arthur Murphy, wrote three plays for it, *The Sleeping Bag, Charlie,* and *Tiger! Tiger!* Other original productions of its early years included *Louisbourg* by its first resident dramatist, Jack Gray, and the highly praised *The Wooden World* by Gavin Douglas.

At first as many as twelve full-scale productions could be seen in a single season's repertory, but by 1970 both repertory and main seasons of more than six plays were rendered impracticable, largely because of the building's limitations. Heinar Piller, who succeeded Major, continued the wide selection of plays from both the classical and modern repertoire. The third artistic director, Robert Sherrin, introduced more internationally known directors and artists. Outstanding productions included Andrew Downie's of *Candida*, Eric Salmon's of *The Caretaker*, and William Davis' of *Long Day's Journey Into Night*. Among Sherrin's own productions, David French's *Leaving Home*, the world première of Michael Cook's *Colour the Flesh the Colour of Dust*, *Peer Gynt* with Heath Lamberts, *The Servant of Two Masters*, and Joe Orton's *What the Butler Saw* were memorable.

The early 70s saw the high point of drama in Halifax. During Sherrin's tenure Neptune ran a Second Stage company for three seasons with the help of L.I.P. grants. Among its notable productions, many experimental and avant-garde, were early performances of Canadian plays, such as *Crabdance, Forever Yours, Marie Lou*, and *Creeps*. Keith Turnbull, who had mounted colourful productions of *The Good Soldier Schweik* and James Reaney's *Listen to the Wind* on the mainstage, assisted Reaney at Second Stage with his famous *Donnellys* workshops. At the same time Pier One Theatre, founded by a prospective Neptune player, John Dunsworth, rivalled Second Stage with many experimental productions: notable were *Endgame, The Maids, The Empire Builders* and *Of Mice and Men*.

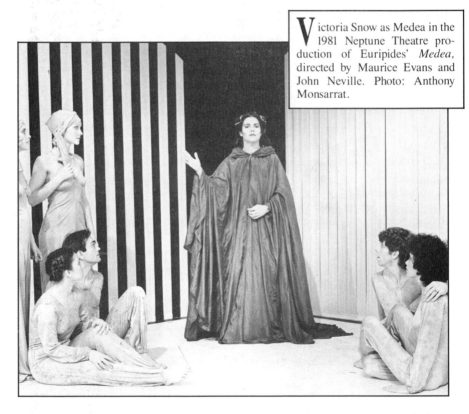

Victoria Snow as Medea in the 1981 Neptune Theatre production of Euripides' *Medea*, directed by Maurice Evans and John Neville. Photo: Anthony Monsarrat.

Constant theatrical innovations and excitement disappeared in the capital by 1974. Though John Wood, who replaced Sherrin at Neptune that year, mounted some ambitious productions, the theatre fell badly into debt. John Neville succeeded not only in eliminating the huge deficit that he inherited in 1978 but in raising the number of subscriptions to an all-time high and restoring the theatre to a sound financial basis. He became full Theatre Director with more complete control over the theatre's departments, a role inherited by his successor, Tom Kerr, in 1983. The Neptune Touring Company also continued its unbroken tradition, and Young Neptune, with its extensive touring of schools, as well as the popular Lunch Time Theatre, were fully developed under Neville. Productions at this time were of variable quality, though *Othello, The Master Builder* and *The Apple Cart* enabled Neville personally to meet the challenge of important acting roles; some of his own productions, such as *The Night of the Iguana*, were worthy if not totally successful. Among the most polished were the Lunch Time productions, particularly *Winners, The End of the Beginning*, and *Reunion*.

A succession of amateur and semi-professional groups have attempted to provide in the city an alternative theatre to mainstage—and invariably mainstream—Neptune productions. Theatre Arts Guild, one of the oldest continuously running amateur theatres in Canada, lost some of its best players with the founding of Neptune. Though rarely regaining the standards of its first three decades, the Guild has managed to keep going, celebrating its 50th anniversary in 1981. Grassroots Theatre replaced the defunct Dartmouth Players. Seaweed Theatre, founded by the imaginative John Culjak, has devoted itself to the production of new Canadian plays. Halifax Independent Theatre attracted much interest and critical praise with its productions in the tiny Crypt theatre beneath All Saints' Cathedral, (1977-81). Bit Players made a brief, over-ambitious bid to establish Theatre 1707. Other companies renting spaces at Dalhousie Arts Centre, Collins Court in Historic Properties, Neptune Theatre or T.A.G.'s Pond Playhouse include Halifax Players, No Name Productions and Dream Productions, their performances creditable if frequently betraying inexperience.

A commendable, though short-lived, experiment in professional theatre was Pop Productions of Paul Ledoux and Ferne Downey, which presented the dinner theatre Stages at Holiday Inn in Halifax, (1980-81), but could not find consistent audiences for its innovative though uneven musical entertainments. Actors' Tryworks is a semi-professional group which has made a bold attempt, if again inconsistent in artistic standards, to establish a viable alternative theatre in Halifax. Initiated by under-employed Neptune players Barrie Dunn and Caitlyn Colquhoun, it has since January 1983 mounted plays such as Sam Shepard's *Buried Child* at Dalhousie's Dunn Theatre and George Walker's *The Art of War* at Neptune Theatre.

One of the province's most original and successful professional companies has been Mermaid Theatre, based in Wolfville but essentially a touring company for young audiences. Founded in 1972 by Evelyn Garbary, and now under the artistic direction of Graham Whitehead, it has won national and international acclaim for its dramatic presentation of local history and Micmac Indian legends, using live music, mime, dance and puppetry, with colourful costumes and masks designed by Tom Miller; more recently it has also presented plays dealing with contemporary problems of youth, such as *Running the Red Lights* and *Shadow Valley*.

Christopher Heide, currently Mermaid's playwright-in-residence, has co-ordinated playscripts for another professional touring group, the Mulgrave Road Co-op from Guysborough County. An essentially grassroots company, it creates its own workshop scripts on local historical and community topics. Though the quality of its productions varies, it has steadily improved in recent years; among

The 1978 Mermaid Theatre production of *The Wabenaki*, directed by Evelyn Garbary and Tom Miller. Photo: Lionel J. Simmons.

its best shows has been Robbie O'Neill's portrayal of the late Leo Kennedy, *Tighten the Traces, Haul in the Reins*, which appeared on national television and won praise on tour in Canada and the U.K. Stage East, founded by Wanda Graham, also tours extensively with efficient, imaginatively mounted productions designed especially for schools and young people. In the fall of 1981 there were five professional N.S. theatre companies touring the province, four of them with N.S. plays: the three mentioned above, as well as Neptune and Young Neptune touring companies.

Touring on this scale has been made possible by grants from the provincial Recreation Department. While relatively small-scale funding is a lifeline for the touring companies, subsidies from different levels of government or the Canada Council have generally been either frozen or not raised sufficiently to meet rising costs. The projected new waterfront Neptune Theatre for which John Neville diligently sought financing has failed to materialize in a time of economic hardship. There is a desperate need of suitable performing space for the alternative theatre in Halifax, as there is for a regularly performing professional or semi-professional company to risk avant-garde productions and for a summer theatre season or even a summer arts festival to attract tourists.

Until the economic climate changes and until the required boldness of initiative backed by sound administrative planning is forthcoming, Halifax will remain unfortunately placed in comparison with other Canadian cities in the quality of its theatre. Courageous artistic enterprise in the 1980s has resulted in the magnificent annual Scotia Festival of Music in Halifax with its artists of international repute. A like initiative is needed to raise the quality of theatre in the city, which in turn could provide a leadership in standards of performance that could be reflected throughout the province.

Richard Perkyns

New Brunswick

Contemporary theatre in New Brunswick arises out of a long and lively theatrical tradition. During much of the nineteenth century Saint John, especially, was a beehive of activity. From early beginnings with the Loyalists, amateur and professional theatre alike developed rapidly. By mid-century an enterprising manager, James West Lanergan, brought a company of American actors to the city and began a twenty-year-long series of annual summer seasons in his Dramatic Lyceum on King Square (1856-1876). During one period in the 1870s three professional theatres were in operation simultaneously, providing year round entertainment to appreciative audiences. In the last two decades of the century and into the twentieth century, touring companies replaced the resident companies and, as they did so, opened up many New Brunswick towns to professional theatre, supplementing the community theatre that always went on sporadically.

In turn the disappearance of the touring company (a victim, in New Brunswick as elsewhere, of movies, war, transportation costs, and economic conditions) gave way to the emergence of vigorous community theatre. The Saint John Theatre Guild offered the first of many presentations in January 1931. That group, which, functioning until 1956, was the most tenacious of the province's amateur groups, demonstrated in its twelve-point constitution a direction for community theatre—including experimention within practical limits, encouragement of Canadian as well as British work, and competition with other clubs of a like nature.

Competition became feasible with the formation of the New Brunswick Drama League in 1933, following upon the heels of the establishment of the Dominion Drama Festival. Five societies, all from the southern half of the province, entered the first Regional adjudications: the University of New Brunswick's Dramatic Society from Fredericton, Moncton's St. George Dramatic Club, Sackville's Mount Allison Little Theatre, Saint John's Community Theatre Guild and the St. Peter's Dramatic Club. Drama League festivals were held annually until 1939 when war broke out, were revived in 1948 and, except for 1973-1978, have been a yearly event since.

University societies have been important contributors. For many years Professor Alvin Shaw was the guiding force behind the University of New Brunswick's Dramatic Society, his technical expertise helping to bring about the winning of more than 40 Festival awards. Today, finely produced drama can be seen in Mount Allison's tiny Windsor Theatre, under the exacting direction of Professor Arthur Motyer, and at the University of New Brunswick's Saint John campus, under Mark Blagrave.

Over the years numerous community groups have arisen, flourished for awhile and then faded away, frequently giving place to others—groups such as the Rexton-Richibucto Dramatic Society, the Saint Andrews Music, Art & Drama Club, the Miramichi Summer Players, the Sackville Theatre Guild, Saint John's Phoenix Players and the Members' Company.

The amateur companies provided an outlet for the creative energies of local playwrights. *Small Potatoes*, by Saint John's Jean Sweet, and *La Tour*, by Fredericton's Jack Thurrell, tied for first place as best plays written by Canadians in the Dominion Drama Festival of 1938; W.E. Dann Ross of Saint John took a host of his own plays on tour with his semi-professional company in the 1940s; Marjorie Thompson wrote for the Rexton players in the same decade; Kay McClure of Moncton wrote one-act plays for Stage Door '56 in the 1950s; and Philip Golding and Frances Parkill produced material for Saint John actors in the 50s and 60s. Two well known writers, Kent Thompson and David Etheridge, have had their plays performed by both amateur and professional actors more recently.

With the beginning of the High School Drama Festival in 1953, high school drama received strong encouragement. Much of it has been of a high calibre. Now, more than thirty years after the beginning of the Festival, approximately 1,000 junior and senior high school students gather in May on the campuses of the University of New Brunswick and St. Thomas University in Fredericton to participate in a programme of performances, workshops, and social events.

Summer theatres have flourished in the province. *Tales of a Loyalist Town*, based on Grace Helen Mowat's *The Diverting History of a Loyalist Town*, provided a panorama of life in Saint Andrews, a leading tourist centre, in the summers of 1948-1950. In 1951 the University of New Brunswick's summer school initiated what became an annual tradition of theatrical performances. Residents of the central part of the province were treated to the first offering of the Miramichi Summer Theatre in 1957, and Stage Door '56 also offered summer seasons in Fundy National Park and in Moncton. During several summers in the 1960s the Rothesay Playhouse was home to professional summer stock. From 1974 Theatre New Brunswick's Young Company has presented daily entertainments of original material and Victorian farce at King's Landing Historical Settlement, while Theatre New Brunswick gave special summer performances in the Playhouse in Fredericton until 1979, also the year of a revue-style entertainment entitled *Potluck* at Shediac, and *The Confederation Musical*, written and directed by Michael Payne at Saint John.

Dinner theatre proved to be extremely popular in the summer of 1982. The Rum Runners Revue of Saint Andrews and the Comedy Asylum of Fredericton offered light-hearted selections from well-known writers, while Saint John's *Reversing Follies*, written and directed by Mark Blagrave, provided a witty revue-style look at the early years of that city and had the longest continuous season of any company in Saint John since the Valentine Players at the turn of the century. The Rum

Runners Revue and the Comedy Asylum have continued to offer summer entertainments in 1983 and 1984, the second group becoming more sophisticated in
its producton and also introducing original material into its repertoire. The opening of Market Square (Saint John's waterfront historic restoration project) in 1983
has provided a natural setting for outdoor summer theatre; Peter Pacey has organized companies there for two seasons, Beacon, Bell & Buoy (1983) and the General
Story Tellers (1984). Pacey's own company, the Callithumpians, performed in
Fredericton.

In the mid-1960s the dominance enjoyed by Saint John in theatrical matters since
the arrival of the Loyalists was successfully challenged by the provincial capital.
When the Playhouse opened in 1964, a gift of Lord and Lady Beaverbrook (the
latter acting on behalf of the Sir James Dunn Foundation), it was the only operating
"theatre" structure within hundreds of miles of Fredericton. Standing in its own
grounds, as one corner of the rectangle bounded by the Lord Beaverbrook Hotel,
the Legislative Building and the Beaverbrook Art Gallery, its front reminiscent
of the architecture of Inigo Jones, the 1,000-seat Playhouse was a fine facility.
Initially the Playhouse did not directly produce or present companies of any kind
(although an amateur group known as "The Company of Ten," under the
Playhouse's first director, Alexander Gray, was an attempt to develop a company);
rather, local groups, especially the Patrons of the Playhouse, sponsored visits from
the Neptune Theatre, the Canadian Players, La Poudrière Theatre, the Canadian
Opera Company, and the Royal Winnipeg Ballet.

Such touring productions continued through the directorships of Gray and his
successor Brian Swarbrick until the arrival, in 1968, of Walter Learning, a dynamic
thirty-year old Newfoundlander, recently a doctoral student in Australia. Learning mounted summer seasons in 1968 and 1969, (the first on nothing but ticket
sales), while making plans to bring Theatre New Brunswick to the rest of the province. In the winter of 1969, through visits to six provincial centres, Theatre New
Brunswick established its patterns of touring productions around the province.
By the end of the third winter tour, records showed that Theatre New Brunswick
had the fastest-growing subscription audience in Canada; ticket sales went from
$12,800 in 1968 to $41,900 in 1971 to $83,500 in 1972.

It was impossible to visit all the towns that wished to be included in the tours,
and Learning's evident success persuaded the Beaverbrook Foundation to fund
transformation of what was essentially a good multi-purpose auditorium into a
versatile, efficient, modern professional theatre. The most noticeable of the million-
dollar 1972 alterations was the addition of a fly gallery. Other changes included
installation of an adjustable proscenium arch, enlargement of the lobby area, installation of new lighting and sound systems, provision of a rehearsal room larger
than the stage area, and new workshop and storage rooms. The renovations prepared
the Playhouse for almost any technical contingency while, at the same time, increasing intimacy between stage and audience. Undoubtedly they also increased
the frustrations of designers, directors and actors who had to play most often outside Fredericton, in halls of various sorts, many of which had only meagre space
and technical resources.

The company, its home and its touring policy firmly in place, Theatre New
Brunswick in 1974 established its Young Company, whose mandate was to visit
elementary, junior, and senior high schools throughout the province to educate

students in live theatre. In the 1977-1978 school year over 250 performances were given in 175 schools before approximately 40,000 students. Most productions were of original material, many of them collective creations. In the summer the company performs at King's Landing.

When Walter Learning left Theatre New Brunswick in 1978 to become Theatre Officer for the Canada Council, Malcolm Black succeeded him as artistic director. His expertise did much to enhance the company's image until 1984 when he was, in turn, succeeded by Janet Amos, formerly director of the Blyth Summer

K enneth Wickes and Barbara Stephen in the 1977 Theatre New Brunswick Walter Learning-Alden Nowlan social drama, *The Dollar Woman,* directed by Timothy Bond. Photo: Ian Brown.

Festival. Black, and Amos in her first year, have essentially kept the mix of comedy, music and drama with which Learning built his audience. *Butterflies Are Free, A Flea in Her Ear, Sleuth, The Diary of Anne Frank, Death of a Salesman, Godspell, Man of La Mancha, On Golden Pond* have been mixed with pieces like *Waiting for Godot* or *The Caretaker* that appeal to a narrower audience and with occasional Canadian plays such as *Leaving Home* and *The Head, Guts and Sound Bone Dance*.

Theatre New Brunswick has also provided some outlet for local writing, first by giving fine productions to three works co-authored by Walter Learning and poet Alden Nowlan: *Frankenstein, The Incredible Murder of Cardinal Tosca*, and *The Dollar Woman*, and more recently with W.E. Dann Ross' *Murder Game* and Norm Foster's *Sinners* and *The Melville Boys*. For the most part, the theatre has functioned within what Janet Amos has expressed as her mandate: to stage fine internationally known works of the past and present, to entertain with good modern works, to bring in good Canadian plays and to develop the region's own. All productions, except the summer season, have been taken on tour to eight provincial centres—Edmundston, Campbellton, Bathurst, Newcastle/Chatham, Moncton, Sussex, Saint John, and St. Stephen.

At times the company has taken productions outside the province, for instance *Dracula* to Toronto, *Death of a Salesman* to the Bastion Theatre and *The Daughter-in-Law* to Truro. In return, New Brunswick has received visiting companies, including ones from Centaur Theatre, Bastion Theatre, Neptune, Theatre Beyond Words, Mulgrave Road Co-Op, and Rising Tide. Janet Amos has said she would like to see Theatre New Brunswick do bigger productions, set up a smaller second stage for plays with limited appeal, add one show to the current five-show season, and extend the length and breadth of the cross-provincial tour, but it is far too early to predict if she will find the energy, resources, and cooperation necessary to accomplish her ambitions.

One fascinating project on the horizon is the restoration of the Imperial/Capitol Theatre (built 1913) in Saint John. Its board of directors, known as the Bi-Capitol Project Inc., has recently raised more than a million dollars from the private sector to purchase the building, has chosen a team of consultants, and is now seeking funds from the public sector for the restoration which it hopes will be complete before the end of the city's bicentennial celebrations in 1985. The restored theatre will provide a fine alternative to the Playhouse and should do much to stimulate theatre in the southern part of the province.

In the only officially bilingual province in Canada, the story of theatre is incomplete without an account of the vigorous drama being produced by the Acadians. As among the English population, university, community, and professional theatres are lively. L'Université Saint-Louis in Edmundston began play production in 1948 under J.R. St. Laurent. From 1953 Saint Joseph's College in Memramcook became a formidable competitor in the Regional Festivals, followed by Sacré-Coeur of Bathurst and Notre-Dame d'Acadie of Moncton. Outside the universities, La Société d'Art Dramatique d'Edmundston expressed "un désir de créer une oeuvre culturelle, de développer au pays du Madawaska le goût du bon théâtre," while on the other side of the province, in Moncton, societies came into being calling themselves Le Théâtre de la Virgule and Le Petit Théâtre de Neptune.

Since the mid-1970s the professional Théâtre Populaire d'Acadie, under director Réjean Poirier, has been performing in the Boîte-Théâtre at Caraquet and also has been touring productions to fifteen francophone centres around the province. In accord with its principal objective of encouraging the writing and production of original Acadian plays, its repertoire combines locally written pieces with at least one classic. Productions have included *Louis Mailloux* (the first Acadian musical), *Cochu et Le Soleil* (an historic tale set in the Acadian post-deportation era), *La Bringue* (about Acadian village life in the 1950s), *Les Sansoucis* (political satire), *Le Rêve de Monsieur Melpiasse* (satiric comedy), and Molière's *George Dandin*. Recently another company, Le Théâtre du Bord d'la Côte, has been established in Shippegan.

The Acadian equivalent of Theatre New Brunswick's Young Company, La Co-opérative de Théâtre L'Escaouette, started tours of French schools in the Atlantic region in 1978, with *Ti-Jean,* an old Acadian story updated with lively political overtones. Working out of Moncton, the company has toured a variety of locally-written pieces including a multi-media production of *Evangeline, Mythe ou Réalité* that toured France and entered the festival in La Rochelle, France, with the assistance of grants from the Department of External Affairs, the New Brunswick Department of Youth, Recreation, and Cultural Resources, and the French government.

Acadian theatres have been successful in encouraging local playwrights, and Antonine Maillet has become the best known among them. In the late 1950s, university societies entered her *Entr'acte* and *Poire Acre* in Regional Festivals. Théâtre Populaire d'Acadie has toured *Gapi*. Moncton's intimate little theatre, Les Feux Châlins, was the setting for the first production of Maillet's *La Sagouine,* the series of monologues of an Acadian woman, daughter of a cod fisherman and wife of a fisherman of oysters and smelt, that made Maillet and Viola Léger, who performed the piece, household words. The production with Léger has toured Canada in both languages for many years.

The roots of contemporary theatre in New Brunswick thus go back to the Loyalist foundations of the province. Although, in the past, interest in theatre tended to be concentrated in the south of the province, during the last few decades it has become a vital force throughout the province in both language groups. New Brunswickers may be justifiably proud of their theatre heritage and look forward with anticipation to the future.

Mary Elizabeth Smith

Quebec

Canada's first theatrical presentation in French took place in Acadia as early as 1606. In that year Marc Lescarbot's *Le Théâtre de Neptune en la Nouvelle France* celebrated the return of an expedition with a brief masque staged on the water. In Quebec, however, 350 years of uneven theatrical activity passed before an authentic dramatic tradition developed. There are a number of reasons for this long delay: a feeling of cultural insecurity after the young colony was abandoned by France in 1760; the influence of an orthodox clergy who imposed a mythical agricultural "vocation" on the people of Quebec and preached against urban temptations, including the theatre; and, finally, various economic and demographic reasons.[1]

In fact, an indigenous dramatic tradition in Quebec got its real start in radio. In 1938, Gratien Gélinas, a young, likable home-grown version of Charlie Chaplin who was fairly well-known for his radio series based on the character Fridolin, decided to try the stage. For ten years, he wrote, directed and acted in the "Fridolinades," a series of light-hearted revues which were tremendously successful. For the first time, audiences were seeing one of their own on stage. The costumes, the frankness of the language and the situations reflected the reality of French Canada, which unconscious modesty—ascribed by some to an inferiority complex, by others simply to good taste—had never before permitted in the theatre.

Another first for Gratien Gélinas came in 1948 with his drama *Tit-Coq*. The hero is an illegitimate son who is deceived in love and resigns himself to his fate. The play's language is picturesque and its situations true to life. The great success of *Tit-Coq* was unexpected: theatregoers sensed the importance of recognizing this realistic reflection of themselves before giving free rein to their fantasies on stage.

Nine years later, in 1957, Gélinas founded the Comédie Canadienne, with which he was associated for the next fifteen years. During that time he produced two of his own plays, *Bousille et les justes* (1959) and *Hier, les enfants dansaient* (1966), as well as the plays of Marcel Dubé, whose *Zone* (1953) gave him an undisputed claim to being the other great Quebec dramatist of that period.

J ean-Pierre Masson, Sylvie Gosselin and Denise Proulx in the 1981 revival of Gratien Gélinas' *Tit-Coq*, directed by the author, at the Nouvelle Compagnie Théâtrale. Photo: André Lecoz.

In those years, playwrights had to confront a fundamental problem: what *language* to write in? Each found a personal solution. Paul Toupin, a classical aesthete, chose a serious literary style enhanced by smooth dramatic action. His cosmopolitan characters speak a so-called "international" French—definitely anti-Gélinas! André Laurendeau, Anne Hébert and the early Françoise Loranger also opted for that uncompromisingly literary quality. Jacques Ferron, the Rabelaisian raconteur, forged his own speech as if he were creating a country. Pierre Perrault's characters echo the nostalgic manner of speaking peculiar to the inhabitants of Ile-aux-Coudres. Jacques Languirand affected a strange, somewhat absurd language, but the experiment was only a formal exercise. Both Gilles Dérôme and Claude Gauvreau cut dialogue to a minimum and concentrate on a muddle of apparently incoherent monologues in which their neurotic characters explore the shadows of the unconscious. And Marcel Dubé in his early "over the back fence" dramas used the language of the working classes.

Mainly because he has been writing for so long, Dubé more than any other playwright shows how difficult it is to create drama when a people—the lifeblood

119

of a nation—speaks its own language and a small élite affects that of a far-off land called France. Once dramatists attained a certain level of culture, they embraced "French" French and from that moment on condemned using the language of the people as a relapse. In so doing they cut themselves off from their roots. Isolated from any source of nourishment, their works remained abstract *jeux d'esprit*. Dubé tried to avoid these pitfalls, but he too slipped imperceptibly into writing bourgeois drama.

It was at this point in the late 1960s that Quebec dramatists, long intimidated by foreign masterpieces, decided it was time to create Québécois characters. Until then they had only been able to escape the abstract by falling into the trivial in the form of insignificant, crowd-pleasing revues. The so-called "great" works had been created in France, or by Quebec writers steeped in a rarefied European cultural tradition, and were aimed at a select audience which was well educated but not sufficiently so to realize that it was only a sub-culture. However, a new phase was inaugurated with the production of Michel Tremblay's *les Belles-Soeurs* in 1968: its success marked the real birth of Quebec theatre.

Along with novelists and polemicists, dramatists were the most involved in the movement to emancipate Quebec society, which was undertaken at the political level during the 1960s. By adopting the daily parlance of Montreal's poor east end and using it in a more conscious and aggressive manner than their elders, young Québécois writers (they no longer called themselves French-Canadians) made a choice that met with criticism from many quarters. Nevertheless, they stood beside poets and singers, whose fame soon spread beyond our borders, to show that the speech of the Québécois, peppered as it is with archaic French terms and mangled English, displays a vigor, truth and, indeed, a harsh, unsettling beauty.

Some call this language "joual," a corruption of "cheval" pronounced with the lips tightly pursed. But with his keen ear, Michel Tremblay has immortalized the language of the working-class area where he was born. Far from apologizing for joual, his plays employ mockery to utter a painful, hallucinatory condemnation of a truly tragic condition. However, Tremblay feels such tenderness for his characters that he may not have fully achieved his desired effect. Still, the fact remains that never before had theatre hit out so violently; never had such large audiences been so angry and impassioned—to the extent that today they realize theatre can also speak to *them,* even when, on the surface, a play appears to be only a bizarre and unreal ritual.

In addition to *les Belles-Soeurs,* other plays by Tremblay such as *À toi, pour toujours, ta Marie-Lou, Hosanna, la Duchesse de Langeais* and *Bonjour, là, bonjour* have been translated and produced in a number of foreign countries, including Japan. His success proves that, contrary to received wisdom, it is possible to move other nations by devoting all your attention to what goes on in your own backyard.

At least three other major writers have followed in Tremblay's footsteps: two of the most prolific are Jean Barbeau, whose forte is light comedy, and Michel Garneau, a poet of the stage, while the enigmatic Réjean Ducharme loves to play with words. André Brassard has staged nearly all of Tremblay's plays, and perhaps not having such a loyal and demanding director to work with throughout their careers explains why the output of the other three playwrights is uneven. Certainly they have not matched the imposing gallery of characters which has made Tremblay's world so familiar and appealing.

As the 1970s drew to a close, playwrights in Quebec ran out of steam, having fought a campaign alongside other Quebec artists which was essentially nationalist in nature. When the Parti Québécois came to power in 1976 intending to gain political independence for Quebec, creative talents—who apparently feel a compelling need to oppose any established order—felt themselves stymied.

In the 1980s a fresh wind is blowing: there is a return to the text but with broader, more universal thematic structures. The kitchen window and the back fence no longer form the only horizons. Jean-Pierre Ronfard toys with history in his saga of *le Roi Boiteux,* while Gilles Maheu explores the world of the imagination in a very modern style by conceptually writing directly "in the space of the stage," in such works as *l'Homme rouge* and *le Rail.* That same world provides insights into the female unconscious in the writings of women working with the Théâtre expérimental des femmes. Either epic or disproportionate, the inspiration — especially in the work of René-Daniel Dubois—is the proof of a burning desire to journey down the road of excess.

Companies

In 1932, Emile Legault, an "avant-garde" priest and professor of French at the Collège de Saint-Laurent in suburban Montreal, set up a theatre company whose members were students at the college. Acquiring a taste for ensemble playing, and fascinated by a certain liturgical mode of theatre, he succeeded over the years in creating a rigorous style—an astonishing feat for an amateur group. All the female roles had to be played by men: while Parisians were cheering Marguerite Jamois (inspired by Sarah Bernhardt) for her performances as Lorenzaccio and Hamlet, Montrealers restrained their emotions (which were real enough, according to the reviews) while watching Athalie brilliantly played by none other than...Edgar Tessier!

In 1937, Father Legault decided that his company should turn professional. Over the next fifteen years, the work of the Compagnons de Saint-Laurent became a benchmark for theatrical excellence as the group presented great works from the classical and modern repertoire intelligently and without pretension. A veritable nursery for theatre practitioners, the group launched quite a few careers, including those of many among Quebec's better-known actors, directors, and writers of the past quarter century.

Later, two important companies widened the trail blazed by the Compagnons. In 1949, Yvette Brind'Amour and Mercédès Palomino established the Rideau Vert, a small, professional theatre. After a shaky start, it eventually became Quebec's most dependable theatre company. Then, in 1951, Jean Gascon and Jean-Louis Roux co-founded the Théâtre du Nouveau Monde (TNM). The masterpieces of classical theatre, especially the works of Molière, were well treated by this young company which boasted an individual style, flawless diction and exacting professional standards.

At this point, it became clear that actors alone, even extremely good ones—in 1955, three TNM productions of Molière were acclaimed in Paris—were insufficient to create a new drama. Playwrights were needed too. But Quebec's population of five million, even though mainly concentrated in the Montreal area, offered little potential for innovation. Depending on box-office success, theatre companies maintained the safe programming of the past.

However, a few amateur and "semi-professional" groups did introduce the avant-garde European playwrights of the 1950s. In Montreal, these groups included the Apprentis-Sorciers and the Saltimbanques (the two joined forces in 1968 to form the Théâtre d'Aujourd'hui) and l'Egrégore; in Quebec City, there was l'Estoc. Even though all the material was "imported," the vibrant, caustic plays of Beckett, Genet, Ionesco, Arrabal, Vian, Weingarten and Brecht fired the imaginations of many playwrights and practitioners in Quebec theatre by the sheer novelty of their staging. Dream-like fantasies, bizarre events and the poetry of objects and games finally became accepted on our stages. But there still remained the task of reconciling this new language with the needs of a society deeply involved in the process of finding its identity.

As playwriting evolved, principally through the efforts of the Centre d'essai des auteurs dramatiques established in 1965, two other factors contributed to an upsurge in activity among theatre groups. First, there was an appreciable increase in the number of theatre courses offered by learning institutions, particularly in the new network of Collèges d'enseignement général et professionnel (C.E.G.E.P.'s) and on the campuses of the Université du Québec. Second, in these same years, government initiatives aimed at reducing unemployment among the young resulted in a series of programs providing grants to the arts, most of them for short-term projects. As a result, many new companies were set up dedicated to what the director Jean-Pierre Ronfard ironically called "théâtre pour" (for children, women, workers, the unemployed, prisoners, adolescents, welfare recipients, chronic-care patients, homosexuals, ethnic minorities, etc.).

Somehow these groups managed to survive with a grant here, a scholarship there, some "real" work (part-time, of course), unemployment insurance, etc. Some found a ready audience by virtue of the causes they espoused, while others were in a less enviable position. However, some longer-lived groups were able to survive, most being members of the Association québécoise du jeune théâtre (AQJT). In time the Théâtre sans fil (giant puppets for adults), as well as la Marmaille and le Carrousel (children's theatres), grew until they have toured all over North America and Europe, introducing foreign audiences to plays by Québécois writers. As a result, one play may run as long as four years in both French and English. In 1984, one sector of AQJT established an association for young people's theatre as twenty-one companies joined together in the Maison québécoise du théâtre pour l'enfance et la jeunesse (or Maison-Théâtre).

Because the companies of the "jeune théâtre" often espouse collective creation, they have popularized a style of acting that may be described as robust, in which the actors withhold nothing while utilizing every part of their body. This style contrasts sharply with the more "intellectual" and refined style of French actors. There is an obvious difference in the way the Québécois and the French play Molière or Ionesco, for example. But because the large mainstream theatres find it too expensive to maintain acting companies and instead depend on an artistic director and professionals hired for individual projects, they have always neglected collective creation. Their preference is for a more compartmentalized structure in which each person brings his or her special talents to create a unified production.

Among the innumerable collective creations that have appeared since 1968, the following deserve special mention: *T'es pas tannée, Jeanne d'Arc?* by the Grand Cirque ordinaire; *l'Histoire du Québec* by the Théâtre Euh!; and *les Enfants de*

Chénier dans un autre grand spectacle d'adieu, which marked the debut of playwright Jean-Claude Germain.

Companies belonging to the "jeune théâtre" do not constitute a solid bloc displaying a uniform style or content, however. Many have made an original contribution to theatre in Quebec by creating a distinctive theatrical language. Such companies spring to mind whenever any aspect of contemporary Quebec theatre is under discussion.

Ginette Morin, Monique Mercure, Anne-Marie Provencher, Louise Ladouceur and Jean-Pierre Ronfard in Ronfard's 1977 *Lear* at the Théâtre expérimental de Montréal. Photo: Gilbert Duclos.

Experimental theatre

Over the years, a few groups of very humble origins—often without a theatre of their own and occasionally even subdivided into smaller autonomous units—have carved out enviable niches in Quebec theatre and attracted a relatively large and loyal audience. One of these is the Théâtre expérimental de Montréal (TEM), whose prime mover is Jean-Pierre Ronfard. Resident initially above a restaurant in Old Montreal, this company made up of smaller self-governing groups has been the wellspring for several ventures. Evicted from its quarters by a feminist theatre group which TEM itself had fostered—an event leading to the establishment of the Théâtre expérimental des femmes—the company became the Nouveau Théâtre expérimental. With a strong emphasis on collective creation, innovative staging and, above all, improvisation, the NTEM appeared in various locations for two seasons—a necessity which gave free rein to its penchant for creation *ex nihilo*. The company's greatest adventure so far has been *le Roi Boiteux,* an immense, tragic and grotesque frieze produced in 1981 and 1982. Most of the work was staged outdoors: it included six plays, a prologue and an epilogue, all of which took twelve hours to perform and required more than thirty actors.

Just as the Théâtre expérimental des femmes was starting out, the Ligue nationale d'improvisation, the brainchild of actor Robert Gravel, also began at the TEM before evolving into a separate company in 1981. Gravel's original idea was a simple theatre game based on the rules of ice hockey involving six "players" on each side, two managers, a referee and a skating rink. Much to the group's surprise, audiences responded very enthusiastically to the improvisation of the actors, just as they had 40 years before to Fridolin's comic sketches, which were also partly improvised. The players at the Ligue, who must elaborate on themes chosen at random in a limited period of time with or without partners using either props or dialogue or both, feel as if they are in a lion's den. If they refuse to resort to a personal arsenal of clichés, the game exhausts them mentally—all the more so since, unlike real hockey players, these "athlètes du coeur," in Artaud's phrase, have to deal with an extremely demanding audience. The "matches" are staged for three months every autumn using six teams of young professional actors who are available only on Friday evenings at midnight and on Mondays at 9:00 p.m. when other theatres are closed. In the spring of 1981, the LNI's first European tour added an international dimension to this unique performance style.

The Théâtre expérimental is not the only company dedicated to theatrical research and experimentation. The Eskabel, led for many years by Jacques Crête, devotes all its energies to creating majestic environmental theatre and relies on the services of a great many actors who have had little or no experience (and who receive little or no pay). The productions are usually adaptations of films or short stories or collective creations cobbled together which blend various elements to conjure up a feeling of magic, ritual and freedom. A splinter group under Pierre Larocque left Eskabel in 1978 to found Opéra-Fête, which considers the early Eskabel productions pure and orthodox and remains faithful to their spirit.

La Veillée, a company under the direction of Gabriel Arcand, derives its inspiration directly from Grotowski and offers a more intimate kind of entertainment. The precise, calculated performances set the audience's nerves on edge with sudden cries breaking periods of silence, occasional gestures and sudden, explosive body movements—all in an untheatrical setting with little or no scenery.

Two other companies, Omnibus and les Enfants du Paradis (now called Carbone 14), are moving the theatre of research more towards mime. But having laid claim to the genre, these groups now repudiate the term mime on the grounds that they are only doing a "different" kind of theatre. Yet Omnibus is run by artists who, starting with its director Jean Asselin, studied in Paris under Étienne Decroux. And Carbone 14 is headed by Gilles Maheu, who also spent a long time studying body mime in France and Denmark. Still, the costumes, sets, sounds as well as the text (occasionally bilingual, a sign of the times) have become prominent in productions which initially revealed the art of physical movement and silence alone. The spectacle is richer, yet the actors have not lost their powers of physical expression.

Venues

Among the important "jeunes théâtres" which cannot readily be classified as research or experimental theatres are those in the mainstream tradition with a fixed address that coexist comfortably with the established order. Such is the case for the oldest among them, the Théâtre d'Aujourd'hui, run for many years by Jean-Claude Germain—playwright, director and well-known polemicist. For the past ten years, all the productions in this tiny Montreal theatre have been written and created by Québécois. Other companies have been forced to move from place to place for a variety of reasons: the Théâtre de la Manufacture staged an extraordinary *Macbeth,* adapted in Québécois by Michel Garneau, in a tiny hall seating sixty before it found a permanent location. On the other hand, companies such as la Marmaille, which puts on productions for children in schools and goes on national and international tours, have acquired a wealth of experience and a great ability to adapt to different situations. La Marmaille's approach is eclectic: at times it works collectively, but it has also collaborated with guest playwrights such as the German writer Rainer Lücker and the directors of Portugal's Teatro O'Bando.

The problem is that medium-size auditoriums remain a relatively rare commodity given the number of groups whose only requirement is a place to stage their productions. The recent phenomenon of "garages" (theatres not belonging to a specific company) such as the Comédie Nationale and the auditoriums on the new campus of the Université du Québec à Montréal, offer only a partial solution. Very expensive to operate, they can only be used for limited periods and not all companies have access to them.

During the 1970s, a number of "café-théâtres" appeared, first in Quebec City and then in Montreal, where they have proliferated. It seems that each time a period of intense artistic activity coincides with a slump in the economy, these small, uncomfortable theatres with minuscule stages spring up where drinks must be bought on top of the price of admission. That sum confers the privilege of seeing plays which are either light, poetic or intimate, often performed by a lacklustre cast with a minimum of sets. This trend explains the popularity of one-character plays, several of which have been performed by women. Certain actresses have in fact made one-man/one-woman shows an art form in itself, a prime example being Louisette Dussault's *Môman.* Another is *la Sagouine* by Antonine Maillet, and the Acadian writer found the perfect performer for her one-woman monologue in Viola Léger, whose personality has been imprinted forever on the character she created.

A more recent solution to the problem of performing spaces, and one encouraged by granting organizations, is cooperation among companies. As a result, the NTEM, Carbone 14 and Omnibus settled into Espace libre (an old firehall) in 1981. Now members of the three companies participate more and more in one another's productions.

The Audience

With their ranks swollen because of the interest in playwrights of the late 1960s, especially Michel Tremblay, theatregoers are no longer drawn exclusively from the leisure classes. Two factors are responsible for this phenomenon: today's plays are less exotic and intellectual in tone, mostly because of the language, and theatres have bridged the distances separating working-class neighbourhoods by decentralizing their locations and through touring. At one time all theatres were located downtown, and it was considered risky to settle in Old Montreal, as les Saltimbanques did, or to follow the lead of the Théâtre d'Aujourd'hui, which established itself a few blocks east of the city centre. When the Nouvelle Compagnie Théâtrale, which for twenty years has devoted itself to repertory theatre for a huge audience of students and schoolchildren, decided to move from downtown to the outskirts of the east end, it was obvious that times had changed. Even though the NCT could count on its loyal audience—"captive" would be more accurate, since thousands of students are bused in accompanied by their teachers—the company proved that it could also rely on support from residents in the area. Proof of this is the popularity of the small Fred Barry theatre which adjoins the main auditorium and is used for experimental theatre. It has served as a testing ground for several plays before they are produced in the larger auditorium or elsewhere.

Following the NCT's successful move to the east end, the Eskabel moved from Old Montreal to the western suburb of Pointe-Saint-Charles. But such a change involved greater risks for a theatre devoted to research and innovation: arsonists set fire to the building in 1982. Today there is a tendency, not just for medium-sized theatres but for café-théâtres as well, to locate just about anywhere in the Montreal metropolitan area. It should be kept in mind that one-half of Quebec's six million-and-a-half population lives in the Montreal area. Given that culture is essentially an urban phenomenon, this fact helps to explain the great importance of Montreal theatre in Quebec.

Outside Montreal, however, there is touring theatre—a specialty of the Théâtre populaire du Québec—as well as several small local or regional companies (the Parminou is the most important). Above all, a network of theatres, largely stagnant today, provides light entertainment in the summertime. This theatrical subculture, whose light artistic fare caters to city-dwellers on the weekends or on holidays, is often found in converted barns which abound in the countryside around the resorts. Although it receives little subsidy (unlike the *other* theatre), summer theatre is the most profitable, in fact the only profitable kind of theatre. Unfortunately, it is also the least significant. Nevertheless, it helps to create an audience for theatre.

There is no doubt that the public has developed a taste for theatre and finds the experience more and more to its liking. Touring companies put on plays in Quebec schools from September to June. In neighbourhoods, on workers' councils and in small towns, amateur and professional groups are improvising, establishing small theatre groups and getting together at festivals celebrating young people's theatre, amateur theatre, children's theatre, women's theatre, puppetry and mime. Theatre is also going into the streets to enlarge its audience, and agitprop in particular boasts skilled exponents. The Théâtre du Quartier and the Parminou create on request for organizers of the Saint-Jean Baptiste day celebrations, held each year on June 24, or for trade union conventions, while l'Escouade de l'instantané presents shrewd political sketches inspired by the medieval mountebanks on the site of Expo 67 or the Floralies internationales.

Similarly, Opéra-Fête will stir up a museum or public place—just as les Enfants du Paradis used to do—by mixing in strange, silent, almost motionless figures with the crowds wandering about in their Sunday best. Their characters are bizarre visions akin to the performance art of the American post-modernists, and they resemble a living statuary peculiar to our century. Players from the Opéra-Fête once spent five hours in a shop window on rue Saint-Denis, attracting crowds of onlookers and stopping several buses. But for Opéra-Fête, unlike other street companies, it is not a question of presenting such a performance as a completed experiment but rather, through a series of interventions in different locations with different audiences, to create a richer work in the theatre. The shop window, the museum and a show in the Great Hall of the new complex at the Université du Québec à Montréal were steps in the development of a work inspired by Dumas, Genet and Arrabal: *l'Usage des corps dans "La Dame aux camélias."* At that rate, it is impossible for the company to produce more than one or two "finished" pieces each year.

In conclusion, even though theatrical activity in Quebec has never been as intense as in the past 15 years, never before has it been so difficult for professionals to practice their craft: ninety per cent earn less than the minimum wage. The abundance of theatre, in fact, underlines the ephemeral nature of the art: its traces disappear without anyone—at least not the members of the theatre community itself—showing much concern. That is why the theatre journal *Jeu,* the only completely independent periodical dedicated to theatrical activity in Quebec, is so important. For the last ten years, *Jeu* has noted the fact that theatre in Quebec is thriving, and the questions it raises have also contributed to that growth.

Michel Vaïs
Translated by Audrey Camiré and Mark Czarnecki

Notes

[1] For a history of the beginnings of a French-Canadian dramaturgy in the 19th century, see Leonard E. Doucette, *Theatre in French Canada: Laying the Foundations 1606-1867.* Toronto, University of Toronto Press, 1984.

Bridging the Two Solitudes: English and French Theatre in Quebec

Despite profound changes in Quebec society since Hugh MacLennan published his novel *Two Solitudes* in 1945, that powerful image is not yet a literary footnote. An essay on the bridge between English and French theatre in Canada must be prescriptive, launch a challenge, for the bridge between the Solitudes is still a narrow foot-path in need of expansion. The history of Canadian theatre is dotted with stories of individual actors, writers, directors and plays crossing the cultural border between French and English, but few people working in either theatre scene today have a solid knowledge of what is happening on the other side. We still look to Paris, London, New York for stimulation, models and acclaim.

I can think of only one good explanation for this state. Theatre is rooted in language, and while English Canadians are striding toward bilingualism at a speed previous generations would never have believed possible, most of those doing the striding are still too young to stay up past curtain time. Their influence is for the future. As for francophones, visitors to Montreal may assume from meeting bilingual bus drivers that "they all speak English," but outside the service industries, that isn't true at all. Nor does the present Quebec education system encourage young Québécois to learn English.

When Quebec actors, directors and plays in translation have turned up in English Canada, one may wonder whether audiences came out of interest in Quebec culture, or in search of an answer to a strictly political query: What does Quebec want? Director Bill Glassco, the man who brought Michel Tremblay's plays to Toronto's Tarragon Theatre in the 1970s, thinks English Canada's interest in Quebec theatre has been politically motivated, and therefore fleeting. "I get the feeling," he told me in early 1984, "that nothing of English culture is of any interest to Quebec, and we aren't really interested in them."

An epidemic of self-doubt hit Glassco's generation in the early 1980s, a predictable post-partum depression after the quite astonishing birth of a national, professional theatre scene in the late 60s and 1970s. Glassco's comment seems to fit that mood, to reflect his personal background more strongly than the facts. Son of an old anglophone Quebec family, he has kept in touch with Quebec theatre during an illustrious career elsewhere, but has not, it seems to me, escaped the melancholy of his fellow English Montrealers whose place in the hierarchy of power has dropped. Nor has he escaped that community's complex ambivalence to French Quebec. He may be right when he says Quebec's current openness to the rest of the world—including English Canada—won't last. But my clippings from the past year alone offer a lot of evidence that theatre *is* challenging fortress Two Solitudes, and hope that something more lasting may come from that challenge. From a Montreal perspective, it seems the mid-1980s could be a turning point in Canadian cultural history, the moment when English and French cultures may finally establish some kind of ongoing conversation, and in that exchange, find new solutions to our problems, new inspiration for artistic projects. The potential is there. Pioneers have already broken the ground.

But first, the evidence. At the Théâtre d'Aujourd'hui, an important venue of new work in Montreal, David Freeman's *Battering Ram* was presented in translation in 1984, a project spearheaded by Ottawa actress Louison Danis. On a trip to Ontario's Blyth Festival, fluently bilingual Danis was impressed by the "strong sense of realism" that pervades much of English Canada's drama, a sensibility

Marcel Gauthier and Michel Côté in *Broue/Brew,* written by Claude Meunier, Jean-Pierre Plante, Francine Ruel and Louis Saia.

she doesn't often find in Quebec. She's currently working on a translation of Anne Chislett's *The Tomorrow Box.* Her ally at Théâtre d'Aujourd'hui is artistic director Gilbert Lepage, whose interest in English-Canadian theatre began when he served on a Canada Council jury with playwright Sharon Pollock. Lepage says more translations are planned.

That same season, actress Sylvie Gosselin performed Linda Griffith's *Maggie and Pierre,* hardly a timely choice, but a good vehicle to showcase her talents. Gosselin enjoyed an extended run. In sum, 1983-84 saw half a dozen English-to-French ventures launched.

From French into English, the translation traffic is considerably greater and this time, largely a result of Quebec initiative. Top of the trend is the mega-hit comedy *Broue* (which means the foam head on beer), a series of sketches set in a tavern that continues to break attendance records. The original *Broue* toured Quebec for five years before the cast/writers hired a translator, learned English and opened at Montreal's Centaur Theatre as *Brew.* They sold out the run, and went on to play before great houses in several other Canadian cities. A second English-speaking touring cast has now been assembled; the originals are working on their Broadway debut by playing small New England theatres.

Michael Sinelnikoff's translation of the hit *Bachelor (Single)* won Toronto actress Rosemary Dunsmore a Dora Award nomination after a successful run at Toronto Free Theatre. *The Guys, Syncope, Remember Me*—some ten Quebec plays were translated for production into English in 1983-84. And Tarragon Theatre has Michel Tremblay's *Albertine en cinq temps* on the playbill (as *Albertine, In Five Times*) just a few months after it opened (in French) at the National Arts Centre. To facilitate the art of translation, Montreal's Playwrights' Workshop under Rina Fraticelli now runs a workshop program of translations-in-progress.

Less obvious to someone passing through town is the number of anglophones working in Quebec theatre. Montreal has a lively performance art, video, avantgarde, and music theatre scene. Almost every troupe has an anglophone member. Espace Libre is the city's most interesting "non-establishment" theatre, a converted firehall in the East End that's home to three companies: Mime Omnibus, Carbone 14, and the Nouveau Théâtre expérimental. Lorne Brass, originally from Toronto, joined Carbone 14 in 1981, and has been a prime force in the troupe's strongly visual, completely original approach to theatre. The Anglo factor was doubled when Jerry Snell arrived from Vancouver a year later. He didn't speak a word of French then. He does now, and well enough to speak a few words onstage.

However, Espace Libre productions don't usually concentrate on the language. The 1984 hit, *le Rail,* an incredibly atmospheric piece of theatre inspired by *The White Hotel,* used English and French with a smattering of German. In the same season, Mime Omnibus achieved an interesting synthesis of Quebec and American theatre styles in a work called *It,* conceived by Larry Smith. A mime actor who spoke no French when he joined Jean Asselin's troupe two years ago, Smith has taken the fluid, dream-like image theatre familiar at Omnibus and used it to reinterpret American family drama. With a stunning set including everything *and* the kitchen sink strewn helter-skelter on four stage levels, *It* managed to encompass just about every possible blood-relation conflict and hold them all together by images without narrative or traditionally developed characters. Written and rehearsed in English, *It* first ran in French. (Yes, they would like to tour.)

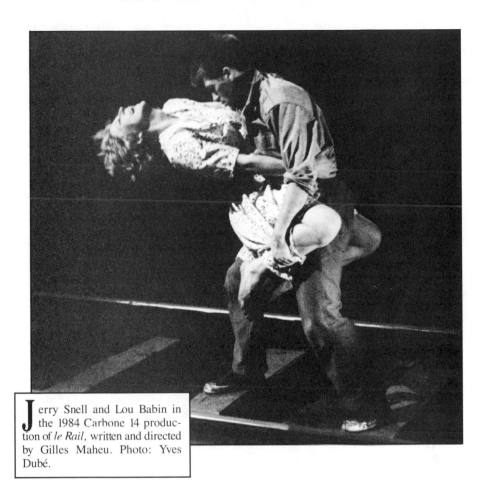

J erry Snell and Lou Babin in the 1984 Carbone 14 production of *le Rail,* written and directed by Gilles Maheu. Photo: Yves Dubé.

Anglos are busy behind the scenes as well. American-born Linda Gaboriau is the dramaturge at Centre d'essai des auteurs dramatiques, a two-decade-old organization that develops new plays and promotes the work of Quebec authors. In 1984, she organized a three-week festival of productions, play readings and lectures about Quebec plays in New York. CEAD publishes (in English) a quarterly newsletter, *Théâtre Québec,* summarizing the Quebec theatre scene, with synopses of new plays.

At first glance, a travelogue of local initiatives from a single season may not inspire a manifesto, or explain why the mid-80s are such an important moment on the always tenuous bridge between English and French-Canadian culture. These points of interest must be seen against a larger stage of Quebec theatre, for they stand out sharply against the conventional (Anglo-Canadian) wisdom about that milieu. The theatre in Quebec, so the patter goes, is (a) generally better, more lively, and more intense than elsewhere in Canada but (b) not nearly as exciting or as interesting as it was during the politically-charged seventies, when audiences and artists were united and fired by nationalism.

As always with conventional wisdom, those points contain some truth but overlook what is original and new on the present scene, and the implications of what is new.

Is Quebec theatre better? The 1984-85 season offered promise and surprise, but night by night a faithful patron saw a goodly number of new plays that seemed like first drafts, revivals of deservedly dead works, unauthentic translations of Broadway hits, and mighty classics that tossed their valiant crews overboard at first lurch. Big, boring fluffy plays sometimes did well, while the off-beat experiment the critics said was brilliant played to an empty room. And listen to actors: They are starving, unappreciated and overburdened with talent, while the public is fickle, or worse, glued to *Dallas.* In other words, much of the activity and many of the arguments here will sound familiar to anyone who follows theatre elsewhere in Canada. Add to that the frequent complaint among press, new playwrights and actors that subscription theatres simply won't risk their precariously balanced budgets on a new Quebec work.

There was good news, though, for those who care to look: A healthy leap forward for commercial theatre; a determination among actors to produce new work at their own risk; and a good new play by Quebec's most popular playwright. Michel Tremblay's *Albertine en cinq temps* premièred at the National Arts Centre in October, 1984 and has been hailed by veteran Quebec theatre critics as his best work to date.

If Tremblay has outlasted, indeed surpassed, the nationalist tide on which his art first gained popularity, that's a much-needed reminder to those of us who get bogged down by the endless debates over institutional politics, grants, cutbacks, etc. Art is a personal journey before it is public property. The marketplace displays trends, public tastes change, theatres come and go, but no amount of political frenzy or well-funded institutions has ever created a great playwright.

Not that Tremblay's plays don't invite, even demand, a fresh interpretation. Last year André Brassard's revival of *les Belles-Soeurs,* 15 years after he directed the first production, received a tepid critical response. Rather wearily, Brassard admitted he was not inspired to find anything new in the text. And Toronto critics have mumbled recently that productions of Tremblay in translation seem static.

A rather obscure 1983 production suggested a more radical approach to the young master could revive some of that original excitement. Théâtre populaire du Québec's musical version of *À toi, pour toujours, ta Marie-Lou,* was fresh, original, and quick to the essence of this eminently musical playwright. The monologues were sung using rock, country and western music, and hymns from the Latin Mass. An original score raised the emotions of the play to operatic proportions, bold and anything but static. TPQ's experiment suggests that music may be the perfect bridge between a lyrical theatre like Tremblay's and English translations of his work.

By now, the stature of Quebec's best-known, most frequently produced playwright exists to some extent independent of the local milieu, yet that milieu has clearly been changed by his presence. From the Brillo pad hairdos of fat ladies in a mime show to laugh-lines in a local stand-up comedian's routine, Tremblayisms have penetrated local pop culture.

He is indeed a popular playwright. A one-woman show based on his novel *C't'à ton tour, Laura Cadieux* has toured the province and packed a local night club that usually features bands and comics. Subtler echoes abound. Since Tremblay pioneered the use of *joual* in the theatre, it is not uncommon to find that accent and vocabulary on stage. But these days it is not *de rigueur* either, and that's something of a relief to classroom-educated bilinguals attempting to find their way around the new plays.

The interests of Quebec playwrights writing today are as varied as the writers themselves, although as elsewhere in Canada, the socially conscious play has been eclipsed by more personal concerns as subject matter. The poles in Quebec are far apart indeed: from René-Daniel Dubois' fantastical *Blamez jamais les bédouins* (a dozen motley characters wandering in the desert—a one-man show) to Marie Laberge's bleak *l'Homme gris* (an encounter between a desolate young woman and her alcoholic father, to whom she never speaks). Also to be watched: Serge Sirois, Normand Chaurette, Jovette Marchessault, Marco Micone.

Because they are less tied to social problems particular to Quebec, these plays may be more easily understood outside the province. Yet as neophyte play translators are discovering, making a Quebec play work in English is more than a matter of finding the right words. Quebec actors have a performing style quite different from most English-Canadian actors—less reserved, more at ease expressing wide poles of emotion. Plays written for that style really need adaptation, or a very special director and cast.

Quebec theatre is particularly adept at the art of adaptation. Both the Théâtre du Rideau Vert and the Compagnie Jean-Duceppe offer several Broadway and West End hits on their seasons each year. Serving middle-class, largely middle-aged audiences, these are two of the most financially sound theatres in Montreal, despite critics in the culture media who campaign relentlessly on behalf of new work.

Commercial hits from elsewhere are usually renovated for the local audience. Most memorable example: a British comedy, *Rattle of a Simple Man,* at Théâtre du Nouveau Monde, starring Yvon Deschamps and Linda Sorgini. Set in Montreal, the language and details were so thoroughly localized that the author's name was the only hint of the play's origin. It doesn't always work—*Foxfire* was a disaster at Rideau Vert. It isn't always tried; Tennessee Williams and Arthur Miller have recently played intact, and rightly so. But by adapting a commercial hit to the local audience, Quebec directors seem to be recognizing a commercial hit for what it is: an evening of theatre that brings pleasure to a wide public, maybe a statement or an *objet d'art,* but not necessarily. If local content is part of that pleasure, then Quebec theatre is willing and able to deliver.

The growth and health of commercial theatre in Quebec is undoubtedly one of the great success stories of the 1980s. Most musicals and popular comedies begin outside the established theatres, typically the creation of actors in search of work. *Broue* was launched in 1977 in a tiny, upstairs theatre in the East End, and moved to the Compagnie Jean-Duceppe's season in 1980-81. After Duceppe, the cast/writers signed with independent producer Jean-Claude L'Espérance. Organized tours of the province between engagements at Montreal's 1,600-seat Théâtre St. Denis slowly built the show into a $1 million a year business. Quebeckers never seem to get tired of *Broue*—a week at St. Denis is usually sold out before opening night. During a recent run, I chatted with the faithful and surprisingly diverse public in St. Denis' lobby one evening. L'Espérance is right. Many have seen the show more than once; most are there on a word-of-mouth recommendation.

133

L'Espérance manages a handful of Quebec singers, musicians, and plays. In 1983-84 he grossed $10 million, more than half that from ticket sales outside Montreal. Some 30 towns and villages outside the metropolis offer an equipped theatre or hall where travelling entertainment is received regularly. Most have independent producers there ready to do the publicity, sell tickets, and greet a touring act. Since 1963, that path has been used regularly by the Théâtre populaire du Québec, a professional company that produces a season exclusively for tour (1984-85: *Twelfth Night, K2,* and a Quebec play). Typically, TPQ likes to cast well-known television personalities in its season, always a draw in parts of the province where TV is the main entertainment.

Broue/Brew hit Quebec's funnybone. While that success hasn't quite been duplicated, the phenomenon has inspired a small industry. A rock musical, *Pied de Poule* enjoyed a single and an LP on the hit parade. *La Déprime* (or *Terminal Blues* as it is called in translation, NAC, 1985 season), made Julie Vincent a star. Both started small, then were picked up by L'Espérance, the most active but not the only member of a handful of entertainment entrepreneurs. Paul Dupont-Hebert of Productions Specdici Inc. produced *Bachelor,* and was encouraged by the success of the English translation, *Single.* He'd like to continue touring the translation across Canada, and hopes to try U.S. theatres.

On the English theatre scene, big experiments and failures vie for headlines with small, quiet projects. Montreal producer Sam Gesser invested close to $1 million in his longstanding dream to turn Mordecai Richler's novel, *The Apprenticeship of Duddy Kravitz,* into a Broadway-style musical. He co-produced *Duddy* with Edmonton's Citadel Theatre in the spring of 1984, and after bleak reviews from the national media, cancelled a planned cross-country tour while it played at Ottawa's National Arts Centre. In true Canadian style, Gesser blamed his country and "negative thinking" for the fiasco, but grudgingly admitted that if he'd started small and taken more time before the black-tie debut, the project might have succeeded. Starting almost-big and giving up too soon was the problem with Encore Theatre, which enjoyed a brief tenure at the Saidye Bronfman Centre before the board of directors decided a $100,000 debt after a season and a half was untenable.

Both projects used taxpayers' money. On the other hand, some of the most promising signs of revival on the English theatre scene are commercial ventures. Two independent companies, Elite Productions and Le Stage are producing seasons of musical comedy and drama at local dinner theatres; both have commissioned new work. After building an English audience at a former disco-bar, Elite ventured into French theatre with a comedy starring well-known Quebec talent (Louise Latraverse, currently artistic director of the Théâtre de Quat'Sous), and later, an original musical satire about television. Le Stage commissioned a stage version of a local best-seller, *The Anglo Survival Guide to Quebec—*a satirical look at English-French relations.

After David Fennario's *Moving* was produced in 1983-84, Centaur Theatre's popular playwright decided to take his theatre back to the people. He began working on a satirical history of Montreal called *Joe Beef,* workshopped and performed by friends at the Black Rock Community group in Verdun, where his other plays are set. A dedicated Marxist, Fennario is disaffected with the "system" that produces subscription theatre. The Centaur, struggling to pay its bills, is hardly a faceless corporation, but in the mid-1980s, it does seem that the only hope for

D on Scanlan, Peter MacNeill, Simon Malbogat, André St-Denis and Lubomir Mykytiuk in the 1978 Centaur national tour of David Fennario's *Nothing to Lose,* directed by Guy Sprung. Photo: Basil Zarov.

the revival of English theatre in Montreal is in these grass-roots projects. The Association of Performing Artists, a semi-professional group at Concordia University; Theatre Schmeatre, a Sunday night improv group on Park Ave.; and a handful of one-time, independent projects are among the encouraging signs of vitality.

Inevitably, the future of English theatre in Quebec depends on the anglophone community now emerging from a decade of political change, a time that saw more than 100,000 of the young and bright, the old and established members of that community leave the province. To date, that community's response has not really been reflected in the theatre. A comedy revue written and performed by ex-Montrealers (now living in Toronto) enjoyed a long cabaret run in 1984 with a series of skits about language tensions and other local political issues. Judging from audience response to *Mad in Canada,* Montrealers are enthusiastic about political theatre detailing their reality. The key word in English Montreal theatre is potential. Centaur Theatre audiences grow older, while their young offspring look elsewhere, to music, dance, film, and French theatre.

French Quebec is open to the world; English Montreal is open to more and different plays. What does it all mean to those in the rest of Canada whose dreams are invested in theatre? It means the moment is right—in Leonard Cohen's wonderful phrase—to renew neurotic affiliations. Any new English theatre venture in Montreal that's good, that captures the particular spirit of the city, would probably find audiences very responsive, and would certainly be treated royally by the local press. That news should interest the prodigal sons and daughters who've been waiting on tables in Toronto.

And if, for the moment at least, Quebec has abandoned the inward-looking attitude of nationalism and is open to new influences, interested in talking to English-speaking Canada, then now is the time to establish a real bridge between the French and English artistic communities. As I've tried to show, good ideas abound on the Quebec scene. Many could work elsewhere, if only theatre people outside Quebec knew about them.

But beyond the practical side are less obvious, more profound reasons why a bridge between Quebec and English-Canadian culture is important to the future of our theatre. Despite the quite different historical origins of both societies, despite the language barrier and the legacy of political tension, the existence of English and French Canada beside an empire to the south is far more precarious than our co-existence in one lumpy political unit.

At the bottom of that dilemma is a powerful argument for more communication between artists. Quebec wonders, Can we survive? An inner voice answers, no, and every act of art seeks to contradict that fear. The rest of Canada wonders, Do we exist? From the din of world-wide Anglo culture, no reply; therein the fear. So English Canadians wander, noses pressed against foreign windows, hoping for a toe-hold, a reflection of the self. And why not wander? The act of becoming needs models, needs to escape the familiar before the familiar can be reinvented as art. New York and London are good places to acquire skills and money—on their own terms—but are ultimately indifferent, impatient with young themes like identity, and poor stops on the journey to the self.

To the curious, the open-minded, the young and adventurous, artists, arts entrepreneurs and intellectuals, Quebec today presents a challenge, if not quite an invitation. Now is the time to rediscover *le nouveau monde* here at home. Build the bridge: Come to Quebec, go to the theatre, make friends who will be your continuing contact with French Canada when you have moved on.

For despite confusion and self-doubt, shadows and misplaced ideals, the New World does have a vision. Old empires do not block the way, must not have the last word. Only the energy and resolve of individuals can build a bridge, or a culture—which is, after all, nothing other than the sound of many inner voices inspired to speak out. And where a place more inspiring than this foreign corner of home? Paris in the 20s. San Francisco in the 60s. Why not Montreal in the 80s, our own *nouveau monde* to be rediscovered, a place where the small, inner voice can be heard and its contradictions shaped in our own image?

Marianne Ackerman

Ontario

There is no logical place to start a discussion of theatre in Ontario. The province is twice the size of France. While almost a third of Canada's entire population is clustered along Ontario's southern border, the closest theatrical neighbour to the Magnus Theatre in Thunder Bay, for example, is an eight-hour car journey away in Winnipeg, Manitoba. Given such a range, both geographically and artistically, there is no "right" place to begin. So, let's go to Ottawa first.

Between 1949 and 1956 the Canadian Repertory Theatre, operating out of the 688-seat auditorium of La Salle Academy boys' school, provided Ottawa with its only professional theatre in the form of weekly rep, the like of which has not been seen in the city since. The standard was relatively high, considering the company mounted as many as 20 shows in a season and aimed to provide something for everybody. Productions included Oscar Wilde's *Lady Windermere's Fan,* Molière's *The Imaginary Invalid,* Terence Rattigan's *The Deep Blue Sea,* Christopher Fry's *The Lady's Not For Burning,* leavened with such potboilers as *Dial M For Murder, The Cat and the Canary,* and the inevitable farce, *See How They Run.*

Many of Canada's best-known actors practiced their craft in that school hall, among them Christopher Plummer, William Hutt, William Shatner, Betty Leighton, and Amelia Hall, the CRT's artistic director. Those were the days before government subsidies, and the CRT relied solely on its box office receipts and the generosity of patrons for its finances. Not surprisingly, it ran into financial difficulties which proved insurmountable. In 1956, with Ian Fellows at its helm, the CRT had to close its doors. It is remembered with affection by those who attended its productions, but its demise set an unfortunate pattern for the future of professional theatre in Ottawa.

For a time, the Theatre Foundation of Ottawa, formed in 1957 with the objective of keeping professional theatre alive in the city, filled the gap. Along with Tremblay Concerts, it provided the capital with touring shows. Later the TFO was instrumental in paving the way for the National Arts Centre, by undertaking feasibility studies. On the advice of Sir Tyrone Guthrie ("You've got to produce!"), TFO formed the Town Theatre in 1967, with Frank Daley as its artistic director and, later, Paul Gaffney as its general manager. The first show was *The Subject Was Roses,* by Frank Gilroy, starring Kate Reid, Bud Knapp and Douglas Chamberlain.

The Town Theatre survived for three seasons, producing among other dramas Jean Anouilh's *Antigone,* Brian Friel's *Philadelphia Here I Come,* Murray Schisgal's *Luv,* and Arthur Miller's *Death of a Salesman,* featuring actors such as Dinah Christie, Tom Kneebone, Betty Leighton, Leo Ciceri, Amelia Hall, Ken James, and Hugh Webster. These stars had to carry the show since the production values didn't always measure up to the acting. The Town met its box office target but its board of directors was unable to raise the additional funding needed. Nor was the Canada Council able to help since it was preoccupied with the anticipated requirements of the National Arts Centre. The Town Theatre closed in 1969, the same year the NAC opened its doors.

Given these splendid early efforts at bringing Ottawa professional theatre, it is deplorable that the National Arts Centre, a three-theatre complex completed in 1969 at a cost of $46 million, has the dubious distinction of being one of the few capital city arts centres without a theatre company of its own. The NAC's original mandate was to act as a showcase for the best in Canadian theatre by bringing in productions from other parts of the country, and by sending out touring productions from Ottawa. The first part of that mandate has proved easier to fulfill than the second.

Jean Roberts directed theatre activities at the NAC from 1971 to 1977 and during that time brought in productions from the Stratford Festival, Neptune Theatre, Toronto Arts Productions, Tarragon Theatre, Toronto Workshop Productions, and Theatre Passe Muraille. Under Roberts, NAC audiences were sometimes intrigued, often outraged, but seldom bored; her programs were, to say the least, adventurous. She produced a fine *Tango* by Slawomir Mrozek, and a curious *The Tempest,* directed by Marigold Charlesworth and featuring John Neville as Prospero, in which actors occasionally used trapeze-like swings against a faintly outer-space decor. Jean Gascon directed a spectacular production of John Coulter's *Riel,* and Charlesworth staged Timothy Findley's *Can You See Me Yet?.* The most memorable event, however, was the occasion when people booed Peter Handke's *The Ride Across Lake Constance* and left the theatre in droves.

Despite the best efforts of Jean Roberts, it wasn't until the 1977-78 season that John Wood, recruited from the Neptune Theatre in Halifax, was able to establish a resident company at the NAC with long-term contracts for the actors. Under Wood's direction, the NAC Theatre Company produced a wide variety of work, with an understandably varying degree of success. Wood's way with Shakespeare was always innovative, often bold, and, with the exception of his *Hamlet,* seldom successful. Wood's productions invariably had a director's vision which, rightly or wrongly, left its stamp on the work. His swan song, before leaving the NAC in 1984, was an impressive production of *The Oresteia of Aeschylus.*

It was Wood, too, who took the company on tour with *Hamlet,* John Murrell's *Waiting for the Parade,* and *William Schwenk and Arthur Who?* which he co-wrote with Alain Laing. Touring predictably proved far too costly a proposition given the size of the country, and the company remained in residence performing such plays as Tennessee Williams' *Camino Real*, Shakespeare's *Troilus and Cressida*, Ibsen's *Ghosts*, Peter Shaffer's *Equus*, and Brecht's *Mother Courage*.

It is worth noting that during Wood's tenure, almost 40 Canadian works were produced at the NAC. Some of the indigenous work was staged at the Atelier, a converted warehouse a few blocks from the NAC. The Atelier provided a venue not only for new work but also for such plays as Tom Stoppard's *Dogg's Hamlet*, *Cahoot's Macbeth*, Edward Bond's *Narrow Road to the Deep North*, and C.P. Taylor's *Good*, and gave apprentice actors and designers a chance to work in pro-

Roland Hewgill as Agamemnon in the 1983 National Arts Centre Theatre Company production of *The Oresteia of Aeschylus*, directed by John Wood. Photo: Murray Mosher.

fessional productions. The Atelier was also the scene of training sessions in voice, movement, and the Alexander method, both for apprentices and seasoned company actors.

Canada's faltering economy and the government's refusal to increase its subsidy to the NAC resulted in the disbanding of the theatre company at the end of the 1983-84 season—a move which coincided with the expiration of John Wood's contract. It is discouraging to note that while there has been a good deal of indignation on the part of the actors at the demise of the NAC company, there has been remarkably little reaction from the general public.

Wood has been replaced by Andis Celms, the NAC's theatre administrator for many years, who assumed the title of producer. Celms' first season consisted of seven comedies: three produced at the NAC on an ad hoc basis, bringing in directors and actors for each show, and four productions mounted by companies from Toronto, Vancouver, New Brunswick, and the Shaw Festival. This line-up drew over 9,000 subscribers—a record number for the NAC but not an overwhelming response from a city of 350,000 inhabitants. In comparison, the Ottawa Little Theatre and the Orpheus Society, both now in their eighth decade of existence, produce, respectively, popular plays and musicals of a near-professional standard and have almost as many subscribers as the NAC's English theatre.

Juxtaposed to the NAC Theatre Company has been its French-speaking counterpart, La Compagnie du CNA. After a brief and stormy start as Le Capricorne, the French venture has had a rather more serene history than its English counterpart. For many years La Compagnie was headed by Jean Herbiet, a former theatre professor at the University of Ottawa. Since 1982 it has been run by André Brassard, the director responsible for staging nearly all of Michel Tremblay's work. In this bilingual city, the French company has 5,400 subscribers. The work is generally good, sometimes outstanding, and is obviously finding favor with its audience.

Today the capital has only one full-time English-language theatre company, the Great Canadian Theatre Company. It, too, is having financial problems. The GCTC concentrates on Canadian plays, mostly with socialist themes. After ten years, the company finally has its own 200-seat theatre in a former auto body shop in the heart of the city's Italian district. The GCTC has been more successful in its choice of actors and designers than in its choice of plays. All too often there is an unfinished feeling to their work. The play's idea may be worthy, but the execution is often indifferent. The GCTC's regular subscribers number less than 1,000, testimony to the limited appeal of their specialized approach to theatre.

Two Ottawa companies which recently expired are the Penguin Theatre Company and Theatre 2000. The future looked bright for the tiny Penguin Theatre Company when, in the 1981-82 season, it moved from a school basement to an attractive 250-seat theatre renovated by and leased from the National Capital Commission. But the following year the company ceased production, alarmed by the state of its finances. It is currently subletting the theatre to other performing groups in order to pay off its debts. Theatre 2000, which operated out of a 120-seat space above a store in the Byward Market area, appeared to have a faithful following, but evidently not faithful enough to make it financially sound.

Both theatres claimed that lack of public interest contributed to their financial failure and influenced their decisions to close. Penguin's fare, though it always maintained a certain integrity, was perhaps too esoteric for Ottawa's theatre-goers;

it produced new Canadian scripts and little-known ones from elsewhere. Theatre 2000 also worked at developing new scripts, but its death is harder to understand since it also staged such popular shows as *18 Wheels, A Streetcar Named Desire, Accidental Death of an Anarchist,* and *Jacques Brel Is Alive and Well and Living in Paris.* Its dark and limited space at the top of a steep and narrow staircase undoubtedly worked against it; so, too, did some poor financial management.

A recent vogue for co-productions among professional theatres has benefited Ottawa, as well as other Canadian cities. Co-productions allow companies to share production costs and reduce artistic risks. Claire Luckham's *Trafford Tanzi,* for example, mounted by the NAC in September, 1983, went on to become one of the hits of the 1984-85 Toronto Free Theatre season, generating more box office revenue than the rest of TFT's season combined. *Country Hearts,* written by Ontarian Ted Johns, had its première at the Blyth Festival, and was subsequently produced by Theatre New Brunswick which brought the show to the NAC in Ottawa. Similarly, the Shaw Festival's production of Labiche's *Célimare* travelled to the NAC as well as to London's Grand Theatre, and its celebrated production of *Cyrano* played Toronto's Royal Alexandra Theatre. The Stratford Festival production of Rattigan's *Separate Tables* also had a healthy run at the Royal Alex. *I Love You, Anne Murray,* by Paul Ledoux and David Young, originally mounted in 1982-83 by Magnus Theatre in Thunder Bay, went on to tour the country under the title *Love Is Strange.*

Magnus Theatre is an unlikely venue for launching a touring production. Situated in Thunder Bay, an isolated industrial town, at the head of the Great Lakes, dominated by pulp mills and grain handling facilities, Magnus caters to what is considered a male-dominated community. Yet its 1983 season was typically venturesome. Included in it were productions of *Trafford Tanzi, The Tempest,* and *The Front Page.* Last season also included such Canadian plays as *When I Wake* by James Nichol, set in northern Ontario, *Shipbuilder* by Saskatchewan writer Ken Mitchell, and *Gone the Burning Sun,* a one-man play about Dr. Norman Bethune, also by Mitchell.

In the same city, Kam Theatre is devoted strictly to Canadian work. The company started life a decade ago with the tongue-twisting name of Kaministiquia Theatre Laboratory and has since produced more than 60, mostly original, plays. Kam Theatre's pride in its locale and Thunder Bay's history as Canada's second largest port, is mirrored in the company's encouragement of local artists. The company is particularly supportive of local writers and one of its ambitions is to become a place where writers can be given a chance to re-work their scripts after a first mounting.

In the northern Ontario mining town of Sudbury (population 100,000), the Sudbury Theatre Centre has a different kind of success story. The theatre claims to have the highest subscription rate per capita of any theatre in Canada, having increased its subscription list over the last few years from a mere 300 to more than 4,000 with a lengthy waiting list. Seven mainstage productions are staged each season in the company's 297-seat theatre, built at a cost of $3 million three years ago. The theatre's program includes such popular fare as *My Fair Lady, Mass Appeal, Educating Rita,* and Agatha Christie mysteries. STC also operates two dinner theatres, and is now in its third summer season, making it a more-or-less year-round operation. A professional company, most of its actors are drawn from the Toronto area. With the help of the Ontario Arts Council, the Department of Northern Affairs, and local corporations, STC has been able to undertake limited tours of other, smaller northern Ontario centres from time to time, taking theatre to communities where it is rarely seen.

The Grand Theatre in London, Ontario, began as the amateur London Little Theatre in the 1930s. It made the successful transition to the professional Theatre London under artistic director Heinar Piller in the early 1970s. Led by Robin Phillips, it became the Grand Theatre Company, named for the lovely old building which was handsomely renovated and modernized in 1978.

Phillips, having resigned after six seasons at the helm of the Stratford Festival, took with him some of its best actors including Martha Henry, William Hutt, and Brent Carver. With extravagant hopes, Phillips mounted an impressive season consisting of *Godspell, Timon of Athens, The Doctor's Dilemma,* John Murrell's *Waiting for the Parade,* and Anouilh's *Dear Antoine,* among others, playing in repertory. While the surface sometimes dazzled at the expense of the heart of the play, the acting was unimpeachable.

London theatregoers, unlike the Toronto press, were not impressed. Phillips' rather cavalier rejection of their beloved subscription series in favor of a repertory system, and his somewhat peculiar (to Londoners anyway) choice of plays, met with considerable resistance. The attention Phillips had gained outside London—due in large part to his personal aura as a *wunderkind* and also the proximity of London to Stratford from which he had been unceremoniously dumped—did not translate into box office support. Phillips resigned after a single season and a large deficit. The Grand Theatre was taken over by Don Shipley, who returned to the subscription format and staged a combination of popular hits such as *An Inspector Calls* and *You Can't Take It With You,* with contemporary plays like *Passion, Painting Churches,* and *'Night Mother.*

The Press Theatre in St. Catharines also produces within the shadow of a nearby summer festival—the Shaw Festival in Niagara-on-the-Lake. The Press Theatre began as a 100-seat community theatre. In the 1930s and 40s, its forerunner, the Civic Drama League, occupied premises above a printing business—hence its present name. From 1945 to 1974 it was known as the St. Catharines Community Theatre. It is now a fully professional company with an artistic director, performing for its 1,500 subscribers in the 500-seat Playhouse of the Brock Centre for the Arts, at Brock University. Its latest season saw productions of *One Flew Over the Cuckoo's Nest, Special Occasions, Dames at Sea,* Sharon Pollock's *Blood Relations,* and *A Day in the Death of Joe Egg.*

This leaves Toronto, indisputably the centre of English-language theatre in Canada. Few would argue that Toronto came to its preeminence as Canada's centre of professional English-language theatre in the four years after 1969—the year that Theatre Passe Muraille emerged from the cellar of Rochdale College on the impetus of Jim Garrard. Ken Gass' Factory Theatre Lab followed in 1970; Bill Glassco's Tarragon Theatre a year later; and Toronto Free Theatre, founded by Martin Kinch, John Palmer, and Tom Hendry, in 1972.

A score of other companies rose and fell in the surrounding fifteen years, each with a number of notable productions to its credit—Open Circle Theatre (*The Primary English Class,* 1977), Studio Lab Theatre (*Dionysus in '69*), NDWT Company (*The Donnellys* trilogy, 1975), Phoenix Theatre (*Fortune and Men's Eyes,* 1975 and *Rexy,*

1981), Theatre Compact (*The Suicide, Da,* 1976), Theatre Second Floor (*Jekyll Play Hyde,* 1978), and New Theatre (*Automatic Pilot,* 1980), to name just a few. All of them made a mark, but none had the lasting impact of the original four.

The mood of the time was rebellious; the tone, polemical. Garrard called for a theatre "free of distinctions between actor and spectator." Gass and the founders of TFT battled for the right to call their respective theatres the Home of the Canadian Playwright. With less fanfare, Glassco turned Tarragon into the most successful of them all by championing such playwrights as David Freeman (*Creeps, Battering Ram, You're Gonna Be Alright Jamie Boy*), David French (*Leaving Home, Of the Fields Lately, One Crack Out, Jitters, The Riddle of the World,* and *Salt Water Moon*), and Michel Tremblay (in translation, *Hosanna, Forever Yours, Marie-Lou, Bonjour, là, Bonjour, The Impromptu of Outremont, Ste Carmen of the Main,* and *Damnée Manon, Sacrée Sandra*).

The enduring legacy of the first four or five years is incontestable as revealed by the number of Canadian playwrights, actors and directors who are alumni of Toronto's small theatres. It would be a mistake, however, to date the birth of indigenous professional theatre in Toronto to 1969. That honour belongs to the year 1946 when Dora Mavor Moore founded the New Play Society "to establish a living theatre in Canada on a professional but non-profit basis." Their first season at the Royal Ontario Museum Theatre opened with Synge's *The Playboy of the Western World,* Strindberg's *The Father,* a Chinese play called *Lady Precious-Stream,* Maugham's *The Circle,* and O'Neill's *Ah! Wilderness.* But the banner season was in 1949-1950 when five of the nine productions were of Canadian dramas—Mavor Moore's *Who's Who,* Harry Boyle's *The Inheritance,* Andrew Allan's *The Narrow Passage,* Morley Callaghan's *Going Home,* and John Coulter's *Riel.*

In 1951 the New Play Society was joined by Jupiter Theatre, run by a number of CBC Radio actors, playwrights, and directors "to produce plays of repute, both classic and contemporary, and to promote the production of plays by Canadian dramatists." Its first production was Brecht's *Galileo,* directed and designed by Herbert Whittaker, with a cast that included John Drainie, Lorne Greene, Margot Christie, David Gardner, and Hugh Webster.

Like the New Play Society, Jupiter Theatre operated in the ROM Theatre producing plays by Sartre, O'Neill, Pirandello, Coward, Tennessee Williams, and Christopher Fry (*The Lady's Not For Burning,* designed by Toronto artist Harold Town and starring Christopher Plummer, was a hit for the theatre in 1953). But it also staged a number of Canadian plays, including Lister Sinclair's *Socrates* (1952) and *The Blood is Strong* (1953), Ted Allan's *The Moneymakers* (a production televised by the CBC one week after its run in December, 1952), and Nathan Cohen's ill-fated *Blue Is For Mourning* (1953). Jupiter's last production in 1954 was Noel Coward's *Relative Values* at the Royal Alexandra Theatre.

By 1956, the New Play Society was channeling its energies into a theatre school it had formed in 1950. Luckily, Murray and Donald Davis and their sister Barbara Chilcott had stepped into the breach by opening the Crest Theatre in 1954 as a professional repertory house. For the next ten years, the Crest would house Toronto's most important productions. The apogee, at least in terms of international recognition, for the Crest company was the night in 1957 when the curtain rose on J.B. Priestley's *The Glass Cage.* The British novelist had written the play expressly for the Davises and their sister. The Crest's successful Toronto production subsequently became the first all-Canadian production to take the boards of London's West End.

Over 90 productions later, the Crest was floundering under a heavy deficit by the early 1960s, as was another Canadian venture based in Stratford, Ontario. The touring Canadian Players had been founded by actor Douglas Campbell and Stratford Festival founder Tom Patterson to keep Stratford's actors busy in the off-season. By 1965, under Jean Roberts and Marigold Charlesworth, the Canadian Players had moved into a semi-permanent home at Toronto's Central Library Theatre, and settled under a large debt. A merger between the remnants of the two organizations was planned. Out of that very short-lived union came the equally short-lived, but more significant company, Theatre Toronto.

Theatre Toronto lasted only two seasons, dying in 1969. But with Royal Shakespeare Company director Clifford Williams in charge, the company gave credibility to the nascent idea that Toronto needed an active professional repertory theatre. This was unavoidably evident after Theatre Toronto's excellent production in 1968 of Rolf Hochhuth's controversial play *Soldiers* starring John Colicos. In fact, with their dedication to professional theatre, Theatre Toronto, the Crest, the Canadian Players, and Toronto Workshop Productions were the midwives to the small theatre movement which grew in their wake.

Ironically, it was against the preponderance of imported dramas in the repertoires of the first three that the movement reacted. That, and against the mainstream entertainments of the O'Keefe Centre and the Royal Alexandra Theatre. The O'Keefe Centre opened in 1960 with *Camelot,* and became the home for visiting Broadway musicals, the Canadian Opera Company, and the National Ballet of Canada, as well as for entertainments as diverse as the circus and Liza Minnelli.

Today, the impetus for small and big musicals has swung to where it belongs—into the hands of Toronto's dozen or so dinner theatres which have sprung up in the late 1970s, and into the hands of independent producers such as Marlene Smith and Tina VanderHeyden who have taken the unprecedented step of raising $3 million to mount an all-Canadian production of the hit London and Broadway musical *Cats* in the refurbished Elgin Theatre. A further sign of the times for independent commercial production is a venture begun by the Toronto public relations firm Marshall Fenn Ltd. President David Butler supervised the bankrolling of a new musical called *Made in Canada* at the Bayview Playhouse in order to expand the firm's corporate base into the arts.

Unlike the O'Keefe Centre, the Royal Alexandra Theatre is no drain on the public purse, but like the O'Keefe Centre it has been treated, somewhat unfairly, as a public nuisance by the city's young theatre professionals. Ideal as a transfer house, something which Toronto still desperately needs, owner Ed Mirvish prefers to offer it as the home of money-making touring productions, unfortunately often featuring second-string or has-been casts. There have been exceptions—notably a production of Harold Pinter's *No Man's Land* starring the preeminent Sirs of British theatre, John Gielgud and Ralph Richardson, and a good touring version of *A Chorus Line*—but not enough for Toronto's smaller theatres to feel any less deserving of the title "alternate." Credit has to be given Mirvish for keeping his 51,000 subscribers happy. But what happens at the Royal Alex has very little to do with the creative heart of Toronto theatre.

Two other theatres which have played a contradictory role in Toronto's theatrical life over the last fifteen years are the resident company at the St. Lawrence Centre (first called Toronto Arts Productions and now CentreStage), and Marion André's redoubtable Theatre Plus. The former gained notoriety under artistic director Leon Major for his extravagant versions of the contemporary classics, in particular a series of over-dressed Brecht plays—*Mother Courage,* for example.

The latter theatre has remained in the public eye for over ten years on the strength of André's policy of producing, in the depressing heat of Toronto summers, morally and politically righteous dramas with good casts although frequently poor direction. Audiences love André's slick productions; critics have often questioned his casting and choice of plays. Indeed, Theatre Plus has become almost inseparable from André's peculiar catholic taste in theatre classics.

Both TAP/CentreStage and Theatre Plus have been the target of attack by other theatre professionals and critics for their lack of commitment to the work of Canadian playwrights and for their tendency to spend considerable sums on less than worthy productions. Yet both centres have given Toronto a number of good moments in theatre. One can point to productions at the St. Lawrence Centre of Trevor Griffiths' *Comedians* (1976), Garson Kanin's *Born Yesterday* and Thornton Wilder's

Ted Dykstra, Gina Wilkinson and Peter Blais in the 1984-85 Factory Theatre production of George Walker's *Criminals in Love,* directed by the author. Photo: Ben Lechtman.

The Matchmaker in 1980, all noted for their fine casts (R.H. Thomson and Toby Robins among the top actors). Certainly Theatre Plus' production of Arthur Miller's *The Crucible* stands out as the best possible interpretation of that rather heavy-handed play (aided immensely by the fine acting of Martha Henry and David Fox).

A lot was expected of Richard Ouzounian when he took control of CentreStage in 1984. But part way through a moderately successful first season, which included an important production of John Murrell's *New World,* he resigned under curious circumstances relating to budget matters. Despite having made two mistakes—co-producing the absurd mystery-comedy *Fatal Attraction,* which seemed only to have playwright Bernard Slade's Broadway name going for it, and letting Robin Phillips fiddle with Coward's *Tonight at 8:30*—Ouzounian deserved a better chance. He had strong credentials as a director, writer, actor, and producer, and possessed commercial acumen—all sorely needed by the troubled company.

Ouzounian's successor is Bill Glassco—the perspicacious former artistic director of Tarragon Theatre, who has established himself as one of Canada's finest directors. As CentreStage's director of theatre, he will quickly have to take the measure of the CentreStage audience and the theatre's board of directors, neither of whom have shown much patience with the intense probing plays favoured by Glassco in the past.

Today, the excitement in Toronto theatre has by and large swung back to the original alternates (although Toronto Workshop Productions has become somewhat mired in old production styles and dated dramatic content), after a brief flirtation with the avant-garde in venues like the Theatre Centre, and with such active companies as Necessary Angel, Buddies in Bad Times, Autumn Leaf, and Actor's Lab. Under artistic director Bob White, Factory Theatre spent a number of years producing a series of "fringe" staged readings called Brave New Works which hoped to give place and voice to new playwrights. Indeed, at least one discovery made the lengthy effort worthwhile—playwright Lawrence Jeffery and his works *Clay* and *Tower* which evoke the sparse power of Samuel Beckett's early plays.

Now White and Factory Theatre have moved back into the mainstream (insofar as a company which produces George Walker's zany dramas can be called mainstream), and into a large rejuvenated theatre on Bathurst Street, with a recent production of George Walker's Chalmers Award-winning play *Criminals in Love* which played to sold out houses and rave reviews. In the meantime, Factory founder Ken Gass has launched a new company called Canadian Repertory with the intent of re-mounting important Canadian works, although again with very little financial backing.

Tarragon Theatre, on the other hand, under artistic director Urjo Kareda has shifted slightly away from the mainstream image with which it had become identified in the later years of Bill Glassco's tenure. The move, however, is for the better, if only because Kareda has given his stage, and his fiercely loyal audience, over to such unlikely Tarragon playwrights as Judith Thompson (*White Biting Dog*), Lawrence Jeffery (*Tower*), Charles Tidler (*Farewell Heart*), and George Walker (*Science and Madness*). At the same time, he has preserved Tarragon's historical respect for the written word (remember George Jean Nathan's definition of drama, "what literature does at night") and presented such gems of dramatic writing as David French's *Salt Water Moon,* Mavis Gallant's *What Is To Be Done?,* and British playwright Caryl Churchill's *Top Girls.*

Greatest attention in Toronto today is paid to Toronto Free Theatre under Guy Sprung. Sprung has produced a series of stunning shows ranging from Middleton and Rowley's *The Changeling* to Brecht's *In the Jungle of Cities* and a number of runs of less auspicious dramas such as Sharon Pollock's autobiographical *Doc* and Sam Shepard's *Fool for Love*. Sprung's strength as an artistic director is the breadth of his taste in drama and his wish to explore various theatrical styles. Indeed, his passion for such exploration, quite apart from the equally necessary search for Candian playwrights, should be the modus operandi of more theatres.

Theatre Passe Muraille, on the other hand, hasn't been quite the same since Paul Thompson handed over the artistic directorship to Clarke Rogers in 1982. Rogers is an able director, but frequently lacks sound judgement in choosing new plays. His two major discoveries—Judith Thompson's *The Crackwalker* and Linda Griffith's *O.D. On Paradise*—can't hide the weak discernment involved in letting such unpolished dramas as *Lost Souls/Missing Persons* by Sally Clark and *Prodigals in the Promised Land* by Hector Bunyan find his stage.

With theatre in Ottawa in decline, London's Grand Theatre backing away from Robin Phillips' brave experiment, and theatres in other cities just holding their own against reduced government support for the arts, the recent burst of creative energy among Toronto's 45 theatres seems all the more startling and needed. The explanations for this liveliness range from the high quality work done by the new generation of actors, directors, and writers to the solid U.S. tourist dollar. Perhaps the proper answer rests with Toronto audiences—they are more discerning and demanding and yet ready to stand behind the honest efforts of any company. This talented audience may be the best legacy of the early 1970s and the work of Toronto's theatre pioneers.

Audrey M. Ashley (Ottawa) and Boyd Neil (Toronto)

The Stratford and Shaw Festivals

Since 1945, as wealth and leisure time have grown, Canadians have been engaging increasingly in cultural pursuits. During the past three decades, dozens of arts festivals have been founded from coast to coast. One of the country's first festivals was dedicated to the plays of Shakespeare. The Stratford Festival began production in its famous tent in 1953. A decade later, a second festival was dedicated to George Bernard Shaw. The Shaw Festival started in Niagara (later called Niagara-on-the-Lake) in the summer of 1962.

The Stratford Festival

Stratford has been one of Canada's most important theatrical institutions for the past three decades. Since its founding in the railway town of 19,300 in southwestern Ontario, it has been the only company consistently to attract international critical attention. Space limitations prevent a complete account of the many outstanding productions during the reign of Stratford's founding artistic director, Tyrone Guthrie (1953-1955), and of the achievements of his successors: Michael Langham (1956-1967); Jean Gascon and John Hirsch (1968-1969); Jean Gascon (1970-1974); Robin Phillips (1975-1980); and John Hirsch (1981-1985).

Yet despite its extensive resources and the stature of artistic directors since the beginning, the Stratford Festival, for the second time in five years, has been overwhelmed by a serious crisis that threatens to cripple its artistic life. As the 33rd annual season approaches, this awesome organization—the largest classical theatre in North America and the second largest artistic company after New York's Metropolitan Opera—faces not only an enormous financial debt but also internal dissension between senior administrators, which is spreading a paralyzing atmosphere of gloom among company members.

Last season was the greatest financial disaster the Stratford Festival has ever experienced. Although the season was budgeted at 73% attendance to break even, actual attendance fell from 73% in 1983 (rather low in the first place) to only 70% in 1984. This decline resulted in a short-fall at the box office of nearly three-quarters of a million dollars. But that considerable disappointment was only half the problem.

The greater share of debt resulted from production overspending that amounted to almost one million dollars. Since three of the 13 productions last season were remounted completely intact from the previous year, this means that each of the 10 new productions exceeded its production budget by an average of $100,000. Some of that overrun was caused by overtime costs for rehearsals, scheduled in off hours for new productions that opened late in the season.

The harsh reality is that Stratford suffered a deficit of $1.6 million last year. As if this isn't bad enough, last year's deficit must be added to the $1.7 million loss suffered mainly during the previous two seasons. That doesn't take into account the $1 million loss that occurred during John Hirsch's first season when a very late start at planning the season—due to the crisis of 1980—created panic spending that went way over budget.

All of that financial misery adds up to an accumulated deficit of $3.3 million. To bring that embarrassing total down a bit, the board of governors reached into Stratford's endowment fund for half a million dollars, reducing the deficit to $2.78 million. That leaves the endowment fund with a total of $2.88 million, just enough to retire the current losses over the next three years.

The fact is that the Festival has suffered a loss in every year of John Hirsch's regime as artistic director—four years in a row. It is ironic that the man appointed five years ago to rescue Stratford from a crisis of leadership seems to have led it since then into financial chaos and artistic blandness. Despite some very fine productions during the past four seasons, the overall programming of plays has been uninspiring. Surely that's the reason for falling attendance.

Hirsch's greatest success has actually been achieved by Brian Macdonald, a distinguished Canadian choreographer of ballet with a world-wide reputation. For the past three years, Macdonald has been staging a mini-season of Gilbert and Sullivan operettas at the 1,100-seat Avon Theatre. These lively updated revivals, directed and choreographed by Macdonald with an abundance of imagination, have been both artistic successes—except in the case of *Iolanthe,* which was grotesquely overproduced—and box-office hits that were repeated on CBC TV in their original form.

Macdonald wisely cast singers who could act and then made them dance. Every step and every gesture of the cast in *The Mikado* and *The Gondoliers* was choreographed with Macdonald's consummate skill and flamboyant imagination. These were world-class productions, austerely designed yet sumptuous-looking. In fact, Stratford's production of *The Mikado* was well received when it played in London at The Old Vic (recently refurbished by Toronto's Ed Mirvish, owner of the Royal Alexandra Theatre) during the winter of 1984.

John Neville, who takes over as artistic director at the end of the 1985 season, is not convinced that revivals of Gilbert and Sullivan belong at the Stratford Festival. Yet the current run, continuing this season with Macdonald's staging of *The Pirates of Penzance,* is not without precedents. During Langham's regime, the same operettas were staged at the Avon Theatre, one each year from 1960 to 1964. The first two were directed by Tyrone Guthrie, followed by Leon Major, Norman Campbell and William Ball.

Despite his negative achievements, Hirsch is responsible for some positive accomplishments during his regime. Perhaps the most praiseworthy has been his commitment to the training of young actors and the re-emphasis on the basics of classical acting—particularly clear, emotionally colored speech. Starting with his second season as artistic director, Hirsch put together the resources for a training program at the 400-seat Third Stage.

With its small thrust stage designed by Desmond Heeley, a near-replica of the platform stage in the large Festival Theatre, this former curling arena became the perfect setting for an introduction to the classics. The Young Company consisted of 14 professional actors in their twenties and thirties with considerable acting experience—especially in contemporary plays—but little experience in classical theatre, particularly Shakespeare. For each of the past three seasons, this company tackled two plays by Shakespeare with varying results. The best work was achieved in the summer of 1983 when Michael Langham supervised the training program and directed both plays.

His production of *Love's Labour's Lost* was a wonderful piece of theatre that caught the play's seasonal shift to autumn with great poignancy. The clear speaking in this production was strong, the result of Langham taking infinite care with his young actors, line by line and phrase by phrase. He was concerned that they speak Shakespeare as if they were thinking it for the first time, discovering the meaning at the same time as the audience in order to make it fresh. Despite its simple staging, this production was beautiful and moving—more satisfying, in fact, than any of the Shakespearean productions at the big theatre.

There is something very important lying behind this training program for young actors. It is Hirsch's desire to improve the skills of all the actors throughout the company. Both Hirsch and Langham have expressed their dissatisfaction with Robin Phillips' neglect of actor training and emphasis on building productions around stars. By the end of Phillips' regime as artistic director in 1980, there was a noticeable reduction in the competency of the middle range of actors.

Hirsch was hoping to infiltrate the Stratford company, starting with the young actors, making a new commitment to basics and upgrading their abilities. Langham's new approach to speaking Shakespeare was to be the first step in revitalizing acting skills. Incoming artistic director John Neville seems just as committed to this principle. In fact, he will take over the supervision of the training program at the Third Stage this season.

During the past three seasons, John Hirsch has revealed a personal fascination with dark interpretations consistent with his Slavic roots in eastern Europe, specifically Hungary. This is by no means a new development for him, but it did allow him to re-approach certain plays that he had directed before and to realize them this time in a way that was truer to his vision.

Even in productions that were not successful, Hirsch demonstrated that he is masterful in his use of Stratford's platform stage. This was obvious in his productions of *As You Like It* and *A Midsummer Night's Dream* where he created magnificent patterns of people filling the stage as well as an enormous variety of scenic moods. His experience of working on that challenging stage over a period of 20 years has given him skills that many younger directors envy.

The problem with Hirsch's staging of these two festive comedies was that his concept of a black court weighed down the productions too heavily. The comic spirit of unity, regeneration, and light-hearted whimsy was never able to lift off the ground. In fact, these productions became depressingly tragic. Nor were the comedies always cast with suitable leads.

Yet Hirsch's dark interpretation worked well in *Tartuffe,* despite his many ef-

forts to dampen down the comedy in order to emphasize the improbable *rex ex machina* ending that rescues Orgon from a disastrous conclusion. By staging this a second time, Hirsch was able to create a mellow golden glow over this eccentric production that still managed to be funny.

This frequent laughter was due very much to Douglas Campbell's restrained portrayal of Orgon and to Brian Bedford's rendition of Tartuffe, not as a masked hypocrite, but as a deliberate villain who looked and behaved more like an escaped convict than a religious man of the cloth. Yet this fine production wasn't half as comic as Jean Gascon's delightfully farcical version in 1968 when William Hutt played Tartuffe as a piously long-faced hypocritical monster.

During Hirsch's regime, other praiseworthy productions have included Jean Gascon's elegantly flamboyant *The Misanthrope,* starring Brian Bedford as an extraordinarily refined but petulant Alceste; Bedford's savage and cynical production of *Coriolanus,* starring Len Cariou in the title role—a production that was memorable for its astonishing image of a throng of pitiful Roman citizens floating in mid-air; Michael Langham's hilarious production of *Arms and the Man,* starring Bedford and Cariou as Bluntschli and Sergius; Guy Sprung's sadly wistful production of Brian Friel's *Translations,* a recent Irish history play about the spiritual defeat of the people when the British colonizers forced the English language on them.

Yet the accumulation of mediocre and wrongly-interpreted productions during Hirsch's regime has had a more serious effect on audience morale than merely the current financial deficit. The cruel result has been the development of audience apathy and indifference to the Festival's plight during the austere 1980s when government funding has fallen to a low of 11%. It doesn't take long for the public to forget what a glorious cultural institution Stratford has been and its theatrical accomplishments over the past 32 years.

That is why it is important now to remember the long and often illustrious history of the Stratford Festival as it has evolved through five distinctive regimes of artistic leadership. When Stratford's board of governors appointed a successor to Jean Gascon in 1974, they immediately plunged into a heated controversy with the vociferous nationalists across the country who demanded that a Canadian run the Festival.[1] Instead, the board chose Robin Phillips, a young British director in his early thirties who had been an impressive boy-wonder at several regional theatres in England. Also, he had been an actor, like Gascon before him.

To defuse criticism from nationalists, Phillips came to Canada a year early to study the theatrical landscape, visiting theatres from coast to coast and observing their work. When he took over control in 1975, Phillips was certainly bursting with fresh ideas. One of his first changes was to remove the Avon Theatre from the ghetto of second-class citizenship by staging Shakespearean plays there as well as at the larger Festival Theatre. Another significant change by Phillips was to import guest stars and to build handsome productions around them. Brian Bedford arrived that first season and stayed continuously for an entire decade, even after Phillips departed. The two of them teamed up that first season for a superb and intellectually strong interpretation of *Measure for Measure* that also starred Martha Henry.

Bedford was astonishingly funny as Malvolio in *Twelfth Night,* directed by David Jones. Bedford turned the disapproving puritan into a ridiculous figure of universal *hubris*, looking up at the audience in the balcony as he spat out, "I'll be revenged on the whole pack of you," before departing from the otherwise unified society of the play. In Phillips' second season, Maggie Smith arrived and graciously stayed for five seasons of often wonderful productions. In particular, she was paired with Bedford for several productions that delivered quite spectacular acting, bravura displays like *The Guardsman, Hay Fever, As You Like It, Private Lives,* and *Much Ado About Nothing.* The greatest of these may have been Smith's charmingly girlish portrayal of Rosalind, complemented by Bedford's two-sided portrait of Jaques as a wryly amusing and despondently sad Monsieur Melancholy. These two ravishing actors, each with that mysterious quality of stage presence, seemed born to play together.

On her own, Maggie Smith portrayed an exquisitely artificial Millamant in *The Way of the World* as well as a searingly realistic and disintegrating portrait of Virginia Woolf in *Virginia* by Edna O'Brien. On his own, Bedford played a ferocious villain in *Richard III* and directed his first play, a savagely dark interpretation of *Titus Andronicus.* Other notable productions during this regime included Zoë Caldwell's austere and elegiac production of *Richard II,* all in white; William Hutt as a sad loser of a nobody in *Uncle Vanya,* cross-dressed as Lady Bracknell in *The Importance of Being Ernest,* and as the proud magician/poet Prospero in *The Tempest,* all of which were directed by Phillips. So was a popular production of

King Lear, starring Peter Ustinov in a misguided interpretation of the king as a funny old fusspot. There was no tragedy in this sitcom figure.

Because he was a workaholic, Phillips increased the number of productions each season from the four or five at the end of Langham's regime, or the eight or nine at the end of Gascon's, to anywhere from ten to sixteen. There was an incredible amount of activity on the boards, with Phillips directing half of the productions himself (or sometimes with so-called assistant directors). Only half of these were successful, yet his average of 50% was still respectable. Occasionally he gave a young director from the regional theatres a chance to work at the tiny Third Stage, but none of these received the necessary training to work on the platform stage. The exception was Peter Moss, the only Canadian who directed a handful of productions on the main stage during Phillips' regime. A failure to develop Canadian directors was the same problem that plagued the directorships of Gascon and Hirsch.

In contrast to Hirsch's current regime, the morale of the company was very good during Phillips' six years. He was idolized by his actors who spoke of the thrill of rehearsing with him. They became dependent on him and he seemed to encourage that. Meticulous with every detail of every production, he made all final decisions about everything, even if this held up the smooth flow of work. Obviously he was not comfortable with delegating authority.

In 1979, just when everything seemed so rosy, Phillips suddenly announced that he was quitting due to illness. It may be that he thought he was fatally ill, since he had suffered from heart disease before taking the job at Stratford. He departed for England and recovered sooner than expected. In the meantime, the board flew into panic. When Phillips returned for his final season in 1980, he suggested he be succeeded by two tiers of artistic committees—an inner and an outer council. He would sit on the inner council as an adviser. However, the plan fell apart when Brian Bedford said he would have no part of what looked like a disaster searching for a place to happen.

This plan was replaced by a single committee of four artistic directors—Martha Henry (actress), Urjo Kareda (Phillips' literary manager), Peter Moss (a Canadian director), and Pam Brighton (a British director). The board hired this artistic quartet at the end of the 1980 season and then fired them only weeks later, using the excuse that their proposed season for the following year was certain to lose money. The real reason was that the board was eager to hire the high-profile British director John Dexter, who admittedly was one of the great directors in the world and happened to be available. Once again, cultural nationalists screamed foul, demanding to know when Canadians would get to run Stratford. This time, the government listened and refused to grant Dexter a work permit until Stratford proved that there were no qualified Canadians available for the job.

That is when Hirsch's name came up. After weeks and weeks of negotiations, he reluctantly accepted the position of artistic director, even though previous commitments to theatres elsewhere prevented him from being at the Festival for most of his first year. But he recognized his duty to save the Stratford Festival from the internecine quarreling that threatened to destroy this inestimably valuable cultural institution from within.

Today, it is ironic that someone must save it once again—from John Hirsch.

The Shaw Festival

The Shaw Festival was the brainchild of Brian Doherty, a retired lawyer living in Niagara in southern Ontario. This charming small town of white-painted Edwardian architecture and a population of 2,620 was an ideal setting for a summer festival and close enough to the U.S. border to attract American tourists from New York State. The drive from Toronto is only two hours, making the town the perfect destination for an all-day outing.

With the example of the Stratford Festival in mind, Doherty conceived the idea of a tribute to the works of Bernard Shaw, whose 50 plays would provide an extensive repertory to choose from. Although the town lacked a proper theatre, there was a nineteenth century court house available right in its centre with a large council chamber on the second floor. And that's exactly what he chose.

The first season began modestly in the summer of 1962 with a company of 10 unpaid actors performing two Shaw plays—*Candida* and *Don Juan in Hell*—for eight weekend performances. Excited by the enthusiastic response to this "Salute to Shaw," Doherty decided to create a fully professional Shaw Festival for the following year. In 1963, he set up the Festival as a non-profit corporation (similar to Stratford) and hired Andrew Allan as artistic director—the man who had created the "golden age" of Canadian radio drama at the CBC during the 1940s and 1950s.

Allan began with a four-week season of four Shavian plays of popular appeal, performed by a company of 14 actors. The repertory included both full-length and one-act plays from all phases of Shaw's extraordinarily long career. By the end of Allan's three-year tenure, he had expanded the repertory to include plays by Shaw's contemporaries (O'Casey, for a start), lengthened the season to six weeks, added to the list a stimulating seminar series, and obtained financial support from the government through the Ontario Arts Council.

Barry Morse, a British-born actor who made a name for himself in Canada before moving to American TV (playing a leading role in *The Fugitive* series), became artistic director in 1966 for the Festival's fourth season. He selected a meaty playbill consisting of three major Shavian plays—*Misalliance, The Apple Cart,* and *Man and Superman,* in which he played John Tanner as well as directed—and inspired a standard of artistic excellence that gave the Festival its theatrical credibility. Besides infecting everyone with his enthusiasm for Shaw's plays, he established a tradition of artistic directors who not only directed the plays but also acted in them (sometimes both at the same time).

Morse was succeeded as artistic director the following year (1967) by Paxton Whitehead, another young and immensely talented British actor who had been introduced to the Festival during Morse's brief tenure. Whitehead expanded the season by introducing at the end a tour of *Major Barbara* to Montreal and Winnipeg, thus establishing a tradition of frequent out-of-season tours. By the middle of Whitehead's decade as artistic director, he had expanded the season to 15 weeks. By the end of his tenure in 1977, it had expanded to 22 weeks, matching the length of Stratford's season.

During his decade of tenure, Paxton Whitehead took a sabbatical only once, in 1975, when Tony van Bridge was appointed acting artistic director. Despite assistance from directors Eric Till and Douglas Seale, van Bridge's year at the helm was artistically mediocre. The reason for Whitehead's sabbatical was his mental fatigue which he incurred during the exhaustive process of opening the new Festival Theatre in 1973. Toronto architect Ron Thom designed this magnificent-looking and wonderfully intimate theatre. Made of red brick and pale cedar, the modernistic and functional building seats 830 people in a spacious orchestra and steeply raked balcony. The new theatre, which stimulated the tremendous growth and popularity of the Festival, was very likely the most important event during Whitehead's regime.

There were many memorable productions throughout the period of Whitehead's artistic leadership. These included *Arms and the Man* in 1967, starring Douglas Rain, Martha Henry and Whitehead himself in the role of Sergius; Kate Reid in *The Circle* by Somerset Maugham in that same season; Jessica Tandy as Hesione Hushabye in *Heartbreak House* (1968); Lila Kedrova and Paxton Whitehead in *The Guardsman* in 1969; Stanley Holloway as Burgess in *Candida* in 1970; Amelia Hall and Alan Scarfe in *Forty Years On* by Alan Bennett in that same year; Elizabeth Shepherd and Tony van Bridge in *Too True to be Good* in 1974; plus both of those actors joined by Powys Thomas and Edward Atienza in *Pygmalion* in 1975.

At times, Whitehead was criticized for seasons that seemed too lightweight, reducing the Festival to the status of straw-hat players in frivolous summer stock. But the few outright farces that he did produce were tremendous hits, both artistically and commercially. These included *The Chemmy Circle* (1968), translated by Suzanne Grossmann from Feydeau's *La Main Passe,* starring Frances Hyland, Jack Creley, Patrick Boxill and Kenneth Wickes; and *Charley's Aunt* (1974), starring Whitehead, Boxill, Norman Welsh and Kenneth Wickes.

Perhaps the finest production of Whitehead's regime occurred in his final year when he engaged the highly respected British actor, Ian Richardson, to play John Tanner in a revival of *Man and Superman.* Besides his handsome chiselled looks, Richardson has one of the greatest, most musical voices in the English-speaking theatre and used it very successfully in this marathon role, in a production (including the "Don Juan in Hell" scene) that lasted almost five hours.

When Paxton Whitehead left in 1977, the Shaw Festival went through two difficult years, experiencing a crisis of leadership. In 1980, to lift the Festival out of the doldrums, the board appointed as artistic director Christopher Newton—a young man in his mid-thirties with a reputation for his work at the Vancouver Playhouse (artistic director for 1973-79) and at Theatre Calgary where he had been the founding artistic director (1968-71). Like Morse and Whitehead before him, Newton was both an actor and a director, with experience on the stage of almost every regional theatre in Canada, not to mention the Stratford Festival. He was trained classically in England, was a versatile actor, and was a talented playwright to boot.

Right from his initial season, Newton energized the Festival with his dynamism and his ensemble approach to building a company of indigenous actors without importing stars from abroad. Above all, he has shown confidence in the talent of Canadian actors. However, he has a weakness for choosing directors—often imported from England—who have not been equal to the task. In particular, the work of young Canadian directors has not been good enough—several times because they were saddled with poor scripts.

A recurring and very prominent part of Newton's theatrical personality has been his impulse to be an *enfant terrible*. He perceives himself as part of the avant-garde tradition that shocks and assaults its audience. That is why he introduced a gratuitous scene of male nudity into his abysmal production of *Saint Joan* in

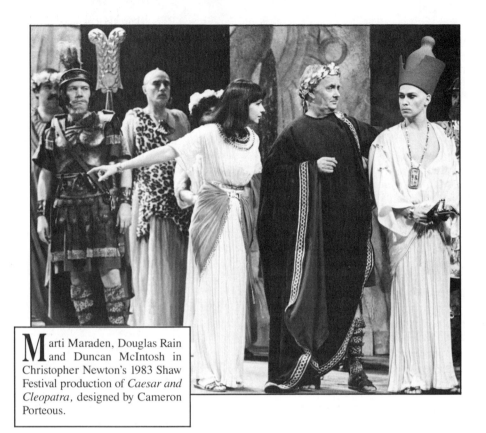

Marti Maraden, Douglas Rain and Duncan McIntosh in Christopher Newton's 1983 Shaw Festival production of *Caesar and Cleopatra,* designed by Cameron Porteous.

1981. It is also the reason why he produced *Camille* by the Scottish playwright Robert David MacDonald in the same season. This dark, decadent look at what really happened in the relationship between Dumas *fils* and his actress mistress (the basis for Dumas' idealized play *La Dame aux Camélias*) tried very hard to be outrageously perverse. The production had the intended effect on audiences and was repeated in the next season.

Newton's craving to shock and assault audiences was realized best by the 1980 production of *A Respectable Wedding,* an early trifle by Brecht which was revived impressively by director Derek Goldby, a man with an international reputation. Goldby had previously staged this story about a suburban wedding where everything goes wrong at the Vancouver Playhouse. This time, the production achieved its nightmarish vision of social decay and material disintegration very well. However, the ending—when the groom tries to rape his bride with a wine bottle—was excessive, misogynist, and far beyond Brecht's intentions. Needless to say, it outraged many spectators. Yet the production was a hit.

Goldby has had some of the biggest successes during Newton's regime, particularly with farce. In fact, Newton has been associated more closely with farce than Whitehead was. This new tradition began in Newton's first season with Goldby's wonderful and brilliant production of Feydeau's *A Flea In Her Ear.* What made this production so remarkable—even astonishing—was the furious frenzy of the pacing (in both speaking and moving about) and the mechanical puppet-like movement of the actors. Beneath the smiling clockwork precision lay a darkly philosophical meaning that implied the characters were the doomed victims of the chaotic plot. The brilliant comic invention of Heath Lamberts (in a double role) enabled him to quickly shoot up to star status at the Festival. In the next season (1981), Goldby and Lamberts teamed up for a British farce from the 1920s, *Tons of Money.* Lamberts was sensationally hilarious in a triple role while Goldby took just as frantic a pace.

This tradition of lively farce continued each year. Lamberts starred in *See How They Run* in 1982 and Ben Travers' *Rookery Nook* in 1983. When Lamberts took a sabbatical in 1984, Tom Wood tried to fill his shoes in the production of *Célimare.* But Wood was not as comically inventive as Lamberts, Eugene Labiche was not as good a *farceur* as Feydeau or Travers, and British director Wendy Toye was not suited to farce at all.

Heath Lamberts' greatest triumph at the Shaw Festival was in Goldby's cluttered and sloppy production of *Cyrano de Bergerac,* which debuted in 1982 and was repeated in 1983 (minus the sloppiness). Lamberts gave life to an extremely flamboyant character who was as witty (though not poetic) as he was adept with a sword. His drawn-out dying was doubly pathetic and as heart-rending as it was gallant. His performance was a *coup de panache.*

Newton's regime has had other fine performances. These have included Carole Shelley as the Polish aviatrix in *Misalliance* in 1980; Goldie Semple as the sluttish courtesan, Marie Duplessis, in the revival of *Camille* in 1982; Fiona Reid as the elegantly mannered Amanda in *Private Lives* in 1983 (though Denise Coffey's production stressed the brittle surface of artifice and missed the soft romantic heart hidden underneath); Douglas Rain and Tom Wood in Shaw's *The Simpleton of the Unexpected Isles,* 1983; Frances Hyland and Geraint Wyn Davies as mother and son in Noel Coward's decadent early drama, *The Vortex,* also in 1983; and Nora McLellan as a dithery but sympathetic maid Sabina in Thornton Wilder's *The Skin of our Teeth* in 1984. In this production, Newton's elaborately cosmetic direction managed to hide the increasing tedium of Wilder's script, which diminishes in impact with each successive act. It was not quite a *coup de théâtre,* but it was still a show with many enjoyable moments.

For many years when the Shaw and Stratford Festivals were young and their seasons short, their artistic directors hoped to lengthen the season to increase work opportunities for their acting ensembles by establishing winter homes for the companies in Toronto. However, it was only in the winter of 1983/84 that Christopher Newton was able to establish a Toronto presence for the Shaw Festival between seasons through co-productions with two theatres in the city. The first was with Young People's Theatre, where Newton directed a large group of actors from the Festival in a production of Dickens' *A Christmas Carol* which ran throughout the holiday season. A year later, this association was repeated in a production of Dickens' *Great Expectations.* In each case, the novels were awkwardly adapted to the stage, the acting was mostly one-dimensional, and the directing was frequently dull. Yet the productions proved to be very popular with YPT's young audiences in search of holiday diversion. And YPT's management was delighted to share the costs with Shaw for one of its biggest shows of the season.

Newton's second co-production was with Toronto Free Theatre. The first "Toronto Project" was a risky venture for adults only and gave Newton another opportunity to play the role of *enfant terrible*. He chose the recent French play *Delicatessen*, written by the actor and director François-Louis Tilly. In 1981, Derek Goldby had directed a controversial French-language production in Brussels which incited a small theatre riot and required the presence of police to allow the performance to take place.

Although its sporadic dialogue was often funny, *Delicatessen* was really only a sordid melodrama with an abrupt violent ending about the mutual dislike and intense conflict between a middle-aged father and his youthful son, a vile unkempt ruffian whom the audience dislikes from the moment he is met urinating into the kitchen sink. Directed by Derek Goldby in a style of infinitely slow super-realism that soon became gnawingly dull, *Delicatessen* nevertheless had audiences looking for seamy sensation flocking to Toronto Free Theatre's 125-seat studio upstairs.

However offensive this production was, it set a precedent for the Shaw Festival's staging of new plays, both Canadian and foreign, in Toronto during its former off-season. By using small casts and a small studio space, production costs are held down while the Festival gains a jolt of creative juice firing through its veins. In March of 1985, the second "Toronto Project" was another co-production with Toronto Free Theatre, *Goodnight Disgrace,* by the Vancouver dramatist Michael Mercer. This memory play about the relationship between Malcolm Lowry and Conrad Aiken included a strong performance by Geraint Wyn Davies as the repugnant Lowry, but was often carelessly directed by Leon Pownall. Certainly, such productions as these would be more expensive to produce on one of the Festival's larger stages—if summer audiences could be persuaded to buy tickets for an unknown new play.

For although purists would be shocked, it is a known fact that Canadian and American tourist audiences frequently take a casual approach to the Shaw and Stratford Festivals. The cultural activity is often only one part of an annual all-day excursion that includes scenic drives through rural settings, languid meandering through green parkland, and hearty picnicking along a riverside when the few crowded restaurants are not available. If the cultural component is not completely rewarding, the other ingredients often make the day's considerable efforts sufficiently satisfying.

As long as audiences take this casual approach to summer theatre festivals, there is no unified public demand for the very best quality of plays and performances. Mediocrity can become acceptable, even expected. Yet perhaps the recent financial problems at Stratford since 1981 are in part a sign that the public has reached a new level of maturity and will not accept mediocre programming any longer.

Richard Horenblas

Notes

[1]For background information on the controversies surrounding the appointment of Robin Phillips and John Hirsch as Stratford's artistic directors, see "The Stratford Controversy", *Canadian Theatre Review,* No. 30, Spring 1981 and Martin Knelman, *A Stratford Tempest.* Toronto, McClelland and Stewart, 1982.

The Prairie Provinces

It all began in the Manitoba capital of Winnipeg. It was here, in the middle of the Canadian prairies, that Canada's first professional regional theatre—the Manitoba Theatre Centre—was founded in 1958 by John Hirsch and Tom Hendry (later one of the founders of Toronto Free Theatre and the Playwrights Colony at the Banff Centre, School of Fine Arts). Hirsch and Hendry expressed the hope that the Manitoba Theatre Centre, a bold new artistic venture for its time, would become the "cornerstone of a decentralized national theatre network in Canada."

Winnipeg, with a metropolitan area population of about half a million, was luckier than most Canadian cities of its size in that it boasted both a thriving amateur company and an emerging professional troupe. The amateur Winnipeg Little Theatre had been active in the community from 1921 to 1937 and was revived by George Broderson, of the University of Manitoba, in 1948. Just starting to make its presence felt was Hirsch and Hendry's Theatre 77—a small company so called because the loft where it performed was located just 77 steps away from the busy downtown intersection of Portage and Main Streets.

But even Winnipeg seemed to be going nowhere in terms of cultural growth until its two theatres decided to form an alliance and expand the scope of their operations. The merger of Winnipeg Little Theatre—which had recently acquired an old movie house for a performing space—and Theatre 77 into what was to be called the Manitoba Theatre Centre marked the beginning of the regional theatre movement in Canada and coincidentally the birth of modern professional theatre in the prairie provinces. The structure, ideology and philosophy of the Manitoba Theatre Centre were to be studied and copied not only throughout Canada but also by theatres in the United States and parts of Europe.

The founding of the Manitoba Theatre Centre, a professional non-profit theatre with a specific regional focus, was followed in succeeding years by the establishment of similar theatres in Edmonton (Citadel Theatre, 1965), Regina (Globe Theatre, 1966), Calgary (Theatre Calgary, 1968) and Saskatoon (Persephone

Theatre, 1974). These cities, ranging in population from about 126,000 (Saskatoon) to 400,000 (Edmonton) are separated from one another by hundreds of miles in the prairie provinces which are bounded on the west side by the Rocky Mountains of British Columbia and on the east by the border lakes of Ontario. It is an area of Canada where the people tend to define themselves according to their pioneering spirit. Because it contains a rugged and somewhat thinly-populated environment where people can symbolically face and come to terms with whatever destiny unites them, the prairie region is viewed by Canadians generally as being separate from the more populous areas of Ontario and Quebec, and different from those parts of Canada—particularly the coastal regions—where the climate isn't characterized by unbearably cold winters and summers that are dry and very hot.

Such geographic and climatic differences have a bearing on the development of distinctive cultural identities in the different regions of Canada. The Manitoba Theatre Centre grew out of a communal desire by theatre lovers and artists in Winnipeg to have something of the life around them reflected in their modes of cultural expression. Similarly in other prairie cities, theatre evolved as a form of homegrown entertainment for communities separated by distance—geographical and spiritual—from the rest of North American civilization. What these cities lacked in the way of culture was not available for hundreds of miles. As a result, they were forced to develop their own cultural institutions, to alleviate the sense of boredom and isolation and to bring cheer to those long winter nights when blizzards and sub-zero temperatures tended to keep residents indoors.

But that's not to say geographical isolation or weather factors alone were what stimulated the growth of professional theatre in the prairie provinces. Many communities in other parts of the world have grown up in a similar state of isolation or snow-bound *angst* and have chosen to remain in a permanent state of cultural deprivation. More significant for the evolution of theatre on the prairies was the mix of ethnic cultures—particularly in Winnipeg and Edmonton—which fomented a sharing of traditions that led eventually to a desire by the residents to acquire imaginative control over their own space, to express artistic ideas more relevant to their own lives than anything television or the movies could supply. For prairie dwellers who had accepted Hollywood culture as compensation for living in a backwater, indigenous professional theatre served to show that their way of life was something to be celebrated, too.

In prairie cities such as Calgary and Regina, professional theatre arrived at a time during the late 1960s when Centennial grants were available from the federal government for the establishment of cultural institutions, and before there was any indication that the cities needed or even wanted such institutions. But they took root in fertile soil. Once the theatres were established, public support followed quickly and they became a focus for all the theatrical energy and resources within their respective communities.

That focus remains central to their operation. In addition to offering annual seasons of plays for adult subscription audiences, the Manitoba Theatre Centre, Theatre Calgary, Edmonton's Citadel Theatre and Regina's Globe Theatre also send out touring productions for children to elementary and high schools, often located several hundred miles away. In addition, they provide steady work opportunities for local actors, directors, designers and playwrights. The Manitoba Theatre Centre, for example, is one of the few regional theatres in Canada that has endeavored to maintain a resident acting company rather than rely on the availability of itinerant talent.

Although theatres in the different prairie cities evolved in response to varying community needs in the first instance, all have now attempted to maintain a regional perspective and address themselves to their local constituencies. Even when staging Shakespeare or Molière or the latest hits from faraway London or New York, theatres in the prairie provinces strive to put their own individual stamps on their productions—either by employing an identifiably Canadian style of presentation in terms of speech patterns and acting techniques, or by setting the work in some kind of localized context.

One example of this was a Theatre Calgary production of Aristophanes' *The Birds,* in which the stage setting was designed to represent downtown Calgary during a construction boom. It wasn't a particularly effective adaptation because it was marred by sophomoric humor and a tendency on the part of the actors to play the comedy as if they themselves found it funny. But it nevertheless did serve to show that even a weak attempt at updating and localizing a classic comedy can remain true to the spirit of the original work while saying something to a contemporary audience.

The Aristophanes adaptation, as it happened, was an unusually radical treatment of a classic by normal Calgary theatre standards. As a general rule, and this holds true for other prairie theatres as well, the classics are done with all due respect for the text because directors are reluctant to match their visions against those of the master playwrights.

Yet slavish imitation of American or English production styles is rarely attempted, except in those instances where a particular theatre—such as Edmonton's Citadel Theatre, which often functions as a Broadway tryout house—is planning to take a show to New York or London after the completion of its local run. The value of such imitation can be measured by the fact that these travelling shows—such as the Citadel productions of Brian Moore's *Catholics,* Cliff Jones' *Hey Marilyn* and Mordecai Richler's *Duddy*—rarely do well after they leave the home theatre.

In fact, even those Canadian plays which are not imitations of American or British models seem to do poorly when they are produced in New York. The American critic John Simon has suggested this stems from what he perceives as a cultural provincialism rampant in Canada which supposedly allows inferior works of art to flourish. However, the fact that several Canadian plays—such as John Murrell's *Memoir,* John Gray's *Billy Bishop Goes To War* and John Herbert's *Fortune And Men's Eyes*—have found favor with audiences in other countries would seem to indicate that the problem of gaining acceptance outside Canada only occurs when a Canadian play travels to New York.

John Murrell's play *Memoir,* a bittersweet drama about the final summer of Sarah Bernhardt, has been translated into more than a dozen languages and has been produced successfully in many European and South American countries. It has also been staged in the Soviet Union. But it hasn't played New York because Murrell is not willing to make the kinds of changes in the script that a Broadway producer seems to think would make it more popular with a Manhattan audience.

Another Murrell play, *Waiting For The Parade,* did make it to New York where it received mainly negative reviews in the daily newspapers. Yet the play has been staged successfully in London, where it was singled out by critic J.C. Trewin for

The cast of the 1980 Citadel Theatre production of Cliff Jones' *Hey Marilyn,* directed by Peter Coe, set and costume design by Lawrence Schafer. Photo: Bill McKeown.

inclusion in his *Best Plays* anthology. It has been produced by many of Canada's leading regional theatres and received critical acclaim for its television adaptation.

Murrell is an American-born writer and teacher, one of several playwrights who have settled in the prairie provinces in recent years and established fruitful associations with theatres in the region. He began his career during the early 1970s as playwright-in-residence at Calgary's Alberta Theatre Projects, a professional company (founded 1972) which places special emphasis on Canadian work, and he continues to make his home in Calgary while his plays—which also include *New World* and *Farther West*—are being produced around the world.

Other prominent Canadian playwrights who have established working relationships with theatres in the prairie provinces include the Governor General Award-winning writer Sharon Pollock, W.O. Mitchell, Rex Deverell and expatriate Joanna Glass, who lives in Connecticut and whose drama *Play Memory* was nominated for a Broadway Tony Award in 1984. These playwrights and others have established links with prairie theatres similar to the attachments developed in other times between Brecht and the Berliner Ensemble, and Chekhov and the Moscow

Art Theatre. Although none of them, except for Deverell in Regina, has written exclusively for one theatre, all have seen a goodly portion of their work produced in the first instance by theatres in the prairie communities where they established their playwriting careers.

Deverell, resident playwright with Regina's Globe Theatre since 1972, is a rare example of a prairie dramatist who has chosen to work with a particular theatre rather than make his services available to any group that commissions him to write a play. A former Baptist pastor, he began his career by writing children's plays for the Globe, which was established in 1966 as Canada's first fully professional children's theatre. Since 1977 he has written adult plays as well, many of them quasi-documentary works—*Medicare, Black Powder* (on mining)—which reflect a left-wing political attitude and deal with social issues of particular relevance to the province of Saskatchewan.

Other playwrights have maintained a strong connection with the prairies in their work, although in some instances their careers have taken them to places far beyond this region of Canada. Saskatchewan-born Joanna Glass, for example, has lived in the United States for more than 20 years and virtually all the plays she has written during that period have premièred there before production in Canada. Yet the influence of the prairies remains strong in her writing. Several of her dramas (*Canadian Gothic, Artichoke, Play Memory*) are set on the prairies and most have found a receptive audience in this part of Canada even when they have failed to generate enthusiasm among playgoers in the United States.

Glass is one of a number of prairie-born dramatists who started writing at a time when it was almost impossible for a Canadian playwright to get work produced professionally in this country. Although by the late 1960s professional theatre was in full swing across the country, it wasn't until the mid-1970s that the major regional theatres began to stage Canadian plays on a regular basis. During its first nine seasons, for example, the Manitoba Theatre Centre presented only four original Canadian works on its main stage, and a similar pattern can be traced at other prairie theatres where, even today, the classics, Broadway and West End hits tend to be the programming staples.

Before Canadian theatres were ready to support native playwrights on a regular basis, prairie writers were forced to seek other outlets for their work. W.O. Mitchell, who was born in Saskatchewan and trained as a schoolteacher, says that when he started writing during the 1940s "there was no theatre except for CBC Radio." As a result, Mitchell began his career as a radio dramatist and short story writer and it wasn't until the mid-1970s—when he was already in his early 60s—that he was given an opportunity to adapt his work for the stage. By 1984, several of Mitchell's radio and television plays had been turned into successful stage plays, and many of these—*Back to Beulah, The Kite, For Those In Peril On The Sea*—had been produced in the first instance by Theatre Calgary, with whom Mitchell has enjoyed an active and productive association. One Mitchell play in particular, *The Black Bonspiel of Wullie MacCrimmon,* has been produced twice on Theatre Calgary's main stage and is one of the most successful shows ever staged by the theatre. It's a slight, folksy play about a Faustian pact between a Scottish-born curling enthusiast and the Devil, but it plays better in Calgary than any hit comedy from Broadway or the West End.

Even though they now have more Canadian theatres to write for, the most successful prairie playwrights find they still cannot make a living out of creating drama. W.O. Mitchell augments the income he makes from playwriting by turning out novels and screenplays, and by teaching creative writing at the Banff School of Fine Arts and at the University of Windsor in Ontario. Ken Mitchell (no relation to W.O.) lectures at the University of Regina and writes plays that are usually produced initially by theatres in his home province of Saskatchewan. Sharon Pollock has held a full-time job as dramaturge for Theatre Calgary while writing commissioned scripts for the stage and CBC Radio.

Pollock, to a great extent, epitomizes the western spirit of pioneering determination that one finds in theatre as in other aspects of prairie life. She began in theatre as an actress and started writing plays because she felt there were stories to be told about Canada's history and nobody was dramatizing them. At a later point, after she had achieved national success with such plays as *Blood Relations, One Tiger To A Hill* and *The Komagata Maru Incident,* Pollock joined Theatre Calgary as a dramaturge and immediately initiated a series of playwriting workshops to provide an opportunity for other, emerging writers to develop an association with the major professional theatre in southern Alberta. Her subsequent appointment as artistic director of Theatre Calgary marked the first time that a Canadian

The cast of the 1977 25th Street Theatre collective creation *Paper Wheat.* Photo: Basil Zarov.

playwright was hired to lead a major regional theatre. Even though the appointment was short-lived (she quit after three months in a dispute over management policy), it showed how one theatre artist can move toward achieving complete creative control over her work.

Other examples of pioneer determination can be found in those "do-it-yourself" alternate theatres that started sprouting on the prairies from 1970 onward. 25th Street Theatre in Saskatoon, for example, was started in 1972 (two years before the establishment of Persephone, now the city's resident professional theatre) by a group of Saskatchewan university graduates who wanted to publish a literary magazine and run a dance troupe as well as present new Canadian plays. The magazine folded after two issues and the dance troupe lasted only a year, but the theatre company has survived hard times to become one of the most important "grass roots" operations of its kind on the prairies. One 25th Street collective creation, *Paper Wheat,* has toured nationally, was filmed for televison, and has been acclaimed as the most successful stage play in Saskatchewan's history. A folksy musical play about homesteading and wheat farming, it will never be regarded as a classic. But it satisfies regional theatre's basic mandate to be successful in the community where it resides.

Other prairie theatres founded by young professionals to provide outlets for their creative energies and supply an alternative to the highly-subsidized establishment companies include Workshop West, Theatre Network and Catalyst Theatre in Edmonton; Prairie Theatre Exchange in Winnipeg, and Lunchbox Theatre, One Yellow Rabbit, Loose Moose and Sun-Ergos in Calgary.

Many of these non-establishment prairie companies have a home base but no permanent theatre (Calgary's Lunchbox and Loose Moose theatres are notable exceptions) and, as a result, they tour extensively. They also endeavor to reflect the character of life on the prairies in their work. While one cannot lump them all into a single category because of the wide range of performing styles and program material they employ, it can be said that in general they offer a perception of the world which has to do with their being rooted in a region where people tend to take a wide-open view of things. What playwright Ken Mitchell calls the "shrunken box" kind of theatre found in London and New York (i.e. the kind of theatre that traffics in the social mannerisms and customs of big-city dwellers) has less relevance in the work of these alternate prairie theatres than it does in the programs of the mainstream companies.

The major regional theatres in the five prairie cities, with the exception of Regina's Globe—which concentrates almost exclusively on Canadian and other plays with social or political themes—tend to offer a choice of repertory that is somewhat timorous and relentlessly middle-of-the-road. A typical six-play season at any one of these theatres will likely include a period classic (Shakespeare, Molière or Goldoni), a contemporary American or English classic (Arthur Miller, Tennessee Williams, George Bernard Shaw), a modern commercial comedy (Neil Simon, Alan Ayckbourn), a small-cast musical comedy or revue, one or two recent hits from Broadway or the West End, and occasionally a new Canadian work. In terms of programming, therefore, these prairie theatres are essentially no different from theatres operating in other parts of Canada.

Nor can one say that an identifiable production style exists which separates the work done on the prairies from shows presented elsewhere. For every experiment with documentary or collective or improvisational styles of theatre, one can find a theatre in Toronto or Montreal that has attempted something similar in the past. At the start of the 1984-85 season, the major theatres in Calgary, Edmonton and Winnipeg were being led by new artistic directors. Yet one could predict that the style and quality of the work would be much the same as in the past.

By the same token, there is a difference between theatre produced here and theatre done in other parts of Canada. It's the new Canadian work that makes the difference and defines the spirit and character of theatre in the prairie provinces. Plays such as Sharon Pollock's *Generations,* which deals with the relationship between a 77-year-old prairie farmer and the land he has tilled for generations; Paddy Campbell's *Hoarse Muse,* which illuminates the travails of a hard-drinking Calgary newspaper editor; or Rex Deverell's *Black Powder,* a stereotypical agitprop piece about a Depression-era coal miners' strike in Estevan, Saskatchewan—in many instances these works, created specifically for prairie audiences, will have little to say to playgoers who live elsewhere. But as long as they speak to their home constituency, it really doesn't matter how limited their appeal might be in other places.

Something about the structure of Canadian theatre does demand that there be a major centre, a grand county fair where everything can be compared and playwrights can determine if their work is good by national standards. But the reverse side of the coin is that audiences in Calgary, Edmonton, Winnipeg, Regina and Saskatoon are relatively unconcerned about national standards; all they ask is that their theatres do a good job for them. The growing popularity of such locally-written plays as Sharon Pollock's *Whiskey Six*—a drama about small-town rum-running which was the top-selling show of Theatre Calgary's 1982-83 season—or John Murrell's *Farther West,* an epic work of operatic proportions about a Calgary prostitute's mythical quest for self-determination—bears testament to the fact that these prairie theatres are still in touch with their communities and responsive to their concerns.

Brian Brennan

British Columbia

Half the population of almost three million in British Columbia lives in the Vancouver area, in the south-west corner. The nearest Canadian cities are 600 miles away, in Alberta. The second city of the province, Victoria, is far smaller; other towns are both small and scattered. Theatre is self-contained and sometimes self-satisfied.

In the 40s and 50s, amateurs provided quantity and continuity. Vancouver had two professional companies for a while with Everyman and Totem, both killed by the arrival of television. Everyman are remembered for their *Tobacco Road* in 1953, when the cast was arrested onstage and prosecuted for obscenity.

The Vancouver Playhouse, supported by the Canada Council as the area's "regional theatre," began in a new 647-seat theatre in 1963. The first ten years saw several artistic directors and many disputes about money and the choice of plays. The middle-class season ticket holders were disturbed by a homosexual kiss in the one-act *Filthy Piranesi* and by the hippie audience drawn to George Ryga's musical, *Grass and Wild Strawberries*. Ryga's next script, *Captives of the Faceless Drummer*, referred to the 1970 October F.L.Q. Crisis and the Board rejected it, overruling the director.

The period also saw struggles to establish seasons of more adventurous scripts in smaller spaces. When Christopher Newton served as director from 1973 to 1979, the Playhouse finally achieved consistently high standards and found an identity. Walter Learning, director since 1982, has increased the number of productions yet still rarely draws big audiences. Like other regional theatres, the Playhouse tries to balance classics (*School for Scandal*), American and British successes (*K-2, Amadeus*), accessible Canadian work (Anne Chislett's *Tomorrow Box*) and sheer entertainment (*Godspell, A Funny Thing Happened on the Way to the Forum*). Learning's view of his choice of plays is that they all "have a common theme, the celebration, renewal and affirmation of life. How each of them does that, is for you to decide."

Though the big subsidies go to the Playhouse, the Arts Club Theatre is at least as important in Vancouver. Founded in 1964 in a 140-seat mission hall, rapid growth (more varied plays and year-round performances) began eight years later when Bill Millerd became artistic director. His explanation of his success is that "our audience can sense the love we have for what we do." In 1979 Millerd opened a 450-seat theatre on Granville Island and later a revue theatre beside it, so that he now operates three spaces. The Arts Club has more comedies and musicals than the Playhouse, yet in recent years has staged *Bent* and *The Elephant Man,* new plays by John Lazarus (*The Late Blumer*) and Ken Mitchell (*The Great Cultural Revolution*), much of Michel Tremblay's work, Allan Stratton's *Rexy,* Sharon Pollock's *Blood Relations* and other Canadian dramas.

These two companies were joined by many more in the 70s, beginning with the formation of the New Play Centre, still a unique B.C. institution. The Centre

The 1974 Tamahnous Theatre production of *The Bacchae* at the Vancouver East Cultural Centre, directed by John Gray. Photo: Brian Clayden.

initially advised on scripts and held Sunday night play readings. When Pam Hawthorn took over in 1972, the Centre added workshops for some scripts and began staging plays. The du Maurier Festival of new plays, usually one-acters, takes place each spring. The Centre became co-tenant of the Waterfront from its opening in 1979. Nearly all the province's playwrights have had their plays workshopped at the Centre, though some have found this useful only for the inexperienced.

Some University of British Columbia drama graduates who wanted to try out new forms of theatre formed a group in 1971 which soon became known as Tamahnous, the Chilcotin Indian word for "magic." Early creations, full of movement and ensemble spirit, were *Dracula, The Bacchae* and *Medea.* The dedicated members at first struggled along on $5 a week: gradually funding was found and Tamahnous settled down to four shows a year, becoming the resident company at the Vancouver East Cultural Centre in 1977. Recent directions for Tamahnous were Brecht and Beckett, *Garage Sale,* a new Canadian comedy by David King, and collectively devised approaches to the subjects of fools and to dreams.

The Great Leap Forward was in 1972-74. The Liberal government in these years countered unemployment with LIP and OFY (Local Initiatives Programme and Opportunities for Youth). Imaginatively, these schemes recognized that actors were among the unemployed and numerous companies formed to claim short-term funds. LIP/OFY groups emphasized the actor more than the works put on or the building used; they showed what was possible with very little money; they mostly looked first for Canadian texts. Only one survives, Ray Michal's City Stage, which performed at lunch-time in an old doughnut store, 5 metres wide and seating 75—attracting a new audience because it was opposite the Stock Exchange. Michal is pleased that "we have introduced a lot of authors and a lot of talent for the first time." His selection included Mrozek's *Enchanted Night,* Pinter's *The Lover,* Orton's *The Good and Faithful Servant,* David Cregan's *Transcending* and Anouilh's *Cecile,* all, both worthwhile and entertaining. In 1976 City Stage built a new 150-seat theatre. Michal sees this as "here for the people who are within fifteen or twenty blocks of the place." Shows now are mainly evenings and City Stage is best-known for the competitive Theatresports on Friday and Saturday nights, so popular that line-ups start long before opening.

Touchstone, another group formed in 1976 from the U.B.C. Drama Department, alternated between Sam Shepard and shows they created on social issues such as rape (*Broken Dolls*) and nuclear energy (*Hot Rods and Heavy Water*). They now share the Firehall and have recently performed Canadian scripts from out of the province, Lawrence Jeffery's *Clay* and Judith Thompson's *Crackwalker.* In 1985 Touchstone expanded its scope with a big box-office comedy, *Sex Tips for Modern Girls.* The Headlines collective, formed in 1981, has presented two pointed revues, examining the housing shortage and disarmament. Crossroads, with plays about multiculturalism, has also found a niche in social comment.

When the Playhouse ceased to tour childrens' plays, two new groups stepped in. Elizabeth Ball set up Carousel in 1975. The program here ranged from Thurber's *Thirteen Clocks* to *The Diary Of Anne Frank* and American treatments of divorce and child abuse. Green Thumb followed the interests of its founder, Dennis Foon: Indian myth (*The Windigo*), Greek myth (*Heracles*), local history (*Raft Baby*), and social issues (immigrants in *New Canadian Kid* and the nuclear war threat in *One Thousand Cranes*). Childrens' theatre had its great leap forward in 1978 with the first annual Vancouver Childrens' Festival, bringing shows from across the country and round the world, together with dancers and singers.

Another Summer Festival started in 1976, at White Rock, on the coast a few miles south of Vancouver, with several plays in repertory. The Shakespeare Festival, three plays in a tent in Vanier Park, began in 1983. Some talked hopefully of it growing to be a western Stratford or northerly Ashland. The Festival planned a longer season in 1984 in a larger tent. Unfortunately audiences averaged 100 and the Festival ended six weeks early, with the third offering one week into rehearsal. The organizers blamed a bus strike and *The King and I,* playing in the city with tickets at $20-$30 soaking up playgoers' money. In fact, starting with six weeks of *Comedy of Errors* was a risk, despite Henry Woolf's frenzied direction and the use of a jazz band. The Festival will nevertheless be back in production in 1985. The liveliest new idea in the city may be the weekly semi-improvised soap operas, drawing on audience suggestions and full of local jokes, at the Waterfront at midnight.

Tamahnous, Touchstone and the childrens' companies created a demand for more space, though John Juliani's Savage God once showed the unimportance of bricks-and-mortar by doing *Happy Days* in a hollow tree in Stanley Park. Vancouver East Cultural Centre, a former church, met the demand first, in 1973. Presentation House in North Vancouver opened four years later, and then an inconvenient multi-use space under the courthouse complex in Robson Square. Groups used a room in the Carnegie Centre, converted from the old library, and the little Kits House in Kitsilano. More significant, when the industrial Granville Island was re-developed, three theatres were included, two for the Arts Club, and the 250-seat Waterfront. When Vancouver's first firehall became empty, it found new life as a comfortable theatre.

Theatre in Victoria, the capital, was amateur till the 60s (the Victoria Theatre Guild, with its own theatre at Langham Court, was the key group). When the national trend to professionalism arrived, Peter Mannering's enterprising Studio Theatre became the Bastion, moving into the old 837-seat Pantages, restored as the Macpherson Playhouse. Bastion programs were influenced by the big building and by the city's conservative tastes, but by the mid-70s included Jim McQueen as Richard III and Ron Chudley's ambitious account of Wolfe and Montcalm, *After Abraham.* In 1976 Don Shipley and Pat Armstrong established the more adventurous 275-seat Belfry. The University Drama Department has also offered several productions annually for the last 20 years. Carl Hare's Company One, a creative childrens' company, arose from the Department; more recently Kaleidoscope has done fine work for young people integrating music, song, movement and simple props.

Amateurs thrive outside the two cities, with some 200-300 groups and some 350 schools active. The geographical range can be shown by naming a few groups prominent since the war: Vernon Little Theatre, Prince George Players, Lake Cowichan Drama Club, the North Kamloops P.T.A. Wing, the Mutual Improvement Association of Dawson Creek. City groups—Tamahnous, Headlines, the childrens' companies—tour, while the Playhouse took *Loot* round the province. The Arts in 1984 played Sherman Snukal's *Talking Dirty* in Kamloops, Kelowna, Penticton, Prince George, Kitimat, Williams Lake and Nanaimo.

Elsewhere in the province, shows loosely resembling Victorian entertainment are staged every summer in the restored Gold Rush theatre at Barkerville. Theatre Energy, of Winlaw, in the Kootenays, enterprisingly created and toured shows on local history and the risks of nuclear power. Williams Lake in 1971 recognized the major dramatist living nearby, opening the Gwen Ringwood Playhouse with her *The Deep Has Many Voices*. The Caravan Stage Company travels each summer in the interior, its speed fixed by the Clydesdale horses who pull the wagons; the National Film Board's *Horsedrawn Magic* catches some of this unique group's appeal. Tom Kerr in 1974 launched the Western Canada Theatre Company in Kamloops, acquiring a new theatre after four years. Eric Nicol's *Free at Last* and *Ma* (about the Lilloet newspaper editor, Ma Murray) both premièred in Kamloops, or, more accurately, were tried out there. At the end of the 70s Michael Dobbin had the company firmly established and well supported.

Ambitious plans for festivals and theatres are announced periodically, the grandest being Barry Morse's for an Elizabethan theatre on the edge of Victoria. Leon Pownall set up a successful festival in summer 1984 in Nanaimo, on Vancouver Island. His Shakespeare Plus staged *Romeo and Juliet, Cabaret* and a new play about Malcolm Lowry by the B.C. writer Michael Mercer, *Goodnight Disgrace*. With a budget of over half a million dollars, Shakespeare Plus played to 86% capacity in Malaspina College's theatre. Though the deficit was bigger than estimated, this festival will be back in 1985.

What have been the achievements of Canadian playwrights? The first post-war Canadian play of note is Elsie Park Gowan's *The Last Caveman*, toured by Everyman in 1947. Lister Sinclair's *The World of the Wonderful Dark*, drawing on Indian myth, earned attention and bewilderment at the first International Festival in 1958. Many playwrights wrote original scripts for their own amateur groups; the Education Department's annual report reveals that in 1953 the Fort St. John Festival had six originals, four of them on local Peace River themes.

A handful of Canadian texts came in the 60s; only in the 70s are they common. The Playhouse in the 60s staged new plays by Nicol (*Like Father, Like Fun* of 1966 was followed by *The Fourth Monkey* and *Pillar of Sand*) and Ryga (his celebrated lament about Indians, *The Ecstasy of Rita Joe*). When, in 1971, dramatists proposed that one-third, or even half, of the plays in subsidized theatres should be by Canadians, this looked unattainable. A few years later at least a third of the plays in Vancouver were Canadian. The Arts showed successes from other provinces (David Freeman's first three plays, Fennario's *On the Job,* Walker's *Gossip*); at the Playhouse plays by W.O. Mitchell and Hrant Alianak were seen on the second stage and three by David French on the mainstage.

Local authors, meanwhile, were encouraged to write by the New Play Centre. They could rarely look to the two main local theatres for performances and most were produced by the Centre, City Stage and Tamahnous. Talon, in Vancouver, published many of these playwrights.

Though the Centre has sometimes preferred realism to experiment, the British Columbian play is difficult to characterize. In 1975 the Centre published five *West Coast Plays;* one drama was set in London, another in Paris, a third in northern Ontario, a fourth in Absurd-Land and the last unlocalized, though perhaps in Canada. Two of the five authors were born in Britain and two in the United States! The quintessential Vancouver play may, in fact, be set in New York (Sheldon Rosen's

Ned and Jack), Paris (Tom Cone's *Beautiful Tigers*) or the American South (Charles Tidler's *Blind Dancers*). No wonder *Talking Dirty* and Richard Ouzounian's *British Properties* were successful—at last we heard jokes about Burnaby.

The situation for playwrights remains discouraging. Writers have come and gone, some of them abandoning writing: Herschel Hardin's *Great Wave of Civilization* is still unstaged in his hometown; Beverley Simons' *Leela Means to Play* unperformed anywhere. Of the province's many writers, hardly one can be confident of having the next script staged, yet the next play by Leonard Angel, Ted Galay, Margaret Hollingsworth and John Lazarus could be an event.

Audiences have grown, unpredictably, in the last fifteen years. Vancouver has three audiences. The conservative old and the professional young keep the Arts

R obert Clothier and Laura Press in the 1978 Vancouver Playhouse production of Seneca's *Oedipus,* directed by Yurek Bogajewicz. Photo: David Cooper.

profitable: they prefer undemanding comedies and musicals. In the Prairies such people go to dinner theatre, which has invariably failed in Vancouver. The Playhouse and U.B.C. have a slightly more sophisticated public who sense that Theatre is Good for You, hence can be allowed to make some demands. The third, more discriminating, audience is readier to go at least halfway toward the performers onstage, while the other spectators sit back and insist that the actors compel their attention. This is the Vancouver East/Tamahnous audience, some of whom have also discovered Touchstone and the New Play Centre. (Metro Theatre, remote in the south-west, where amateurs perform comedies, and in part City College have *local* audiences which treat their theatres as people treated their local movie-house in the pre-television age.)

Most of the population falls into none of these groups (Kayla Armstrong at Capilano College found students enrolled in her acting class who had never seen a play). A few companies have tried to go to where the people are, acting on beaches in the heyday of LIP/OFY idealism. Lately only Headlines have concentrated on reaching new audiences, playing to half the population of Hazelton. Foon and Green Thumb argue that the new audience is schoolchildren, captive now but potentially a bigger, better audience.

Theatre is too often discussed in isolation. The growth of theatre is paralleled in Vancouver by the growth, and the struggles, of the Symphony, the Opera and the Art Gallery. The New Democrats, in office in the early 70s and in opposition in the mid-80s, often stressed cultural policy, especially equal access to the arts. Currently the economic benefits of the arts are being argued, for they are "labour intensive," drawing tourists and encouraging spending on restaurants, clothes, parking and babysitters.

I have noted the role of new buildings. The old theatres were not valued: the Opera House of 1891 was demolished in 1969 and the York Theatre, built in 1912, is empty and in danger. The Orpheum, a huge ornate hall of 1927, was restored and is now the Symphony's home. School drama was already well established before the Second World War and has expanded. U.B.C.'s Summer School has developed into a large Department and the Playhouse Theatre School, started in 1975, provides an intensive two-year training for twelve students.

The most memorable production I have seen in twenty years in Vancouver was at the Playhouse, Robert David MacDonald's *Camille,* directed by Christopher Newton, with one of Cameron Porteous's many fine sets (the production was repeated at the Shaw Festival). The best version of a Canadian script was Brian Richmond's of Tremblay's *Impromptu of Outremont* at the Arts; the best of a new Canadian play Larry Lillo's of Sharon Pollock's *Komagata Maru Incident,* presented by the Playhouse at Vancouver East. My favourite actress was Blair Brown as Nora in *A Doll's House,* again at the Playhouse. From distinguished male performances by such visiting stars as William Hutt and Heath Lamberts, and by such local actors as Allan Gray and Peter Haworth, I select Newton as Henry Carr in *Travesties* and Alan Scarfe and Neil Dainard in Stoppard's *Rosencrantz and Guildenstern.* Stephen Katz and Mary Kerr created colourful and imaginative costumes for *Mandragola* at the Playhouse. The greatest moment in experimental work was in Tamahnous's second show, *The Bacchae.* At the start the audience were persuaded to join in a celebratory dance, then suddenly Pentheus (David Petersen) appeared on a high balcony, commanded the musicians to stop, ordered us all back to our seats, denounced our worship of Dionysus. Shame-faced, uncomfortable, we quietly, guiltily returned to our seats.

As I write, Bill Millerd's Arts flourishes. He succeeds at almost everything, giving his loyal audience what it wants, then gently taking it a little further. The Playhouse still fails to have the central role in the city that might be expected. For all Learning's energy, there's uncertainty about how to attract audiences, uncertainty about seeking stars, uncertainty about the commitment to Canadian work. Ray Michal at City Stage has had two hits in 1983-84, *Piaf* and *Sister Mary Ignatius Explains it all to you.* With less resources he still finds rewarding plays and talented younger actors. Green Thumb's work always promises originality and excitement.

Alternatives are fewer and less audacious. Tamahnous, after fourteen years as a collective, now look to an artistic director, Morris Panych, to guide them. Though the New Play Centre struggles with limited resources, the annual new play festival is always worthwhile. One alternative on view this summer is Dermot Hennelly's Open Theatre, with two Shakespeares. Touchstone, Headlines and Crossroads appear infrequently, always seeking support. Alertness is needed to catch the under-publicized semi- or would-be professionals of Kico Gonzales-Risso's Kitsilano Company and Joanna Maratta's Theatre Space. In times of restraint and conservatism, one cannot expect much risk and experiment.

For the future I would like to see more Canadian plays, and especially for it to be easier to present such epics as Pollock's *Walsh.* The example of Headlines points to touring, social comment, and reaching new audiences. I particularly wish it were easier for enthusiastic actors to come together to attempt whatever they most want to do. Though quantity and quality are far higher than fifteen years ago, we risk having a static, middle-aged theatre.

Malcolm Page

PART THREE

The Electronic Media

A National Radio
Drama in English

It is a striking feature of Canadian theatre that its major formative influences were in eccentric genres. Because of the early monopoly on our stages of two mature theatre traditions, the British and the American—personified by their touring companies—the most important initial development of an indigenous Canadian drama and theatre took place not so much on the stage but in three new technological communications media: the cinema, radio and television. The National Film Board made a notable contribution to Canadian drama and documentary from the 1930s on. And Canadian anthology television drama of the late 50s and 60s was the most active theatre of its time in the country. It employed many of our theatre professionals, and attracted to its individual productions audiences far larger than any traditional theatre could hold at one time.

Perhaps the most crucial contribution, however, was that of CBC radio drama, which paralleled the growth of Canadian cinema in the 30s, and in its heyday spoke to much larger audiences (as large as those later for television). The Radio Drama Department embarked on several ambitious national and regional series in the late 30s and early 40s. These activities gave it the deserved reputation of our first "national Canadian theatre" and launched the "golden age" of Canadian radio drama which lasted almost two decades. By the end of the 40s, and before the coming of television to Canada, the Drama Department was firmly entrenched as the major locus and the primary force in Canadian theatre. It gave our theatre professionals the competent training and experience which provided the solid base for the growth of professional drama in the 50s, both on television and on the legitimate stage. The CBC TV Drama Department and the Stratford Festival were both beneficiaries of the best talents of CBC radio drama. Of the three media which contributed most to the birth of professional Canadian theatre, radio's influence was strongest at the most crucial period: during the decade or so just *before* the first growth of our professional stage companies and the birth of television.

The Nature of Canadian Radio Drama

It will be objected that radio drama has only a tangential relation to the mainstream of theatre, because its aural medium puts strict limits on what may be tried in subject and expression. This is a misconception to be corrected at the outset. It is, of course, true that the radio play can only communicate through sound. It has no recourse to the visual language of drama, which communicates through the physical surroundings of the theatre, the stage and its landscapes, the actual presence of the actors, their dress, gestures, expressions, movements and so on. For the not inconsiderable loss of these heterogeneous visual effects, the radio play, on the other hand, substitutes a refining of communication down to a sequence of sounds, which forcibly concentrates the auditors' attention in a way impossible on the stage (or in the other visual media). Moreover, this concentration through sound is a tap, through which can pour much of the information and effects of which traditional drama is capable. Radio drama has developed its own *language.* Once that language is understood, the writer may deal with any subject, and can invoke the full range of dramatic expression. In turn, the listener's imagination is stimulated to supply an internal vision of reality far more realistic than any traditional stage illusion could achieve.

The typical Canadian radio drama's manipulation of sounds involved a whole battery of effects, especially those of the voice, with its infinite variations of pitch, timbre, accent and emotional expression. Since these distinctions of voice are so crucial, the acting style for these plays was typically understated and intimate; the actors spoke directly and personally to each auditor. Sound effects are a second crucial element in the language of radio drama. The art of reproduction of the natural sounds which normally help us to identify scenes, people and objects was developed and perfected as part of the Canadian golden age radio-drama symphony. The language of sound effects added a unique psychological authenticity to the re-creation of reality in the radio play.

Music is a third primary element of communication in this medium. During the golden age of Canadian radio drama, flexible and imaginative composers like Lucio Agostini and Morris Surdin were routinely commissioned to compose musical accompaniments to the scripts, which they conducted live, as part of the symphony constituting a radio drama production. These composers used music not only to bridge scenes, but also to paint in an infinite variety of possible emotional and other qualities in scenes, characters and speeches. Indeed, the range in the best scores could move from sentiment through irony to tragedy. The differentiation among characters established by variations in their voices was reinforced by the related musical technique (familiar also in opera) of identifying each character by a particular melodic theme, and then helping to advance the drama by appropriate variations on each theme. These techniques are familiar from the sound tracks of cinema, but it is important to underline the real difference in radio drama: without the visuals, the effects of the music are far more concentrated.

These techniques in radio drama go far to replace the visual effects of the stage play. The point must be emphasized, however, that radio plays have an *advantage* over stage plays. The limitation of the radio drama to sound, in fact, frees it from the artificial limitations in time and space typical of the stage play, as well as the latter's striving for artificial illusions of physical reality in scene, figure and dress. This helps to explain the expressionism typical of many Canadian radio dramas.

In its best examples, it is an interior drama, unfolding in the minds of its characters, proceeding by the recording of fine emotional changes. Alternatively, in its intellectual form, the Canadian radio play is a battle of minds, full of verbal irony, communicating serious didactic purpose in the play of wit. These two types of drama were developed on our CBC networks during the 1930s and 40s, when Canadian radio drama was on the leading edge of development and achievement in North America, as witnessed by the frequency with which it won the annual Ohio University Radio Drama Awards.

The 1930s: Foundations

Canadian radio drama had its first foundations in Jack Gillmore's *CNRV Players* series over CNR Radio from Vancouver. Between 1927 and 1932 Gillmore produced and directed over a hundred plays. These were heard not only in the Vancouver region but eventually over an informal network which included British Columbia and the prairies. These radio dramas included adaptations of popular British and American plays, some locally-written plays, and several Shakespeare productions. With few precursors, Gillmore developed the new techniques of dramatic communication over this purely aural medium.

The second of the fathers of Canadian radio drama was the same Tyrone Guthrie who also gave us our Stratford Festival. Guthrie was commissioned to produce the *Romance of Canada* series over CN Radio in Montreal during the 1931 season. This series, written by Merrill Denison, was the first ambitious attempt at an original Canadian series of historical dramas. It was very popular across the country, and it had a strong and continuing influence on the dramas which followed in this medium. Rupert Caplan, a young professional Montreal actor who worked under Guthrie that first season, took over the production-direction of the second series the following year. Caplan provided the professional continuity among the CN, CRBC and CBC Drama Departments, working in Montreal as producer (-director) in the medium until his retirement as senior Montreal producer in 1969.

Meanwhile, in the 30s there was active radio drama production in several other regional centres: in Vancouver, of course, where others carried on Gillmore's tradition; but also in Toronto, Winnipeg and Edmonton. In Toronto, the CRBC was originating many interesting play series, some written by their script editor, Horace Brown. A private Toronto station, CFRB, also produced radio plays, often the work of the young Andrew Allan, who would later become the CBC's National Drama Supervisor. In Winnipeg, another director who was later to gain national fame, Esse W. Ljungh, was producing plays for both the stage and radio. In Edmonton, the University of Alberta's radio station CKUA was broadcasting radio dramas, including a large number of original Canadian plays, all through the 30s. Sheila Marryat was their producer, and they gained a wide audience over an informal western regional network, eventually being carried on the CBC regional and national networks.

The Golden Age of Canadian Radio Drama

By 1939 the CBC's development of strong regional radio drama production centres was almost complete, with Andrew Allan as drama supervisor in Vancouver, Caplan in Montreal and Esse Ljungh in Winnipeg. Major regional drama series were established in those cities, as well as in Toronto (Rupert Lucas), Halifax and Winnipeg. But the founding of our first Canadian national theatre did not occur until the early 1940s, when the CBC's original regional impetus gave way to a strong centralizing thrust. At the end of 1943 Andrew Allan, who had made his reputation in Vancouver as a daring and innovative producer, was posted to Toronto as National Supervisor of CBC Radio Drama. Frank Willis, the broadcasting hero of the Springhill Mine disaster and a distinguished Halifax broadcaster, had already been brought to Toronto as Head of Features and to join the senior drama production team being assembled there. Esse Ljungh was brought from Winnipeg to join the team in 1946, and Rupert Caplan was also urged to do so. Caplan, however, chose to retain his autonomy in Montreal, though he did make a major contribution, along with his Toronto colleagues, to the creation of our first national theatre.

Together, these four senior CBC producers, along with several hundreds of regional drama producers across the country, and some 1,300 playwrights, created almost eight thousand drama broadcasts in the two decades from 1939 to the end of the golden age of Canadian radio. Some 3,500 of these were original Canadian plays. Much of this vast national drama treasure has been forgotten or ignored in the intervening years, mainly because less than two hundred have ever been

Chris Wiggins, Tony Van Bridge, Frances Hyland and Andrew Allan examining a script for production on CBC *Tuesday Night,* September 19, 1972.

published. (The Radio Drama Project at Concordia University has set up a working Archives to collect, index and study these materials.[1] The first comprehensive descriptive bibliography of Canadian radio drama has been published, which serves as the instrument of access to the Archives.[2] And the first history of Canadian and American radio theatre has also been published.[3])

It was, of course, Andrew Allan who led the team. His first act was to create the national weekly series called *Stage,* subtitled "A Report on the State of Canadian Theatre."[4] *Stage,* which began as a half-hour series in January, 1944, and expanded to a full hour in 1947-48, was a showcase for original Canadian plays (from fifteen to thirty per season). It gave training, experience and continuing employment to a large number of Toronto theatre professionals. When Allan retired as National Supervisor in 1955, Esse Ljungh took over, and continued *Stage* until his own retirement in 1969. *Stage* has existed in some form to the present. *Wednesday Night* (later *Tuesday Night*), an evening-long weekly CBC cultural program begun in 1947, included an open-ended full-length play. All four of the senior CBC producers contributed to it, and its plays included the whole range of classical and modern drama, though fewer original Canadian plays than *Stage. Wednesday Night* continued until 1976. In addition to these two major national anthology drama series, the several senior regional anthology series continued to feature dramatic talents from across the country.

Towards the end of the golden age, two influential new producers began their work, Gerald Newman in Vancouver and John Reeves in Toronto. Newman carried on the golden age tradition of radio drama during the 1960s and 70s. His interests were mainly in contemporary world theatre, and his technique was purified of "extraneous" sounds like music, emphasizing the effects of words, rhythm and silence. John Reeves reflected the new European (especially German) experiments in radio drama, more lyrical, more in the nature of musical compositions, and freer in time and space. Reeves' producing history continues to this day.

Andrew Allan's first star-playwright was the young Fletcher Markle, whose renowned scripts for Allan's 1942 Vancouver series, *Baker's Dozen,* excited Canadians by their demonstration of the potential of drama in sound: its intimacy, its flexibility, its surrealism and its textures of reality. Markle also wrote the opening play for *Stage, 29:40.* He had some forty original plays and ten dramatizations to his credit during the golden age. Many of these are on popular themes, and all have Markle's flexible touch.

The writer whose serious social commentaries inspired Allan to create the *Stage* series was Len Peterson, whose experimental dramas captured many Ohio awards for the CBC. After Allan's retirement, Peterson's prolific radio drama career continued with the producer Esse Ljungh, and indeed Peterson continues crafting radio plays to this day. Peterson wrote almost two hundred original plays and twenty adaptations for CBC production during the golden age. His plays range from documentary through comedy and witty satire to dark tragedy. Among his best works are *Man with a Bucket of Ashes,* a mythic tragedy in a realistic rural setting; *Within the Fortress,* an imaginative and objective play about war seen from the enemy's viewpoint; and *Paper in the Wind,* a post-war social critique. In these plays Peterson combines the flexible resources of radio drama with modern expressionism and a serious didactic purpose which often has a wide social reference. Peterson's best-known play, the experimental 1946 *Burlap Bags,* which

E sse W. Ljungh directing on
CBC radio in the mid-1960s.

has been compared to Beckett's *Waiting for Godot,* anticipates that play by several years.

The "intellectual" among Allan's senior playwrights, who also came with Allan from Vancouver to Toronto, was Lister Sinclair. This playwright wrote about a hundred original plays, and some fifty adaptations and dramatizations including those from Shakespeare, and Greek, Renaissance and modern classics. Sinclair's original plays are (like Peterson's) varied in genre, including comedy, satire, documentary-drama, and serious drama. Sinclair, however, leans towards more traditional realistic and satiric modes, and towards verse drama; his themes are often more universal than social commentaries. His best-known works include *Socrates,* an ambitious verse-drama about the trial and death of the Greek philosopher with modern implications; *Hilda Morgan,* a realistic play with a feminist theme; *The Blood is Strong,* a play about Scottish immigrants; *All About Emily,* a comedy; *We All Hate Toronto,* a typical Sinclair satire; and *Return to Colonus,* a mythic play about the confrontation between nature and civilization. In all his works, Sinclair blends intellectual commentary with a sharp, ironic dramatic sense.

Gerald Noxon wrote one of the most best-remembered scripts on *Stage: Mr. Arcularis.* Though it was an adaptation from a short story by Conrad Aiken, Noxon not only created a gripping dramatic framework, but tapped what must be a set of primarily Canadian archetypes—a mythic trip through the absolute zero of space. *Mr. Arcularis* stands as a central document of our culture. Noxon wrote about forty original plays and five dramatizations (the majority from Aiken's fiction), including comedies and satires, histories, documentaries and serious dramas.

Another playwright who continues his craft to the present is W.O. Mitchell. Author of the famous *Jake and the Kid* serial—that hilarious but accurate and pertinent picture of prairie life—Mitchell also wrote full-length plays. His serious drama *The Devil's Instrument* concerns the journey of a young prairie Hutterite to freedom from his religious community. *The Black Bonspiel of Wullie Mac-Crimmon* is a satire about a curling match against the devil's team. Another well-known play of Mitchell's is *Who Has Seen the Wind*, a drama about the growing up of a prairie boy. As exemplified by his comedy *Chaperon for Maggie,* Mitchell's type of satiric commentary is slow and understated, but devastating, and his dramatic sense is very sure.

Allan King was a prolific and popular radio dramatist who honed his skills as an actor. He had nearly 250 produced plays to his credit in the golden age, including twenty adaptations. These include documentary, biographical and historical dramas, a number of witty social satires, notably *Who Killed Cock Robin;* and some serious social dramas like *The Way Through the Wood*, about a post-war woman's rebellion against current marriage and other social norms. King's serial on the nature and history of drama, *A Touch of Greasepaint,* had a measurable effect in popularizing the theatre in this country.

Tommy Tweed, like Allan King, wrote many historical and documentary dramas, but also a number of mordant satires, among his seventy-five original plays and forty radio-dramatizations. His satire on the prairie naval battle of the Riel Rebellion, *Full Speed Sideways,* is full of comedy and dramatic tension; its final effect is to satirize the Canadian efforts in the war. Tweed's clever documentary, *The Brass-Pounder from Illinois,* on William Van Horne, and the human and hilarious treatment of Prime Minister Sir John A. MacDonald, *The Honorable Member from Kingston,* are justly famous. Tweed's *The Man from Number Ten* is a satire on Newfoundland in Confederation. Another such satire is the *Secret Treaty* in which Canada is offered back to the Indians; but because it is in such bad shape, they refuse to accept it.

Joseph Schull wrote for all four of the senior CBC drama producers. His dramatic career spans radio, television, the cinema and the stage, though his finest work was done for radio. Schull wrote almost a hundred original plays and thirty adaptations for radio, including not only serious drama (his forte) but also comedy, satire and documentary. Among the best is *The Jinker,* a social and personal tragedy about rivalry to the death of two young Newfoundland sealing captains. The play projects some central Canadian cultural archetypes, including the primitive symbols of the sea, the glaciers and the harp seals. Schull's *Almighty Voice* depicts the tragedy of the Cree in conflict with impersonal civilization. *The Fall of Quebec* is one of Schull's polished historical dramas, while *Laurier* is his famous biography of our Prime Minister. *The Flower in the Rock* is a moving drama of prairie life with a mystery at its centre. Two of Schull's best satires are *The Heat Wave,* about the nuclear holocaust, and *The Land of Ephranor,* a fantasy concerning human political idealism.

Among the well-known Canadian poets who wrote occasionally for the Drama Department, Earle Birney was the most prolific during the golden age. He wrote fourteen originals and adaptations, which were broadcast from Vancouver and Toronto. These included dramatizations from Tolstoi and Conrad, a number of modernized dramatizations from early English poems, like *Beowulf, Everyman* and *The Faerie Queene,* "occasional" plays like the one for Remembrance Day, *November Eleven 1948,* and an original poetic drama, the best play he wrote, *The Damnation of Vancouver: Trial of a City.* The latter is a wonderful verbal satire containing his social concerns and his poetic and dramatic genius.

Patricia Joudry wrote twenty-four original radio plays and seven adaptations, most of which were produced in Toronto, but a number in Vancouver, Winnipeg and Montreal. The radio works of this stage playwright were mostly serious dramas, but they included some lighter plays. Her realistic social drama *Mother is Watching* speaks eloquently for the position of women in the family.

Mac Shoub's radio plays were most often produced by Rupert Caplan, who considered Shoub his "golden-haired boy." But Andrew Allan also produced the occasional Shoub play. Shoub wrote over ninety original plays and twenty-five adaptations during the golden age, including tragedy, comedy, satire and documentary. *Ashes in the Wind,* considered Shoub's masterpiece, is a realistic and moving play about a family dealing with the problem of a seriously ill mother. His *In the End is the Beginning* is a psychological drama about the last days of the survivors of a plane crash at sea. Among Shoub's best-known adaptations are Eugene O'Neill's *Long Day's Journey into Night,* Franz Kafka's *The Trial,* Chekov's *The Three Sisters* and Thornton Wilder's *The Matchmaker.*

Reuben Ship's work for radio drama was not extensive, but he made a strong impression with several satires. The best-known radio play of this refugee from McCarthyism is *The Investigator,* which imaginatively and mercilessly satirizes the Senator, in a trial in which God Himself is finally "investigated." Ship's *The Man Who Liked Christmas* is a comedy satirizing commercial attitudes towards the holiday, and social prejudices generally.

These are only the foremost of over 1,300 Canadian radio dramatists (counting only to the end of the golden age); and only a general impression can be given of their large and varied production. It is clear that, while several of them succeeded at serious drama, one of the major modes for the frequent expression of social concerns was satire and satiric comedy of a kind which left little of the critique unclear. This is significant when the later history of CBC radio drama is considered. With the coming of the Stratford Festival and other legitimate theatres, as well as television drama, the dedicated national audiences for radio plays began to disappear. The strong social concerns of radio drama became less relevant as the institution of radio drama lost its great popularity. What followed was, first, the turning away of the golden age generation of radio drama professionals to more private and extreme experiments. Secondly, playwrights with stage experience began to write for radio—sometimes creating more traditional plays.

Of the Canadian playwrights who became active in the 1960s, the majority wrote radio plays at some time. Though their legitimate plays are better known, their radio drama achievements must also be taken into account. The two best known of these just-post-golden-age playwrights are Michael Cook and George Ryga. Both have written extensively for the Radio Drama Departments, regional and national. Ryga has said that for each of his plays produced on the stage, he has had ten accepted for radio. Other Canadian dramatists have not written so extensively for the medium, but the vast majority of them, from David French to Sharon Pollock, have produced radio plays.

Contemporary Canadian Radio Drama: The Renaissance

As described above, radio drama went into something of an eclipse—at least in interest, if not production—in the 1960s and the early 70s. However, as the radio of words and ideas continued to regain Canadian and American audiences, CBC radio drama began a renaissance on the airwaves. This phenomenon became unmistakable on the national network starting in 1980, under a new National Supervisor, Susan Rubes. First, a horror anthology series called *Nightfall* began on the national network that year, produced from Vancouver. And in the following year two new imported popular drama serials began nationally: the American *Star Wars* and the British *Lord of the Rings*. In 1982, a traditional detective series began production in Toronto: *Nero Wolfe*. Though *Festival Theatre,* an anthology series of two-hour plays begun in 1978, was cancelled in early 1981, a new half-hour anthology series called *Playdate* was begun in early 1982 (it only lasted, alas, a few months). Meanwhile, the *Stage* series had continued its tradition of mainly original Canadian radio plays, renamed *Sound Stage* in 1979 and becoming *Sunday Matinee* in 1980. Finally, in Vancouver, an excellent regional anthology play series, *The Hornby Collection,* which had begun in 1977, was continuing, though it was never heard over the national network.

Two new serious national series were begun: *Saturday Stereo Theatre* in 1982 and *Sunday Stereo Theatre* in 1983. The *Sunday* series began with a sequence of dramatized trials, *The Scales of Justice,* followed by serial dramatizations of novels. The *Saturday* series, promisingly, featured original Canadian plays. Thus by mid-1982 there were two Canadian anthology play series on CBC: *Sunday Matinee* and *Saturday Stereo Theatre.* Malcolm Page, who has commented at some length on these series, counts some seventy new plays in both these series during 1981-82, of which fifty were Canadian originals.[5] Though Page was not sanguine about the quality or social relevance of many of the scripts, he did praise the excellence of much of the production, and he responded to the indications of a groundswell of new Canadian radio drama: "In the near future the quantity of (anthology) radio drama is assured along with a high proportion of Canadian work."

I am sorry to say that Page's optimism was premature. *The Hornby Collection* had already been cancelled in early 1983, and *Playdate* even earlier. As of October, 1984, most of the newly-established series have disappeared, owing to budget cuts. The only series which have survived (after a fashion) are the old *Sunday Matinee* (formerly *Stage*) on AM and *Sunday Stereo Theatre* on FM. Neither of these is now an original anthology series. They both feature episodic drama-serials from novels, and indeed they are both presently offering episodes from the same historical novel, *The Canadians.* The quality of the acting and the productions in general are up to the best traditional CBC standards, and Lucio Agostini composes and conducts the music every bit as well as on the golden age *Stage* productions. On the other hand, there is no longer a national anthology showcase for original Canadian plays on the CBC, for the first time since the early 1940s.

A new popular mystery-fantasy series called *Vanishing Point* has just begun this fall. It will include adaptations from plays and short-stories, British, European and South American (an early broadcast featured a Borghes story), as well as the winners of the latest CBC playwriting competition. The productions, as usual, are impeccable. It shows promise, but there is no indication in which direction it will develop. Meanwhile, Peter Gzowski's daily *Morningside* program has begun featuring short episodic serializations of novels since last fall, though it recently included a five-part original mini-series by George Robertson, called *Changes.* And the decade-long run of our traditional comedy-variety drama, *The Royal Canadian Air Farce,* shows no sign of flagging.

The 1980-83 renaissance of Canadian radio drama is definitely over, together with the long history of *Stage* anthology drama. But radio drama has been down before, and revived. A retrospective series of new productions of original *Stage* scripts is being planned by the CBC Drama Department for 1986, to celebrate CBC Radio's fiftieth anniversary.

Howard Fink

Notes

[1]See the scripts and correspondence in the CBC Radio Drama Archives, Centre for Broadcasting Studies, Concordia University, Montreal.

[2]Howard Fink, with Brian Morrison, *Canadian National Theatre on the Air 1925-1961/CBC-CRBC-CNR Radio Drama in English/A Descriptive Bibliography and Union List.* Toronto, University of Toronto Press, 1983.

[3]Howard Fink, "The sponsor's v. the nation's choice: North American radio drama" in *Radio Drama,* ed. Peter Lewis. London, Longman, 1981.

[4]Andrew Allan, *A Self-Portrait,* ed., intro. by Harry Boyle. Toronto, Macmillan, 1974.

[5]Malcolm Page, "From 'Stage' to 'Sunday Matinee': Canadian Radio Drama in English, 1981-82", *Canadian Drama* Vol. 9, No. 1, 1983.

Television Drama
in English Canada

The first fact of Canadian television drama is that Canada finds itself sharing the longest undefended electronic border in the world with the dominant power in the West—the United States. For fifty years, in the absence of a film or music industry or a national theatre, first radio drama (which had achieved world-class stature in the late 1940s) and then television drama have been the primary channels through which we have told stories to ourselves about ourselves. Radio and television have helped to define our borders, to create an indigenous culture as opposed to imitations of American or British popular culture.

A brief outline of the history of television drama in Canada is virtually the history of the CBC. Unlike Britain's Independent Television Authority, the Canadian Radio, Television and Telecommunications Commission has been unable to persuade or coerce the independent networks to plough any significant proportion of their huge profits into expensive drama programming. There have been seasons when their average output in drama has been one half hour for the entire year. As recently as the 1983-84 season, CTV, the largest privately owned network, produced one abysmal sitcom called *Snow Job,* and one competent drama. The new money being pumped into private production houses by the telefilm policy of the government may change that. The smaller Global network is committed to broadcasting 26 half-hour dramas based on Canadian short stories over a two year period. However, to date, by far the largest share of the co-productions is supported by the CBC.

Television broadcasting began in Montreal and Toronto in 1952. In this huge country of two languages and a small population scattered over thousands of miles, most antennae were already pointed to American border stations. Moreover, there was no microwave relay system to send broadcasts across the country. However, there was a remarkable level of accomplishment in both languages in the challenging forms of radio drama. For both popular series and for more demanding fare like the famous *Stage* anthology, there were large, responsive, often vocal audiences.

When CBC television opened up shop, facilities were shared by the two languages in Montreal. The beloved *Les Plouffes,* a series about a working-class family, went out twice a week, using the same script, once in French and once in English. Francophone playwrights were translated into English for production in the 1950s and early 60s so that scripts set in Quebec or Acadia or Manitoba (some by anglophone writers) appeared fairly regularly. There was much less traffic the other way until taping and dubbing were common. Ironically, as the political climate changed and the need to understand one another's imaginative landscapes increased, as far as television *drama* was concerned, contacts between the two cultures steadily eroded.

In English Canada, radio playwrights like Len Peterson, Mavor Moore, Joseph Schull, Patricia Joudry, and playwrights learning to master the new medium like Arthur Hailey, Mordecai Richler and Bernard Slade supplied the Canadian content for early live television. Their work was presented on the same CBC channel as *Studio One* and *Kraft Television Theatre.* By 1955, the very prestigious short anthology of television drama, *First Performance,* featured scripts specifically commissioned from Canadians, often on topical themes. *Folio,* which was unsponsored, featured Canadian plays of a serious or experimental nature as well as concerts, ballet, opera, and plays from the international repertoire. Under the guidance of Sidney Newman, *G.M. Presents, On Camera* and *Playdate* provided somewhat more topical fare. However, the territory was not as strictly divided up as one would expect: for example, *Folio* presented revues and original musicals (*Anne of Green Gables* started that way), *G.M. Presents* did a two part adaptation of Coulter's *Riel* and *On Camera* took some of its more serious scripts from newspaper headlines.

By 1956, the regions were adding drama with a local emphasis to the national mix. Montreal's two languages and somewhat more sophisticated audiences left their mark on *Shoe-String Theatre* and its successor, *Teleplay,* which kept its small but faithful audience up until midnight to watch adult content—often presented in experimental ways—from William Bankier's *Pea Soup and Porridge,* a successful parody of theatre and cultural miscues between French and English written partly in blank verse, David French's evocative little horror tale about a psychotic young girl, *The Willow Harp,* and Dennis Donovan's *Laurie,* a sympathetic and thus very controversial account of a love affair between a 13 year old and her teacher, concentrating on what happens to him in prison before his trial. Some of those scripts including *Laurie* appeared on the network in the 1969-70 season of *Playbill.* Winnipeg, Regina and St. Johns have also produced some fine television drama intermittently for the network over the years.

In 1961, Vancouver ignored the dictum from the CBC that film must be left to the National Film board to produce. The second and subsequent seasons of *Cariboo Country* were shot on location, on film. This series, one of the consistently best examples of television drama I have ever seen, came to birth in 1960 when there were 24 westerns a week in prime time on NBC, ABC and CBS. Setting a pattern for subsequent Canadian television successes, it bent or broke every known convention of the genre, in this case the adult western. It was a "series" with continuing characters, but an anthology in the continual shift of focus from continuing characters to new ones, the refusal to allow an audience to identify with one leading character, and in its use of plots that ranged from slapstick to tragedy.

It also broke the specific conventions of the television western by being contemporary, realistic, wry and by treating Indians, Metis and Whites from varied backgrounds without sentimentalism but with affection and respect.[1]

Canadians have often adapted the television forms developed and made popular elsewhere: the serial and the various genres of series—sitcoms, copshows, family-adventure programs, the "professional" shows featuring doctors and lawyers. However, our versions often focus on the new characters introduced specifically for that episode rather than on the continuing characters. When the series form works in this country, it is usually because the writing as well as the production values and performances are good. The series will also have a strong sense of a particular location and of the habits of speech and thought which divide region from region, city from country-side, class from class.

Recent examples would include the trilogy *A Good Place to Come From* (about growing up Jewish in the northern steel town of Sault-Ste.Marie during the 40s) as well as some episodes of the family-adventure series *The Beachcombers,* specifically episodes dealing with Jesse's search for his Indian heritage, Margaret's coming of age in an attempt to swim the straits, Nick's rediscovery of his Greek father and the two episodes which reminded the audience of the shameful deportation of Japanese-Canadians into the interior of B.C. during World War II. The intricate social nuances of a small town in Ontario during the Boer War in *A Gift to Last,* and the gritty texture of life at a run-down racing track in *Backstretch* also show the range of period, place and tone which distinguish the better programs in both limited and long-running series.

Habits of ambivalence, deprecation, allusion and irony together with many of the unpredictable, occasionally down-beat endings also characterize the best of the episodes in CBC series. This willingness to break with formulae is evident as early as *Wojeck,* an innovative and immensely popular series about a city's chief coroner who grapples with the social abuses of the day (1966-68). It still contributes to the success of *Seeing Things,* the hybrid of mystery, sitcom and Chekov which is a new favourite, growing steadily in popularity since 1982 and sold abroad.

In the early days of the 1950s, television as a medium for dramatic expression struggled to be seen and not just heard on sets which gave pictures with low visual definition and a tendency to flip, break up into "snow" or fade. The broadcasts were equally primitive. Television drama was performed live in front of huge and clumsy cameras in cramped sets, then using the paradoxically named "live-to-tape." This early tape permitted directors and actors to stop and start but was virtually impossible to edit. In the 1966-67 season colour arrived and the CBC was allowed to make more extensive use of film, with its higher visual resolution and capacity for easy editing. More easily edited tape followed by the mid-70s, which permitted directors to check scenes as soon as they were shot—then more sensitive film stock and lighter and more flexible equipment which allowed stories to be set in new locations, seasons, times of day.

At present, the CBC is locked into using tape whenever possible on the series which are the staple of a season because of its investment in studios and equipment, even though tape is now no less expensive than film. However the equipment is so antiquated and unreliable that writers and producers are refusing to think in terms of tape when they propose projects. Just as the move to film and

California's post-production facilities has shaped American television drama—and the huge complex of studios available to the BBC has always tilted the balance of BBC anthology drama toward studio production—technology (or the lack of it) continues to shape television drama in this country. Radio-Canada has had excellent facilities at its broadcasting centre in Montreal since the early 70s but the English facilities have been grossly inadequate for 30 years.

The eight years from 1952 to 1960 were the golden age of television anthology in the United States. However, partly in response to television's growing popularity and the fact that audiences could be delivered more reliably to sponsors by filmed series featuring one or two major characters and a continuing supporting cast, safely conventional genres like the western or the copshow replaced the unpredictability of live anthology television drama in North America. Yet even though studio space for the English network has always been in short supply, the CBC did not abandon anthology (usually recorded on tape) until the mid-70s. Indeed, anthology drama using tape in studios and on location is reappearing with considerable success, for example, in the period dramas focussed on Canadian political issues, presented under the ironic title of *Some Honourable Gentlemen,* now sacrificed to the $85 million budget cut demanded by the new Conservative government. A limited but very successful form of anthology has been the half dozen topical dramas on film appearing under the umbrella title of *For the Record* every season for the past eleven years. However, very successful but costly "specials" like *Gentle Sinners* and *Charlie Grant's War,* co-productions and even pilots for new programs are likely to be seen no more as the CBC endures the lion's share of cutbacks in the arts.

With *Folio* (1954 to 1959) and *Festival* (from 1960 to 1969), the CBC provided a weekly music/drama/ballet anthology where a viewer turned to see all of Chekhov's plays brilliantly directed by Mario Prizek, or a *Galileo* praised by Helene Weigel (and now in the archives of the Berliner Ensemble), or plays for the stage or television by Pinter, Saunders, Clive Exton, Pirandello, Sartre, John Webster, Molière, Shaw, Arden, Wesker, Beckett, Miller, Anouilh, Giradoux. In a country where there was no classical or contemporary theatre available, outside of three or four centres, and no indigenous performing tradition of well-known classics, this repertoire, under the guidance of supervising producer Robert Allen, was absolutely vital to the development of writers, actors and audiences for the theatre to come.

Festival challenged the prevailing temper of the times with a whole range of plays critical of war during the coldest depths of the cold war—including Eric Till's remarkable production of Marghanita Laski's *The Offshore Island* (1962). It also presented a few of the many plays by Quebec writers in translation. Some of its best productions were adaptations of short stories like the beautifully lyrical, expressionist production of Katherine Anne Porter's *Pale Horse, Pale Rider* and Chekhov's *Ward Number Six.* In the 1959 *Folio* production of Mac Shoub's adaptation of *Ward Number Six,* producer Harvey Hart used the black and white contrasts of early television, the interplay of light and shadow, as an effective metaphor for the interplay of madness and sanity. The clumsy technology of that period did not preclude excellent camera-work full of sudden discoveries or the unexpected, off-centre framing of a shot. The distinctive visual style adapted by Hart did justice to the complex set and the detailed characterizations.

The 1957 production of playwright Arthur Hailey's *Flight Into Danger* altered the structure and tightened the pace of television suspense stories in Britain and the United States where the production was broadcast to considerable critical praise. Ron Kelly's 1963 experiment *The Open Grave* created a storm of controversy in Canada before it was broadcast. The program was an exercise in *cinema verité*, a very unusual mode for television then. It was also a sharp look at how the broadcast media cover a suddenly breaking story, in this case the Resurrection, a subject whose controversial content obscured the critical response to the piece in Canada. Later, it won international prizes and was telecast without incident all over Europe.

Ten years later, amid the euphoria of the Centennial year, Timothy Findley wrote a blackly witty script, directed by David Gardner, called *The Paper People*. It is a piece of fiction about the making of a documentary on artist Jamie Reed who films the burning of his *papier maché* sculptures and sells both films and ashes. Ironically, the truth about the artist is available only to the audience of the "fiction," not to the maker of the "documentary." *The Paper People* is also an anatomy of the dilemma of the artist in Canada and of our ambivalent relation to the cultures which gave us birth. This production was not sold abroad. In fact, until a reassessment of its achievement in 1980, all of those concerned in its making thought of it as a critical failure, an ending to a brief hope that full-length films would be created for television in Canada.[2] There is much to admire in it—but it has not been rebroadcast, on the CBC's sporadic "golden oldies" series, *Rear View Mirror,* as *The Open Grave* and *Flight Into Danger* have been. In Britain there is justifiable pride in accomplishments of the BBC and ITV. In America, most television, including films for television, appear in reruns eventually. In Canada, opportunities to reassess television drama are very rarely provided by the CBC.

In the 1960s and early 70s, experiments and risks found a home on producer Daryl Duke's *Q for Quest,* Mario Prizek's *Eyeopener,* Paddy Sampson's *Programme X* and finally *Peepshow.* An experimental 30 minute slot has been one of the casualties of a merciless and short-sighted governmental budget squeeze now almost ten years old. Another casualty of the mid-70s is a "window" on the world theatre scene like that provided by *Festival.* Even television adaptations of suitable Canadian theatre hits are now very rare. It is true that both the forms of television and the definition of what is acceptable content have broadened over the years, thanks in part to the CBC's fairly consistent refusal to censor itself. Yet in the sense of television drama challenging its audience to argue, to protest, to care passionately about what they see, to connect it with their own lives in an ideological as well as a personal way—as still happens sometimes in other countries—in the last 15 years, the CBC has failed. In some ways it is more conservative than it was in the torpid days of the 50s.

The many delightful, sometimes stridently nationalist, occasionally thoughtful dramatized histories of the 50s had given way by the 70s to the topical and to rather tame biographies of Van Horne, Beaverbrook, Emily Carr, L.M. Montgomery. Increasingly television's myth-making functions were neglected, with the notable exception of Imperial Oil's centenary gift to the nation, *The Newcomers.* This anthology about the various waves of immigrants to Canada, beginning with the French in 1740 and ending with the Italians in 1978, used some of our best writers: Charles Israel, Alice Munro, George Ryga and Timothy Findley; directors like Eric Till and Claude Fournier; and a blend of the older generation of actors like Martha Henry, Bruno Gerussi, Chris Wiggins, Hugh Webster, Budd Knapp with newer ones like R.H. Thomson, Ken Hames, Richard Donat, Kenneth Welsh, Diane D'Aquila.

The least successful in the series, *The Prologue,* told the pre-contact story of the Native people, the Git 'Ksan in the interior of British Columbia. Nevertheless, some of the best of our television drama *has* tried to come to terms with the first peoples but focusses on their life and struggles in contemporary Canada. Writer Paul St. Pierre and director Philip Keatley took characters from *Cariboo Country* for *Festival* and created two splendid specials: the tragic, award-winning *The Education of Philistine* and the wry, tragi-comic *How to Break a Quarterhorse,* both starring Chief Dan George. Writer Philip Hersch, director Ron Kelly and producer Ron Weyman did a superb anatomy of an Indian man's suicide in *The Last Man on Earth* (on *Wojeck*) with Johnny Yesno. Claude Jutra directed George

A nne Anglin and Janet Amos in Claude Jutra's *Ada,* broadcast on CBC TV's *For the Record,* February 6, 1976.

Clutesi as a Shaman who tries and fails to save a white runaway child in Cam Hubert's sensitively scripted *Dreamspeaker*. The latter was made in the only surviving anthology on Canadian television, the topical docudramas of *For the Record*, for which well-known Canadian film-makers Don Shebib, Claude Jutra, Donald Brittain and Allan King have directed 60 minute or 90 minute films.

After 1967, nationalism took on new life in Canada. We already had a new and increasingly prolific generation of poets and novelists, and were finally developing a new generation of playwrights, actors, directors and theatres. Ironically, as theatres and itinerant companies flourished, the national theatre of the air, the CBC, was going through a period of low morale, resulting in very uneven production (1968-71). Bureaucracy, always a factor, now proliferated. Resources shrank and costs rose. The CBC sought and found new energy in John Hirsch (Head of TV drama 1972-76) who swept many people out, tried to train new directors and find new playwrights, did a few European plays and broadcast a lot of television adaptations of scripts from the flourishing alternate theatres, finally providing Canadians with a chance to see what was stirring across the country.

He also tried to refurbish the popular formula drama with *King of Kensington*, a sitcom, and *Sidestreet*, a copshow. Unfortunately both became more imitative as time went on. The non-violent mediators of *Sidestreet*'s first season often reverted to car chases and fights. The rich ethnic mix and topical humour of *King of Kensington* yielded too often to standard sitcom plots and stereotyped characters. *For the Record* is probably Hirsch's most valuable legacy.

Eric Till's production of Brian Friel's *Freedom of the City* on tape (1975) was the most innovative and exciting individual production of that period. Using an adaptation by Hugh Webster, Till managed to use television itself to extend the metaphorical levels of the play: for example, Till's counterpoint of music from the funeral with a lament of the singer in a bar which mythologizes the death of the three Irish working-class victims, even as the event itself is still unfolding on the television set in the corner; or the juxtaposition of the three victims speaking out of a spatial limbo about how they died, intercut with flashbacks, freeze frames, fragments of events and a painstakingly useless "inquiry" about their deaths.

The 70s saw the last regularly scheduled anthology, *To See Ourselves*, based on Canadian short stories, and *The National Dream*, a mixture of contemporary footage and dramatization of the struggle to get the railroad across the land in which the superbly photographed landscapes both upstaged the action and underlined the heroism of those who fought to pull the pieces of a nation together. There was also a highly publicized, costly, but quite incoherent version of *Jalna*. The crisply plotted, ambivalent look at the War of 1812-14, *Ambush at Iroquois Point*, was the last full-scale historical drama for several years. There was also the clutch of biographies already mentioned, using a variety of conventions from experiments with direct address, mime and surrealistic settings to chatty entertainments with a little history thrown in. An overdue and searching look at Bethune was offset by an inadvertently sexist treatment of feminist Nellie McClung.

Hirsch's successor, John Kennedy (1976 to the present), responded to the shrinking hours and dollars by deliberately concentrating on contemporary Canadian material. Excellent topical dramas of the 70s, which have outlived the headlines which sparked them, are Robin Spry's *They're Drying up the Streets*, a brutal, cliché-free anatomy of the drug scene and its links to child prostitution and child-pornography; Ralph Thomas' *Cementhead,* an unsentimental look at professional hockey, distinguished by a strong sense of place, wry humour, rounded characterizations and an ear for the many ways ordinary people actually speak; Allan King's *Maria,* a provocative yet balanced study of a young woman's attempt to organize a union; and Claude Jutra's *Ada,* where a subjective camera, a superb script, sensitive performances and an ambivalent ending lift this glimpse behind the wire-mesh windows of a hospital for the mentally ill well beyond didacticism into art.

Diane D'Aquila (standing) as the Italian-Canadian union organizer in Allan King's 1976 CBC TV film *Maria,* scripted by Rick Salutin.

With satellites and dishes, the skies are now as open as our borders have been to signals from all over. The 80s have seen all television systems everywhere entering what is now called the "third age" of broadcasting—the phase of audiences fragmented by cable and by the direct broadcast satellites which will finally link the continents. Both will provide viewers with dozens of channels. However, many channels does not mean many choices. Most of those channels may well be broadcasting *Bonanza* reruns, if there is not the money or the political will to make sure that programs reflecting our different selves are made—with the result that television viewing may well decline.

Yet the qualities which make good television drama that millions of people will choose to watch have not changed. Canadian experience has shown that when we imitate other cultures we generally do it badly. Moreover, Canadian viewers can get their *Magnum P.I.* and *Dynasty, Smiley's People* and *All things Great and Small* directly from cable and dishes which bring American channels (including PBS) to their doorstep.

Pay TV in Canada is so uneconomic in Canada at present that there will be very little Canadian television drama, other than one-person shows like *Maggie and Pierre*, for a long time to come. Tiers of specialized stations—sports, religion, music—offer choices but not in television drama.

Equally restrictive is the fact that, next to the United States (where 99% of the programs on the commercial channels originate) Canada has one of the most closed television systems in the world. We see very little from the BBC or ITV, Australia, virtually no dubbed European or Japanese television, and none from other countries. Cassettes and satellite dishes may bring us more from other countries. That remains to be seen. On the networks, we will all be seeing more international co-productions, which have worked very well when the story is distinctive and the writing is good, and have been disastrous when the story is set in mid-Atlantic to "guarantee foreign sales" and the plot is replaced by car chases. *The New Avengers* (1976) and *Danger Bay* (1984) come to mind.

With the new developmental money from the federal government, independent Canadian production companies, which have often starved over the years, are now getting a chance to do more specials, series and anthologies such as the Oscar-winning *Sons and Daughters*, based on fine adaptations of first-rate Canadian short stories (and one poem). A new set of six is in the works for the CBC and another set of short story adaptations is set for broadcast by the Global network. *The Painted Door,* produced by Atlantis Films in collaboration with the National Film Board in association with Global TV and Telefilm Canada, was nominated for an Oscar in 1985. Global, our newest privately owned network, jettisoned all Canadian content outside of news and game shows for several years in favour of nightly reruns of *Loveboat* and rather weak British sitcoms. The new anthology represents a real change in policy. CTV, the other private network, has not yet announced any firm plans to produce or co-produce any Canadian television drama.

During the 1970s, Canadians acquired more cable per citizen than in any other country on earth. We became a world leader in communications satellites and developed expertise in fibre optics and Telidon (interactive teletext). We also tried in this period, with increasing difficulty and mixed success, to remain an independent culture with an open border and an open sky. A few of us bought video disc players. For television viewers, earth dishes which bring in dozens of channels directly from satellites and video cassette recorders are radically altering the viewing habits of thousands of people. They will alter permanently the structure of the old delivery systems, the networks.

Despite Canadian content regulations, most Canadians have had virtually unlimited access to American television since 1952. Direct broadcast satellites and pay television add to the choices by offering "arts and entertainments," sports or music channels, all originating in America. If enough Canadians really do not care about whether they ever see themselves on their sets, and no one knows the answer to that, then Canadian television drama will disappear. On the other hand, if the political will exists to find the means to produce television drama that is popular and/or excellent, it will be "Canadian" whether the subject is labour relations in the logging industry or Molière's *The Misanthrope*.

Not all of the new technology is threatening. The growing numbers of VCRs in Canada could at last give our television drama a sense of tradition, even though, at the moment the CBC drama videocassettes made for sale abroad are not available in Canada — incredible as that may seem. Intelligent use of the available technology should mean that students can look again at assigned programs. Television critics can compare performances, direction, acting, design, editing and cinematography, get a sense of context, sharpen their ears and eyes with replays and give to good television drama the meticulous attention that up to now has been reserved for good films. Academics and critics writing for periodicals might even engage in the kind of serious debate about the nature of television drama that has been going on in Europe and the United States for years.

Meanwhile the 80s are half over. Even though the Corporation shows the same old lack of confidence which results in poor scheduling (*Judge*, an adult series at 7 p.m. Saturdays), the CBC drama department shows a new willingness to take risks. After nearly a decade of "realism" as the prevailing visual style, the CBC is again widening its stylistic range to include decadent opulence, fantasy, biting political satire disguised as history, multiple narrative points-of-view, intense lyricism, surrealistic use of editing time and space into strange juxtapositions, and a mix of film and tape conventions. I would hope that the subject matter will also broaden and will include again the troubles and triumphs, history and politics of other countries as seen through our eyes. I also think the time has come again for intensely private and highly personalized perspectives on society to replace the more collective, rather balanced, sometimes didactic tone.

For the sake of the future of television drama in Canada, I hope that the CBC will follow in the directions already intimated by the varied tone of the anthology *Some Honourable Gentlemen*; the stylistic innovations of *Blind Faith* and *Rough Justice*; the unabashed entertainment values, acute observations of the tensions in our society and good scripts of *Empire Inc.*; and complex emotional landscapes like the intense love/hate relationship between a teenage drop-out and a sadistic cop in *I Love a Man in Uniform*. We must find our sense of humour again, outside the confines for formula comedy shows, as Vancouver region did with *Last Call*, when they adapted an alternative theatre cabaret on the nuclear nightmare into a bitterly amusing television variety special, not yet seen on the network as a whole. The new Toronto facilities promised in 1987 may free artists like Eric Till (*Gentle Sinners*) to make more drama, in the studio, on tape, on film, on location, or turning full circle and, knowing this time, where we have been—to do some television drama "live".

Popular culture derived from television drama is the only true manifestation as yet of McLuhan's global village. No wonder such a vision of community came from a Canadian scholar. But as McLuhan also pointed out, no one person in a village is identical to another. Whatever the conventions of a medium or genre, no one tells the same stories in exactly the same way. Human beings do not like to be bored, or even reassured, all the time. In Canada, as elsewhere, there will always be room for excellence, for distinctiveness and, most important of all, for the "shock of recognition" which stories about our individual and collective experiences can bring.

Mary Jane Miller

Notes

[1] See Mary Jane Miller, "*Cariboo Country*: The Canadian Response to the American Television Western", *American Review of Canadian Studies*, Vol. 14, No. 3, Fall 1984.

[2] See Mary Jane Miller, "An Analysis of *The Paper People*", *Canadian Drama*, Vol. 9, No. 1, 1983.

Radio and Television Drama in Quebec 1945-1985

The four decades from the end of World War II up to the present have been a period of profound political and social, as well as cultural, transformation for Quebec and its over five million francophone inhabitants. Among the factors which have contributed to changing the face of this province, two major cultural developments stand out: the advent of television followed by a change of direction in radio—and the growth of Quebec drama. If one wants to understand the role that radio and television have played in the evolution of Quebec theatre since the last war, it is important to analyse the relationship between these two forms of cultural expression since then.

In 1945, radio was in the midst of its golden age. Thanks to the war, it carved out a place for itself in homes throughout Quebec, where the habit of regularly catching the news and commentaries had taken hold. But the war also brought a need for diversion during difficult times. So, in addition to music and popular songs, radio serials were broadcast. These drew people into the world of fiction and fantasy. In this way, a first experience with theatre took place in remote and rural regions[1] where often the only public contact with drama had been through melodramas such as *Aurore, l'enfant martyre* (which was revived in Montreal in the autumn of 1984, reflecting the infatuation with the past which has spread through Quebec these past few years), and burlesque revues performed by touring groups.

In urban Quebec the impact of radio was somewhat different; despite a difficult socio-economic situation, a segment of the public already attended theatre regularly by the time radio arrived on the scene. Indeed, this audience was surprisingly large for that era, particularly in Montreal. Few plays presented, however, were Québécois.

The first radio producers had to start from scratch. They brought to life characters, places and events which appealed to the imagination of the listeners. By 1945-50 they had succeeded in creating veritable small masterpieces of "radio-couleur," to quote an expression coined by Guy Mauffette, producer of dramatic series such as *Le Ciel par-dessus les toits, Les Belles Histoires des pays d'en haut,* etc. Several parallel developments took place: actors had learned the techniques of the radio studio, programming became more diversified, and theatre was already carving out a respectable niche on radio. From 1945 to 1952, one could hear two, or sometimes three plays a week on Radio-Canada,[2] the other stations concentrating more on variety programming and light entertainment. This "golden age" was to last until about 1957, which is to say until television had secured its place in Quebec homes.

In order to do justice to the role that radio has played in Quebec dramaturgy, one must recognize the importance of serials—a form long neglected by critics. As a matter of fact, serials effected the transition from prose to dialogue in stories rooted in Quebec. One could characterize them as initiating a long process of sensitization through which people became ever more attuned to various forms of artistic expression, including theatre.[3] From 1945-1960, from ten to fifteen radio serials were broadcast daily, providing approximately three hours a day of original Québécois productions, not counting the two or three individual Quebec plays broadcast every week, and the adaptations of foreign plays. There were also well-done, popular dramatized historical series.[4]

For all those unacquainted with the classical repertoire and those who couldn't go to the theatre (that is to say, the majority of the population), the radio serial was an ideal way of making contact with the world of drama. Besides, this genre had far more in common with radio drama than with the novel (as in "*radio-roman*"), and the language used was identical to speech in radio plays. The essential difference consisted in the fact that the radio serial was not confined to a series of episodes leading up to a dénouement, but rather was an open-ended sequence of scenes comprising episodes. The characters had direct contact with the listener; they weren't described or explained by a narrator. Thus, the kind of communication that occurred was similar to that of the theatre.[5]

Between World War II and the end of the Duplessis era, radio provided an opportunity for young authors as well as actors to make a living and learn their craft. New playwrights thus made their appearance, among whom several would subsequently write for the stage: Guy Dufresne, Félix Leclerc, Pierre Dagenais, Françoise Loranger, and Marcel Dubé (who had already begun writing for the amateur stage in 1951) made their radio début in series such as *Le Théâtre de chez-nous, Le Radio-théâtre de Radio-Canada, Les Nouveautés dramatiques, Quatuor, Le Radio-théâtre Canadien,* and *Le Théâtre populaire.*

It was a real challenge to successfully maintain a network of uninterrupted, cultural communication with a geographically dispersed, politically exploited, and intellectually dulled public. Radio drama, though, met the challenge brilliantly up until around 1955. In an era in which no economic or political achievement was powerful enough to give a stimulating and positive self-image to the people of Quebec, this genre brought to a mass audience a very distinctive set of Québécois images which contributed towards the gradual creation of a national identity. Perhaps these were flawed, but without them the masses would have found themselves in a cultural vacuum which would have been filled by inferior American products.[6] It is important here to emphasize the role played by radio in this epoch by upholding a high level of the French language in Quebec, and consequently making it possible for authors to write in French. Radio created a linguistic and cultural environment which brought to the fore long suppressed and denigrated desires for self-expression,[7] and revitalized a language that was in decline. Radio stimulated the use of the French language among a people who, in large urban centres such as Montreal, heard English spoken all around them.[8]

One can say that more than the written word, the broadcast word won the battle of linguistic survival among the masses and strengthened a cultural ego vitiated by a colonial situation. Thus, a taste for theatre took root, and it is not surprising to see the creation of many new theatre companies in the 1950s and 1960s. (The Rideau Vert in 1949, the Théâtre du Nouveau Monde in 1952, the Comédie Canadienne in 1957, the Egrégore in 1959, etc.)

In his monumental study devoted to radio drama, Pierre Pagé does not hesitate to state that it is the source of the Québécois theatre of today, for it allowed the public to familiarize itself with drama on a regular basis.[9] Radio thus forged a sound link between dramatic works and the public. While stage plays were evaluated in a culturally alienating way according to their degree of conformity to European French models, radio drama was right from the start an indigenous product for an immediate audience. In their works, the authors looked at the problems of their environment (perhaps their focus was limited too much to Montreal) and tried with varying degrees of boldness to use Quebec speech.[10] Thus, a dramatic tradition of original writing developed, as well as an artistic meeting place for authors where they could find others in the field as models and compare each other's aesthetic experimentation.[11]

One must remember that the growth of a culture and a theatrical tradition do not begin with masterpieces, but in a modest way, through a slow accumulation of works relevant to a particular environment.[12] It is therefore no exaggeration to say that radio constituted a cultural medium which was, on the whole, more important than the stage during the period preceding the Quiet Revolution in the 1960s. Above all, radio reached a far wider audience. From this perspective, the years from 1945 to 1960 can be considered as a single distinct period, as far as the function of radio is concerned. Since then this function has undergone a fundamental change.[13] During the 1950s, Quebec society was in a somnolent stage, stuck in the rut of post-war security and the Duplessis regime. When television arrived in Quebec in 1952, it quickly gained a large audience, which radio had prepared for it over the years.[14]

Helped by radio, television quickly activated dramatic writing, especially in the Montreal area. From its very first season, TV helped young authors such as Marcel Dubé and Claude Jutra. Then, in the following years, Guy Dufresne, Yves Thériault, Pierre Dagenais, and Félix Leclerc produced television plays. Later, Quebec novels (*Les Plouffe* by Roger Lemelin, *Le Survenant* by Germaine Guèvremont) started to appear in serial form on television. The first producers of these serials came from the film industry while many of the authors had already written for the stage. The new medium offered them a certain security and at the same time brought their works to a wide audience.[15]

Like the radio serial, the television serial is akin to the stage drama in that it uses dialogue and dramatic structures, including the division into acts. Conversely, it extends the duration of the action considerably.[16] In his assessment of the first five years of television, Gérard Laurence reminds us that even though television seemed to be the natural heir to the theatre, it nevertheless constituted a different mode of communication.[17] It was a matter of *transforming* the materials of the stage, rather than *transposing* them to the TV screen. Those years thus witnessed the search for a policy for TV drama, specific formulas for the new medium (whose possibilities were only gradually discovered), and the development of a repertoire of Quebec plays. Fortunately an audience in the making showed a good deal of tolerance towards the groping errors which occurred. During this period, 108 thirty-minute scripts and 20 ninety-minute scripts were produced by Quebec's own authors. In other words, Quebec TV drama made up 47.3% of broadcasting time devoted to theatre.

The desire on the part of the first TV producers to create a drama distinct from radio serials led to an obsession with the image. This was also due to the fact that these producers had first worked in film. But soon, the conceptions of the stage seemed to intrude, and it was difficult to discover the unique character of the new medium, somewhere between cinema and the stage. A period of confusion followed one of experimentation, and then a degree of mastery of the medium was attained. By 1957, five years after the beginning of television, the major remaining problem was the paucity of Quebec plays suitable for adaptation to the small screen, which would also be "morally irreproachable." (This was during an era when morals, ideology and language were still subject to censorship.) At the time local dramaturgy hardly existed. So, one could no longer call upon the rural idyllic *oeuvres du terroir* to fill the space reserved for theatre in the TV schedules. People expected the new medium to attract new authors. But it was soon realized that this was no easy task. Finally, in 1956 Radio-Canada opened a script department which collected plays, evaluated them, and then gave advice to authors. In this half-decade, Québécois scripts took a total of 27.6% of the broadcast time allotted for television drama. Altogether, 56 writers participated in this upsurge of literary production.[18]

Until 1972, the efforts of Radio-Canada, the main sponsor of TV drama, did in fact promote new authors and original works. And a veritable explosion occurred, resulting in an average of one original TV play being shown every two weeks. Some of these were outstanding, for example: *Zone* (1953), by Marcel Dubé; *Au coeur de la rose,* (1958), by Pierre Perrault; *Sous le règne d'Augusta* (1963), by Robert Choquette; *Tuez le veau gras* (1965), by Claude Jasmin; *Un cri qui vient de loin* (1965), by Françoise Loranger; *Table tournante* (1968), by Hubert Aquin; *Trois petits tours* (1969), by Michel Tremblay; *Une maison, un jour* (1970), by Françoise Loranger; and *Double sens* (1972), by Hubert Aquin. Several plays of this period were notable not only because of their intrinsic qualities but also because they made great strides in developing specific televised forms of theatrical production.[19]

Because of the growing success of television, radio broadcasting of the 1960s and 70s had to undergo various changes. It ceased to be a major medium for literary texts (which were then taken over by the FM network of Radio-Canada); it focussed on music and news, politics, and open-line shows (which one could call a form of drama). In short, radio was mainly concerned with day-to-day events.

From 1965 to 1967, Quebec drama practically disappeared from radio. From 1968 to 1973, however, original plays were on the rise again, even though their relative weight was less than it had been up to 1960, when drama comprised the major part of literary programming. There were many reasons for this decline, including prohibitive costs, a lack of good scripts and the indifference of playwrights

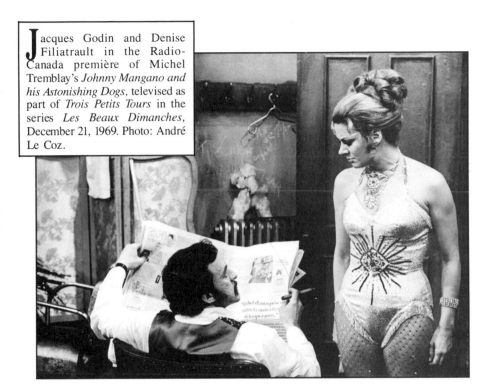

Jacques Godin and Denise Filiatrault in the Radio-Canada première of Michel Tremblay's *Johnny Mangano and his Astonishing Dogs*, televised as part of *Trois Petits Tours* in the series *Les Beaux Dimanches*, December 21, 1969. Photo: André Le Coz.

to this medium. But a more basic cause may have been the attitudes of the supervisors of radio drama, who harboured elitist and narrow conceptions of culture, and, therefore, of theatre. This is the theory put forward by Pierre Lavoie in his assessment of the 1968-1973 period in radio.[20]

As for television drama, the rapid expansion of its first decade was followed by a sharp fall. From 1965 to 1973, this situation was quite bleak, with an average of 4.4 original plays per year. The graphs on the following demonstrates the vicissitudes of Quebec drama on the TV screen, as well as on radio and the stage for the same period.[21]

A tabulation for the 1978-79 television season reveals that 20 Québécois scripts were screened, which adds up to 74% of dramatic programming, compared to 31% in 1957. This is indicative of the resurgence at the end of the 1970s of Quebec drama which was very promising, thanks in part to the launching by Radio-Canada of *Scénario,* a program which relied on little known authors and producers.[22] Radio-Québec took a similar step with *Contrejour,* in 1979. Unfortunately, these two programs have since been withdrawn.

In the course of the same season in radio (1978-79), 89 Québécois scripts were broadcast, the equivalent of 61.8% of the total dramatic output. 85% of these scripts were original productions. This translates into a weekly average of three drama scripts filling three programs devoted to dramatic writing. (One can also observe that production was becoming decentralized—many programs were produced by affiliated stations outside of Montreal.)

These data reveal that at the end of the 1970s, Quebec dramaturgy was in the process of reclaiming the position which it had lost from 1960-1973 as a vital cultural sector.[23]

Currently, as part of the 1984-85 season, there are two Québécois TV drama programs on Radio-Québec, seven on Radio-Canada, in addition to many documentary drama serials (*Duplessis,* etc.) and seven drama serials on Radio-Canada. The private Télémétropole network has also scheduled six drama serials. This genre, which had fallen out of favour in the 1970s, seems to be regaining ground. Of these drama serials, several are devoted to the pre-World War II era, World War II, or the post-war era (and in certain ones, one can see the importance of *radio* in family life of the period).

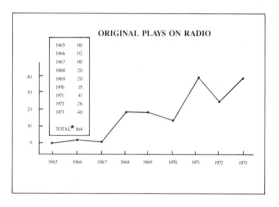

* This total is incomplete because it was impossible, in some cases, to know the title or the author of a play. Nevertheless, there were few such instances and therefore the general trends indicated here are exact.

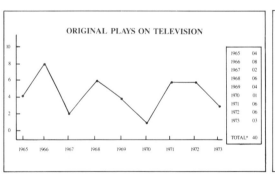

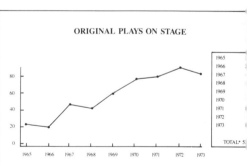

As far as CBF-FM is concerned, two programs a week broadcast Quebec drama in addition to an annual radio play competition.

It is difficult to evaluate accurately the real influence which dramatic texts exerted on television. What is certain, though, is that what was lost in intensity was made up for by the cumulative effect of a series of programs, especially drama serials. The TV serial, to its credit, is more popular, though less intense than the individual televised play. No outstanding TV play, no matter how powerful, could ever have reached as many people as, for example, *Les Belles Histoires des pays d'en haut,* by Claude-Henri Grignon, in which viewers rediscovered their rural roots.[24] Pierre Gauvreau's *Le Temps d'une paix,* currently showing on Radio-Canada, has had a similar impact.

Yet, in spite of the undeniable role which television has played and continues to play in the coming of age of dramaturgy, this medium still has its limitations. Besides being tied to the ratings, which influence programming decisions, television can never be a substitute for the live physical contact which an actor establishes with a theatre audience.[25] Also, a play on a the small screen basically functions as light entertainment, that is to say, as an escape.[26] When one watches a TV show at home, one cannot be expected to have the same degree of receptivity as during the deliberate act of setting out for the theatre and buying a ticket. As well, the TV viewers' isolation can easily lead to conformity of thought, not to mention the shorter attention span caused by the telephone and other domestic intrusions. Television's future development will have to be cognizant of these constraints and ambiguities.[27]

The Radio-Canada television network has played a most active part in promoting Quebec plays by Montreal writers.[28] It built on the achievements of radio which had already secured a place for drama in cultural life, and created a sort of social and family ritual around it.[29] Dramatic writing expanded its scope, thanks to television, and has had a profound influence on our society. Through this medium, drama took on a much greater and unique social importance. That is why it is important to examine and to evaluate periodically the trends in TV scripts.[30]

One can still deplore, however, the fact that, unlike radio, television has not kept up with the pace of progress of stage drama. "If these three means of dramatic expression were functioning in harmony, we would probably have one of the most impressive forms of dramaturgy in the world," suggests Pierre Lavoie.[31] We need a radio and TV policy stressing the development of our own autonomous culture. Such a policy would by no means exclude foreign scripts, but, rather, give an equal place to Quebec texts. There is no doubt that by developing Quebec drama, television makes it possible for viewers to develop a self-image which, under the right circumstances, can strengthen their cultural consciousness. What matters is to determine what kind of self-image and what kind of culture one wants. Thus, we have reached a point where we need to reflect on our experiences and define them.[32]

Such a concerted effort, the absence of which is deplorable, has or will become even more necessary with the advent of "cablevision" and Pay TV (both of which attract viewers to foreign programs), as well as the growing popularity of the video cassette which allows viewers to make up their own TV schedule. For Quebec dramaturgy to continue to develop vigorously, it is essential to note here the need for critics who will in the future be attuned to all forms of literary production broadcast on radio and television. The lack of critical reflection on this area has allowed broadcasters to produce whatever they please. Courses on Quebec literature in our schools should include a study of radio and TV drama.[33] This raises the thorny question of archival conservation of cultural documents and their accessibility, and the urgent need to examine the history of our dramaturgy in an all-encompassing manner.

Solange Lévesque
Translated by Elliot Shek

Notes

[1] Pierre Pagé, *Répertoire des oeuvres de la littérature radiophonique québécoise 1930-1970.* Montreal, Fides, 1975. pp. 13-81.

[2] Claude Gonthier, "L'Influence de Radio-Canada sur les dramaturges montréalais", *Critère,* No. 21, 1978. pp. 57-80.

[3] Pagé.

[4] Gonthier.

[5] Pagé.

[6] Idem.

[7] Idem.

[8] Louise Blouin, *Répertoire du théâtre français et étranger à la radio québécoise 1939-1949.* Mémoire de maîtrise en lettres, U.Q.T.R., 1979.

[9] Pagé.

[10] Idem.

[11] Gérard Laurence, "La Rencontre du théâtre et de la télévision au Québec (1952-1957)", *Etudes Littéraires,* Vol. 14, No. 2, August 1981. pp. 215-249.

[12] Pagé.

[13] Idem.

[14] Gonthier.

[15] Idem.

[16] Renée Legris and Pierre Pagé, "Le théâtre à la radio et à la télévision au Québec", *Le Théâtre canadien-français.* Archives des lettres Canadiennes, Vol. 5. Montreal, Fides, 1973. pp. 291-318.

[17] Laurence.

[18] Idem.

[19] Legris and Pagé.

[20] Pierre Lavoie, "Québec/bilan tranquille d'une révolution théâtrale", *Jeu,* No. 6, 1977. pp. 47-61.

[21] Idem.

[22] Pierre Lavoie, "'Ici Radio-Canada'", *Jeu,* No. 12, 1979. pp. 89-100.

[23] Idem.

[24] Pierre Pagé and Renée Legris, *Répertoire des dramatiques québécoises à la télévision 1952-1977.* Montreal, Fides, Coll. Archives québécoises de la radio et de la télévision, Vol. 3, 1977. pp. 13-40.

[25] Idem.

[26] Laurence.

[27] Pierre Pagé and Renée Legris, *Répertoire des dramatiques québécoises à la télévision 1952-1977.*

[28] Gonthier.

[29] Renée Legris and Pierre Pagé, "Le Théâtre à la radio et à la télévision au Québec".

[30] Pierre Pagé and Renée Legris, *Répertoire des dramatiques québécoises à la télévision 1952-1977.*

[31] Pierre Lavoie. "Québec/bilan tranquille d'une révolution théâtrale".

[32] Idem.

[33] Renée Legris and Pierre Pagé, "Le Théâtre à la radio et à la télévision au Québec".

PART FOUR

The Canadian Performing Arts Mosaic

Indigenous Theatre: Indian and Eskimo Ritual Drama

The ritual dramas of Canada's indigenous peoples, although unique to the Indians and Eskimos[1] of this country, are part of a much larger complex of great antiquity—the universal ritual drama of *homo sapiens*. Modern performances must be understood in the context of the past.

We can see the ritual dramas of the first of our species on cave walls deep under the earth: pictures of dancers in animal heads, skins and horns who try to control the birds and the beasts, weather and fire, the hunt and fertility. These rituals spread over the world after the ice ages, reaching the Americas with the tribes who came over "the Aleutian bridge."[2] Antique rituals became the origins of all later theatre, yet in different ways in different places. The same type of ritual drama continues today wherever farming and commerce have not spread: Siberia, central Australia, the Kalahari, remote South East Asia, and inaccessible parts of America. Annually, however, these areas are reduced and the ceremonies dwindle. Fortunately some Eskimo and Indian performances retain their past glories. Essentially religious events, they also contain proto-theatrical elements of the kind upon which modern theatre is based.

Ancient Hunting Ritual Dramas

In antique times, rituals and myths were one: they were *ritual-myths*. The myth (story) *was* the ritual (action) and vice versa.[3] They concerned the spirits. The everyday world was an illusion while the world of the spirits was the "other reality."[4] Spirits lived both in the sky and under the earth—"upper world" and "lower world"[5]—to be joined by the dead as "ancestors," and all such spirits had powers that might help or hinder the living. The first ritual-myths are known as "origin myths" because they told of the creation of the cosmos and all of life through spiritual powers.

The hunter's priests are known as shamans, magicians, sorcerers, or "doctors."[6] Shamans worked for the tribe's benefit:[7] they cured sickness, brought rain, controlled fire, forecast annual events, and so forth. Shamans performed two kinds of ritual, both through ecstatic possession. In the first they were initiated in a death-and-resurrection ceremony: their mundane personality was "killed" and a new shamanic personality was "re-born." Second, they performed rituals to help the community: in out-of-body experiences their souls travelled to the "other reality" bringing back effective power for the people. Both types of shamanic ritual are pictured on the walls of the paleolithic caves, on Ayres Rock in Australia, in Bushman rock art in Africa, and on thousands of rocks all over North America.

The people also had their own ritual dramas. Each tribe developed "secret societies," or "clubs:" age groups of one sex. They had two kinds of ritual. In the first, like the shamans, they were possessed when initiated into a "society." Second, each "society" enacted its own ritual-myths in which the spirits performed in masks, costumes, and with theatrical effects. The audiences for these spirit-plays and dances were "witnesses" in the biblical sense rather than spectators.

The rituals of the shamans and "societies" were performed all over the pre-historic world. Although they had similar *structures* (initiations, shamanic cur-ing, and spirit-plays and dances) and similar *themes* (e.g. death-and-resurrection), their *plots* and *performance styles* differed with the demands of the environment and the needs of the tribe. These similarities and differences can not only be seen when we compare one culture with another (Siberia with North America, for example); they also affected the ways in which the art form of theatre emerged in later cultures.[8]

North America

When the white man arrived, each native tribe on the continent had evolved its own rituals based on the ancient traditions: the Central American civilizations mingled hunting and farming rituals into great dramatic festivals, as with the modern Hopi of Arizona; the Plains Indians, dependent upon the buffalo, centered their ceremonials on animal life; the North West Coast whalers and fishermen had an abundance of food and leisure to enrich their ritual dramas; in contrast, Eskimos, always on the edge of subsistence in their extreme climate, developed smaller but no less powerful ceremonies. Nowhere, however, had the theatre form completely evolved.

The white invaders seriously affected the indigenous performances. The mis-sionaries regarded them as "pagan" while the deliberate destruction of native cultures and the spread of European diseases so reduced the population that some performances disappeared. Others became secret under threat of punishment. Still others became disused when the native people found them ineffective before the white man's "progress." By the early twentieth century, the native ritual drama was at its lowest ebb.

In recent years, however, the ceremonies have been revived, particularly in the Canadian West. This does not so much apply to the shamanic rituals as to the spirit-plays and dances. But given the wide variety of peoples and performances across this huge country, it is impossible to describe them all in one essay. However, two vivid examples can be given: shamanism in the Arctic and the spirit-plays of the Pacific Coast.

The Shamanic World of the Eskimo

Shamans arrived with the first Eskimo tribes that came across the Bering Strait at least five thousand years ago to occupy the coasts of Alaska, large areas of the Canadian Arctic, and parts of Greenland. Eskimo shamans (called *angakok*), unlike those in some other cultures, included women. Their initiation was frightening and painful: in a trance state the initiate faced a spirit with great power (often a great white bear) who devoured his flesh; the initiate then acquired the power to see himself as a skeleton and to give each individual bone its secret name; the great spirit then spewed him out and he was "re-born" as a shaman with spirit power. The greater the suffering the more he could later control his body and mind in the service of others.

While initiations were conducted in isolation, the shaman's rituals on behalf of the community were public—indeed, a "witnessing" audience was imperative. To cure the sick, for example, he went into a trance, his soul travelled in the "other reality" and he transformed himself into animals, birds or fish, or fought evil spirits; the power he gained was used to cure the patient. Throughout the Arctic, the shaman was a "transformer" who took on roles. The most powerful was a consummate actor: he used many different voices for the spirits, sometimes using ventriloquism to project the sound; he donned various masks and used great mimetic skill in his gestures and bodily movement. It was a "one man show" of the greatest ability. The audience participated in his theatricality through singing, encouraging him, interpreting his behaviour and speech, and by entering into dialogue with him. In fact, the Arctic shaman is an originating metaphor for all later actors.[9]

The Alaskan Eskimos had many spirit-plays but they were less common in Canada although spirit-dances were regularly performed. The major Canadian exception was the Sedna festival where shamanic and spirit-play performances were combined for three days each fall. Celebrating the ritual-myth of Sedna, a mermaid-like spirit, the shamans used various dramatizations: with a coiled rope imitating a hole in the ice, a shaman could enact the spearing of Sedna as she rose to the surface; or the leading *angakok* impersonated Sedna, was harpooned by the others, and was hauled along at the end of a drag-line. Of the various spirit-plays, one included a ritual battle after which those who were killed were resurrected through water and then questioned about the prospects for hunting.

The Eskimos built special winter igloos for ritual dramas: rectangular *kasim* in Alaska and circular *kazgi* in the Yukon. They had a special acting-area and seats arranged according to social status and were, thus, forerunners of the secular playhouse.

A great many ritual dramas have been lost among those contemporary Inuit who have been "modernized." Yet shamans still practice their arts in the more traditional tribes; indeed, a non-Eskimo francophone female student of mine was initiated as a shaman in the late 1960s. Rare secular troupes that present performances in the rest of Canada do not (obviously) include genuine shaman's rituals; however, the acting skills of the performers can reflect shamanic traditions. Most such troupes demonstrate spirit dances and occasional elements of spirit-plays. This was the case, for example, with the recent Inuit ballet, *Aksaliak,* which was based on several "origin" ritual-myths: of sun, moon, the cosmos, human and all other life.

The Dramatic World of the North West Coast Indians

On Canada's Pacific Coast, most of the ancient shamans have disappeared—there are more to the north, fewer to the south. But these Indians have maintained a strong spirit-play tradition which, linked to feasts, was used to confirm a major change in social status of particular tribal members. The most well-known forms of this communal drama are: (1) the Spirit Dance of the Coast Salish; (2) the potlatch; and (3) the Mystery Play, called "the winter ceremonial" in the anthropological literature.[10]

**Coast Salish
Spirit Dancer**

The Spirit Dance is unique to the Coast Salish on southern Vancouver Island and up the Fraser River. Although every American Indian engages in "a spirit quest" at puberty,[11] the Coast Salish developed this trait into a communal drama. At initiation, the initiate (man or woman) is seized, manhandled and half-suffocated for four days to induce a spirit appearance; subsequently he is given his costume and accoutrements before performing as "a new dancer" amongst the community in the longhouse. In the past, these events were held nightly throughout the winter season (November to April) but today they occur on Saturday nights during the same period.

The "new dancers" wear a heavy woollen headdress and costume,[12] with magic deer-hooves on the ankles, symbolic emblems in one hand and, in the other, a long staff with rattles. At "the gathering," they enter the longhouse in a semi-trance, led by a helper who restrains their ecstasy by hanging on to the strands of the woollen costume.[13] Sitting on the bleachers amongst the community before the two fires on the earthen dancing-floor, the "new dancers" throughout the night shake their rattling staffs and give out their spirit cries, providing the whole event with a very particular aural atmosphere. A group of drummers (up to about fifty) encourages the initiates to "come down" onto the dancing-floor and rehearse their performance in turn for a few moments. "The gathering" is then over. After various other ceremonies and dances, and the consumption of plates of food passed around the longhouse, the major ritual takes place. Individually each "new dancer" dances anti-clockwise around the two fires and returns to his seat; while performing, each attempts full possession to "meet" his spirit—wolf, killer-whale, thunderbird, or serpent—but the dance is more a kind of general *mimesis* than an imitative mime. This is followed by dances of those already initiated ("the old dancers"), further ritual testing of the initiates, and a final emergence into the cold winter dawn. The Spirit Dance, therefore, is simple in structure and, while it has some elements of the spirit-play, it is founded on "the spirit quest" and the possession of the shamans.

The potlatch was a version of the feast, the ritual and communal sharing of food.[14] It was hosted by a chief to announce a new status for his son while the guests witnessed this change in status. There were several days of feasts, spirit-plays and dances after which the chief literally gave away all his property to the guests so that they would confirm and remember the occasion. Rarely performed before the arrival of the white man, potlatches rapidly increased as the Indians acquired additional goods from the Europeans. By the end of the nineteenth century, potlatches became fantastic displays of wealth: each chief tried to out-do the rest and, as the giver of the potlatch expected a recipient, when he potlatched, to return twice the value of what he had received, this eventually destroyed the indigenous economy of the coast.

The last massive potlatch of the Nootka was given by George Clutesi's father for his son who, now a famous dancer, actor, painter and writer, has described this magnificent ceremonial in his book, *Potlatch*. Over several weeks there were many spirit-plays and dances with spectacular costumes and brilliant theatrical effects. Today, however, a potlatch is usually a one night event in a truncated form; on occasion, also, ritual dramas that were part of the Mystery Play in the past have been incorporated.

The Mystery Play was the most complex dramatic event on the coast; indeed, it was probably on the verge of taking a genuinely theatrical form when Captain James Cook arrived off Nootka Sound in 1778. It may have originated with the Nootka, on the west coast of Vancouver Island, and been transmitted north up the Island as well as the mainland to the Kwakiutl and all other coastal tribes. Yet it was not acculturated southwards to the Coast Salish.[15]

The structure of this ritual drama was massive. It was one over-arching sequence of smaller spirit-plays and dances that lasted throughout the winter season. To complicate things, parts of each spirit-play were performed some months apart. The whole was a rite of passage for the community while each spirit-play was a rite of passage for a particular "society."

In each play, the ritual enacted the myth of the "society:" a hero left the tribe (an initiate was "captured" by the spirits); he spent a long time in the spirit's lair (the initiate was in the wilderness); he captured the spirit's power and brought it back to the people (the initiate returned to demonstrate his new power through dance and song). With such a plethora of spirits, it took the whole winter for all the spirit-plays to be performed. Spirits were ranked in hierarchies according to power although this differed from tribe to tribe: amongst the Nootka the highest was the Wolf, but for the Kwakiutl it was the Cannibal Spirit—and it was to these highest "societies" that the chief's family belonged.

On the first night of the winter season, "The Assembly" of the Nootka occurred: they gathered in the longhouse, altered their summer names to winter ones, painted their faces and danced. On the following night, the beginning section of the highest-ranked spirit-play was performed: Wolf spirits captured the Wolf initiates and carried them away into the forest much to the consternation of the community. At subsequent dates the opening of each other spirit-play was presented, together with spirit-dances by the already initiated who imitated various species and spirits. Towards the end of the winter season, the community performed a four-day ritual called "The Resurrection" in which various mythical details were enacted, there was much horseplay including ritual obscenity and, finally, "The Calling"— massed singing and drumming that so shook the universe that it signalled the power of the

**Southern Kwakiutl
Cannibal Spirit Dancer**

people to "the other reality." In subsequent four-day sequences, each group of initiates returned to the longhouse where they demonstrated the power they had secured. There was a great feast on the final day when "the sacred red cedar bark" was passed to the chief who would host the following year's ceremonial.

The five-month performance of this ritual-myth had qualities and a length that bears comparison with the medieval Mystery cycles. Both told of a past hero who died and was resurrected to bring spiritual power to the community. Both were explanations of, and judgements upon, human events and destinies within a spiritual world. Both had gone beyond the merely awe-inspiring stage of their religion; they thereby allowed secular relaxation within the ritual structure—in both, clowns performed slapstick comedy. Both had a symbolic ritual that centered upon the fundamental relationship of father to son: in Europe it was God and Christ, but on this coast it was the chief and his son—the initiate who represented the whole community. Both were also the main oral method of transmitting the basic cultural values to society as a whole. The major difference was in the use of words: for Israelites, Greeks, and medieval Christians, "In the beginning was the Word;" but on the Pacific Coast the focus was upon the dramatic dancer supported by others who spoke and sang.

The Theatrical World of the North West Coast Indians

It was this Mystery Play that had almost reached theatrical form when the white invaders arrived. The Indians' dramatic universe had so expanded their available ritual forms that elements had, indeed, become genuinely theatrical. Danced acting, for example, had become theatrically distanced: whereas the Coast Salish were genuinely possessed, in the Southern Kwakiutl Mystery Play the performer was *supposed* to be possessed yet was, in fact, well aware of his skills and techniques.

Indeed, actor-training still exists. Masks and costumes of the Mystery Play, seen in the flickering firelight, were designed to be theatrically effective: costumes were both realistic and emblematic; and masks were vividly carved and painted, some with moving parts, for maximum impact upon the audience.

Acting-areas had also evolved towards theatrical form. Where the possessed Coast Salish performed in the round, in the Mystery Play the Kwakiutl used both open- and end-stages, although proscenia were not known to have been used.[16] While the Coast Salish audiences were genuinely participating "witnesses," the returning Cannibal initiates acted "as if" they were possessed, and this was known to the audience.[17]

The stagecraft of the Mystery Play was full of theatrical wonders. There were miraculous illusions like the sudden appearance or disappearance of gigantic monster-spirits. Spears with retractable blades burst bladders of blood hidden with the victim's clothing so that he appeared to die with blood-curdling screams. Large quartz crystals that gave off light flew around the longhouse, as did various colored birds and diverse magical puppets. A set of large Kwakiutl screens still exist that operated in four parts, dividing both horizontally and vertically; it thus resembles Inigo Jones' double shutters for *Salmacida Spolia* (1642), the last Stuart masque, except that Jones had the advantage of Renaissance mechanics whereas the Kwakiutl screens were operated entirely by hand!

Southern Kwakiutl Hohok Dancer

But perhaps the best illustration of how the depth of dramatic expression in the Mystery Play had so extended the ritual form that it had become theatrical is shown in the Cannibal Spirit performance of the Southern Kwakiutl, one of the most spectacular ceremonials in the world. The dramatic myth tells how the hero killed the Cannibal's three great bird spirits (Raven, Hohok, and Crooked Beak) followed by the Cannibal Spirit itself; he then returned to his people with the spirits' powers, symbolized by the captured masks, whistles, sacred cedar bark, songs, and other paraphernalia. In the spirit-play performance the initiate returns to the village "as if" he is possessed by the Cannibal Spirit. He enters the longhouse "wild," crouching and hopping, and tries to bite anyone near him; his frenzy is (supposedly) so great that helpers have to restrain him with ropes; he then dances four times round the fire only to disappear behind the *mawil* (painted screen or curtain). He reappears from the other side as Raven—the gigantic, flapping, feathered bird with an enormous head-mask that clacks its beak—to dance round the fire four times and go behind the *mawil*.[18] Cannibal reappears slightly less frenzied, dances four times round the fire—followed by Hohok—followed by the Cannibal even less frenzied—followed by Crooked Beak—and finally the Cannibal once more, but now "cleansed" and "fully human."

In this sequence of roles, the performer provides a kernel metaphor within which the Indian on the Pacific Coast views existence. The double-meaning of the ritual-myth is encapsulated in the theatricality of his performance, in his communication with the audience. With a symbolic meaning that parallels the contemporary theatre metaphors of Pirandello, the Kwakiutl performer posits a world focussed on the paradox of reality and illusion: we live a dramatic existence in which we have a variety of roles, or masks, as diverse as Raven, Hohok, Crooked Beak, and the Cannibal Spirit. In our self-presentation, who are we?

The 1972 touring production of *'Ksan* at the National Arts Centre. Photo: D. Tozer.

Spirit-plays and dances are performed in West Coast longhouses today. Secular performances are far more rare, yet they do occur. Only the very occasional Coast Salish group will demonstrate secular parts of their Spirit Dance in playhouses. Segments of potlatch performances or even Mystery Plays can be rearranged for public entertainment. The occasional white playwright can write a major script based on the spirit-plays, such as Eric Nicol's *The Clam Made a Face.*

Perhaps the most remarkable modern theatre piece that has arisen from the Mystery Plays has been *'Ksan,* a two-hour theatrical presentation of a number of spirit-plays and dances arranged by the 'Ksan people (Tshimshian), near Hazelton, British Columbia. In their village, this presentation can be viewed by tourists but it has also toured. With its brilliant dancing, poetic speeches and songs, superb costumes and gigantic colourful masks, as well as its spectacular stage effects, it received a standing ovation after every performance at the National Arts Centre in Ottawa.

Conclusion

Canadian ritual drama, with traditions as old as the origins of human kind, has evolved to highly significant metaphors: first, the shaman's ecstatic rituals that symbolize all human dramatic action, both in life and art; and second, the spirit-plays which encapsulate this action in a form that is (almost) theatrical. By reinterpreting them for the modern playhouse, the native peoples have shown extraordinary abilities to adapt to the dominant culture.

Similarly, a great change has come about in the attitudes of white people to the ceremonies. In the past they were condemned and even regarded as criminal. Today, however, there is the greatest respect for the native peoples' needs to continue their ceremonial traditions; indeed, all levels of government provide funds for the development of these means of cultural expression. Moreover, increasing numbers of non-natives are coming to appreciate the great skills and abilities of the Eskimo and Indian theatre artists. Some of us who have witnessed them have been humbled by awe-inspiring performances and take great pride in their contribution to the Canadian theatre.

Richard Courtney

Notes

[1] In this essay anthropological terms will be followed. Thus "Inuit" refers to specific groups while "Eskimo" is inclusive of all such peoples. Also the more specific term "Nootka" is used instead of "West Coast" to prevent confusion.

[2] The land around the modern Aleutian Islands was higher in pre-historic times than it is today.

[3] Only with the later development of agriculture did myth and ritual separate. This occurred in the ancient Near East and the process was hastened by the invention of writing: we can see the beginnings at Ugarit and the final separation of myth with Homer (see T.H. Gaster, *Thespis.* New York, Doubleday, 1961).

[4] The "other reality" has been given popular expression in Carlos Casteneda's books about the Yaqui shaman, Don Juan. Although they have been criticized by some anthropologists, I asked a Canadian Indian shaman about them and he replied, "Casteneda tells it as it is!"

[5] The shamanic "upper world" and "lower world" changed with agriculture to the concept of Heaven and Hell. The tradition that the dead can live in both "worlds" continues into

the present Christian traditions where, although the dead are assumed to go to Heaven, wreaths are laid on their graves.

[6]The shamans as "doctors" infused the medieval church drama (see Benjamin Hunniger, *The Origin of Theater.* New York, Hill and Wang, 1964) and outcropped as "Il dottore" in the *commedia dell'arte.*

[7]For example, African witch-doctors are known to "doctor" (e.g. to cure, or to correct) witches.

[8]In the ancient Near East, when the hunting and agriculture ritual-myths had mingled, the Mesopotamian and Egyptian ritual dramas had similar structures and themes but developed different plots (Innana and Damuzzi/Osiris and Horus) and varied types of enactment (Babylonia emphasized words/Egypt stressed action). Yet neither resulted in theatre as an aesthetic form. This had to wait until the shamanic Dionysos met the agricultural Olympians and Homer's heroes so that the genius of Aeschylus could create tragedy. In pre-historic Britain, the hunting and farming rites also coalesced; their traditions have come down to modern English mummers' plays and horse rituals which, part of living folklore, vary widely in plot and performing style yet share structures and themes. There are many other variants too: for example, the Japanese *Noh* has its origins in ancient shamanism yet the Indian *Kathakali* has a spirit-play structure overlaid with Hindu plots.

[9]In structure, the Inuit shaman's performance may well have been much like the Dionysian dithyramb in ancient Greece. However, we do not know of an Eskimo chorus of women who commented upon their leader's actions—which was the case amongst the eighteenth century Lapps.

[10]This was so named by Franz Boas and other anthropologists in the nineteenth century. Amongst Indians, the name varied from tribe to tribe.

[11]In most "spirit quests" the adolescent voluntarily spends weeks in the wilderness alone, attempting to meet the particular spirit that will give him power—a dangerous process because he can equally well meet an evil spirit as a good one. This power is embodied in a song and dance which he performs when he returns home.

[12]The costume of the spirit dancers bears a curious resemblance to "the papers" worn by the Marshfield Mummers in Gloucestershire.

[13]The helper of the spirit dancer holds on to the strands of the costume to restrain the possession of the dancer. The helper of the Cannibal Spirit dancer restrains him through ropes. Both may possibly have a common origin.

[14]The ritual and communal sharing of food in the potlatch is a trait shared by many proto-theatrical forms from Sumer to Greece.

[15]Except for a small group at Comox.

[16]In a remarkable coincidence, the last known elevated platform at Cowichan that was used for the "giving-away" of the potlatch, was set against the outside of the longhouse with the following dimensions: 60 feet long, 3 feet wide, and 12 feet high. Thus it had a striking similarity to the early wooden Theatre in Athens as well as the medieval stage at Valenciennes.

[17]The father of the initiate often paid members of the audience to pretend to be bitten by the *supposedly* possessed dancer. This and hundreds of other instances show that the Southern Kwakiutl were fully aware that the Mystery Play was fictive and not actual.

[18]In recent years, instead of the initiate performing all these roles, a surrogate might be used for the three spirit birds. This was not only because of the stamina required to sustain such a lengthy performance but also because of the great weight of the bird masks.

A Coat of Many Colours: The Multicultural Theatre Movement in Canada

The term "multiculturalism" means different things to different people, though it is scarcely a new concept. Canada had been a pluralistic society even prior to European contact in the 16th century.

It is the official recognition of multiculturalism as an inherent part of our social fabric, our human and civil rights, that is new, though the steps that led to its implementation can be traced as far back as the 1949 Massey Commission. It was not until 1963, however, that appreciable progress was made with the Royal Commission on Bilingualism and Biculturalism, established primarily to ease the factionalism between the founding British and French cultures. The commission also took as its mandate to deal with "the contribution made by the other ethnic groups to the cultural enrichment of Canada and the measures that should be taken to safeguard that contribution."[1]

On October 8, 1971, a definition of multiculturalism as an equality of status for all groups was instituted when Prime Minister Trudeau stated that "although there are two official languages, there is no official culture, nor does any ethnic group take precedence over any other....Every ethnic group has the right to preserve and develop its own culture and values within the Canadian context."[2] Since 1972 there has been a minister of state responsible for multiculturalism as well as a Multiculturalism Directorate within the Department of the Secretary of State which has carried on liaison activities with ethnic communities and the ethnic media.

If there is any doubt that multiculturalism has become a very perceptible part of our lives, one need look no further than the daily newspapers for a reminder. We encounter it throughout the media, television, entertainment, government, festivals, city celebrations, carnivals and caravans. Concomitant with this, the multicultural theatre movement has grown in stature and importance through the years and has expressed our various cultures as no other art form.

Prior to World War I, indeed since the turn of the century and the time of mass immigration, immigrants gathered in church basements and ethnic community halls to watch dramas performed in their own language. This sharing of culture in one's own tongue in a foreign land was the greatest buffer the newcomer had between himself and a country which was still alien and represented a possible destructive force to his own culture. While there was much theatre performed that served as a tool for expressing the nationalist or socialist beliefs of key individuals who directed the groups, one should not assume that only political theatre was popular. Immigrants also welcomed sacred and folkloric theatre as well as comedies which spoofed their own situations as newcomers. As might be expected, pre-war immigrant theatre productions never intended to reach outside the immediate ethnic group and were therefore always held in locations which served as a social gathering place for the particular community.

In the years following World War II and the subsequent immigration waves that brought thousands of Lithuanians, Germans, Greeks, Chinese, Latvians and Yugoslavians to Canada, there was a shift from the more heavy-handed political and propaganda theatre to theatre which instead focussed on political satires, traditional and contemporary dramas, musicals and historical plays. The popular folkloric dance and choral groups remained as important as they had been at the turn of the century and as they still are to this day. Though socialist drama and political immigrant theatre had reached its peak in the 1930s, the newer immigrants of the post-World War II years possessed as much a need to share a common national identity in their new land as their forbears had. The number of displaced persons who had survived the trauma of prison camps with the help of amateur dramatics and folklore which strengthened their "nationhood" in the face of destruction, were legion.

One of those artists was Sándor Kertész who organized performances as a prisoner-of-war under German, Rumanian and Russian captors. A professional actor and director for many years in his native Budapest after graduating from the National Theatre Guild School, Kertész emigrated to Toronto in the mid-50s and founded the Hungarian Art Theatre in 1958 in "the most Anglo-Saxon city in North America."[3] Amid many difficulties, Kertész persisted, helped by his wife, Alice, and the great number of professional Hungarian artists who came to Canada in 1956.

Kertész has deliberately avoided political plays—"There are so many beautiful plays we like better"—as well as very modern Hungarian plays which talk about issues which would be unfamiliar in Canada. His repertoire over the last twenty-six years has consisted of Kalman, Strauss, Lehar and Schubert operettas, Neil Simon and Bernard Slade comedies (*Same Time Next Year* has been one of their best received presentations) translated into Hungarian, Molnar and Pirandello and the very occasional serious modern drama such as Peter Muller's *Gloomy Sunday,* a true story based on a Jewish musician in Hungary during World War II.

The Hungarian Art Theatre's productions are produced in a local high school auditorium. This is where many of the present day ethnic production companies are likely to be found, having long ago traded in their former community hall environments for larger and better equipped theatre spaces.

Though Kertész' theatre stands alone as the only Hungarian company in the U.S. and Canada, several aspects of his operation are common to other established ethnic theatres. Many of his actors have been professional artists in their former country (Kertész has always paid his actors), several of his stars have been imported from the U.S. and Europe for special roles, and it is chiefly his commitment and driving force that has kept his theatre alive. Kertész realizes that once he stops there probably won't be anyone else willing to continue what he's done through the years. "It's getting harder," he admits. "The audience is slowly dying out and the actors are, too. Before we had 3,000 people who came to see a show—now we only have 600. It was a miracle for twenty-six years."

One wonders how important the thriving ethnic theatres will be in time to younger generations who have become assimilated into Canadian mainstream culture, who have felt the impact of the electronic age, films and television and who may reject a theatre tradition, as Robert Harney phrases it, that "in most cases is so tied to the language of the homeland."[4]

The same year that Kertész emigrated to Canada, the dynamic Dora Wasserman founded the Yiddish Drama Group in Montreal, located since 1972 at the Saidye Bronfman Centre which also sets its budget. Wasserman, a graduate of the Moscow Art Theatre, drew her first company from among graduates of the Jewish People's Schools and Jewish Peretz Schools. Her founding philosophy was simple: "With the French and English here we had a great opportunity to be ourselves." The company, which produces two plays a year, has a repertoire comprised of musicals, classical Yiddish plays, original adaptations, commissioned works and Israeli plays. Among the authors featured over the years have been Sholem Aleichem, I.L. Peretz, Sholem Ash, Isaac Bashevis Singer and Abraham Shulman.

As in the case of many ethnic theatres, there is a constant attrition of actors, especially those who speak the minority language, so Wasserman is constantly regenerating her group and frequently teaching young performers the Yiddish dialogue through taped recordings. Montreal has a larger Yiddish speaking Jewish population than other Canadian cities such as Toronto whose Yiddish theatres have not fared as well nor certainly as continuously as Wasserman's, except during the first two decades of the century. To reach Yiddish speaking audiences, Wasserman has toured her company to Jewish communities in Toronto, Boston, Quebec City, Winnipeg and Ottawa.

Contemporary Jewish theatre, for the most part, may best be defined as those kinds of English-language productions which reflect a Jewish consciousness, sensitivity and flavour. "We are considered an ethnic theatre" says Reva Stern, artistic director of the Leah Posluns Theatre, founded in 1977 as part of the Jewish Community Centre in North York, Ontario. But she qualifies this with the theatre's ability "to deal with the general community." The springboard resident theatre company of the Leah Posluns Theatre, the amateur Art Theatre Production Company, now only acts as a producing company for the professional productions, many of which feature top name actors. Since its inception, the theatre has always had a subscription series of five shows with a wide range represented, including Canadian premières of plays by William Gibson (*Golda*), Henry Denker (*Horowitz and Mrs. Washington*) and Isaac Bashevis Singer (*Yentl*) to musicals such as Fredelle Bruselle Maynard's *Raisins and Almonds*.

The reasons that many of the ethnic theatre companies have remained healthy throughout years of operation, along with others that have had renewed interest from the community or sprung into existence during the last decade, are as manifold as the reasons that many other companies have faltered or ceased to exist after long life-spans.

Ontario's Estonian National Theatre is thirty years old and still going strong. So is the fifteen year old New Czech Theatre which has a regular subscription season of six productions ranging from Czech classics to adaptations of such contemporary American classics as Thornton Wilder's *The Skin of Our Teeth*. Recitals and poetry readings are also presented for a total of less than 13,000 Czechs living in Toronto. Winnipeg's Tara Players, the Toronto Irish Players, the Irish Newfoundland Association and Edmonton's Shamrock Players all promote an appreciation of Irish cultural heritage through their theatrical presentations. Toronto's Armenian General Benevolent Union and the Hamazkain Armenian Cultural Association are no strangers to the provincial multicultural festivals. Nor is the Finnish Social Club, the Finns being involved in the theatre movement throughout Ontario since the 1930s.

The rapidly growing Hispanic community in Toronto can enjoy theatre productions in Spanish provided by the Open Experience Hispanic Canadian Theatre, which also does bilingual productions and generally incorporates choreography and music in their works highlighting Hispanic playwrights. The Alianza Cultural Hispano-Canadiense at the University of Toronto presents plays as part of its numerous cultural activities while the Spanish Language Theatre based at the University of Calgary fills an educational void for the community at large in depicting the life and people of Spain and Latin America. The Teatro Valle Inclán in Montreal is a ten year old group which presents only Hispanic works, and the eight year old Teatro Experimental Horizontes, founded by Ruben Garcia in the same city, is dedicated to performing South American plays, many of them of a political nature, in Spanish, French and English.

While the majority of multicultural theatre companies in the country perform western-style drama, the Chinese United Dramatic Society of Toronto has been performing Cantonese opera in the city since 1933. The elaborate productions, which are presented twice yearly, feature lavish costumes designed and made in Hong Kong and professional actors brought in from the U.S. and Hong Kong to augment the mainly amateur but highly skilled cast. The Society's 800 members and the Chinese community support the Cantonese operas, many of which are over 1,000 years old. Other Chinese opera societies exist in Montreal and Vancouver.

In the active Ukrainian communities of Toronto, Winnipeg and Edmonton, theatre and folkloric companies continue to flourish and one senses not just a commitment but a compulsion to keep language and culture alive. Andrey Tarasiuk, a busy Toronto-based director/producer who has directed for English language professional theatres and CBC television as well as the Ukrainian Bulava Dance Ensemble says, "For people who have a country, it may not be as important to preserve the culture. But the Ukraine is a non-country, it doesn't exist any more and for Ukrainians their country resides in their children."

The Ukrainian Story Theatre for Children in Edmonton was formed as an amateur theatre group in 1979 as an International Year of the Child project. The group is comprised mainly of educators involved in the Edmonton area bilingual school program who are committed to the preservation of the Ukrainian language and culture and to providing quality theatrical experiences for children. While the content has been taken from Ukrainian folklore, both English and the Ukrainian languages are used, an integration which has proven successful for school children first experiencing a second language. A Ukrainian Children's Theatre can also be found in Winnipeg. In Toronto the twenty-eight year old Ukrainian Dramatic Ensemble "Zahrava" still produces dramas regularly while the younger Canadian Ukrainian Opera Association founded in 1974 has as its goal to bring Ukrainian opera authentically and professionally to the Canadian stage. For its spectacular productions done every two years which cost upwards to $225,000, star performers who have appeared in opera houses throughout the world are employed, along with the Canadian Ukrainian Opera Chorus and the Vesnianka Dance Ensemble. The company has also appeared in gala concerts at Massey Hall, Roy Thomson Hall, Hamilton Place and Carnegie Hall. Their future plans include a half-million dollar production of the 19th century opera, *Taras Bulba,* which calls for a cast of hundreds and is scheduled to be produced in 1988 to celebrate the Ukrainian Milennium—1,000 years of Christianity.

The Deutsches Theater of Toronto has experienced a rebirth since 1979 under the direction of Gerhard Hauck who has built the company from the University of Toronto Victoria College drama course in the German department. Germans are Canada's third largest ethnic group after the French and English. There has nonetheless been a stop/start cultivation of German drama through the years, due to, Hauck feels, the more rapid assimilation of the German immigrants after World War II. Hauck reorganized the theatre, drawing on native speaking actors from the community as opposed to students of German, but continued to utilize the university facilities. To date the blossoming Deutsches Theater has produced such plays in German as *It Was the Lark,* a comedy by Israeli playwright Ephraim Kishon about Romeo and Juliet thirty years later, Schiller's *Intrigue and Love,* Peter Weiss' *Marate/Sade* and C.D. Grabbe's 19th century satire, *Wit, Satire, Irony and Deeper Meaning.*

While Toronto has experienced sporadic community support for its German cultural endeavours, this has not been the case with the Deutsches Theater in Montreal, founded in 1952 by Sasha Djabadary as the German Academy Theatre. In 1958 the company occupied the Montreal International Theatre, La Poudrière, specifically set-up to present multicultural theatre productions with German, English, French, Spanish and Italian groups performing on its stage. The German theatre, then under the direction of Fred Dolderlein, a professional who had worked with Max Reinhardt, prospered, presenting shows on a regular basis. When funding for La Poudrière collapsed in 1976, the group took the name of Deutsches Theater and has since performed at the Centaur Theatre in addition to touring its shows across Canada and to Germany's Black Forest region. Many of the group's members have been working together for the past twenty-five years playing classical works and contemporary comedies to Montreal's German, Austrian and Swiss population, as well as to a supportive student audience.

Other established German theatre groups in the country are British Columbia's Deutsches Theater, a fifteen year old company which alternates productions in English and German; Winnipeg's Deutsche Buehne, a twenty-five year old company which produces mainly comedies; and the Winnipeg Mennonite Theatre, a twelve year old company that produces classics (Molière and Brecht), large-scale operettas, comedies such as Noel Coward's *Blithe Spirit,* and new Canadian plays such as *The Immigrants* which has as its subject matter Mennonite immigration.

Many ethnic theatre founders such as Elena Kudaba have expressed their fear over the disappearance of their culture due to the vanishing of their former homelands. To Kudaba, a professional performer who, since 1950, has produced plays and concert programs for the Lithuanian Theatre Company, Aukuras, in Hamilton, Ontario—a record achieved by no other North American Lithuanian Theatre—there is also an added fear that the newer generation will never "be able to carry out the same kind of work that we carried out."[5]

The 1978 Latvian D.V. Theatre production of *The Witch of Riga*, directed by Osvild Urstains.

Attempting to circumvent that problem, Toronto's thirty-four year old Latvian D.V. Theatre company has embraced the younger generation in many of its cultural activities. Inta Purvs, one of the group's founders, singles out the Latvian Student Theatre and the local Latvian high school which has a drama program as efforts to involve young people. "We use theatre as a teaching vehicle for the language," she points out. She also feels that a group has a better chance of surviving if it doesn't depend on one person. Thus the Latvian D.V. Theatre uses four different directors. The company is the only Latvian theatre group in North America and has toured extensively to Latvian communities in Canada, New York, Cleveland, Boston and Washington. Their program is a mixed one of four to five plays a year in Latvian ranging from classical works to very avant-garde plays, comedies such as *Plaza Suite* and world premières of Latvian plays such as Gunars Grieze's *A*

Widower Once More seen at the 1984 Ontario Multicultural Theatre Festival.

Many large ethnic communities which had thriving theatre groups at one time have stopped producing though other cultural activities are still being successfully programmed. The once energetic Polish theatre which was represented in Ottawa by the popular Teatr Polski from 1952 to 1976 and Toronto's shorter lived "Arabeska" company founded in 1970, are now both dormant. Of Toronto's two exciting Italian theatre companies, Piccolo Teatro, founded in the 1950s by Bruno Mesaglio, ceased operation in the late 70s and La Compagnia dei Giovani, founded in 1969 by Alberto di Giovani, is now in abeyance. Two of the most lauded of Toronto's ethnic theatre companies, Piccolo Teatro produced the works of Eduardo de Fillipo Pirandello, De Benedetti and many of the works of Goldoni for which they won the City of Venice Lion of San Marco Award in 1960, while La Compagnia dei Giovani produced plays by Machiavelli, Goldoni (with Mirandolina portrayed as a feminist), Dario Fo and Ugo Betti. La Compagnia also translated Canadian plays into Italian (Michel Tremblay's *Forever Yours, Marie-Lou* was toured to Rome for four days). After a feverish thirteen years of activity and despite Toronto's huge Italian population, the group suspended activities in 1982. "We could have developed into a professional group," says Giovani, Director of Programming for the Canadian Centre for Italian Culture and Education, "but many of the actors felt it was impossible to devote all of that time to it."

Since the 1970s there has been more of a blurring between the terms "ethnic" and "multicultural" theatre due to the fact that ethnicity as we now perceive it refers to any one of our many Canadian cultures. "We are all ethnics," says Jerry Polivka, Executive Director of the National Multicultural Theatre Association (N.M.T.A.), whose organization comprises some 350 community theatre groups, many of them French and English.

The first provincial multicultural theatre association in Ontario (O.M.T.A.) was founded in 1970 with a nucleus of six groups from the Toronto area. Now representative of some 60 multilingual theatre companies, the O.M.T.A., the oldest and largest of the provincial multicultural theatre associations, celebrated its 13th Annual Multicultural Theatre Festival for three weeks at Toronto's Adelaide Court Theatre in the fall of 1984. It has a chapter in Hamilton and one composed of native groups and was already in existence when the N.M.T.A. was formed in 1975. Included in the O.M.T.A.'s list of objectives were the promotion of dramatic presentations among the performing groups of Canada with a view to preserving, developing and advancing the cultural heritages of the Canadian people and the fostering and appreciation of the lingual, racial and national groups. Subsequent to its formation, the N.M.T.A. was instrumental in the creation and development of the British Columbia, Quebec, Manitoba and Alberta multicultural associations whose main activity is the organization of the annual provincial multicultural theatre festival. In provinces where multicultural theatre groups do not exist, the N.M.T.A. involves the majority community theatre associations in its activities.

In addition to pursuing the multicultural objectives of the federal government as stated on October 8, 1971, the N.M.T.A. acts as a liaison between its provincial associations, disseminating ideas and news, promoting the exchange of productions, personnel and material, and establishing a national publication. The annual N.M.T.A. Theatre Festival, the Association's main project, which is held in a different province each year, is the only national event of its kind in Canada. The

N.M.T.A. is also deeply involved in the promotion of national playwriting competitions through which it searches for plays for children dealing with tolerance, cooperation and multiculturalism.

Though the N.M.T.A. is only nine years old, its record of achievements is impressive. In 1979 it was officially appointed the organization to represent Canadian amateur theatre, replacing the now-defunct Theatre Canada. As well, the N.M.T.A., with representation in the International Amateur Theatre Association, hosted and organized the "World Theatre Mosaic" in 1983 in Calgary, the first International Community Theatre Festival ever held in Canada. In 1980, together with Toronto's York University, the N.M.T.A. sponsored the first Indigenous Theatre Celebration to be held in Canada, attended by 300 indigenous/native peoples.

If there is any new dimension in multicultural theatre, it is the depiction of cultural clashes in the new land and the immigrants' experience within the immediate Canadian or North American context. And it is precisely in this area where theatre companies become less "ethnic" and more multicultural/community oriented. The two year old Canasian Artists Group, an umbrella group for Asian-Canadian performers and writers, has had only two productions to their credit, both well received by the general public: Rick Shiomi's *Yellow Fever* and David Henry Hwang's *F.O.B.* (Fresh off the Boat). Both shows have been presented at Toronto Free Theatre and have given Asian-Canadian actors opportunities to perform in major productions. Hwang, however, in his program notes for *F.O.B.*, an American play which won an Obie Award in 1981, unequivocally states that the term "ethnic theatre" is redundant. "All theatre, indeed all literature is 'ethnic'," writes Hwang. Feeling that the term "ethnic theatre" is often manipulated to mean "inferior theatre," he adds, "That is what we will fight as we build an Asian theatre. We will attempt to exert a permanent influence on the stages of our nation, for we will ask that they represent our societies truthfully—as pluralistic, multicultural worlds, where all have an equal claim to their humanity."

Hwang's contention that "we are merely exploring specifics which have been ignored on our stages up to now," could apply to many companies, certainly to all of the Canadian black theatre companies which present the experiences of blacks existing in a predominantly white society and promote black culture, black playwrights and artists. One of the oldest companies started in Montreal was the Black Theatre Workshop which presented play and poetry readings and eventually original productions such as Lorris Elliott's *How Now Black Man?* The Workshop incorporated in 1972, drawing upon all the black communities in Montreal. The now professional company presents three plays a year including new and contemporary Canadian works, such as Hector Bunyan's *Prodigals in a Promised Land, Rum and Coca Cola, Smile Orange,* and non-Canadian plays such as *On the River Niger, My Sweet Charlie* and Pinter's *The Caretaker.* The company also presented a Festival of Black Theatre in the summer of 1974 with the assistance of a Canada Council grant.

In Toronto, Professor Jeff Henry founded Theatre Fountainhead in 1974, his intention to develop and produce the works of black playwrights. His professional company has presented works such as *The Swamp Dwellers* by Wole Soyinka, *Africa in the Caribbean* by Jeff Henry, *See Skengo* by Errol Sitahel, *Waiting for Godot*—with a mixed cast—and recently Barrie Keefe's *SUS* and Linda Ghan's *Coldsnap,* a sensitive and humorous portrayal of the West Indian immigrant faced with the complexities of coping in Canadian society. The company has also toured schools.

Black Theatre Canada in Toronto, a twelve year old professional company founded by Vera Cudjoe, who is also its artistic director, has had a continual struggle

Cecile Frenette and Dave Wignal in the 1984 Black Theatre Canada production of *One More Stop on the Freedom Train,* written and directed by Leon Bibb. Photo: Francine Dick.

through the years with insufficient funding as well as finding a permanent house in which to stage productions. Cudjoe's goal in pioneering black theatre in the city was to share the culture of black people with the larger community. Starting with a series of workshops which employed black youth in a theatre-training environment where they also studied the works of black writers, poets and playwrights, the company's first full production was in 1974, Roderick Walcott's *Malfinis,* an award winning play in Jamaica and St. Lucia about three men tried in purgatory for the murder of a young boy.

As Theatre Fountainhead had also experienced, Cudjoe ran into obstacles with government granting bodies when some of them turned down the company because they were professional while others rejected their applications because they used community actors and had workshop productions that used youth. Cudjoe's answer to the situation was typically direct: "The arts councils cannot resolve this situation at all—they either have to say that you are professional or amateur, which is a very ridiculous situation.... When I use the word professional, I'm talking about the quality of the work."[6]

Nonetheless, Cudjoe persevered, bringing black theatre productions into the schools, conducting workshops, and producing a number of new works, among them, Bobby Ghishays' *Bathurst Street,* Trevor Rhone's *Story Oh,* Peter Robinson's *Holes, Dem Two in Canada, More About Me,* a multi-ethnic musical foray into the "new" Toronto written by Daniel Caudeiron, and a "liberated" Shakespeare, *A Caribbean Midsummer Night's Dream.* Their most recent production, a musical about the early underground railroad period in Ontario, *One More Stop on the Freedom Train* by Leon Bibb, is being scheduled for a 1985 spring tour across Ontario.

Other black theatre companies of note are Winnipeg's Caribbean Theatre Workshop, which generally produces the works of new West Indian playwrights, and the only black theatre group in the Atlantic Provinces, "Kwacha" (Zambian for "Dawn of a New Day"), recently incorporated under the artistic direction of Walter Borden. The Nova Scotia-born Borden, a graduate of the Circle-in-the-Square Theatre School in New York, premièred his company in 1984 with a 1927 gospel musical by James Weldon Johnson, *God's Trombones. Tight Rope Time,* written by Borden, was presented at the 1984 National Multicultural Theatre Festival in St. John's. An all-black Nova Scotian drama about the quest of black people for a place in the Nova Scotian/Canadian mosaic, Borden's play and his work in it were acclaimed as one of the best artistic efforts presented at the Festival.

While established multicultural theatre companies tend to vary their programs with plays that extend the recognition of their root cultures to the community at large, along with new works that specifically zero in on the immigrant experience in the new homeland, a number of individual works produced have dealt with the cultural clashes that come about within a given ethnic group when older and new generations lock horns. Plays such as Dennis Foon's delightful examination of a young person's adjustment in a strange land, *New Canadian Kid,* originally produced by Vancouver's Green Thumb Theatre, has toured to school groups across the country and was featured in the 1984 Ontario Multicultural Theatre Festival. Ted Galay's dramas about a Ukrainian family in a small Manitoba town confronting cultural and generational changes, *After Baba's Funeral* and *Sweet and Sour Pickles,* began as an O.M.T.A. amateur entry to a Theatre Ontario Festival before they went on to professional productions at Toronto Free Theatre and the Prairie Theatre Exchange.

In Chrysta Theatre Productions' 1984 comedy revue, *Just a Commedia,* based on the theme of growing up Ukrainian in Canada or growing up Canadian in Ukrainian Canada, nearly every kind of immigrant experience and generational gap is examined with humour and style. The appeal of the revue lay in its accessibility to all audiences no matter what their background. Writer Niki Rylski was chosen to piece together the collaborative effort because she was not Ukrainian, providing a necessary third eye. Rylski felt that the experiences she had in growing up Polish in Canada were exactly the same as those of the Ukrainian cast members. Her original script, in fact, was written with Polish references, then changed by the actors to Ukrainian references in rehearsals. It didn't change the mirror image of the experiences themselves, however, and for Rylski it was a cultural purgation. "Growing up ethnic is growing up schizophrenic," she says. "I wanted to talk about it. I'd never seen my experiences on stage."

Just a Commedia finishes with a song that illustrates the challenge of what is not always such a harmonious intermarriage after all: growing up between two cultures. It is a logical note on which to end. The third and fourth generation Canadians whose grandparents sat in ethnic community halls and church basements watching comedies which satirized their life in the new land have only taken multiculturalism one step further, embarking on a different path in order to share their cultural backgrounds with a wider audience. As multiculturals in a promised land, we have completed the circle.

Jeniva Berger

Notes

[1]Royal Commission on Bilingualism and Biculturalism. *Report.* Ottawa, Queen's Printer, 1967. p. 173.

[2]*House of Commons, Debates,* October 8, 1971. Vol. 8. Ottawa, Queen's Printer, 1971. pp. 8545-46.

[3]Sándor Kertész, *Curtain at Eight.* Toronto, Author, 1981. p. 649.

[4]Robert F. Harney, "Immigrant Theatre", *Polyphony,* Vol. 5, No. 2, Fall/Winter 1983. p. 13.

[5]Milda Danys, "Lithuanian Theatre in Canada After the Second World War", *Polyphony,* Vol. 5, No. 2, Fall/Winter 1983. p. 21.

[6]Lorraine D. Hubbard, "Black Theatre Canada: A Decade of Struggle", *Polyphony,* Vol. 5, No. 2., Fall/Winter 1983. p. 59.

The Enduring Vitality of Community and Grass Roots Theatre

"I like to describe what we do as 'community theatre;' we serve our community, after all."
Jeannine Butler, past festival chair, Association of Community Theatres, Central Ontario.

"I prefer to use the terms 'recreational and vocational,' rather than 'amateur or professional.'"
Richard Ouzounian, former artistic director, Manitoba Theatre Centre; former producer, CentreStage, Toronto.

"I like the word 'amateur;' the Latin roots of the word reflect how I feel about my theatre work—I love it."
Actress, Theatre Nextdoor, Toronto.

Whatever the title or the attitude toward it by a now well-established professional theatre, amateur/community theatre has more than held its own since the beginning of the century. Its tenacity and strength has built the base of what we have come to accept as our theatrical heritage. Just about everyone who is anyone in Canadian theatre today, at one time struggled up through the once powerful amateur ranks. The most highly visible national profile community theatre ever had was in the golden days of the Dominion Drama Festival, a time when a country often divided through distance and politics was briefly united by means of the arts. It was in 1933 that eager thespians came to Ottawa to compete in the final stages of the first DDF festival; they travelled from Vancouver, Winnipeg, Saskatoon, Quebec City, Toronto, New Brunswick, Medicine Hat, Halifax, and Montreal. DDF Chairman Vincent Massey, in addressing an excited audience at the Ottawa Little Theatre on the opening night of Monday, April 24, said: "Eight provinces are represented here at the Festival. The number of individuals who will take part have become a rather formidable army. If the Festival was held in Europe, teams would have come together from as far apart as Constantinople, Warsaw, and Algiers. That gives you an idea of the geographic dimensions of the Dominion Drama Festival."[1]

On that auspicious occasion theatre aggressively took a centre stage position under the benevolent sponsorship of both the Governor General and Prime Minister, and in doing so put itself as never before in the forefront of public consciousness. What previously had been viewed as a social activity of little serious consequence, suddenly took on a respectability few could deny. It was only much later, when the sheer size of administrating such disparate groups across the country overwhelmed the Festival, that the long fought-for dream began to wane. The Dominion Drama Festival gave its final gasp in 1978, when Theatre Canada (it's official survivor), closed the doors—finally defeated by time, politics, and an ever strengthening professional theatre. Yet in 1933 things were very different: no one questioned the stature of the activities, or attempted to devise a class system—this was, quite simply, the largest, most ambitious, and most successful theatrical venture to date. And for 33 years (the Festival was suspended during World War II), as companies came and went, the Dominion Drama Festival remained at the forefront of Canada's theatrical family. As Governor General Lord Bessborough declared in 1935, "Drama Leagues [have] sprung into being all over Canada. Instinctively and without any prompting or previous consultation, Canadians laid the foundations of a peoples' theatre."[2]

As early as 1906 there had been enough theatre production to warrant festival activity. Between 1907 and 1911 the Earl Grey Musical and Dramatic Competitions (named after the current Governor General) were held every year "with a view to encourage the sister arts, Music and Drama, throughout the Dominion of Canada." Trophies were presented—one each for the two categories—in the form of sculptures designed and executed by artist Louis Phillipe Hébert.

In 1907, the first year, six companies entered. There was the St. Mary's Dramatic Class of Halifax (who won with their production of *Captain Swift*), the Toronto Garrison Dramatic Company, the Garrick Club of Hamilton, the Ottawa Dramatic Club, Montreal's University Dramatic Club, and the Winnipeg Dramatic Club. Toronto critic Hector Charlesworth adjudicated.

The inclusion of theatre professionals as adjudicators at competitive festivals (be they critics, directors, or teachers) is a tradition as old as the festivals themselves. Despite the sometimes antagonistic relations between performer and critic, the partnership will undoubtedly continue until the last festival has played itself out. There is, and always has been, a desire for professional feedback within community theatre circles—a serious interest in learning and developing a complex and demanding art form. Consequently, the amateur does not take lightly the often belittling comments made by professionals; the dismissive attitude that they are unnecessary to this country's "real" theatre.

Adjudicators, who for the most part do recognize little theatre as an important grass roots movement, have watched community theatre grow in leaps and bounds over the years. As far back as the 1911 festival, Charlesworth was noting improvement in the choice of plays and standards of performance. (It was also at the 1911 festival in Winnipeg that theatre pioneer Dora Mavor Moore won an honourable mention acting award.)

Groups were springing up all across the country in those days: in 1918 the Dramatic Club of the University College Alumnae Association (University of Toronto) opened with Molière's *Les Femmes Savantes*. On their heels came Hart House Theatre, also at the University, with a resident company called the Players Club. In Winnipeg, the Community Players came into being, and in 1921 the Vancouver Little Theatre was born. In 1928 the Ottawa Little Theatre successfully raised funds for a $60,000 permanent space, and a year later Nova Scotia spawned the Theatre Arts Guild of Halifax. In 1930 the Alberta Drama Festival held a competition in which groups from all over the province participated.

It would be impossible to detail all the activity from the 1920s to the 1960s in an essay of this nature. Theatre, amateur though most of it was, exploded during that time onto stages all across the country, including the province of Quebec. It was for a very long time the only indigenous theatre—the professional work being British or American road shows. It was not, from our modern perspective, always the sort of theatre one would wish to emulate (or sometimes even attend), but it gave birth to many of the artists who were destined to form the body of our national theatre.

Among the playwrights who molded both our national sensibilities and our early dramatic literature in English-Canada were: Merrill Denison, Herman Voaden, John Coulter, Gwen Pharis Ringwood and Robertson Davies. Alongside them were many of our important actors and directors, to mention a few: John Colicos, Kate Reid, William Hutt, Leo Ciceri, Andrew Allan, Allan King, Eric House, Amelia Hall, Frank Shuster, Johnny Wayne, Lorne Green, Douglas Rain, Jane Mallet, Ted Follows, William Needles, and Paul Soles.

It was a golden time in which there was no shame attached to working as amateurs, and no one around to cast aspersions on those doing it "for love." Only later, during the post-war years, as professional theatre finally took hold and began to grow, did the amateurs for the first time begin to lose steam. No one could blame those who took paying work in place of the non-paying, and there was even a fierce pride in the fact that, finally, some Canadians were able to make a living at their art. But those left behind began to suffer from more than a thinning in their ranks: they sensed that their theatre was slipping in stature—at least in the perceptions of their professional kin.

With the emergence of such professional companies as the New Play Society, Jupiter Theatre, the Crest, and the Canadian Players in Toronto, the Canadian Repertory Theatre in Ottawa, Everyman Theatre in Vancouver, Newfoundland's London Theatre Company, and Stratford, a class system emerged for the first time. Even the fact that many of the newly hatched professionals were of recent amateur standing did nothing to alleviate the growing tensions. The split began to deepen and before long there was enough ammunition on both sides for a bitter philosophical debate.

Professionals argued that, whereas once community theatre was the *only* outlet for indigenous theatrical activity, now there were other options. It was now possible for a large number of professionals to make a living at their craft—meager though that living might be. It was no longer necessary for them to work "for fun."

Today community theatres counter that much of what is wrong with professional theatre is precisely that absence of "community spirit" and enjoyment. They also stress that despite an emphasis on recreational rather than vocational theatre, they resent the implicit attitude that lack of payment necessitates poorer quality work.

In a recent cross-country survey for this article, community groups were asked to define the prime difference between community and professional theatre. The unanimous response centred around the issue of payment. They felt that the paycheck was the harsh dividing line. Some also pointed to the term "community theatre" as outlining another essential difference. The feeling was that amateur theatres, reliant as they are on community support and funding, take the needs of their public much more strongly into account whereas professional theatres can (and sometimes do) exist in a vaccuum designed by one person's vision—that of the artistic director.

Group after group sadly admitted that the professional theatres in their community want nothing to do with them, and that it is the amateurs themselves who try and reach across that seemingly bottomless chasm. Yet a cross-over between professionals and amateur companies actually does take place quite regularly. Professionals are willing to access their community theatres in times of unemployment, but are hesitant to admit a connection, or to encourage it, once back in the professional sphere.

Theatre 9 Productions in Winnipeg claims that 2% of their actors are professionals. Theatre Amisk of Dauphin, Manitoba, estimates a cross-over of slightly less than 20% in their six-decade history. Theatre 80 Society of Calgary reports they have a growing body of semi-professionals who take union jobs when available and spend much of the rest of their time working with community theatres. Stage Centre Productions, of North York, Ontario, have three or four professionals in their midst at any one time. Workshop Theatre in Calgary sees a fair amount of back and forth in their group, where some members are semi-professional and many fully so.

The actual working relationship between the two groups overlaps more than is evident at first glance. (No information on Quebec was available at the time of writing, so the visible trends referred to here apply to English-speaking Canada.) Since on the surface there appears to be so much cooperation, it is frustrating, to see the lack of comradeship—especially as the ultimate goal of both is the same: to provide the best possible theatre for a paying public. Perhaps professional theatre in this country is still too young and perhaps its artists are still too insecure; perhaps also, given the paucity of jobs and the competitive nature of the stage, this is how it will always be.

One thing is certain—there are myths which are hard to kill. Critics of community theatre are fond of decrying the quality of productions—yet when questioned it is amazing how little of the work they have actually seen. The popular idea that professional theatre is worthy and amateur is not, should by now be laid to rest. True, some of the productions are poor, and community theatre folk are the first to admit it (but then so is some professional work). Productions tend to be more uneven in quality because the necessary talent is not always available. But the sheer volume of activity also guarantees the emergence of some extraordinary theatre.

Samuel French published statistics in 1972 which claimed that Canada had 500 active little theatre groups. They also listed 10 amateur children's theatre groups, 1,238 high school drama groups, 120 university drama groups, and 200 community college drama groups. They estimated, in total, 31,000 active members, and calculated that their productions reach an average of 2,790,000 people—or an equivalent of one tenth of the Canadian population. They went on to estimate that only a total of between 50 and 60 semi- or fully-professional companies were then in existence.[3]

With the volume of activity generated by these staggering figures, *good* community theatre is not hard to find. Several provinces continue to have their own festivals, even without the unifying force of the DDF. British Columbia, Alberta, Nova Scotia, Ontario, Manitoba, and Newfoundland, host yearly competitions, as well as regular seasons. And while other interesting work does take place during the season's run, it is still the festivals which carry the profile and make the work most clearly visible to those outside community circles.

Theatre Ontario, a community theatre umbrella organization, runs the most complex of these festivals, with a two-tier play-off system that closely resembles the

Dorothea Painter, Trevor Stanley, Wayne Watts and Louise Queen in the 1973 Richmond Hill Curtain Club production of Donna Jean Arnold's *Six Tales of Canterbury,* directed by Cicely Thomson. Photo: Ramon Stringer.

DDF structure. The festival includes four regions: Quonta represents northern Ontario, while the Eastern Ontario Drama League (EODL), Western Ontario Drama League (WODL), and the Association of Community Theatres—Central Ontario (ACT-CO) cover the rest. ACT-CO even holds two festivals within the one—they have a musical and drama category, each with its own adjudicator. Between the two, upwards of 30 productions are staged yearly, making for a very large selection in the region.

The final stage, known officially as the theatre Ontario Festival, showcases the four strongest plays — one from each region. (The regions have their own awards ceremony in which the entry for the finals is selected. ACT-CO has a ball attended by some 1,000 people.) Also included is the Multicultural Theatre Organization, which organizes its own preliminary and makes up the fifth entry for the finals. Here professional theatre continues to connect in a hands-on fashion with its brethren. The adjudicator, (last year Marion André, artistic director of Toronto's Theatre Plus) chooses award winners. One of the prizes of the festival is a series of Stratford auditions for the most promising actors.

The scope is obviously large, the work often very good indeed, sometimes better than its professional counterpart. The 1984 winner of the ACT-CO Festival Drama Division was a stunning rendition of *The Taming of the Shrew*. Directed

The 1983 Brampton Musical Society production of *The King and I*, directed by Eleanor Calbes, Tom Mitchell, musical director.

by Ken Peterson, and produced as part of the Theatre Etobicoke season, it out-shone several of the Stratford versions. The production values, from a simple yet arresting set consisting only of doors and platforms, and costumes made by hand, to an evocative lighting plot, all placed this production in the realm of professional work. A year earlier, Brampton Musical Society took the Best Musical Award with an utterly charming version of the *King and I*. Designed with verve and performed with gusto, this old favourite swirled across the stage to capture the hearts of even the most cynical viewer. On its heels came the action-packed *West Side Story* produced by Scarborough Music Theatre. Choreographed with astounding success, this show could have stood anywhere without apology. On the other end of the spectrum were two very different but equally dynamic productions of *Lion in Winter*. Aurora Theatre and Georgetown Little Theatre cast the shows with sensitivity and performed them with clarity and aplomb. Both productions gave lie to the myth of community theatre as inferior stagecraft.

If there *is* an overall weakness at this stage in the development of community theatre, it is too much reliance on the old chestnuts and mindless crowd pleasers. Too many companies still believe a British or American farce is easy to stage and will fill seats. Often they find it is neither. And too few have been exposed to the basic techniques of group creation and new play development, although Canadian scripts have happily taken a firm foothold. With ongoing workshops (provided by professionals) and the development of audiences which demand more, this too will come. Some years ago an aware committee executive in ACT-CO added an award for "Best Production of a Canadian Script," and that generated a healthy interest in Canadian writing. Others too incorporated this award with good results.

Perhaps one day soon someone will add an award for "Best Original Play" and yet another hurdle will be taken. Newfoundland and Labrador, isolated as they are geographically, have an extremely vital community theatre movement characterized by active playwriting on the part of their own members. In a province that still suffers from a lack of professional outlets, community theatre has shown itself to be not only a viable alternative, but a strong cultural force in its own right.

Newfoundland also has a sizeable high school festival, as does Nova Scotia, Ontario, Manitoba, Saskatchewan, British Columbia and Alberta. Student theatre is dismissed even more readily than community theatre yet it flourishes and has done so for decades. Ontario hosts the largest of these festivals (and the oldest, ongoing one), in operation since 1946, when Ken Watts first conceived of the idea. Watts was organizing youth clubs under the auspices of the Robert Simpson Department Stores and came to the conclusion that drama might be the very force to unite a restless post-war student population. He rented the Al Purdy auditorium (Orange Hall) in Toronto, brought in four schools to compete, and hired his first adjudicator, Dora Mavor Moore. "The First Annual Drama Fiesta" was a resounding success, so Watts approached Simpsons about sponsorship of a yearly festival. They agreed and the Simpsons (now Sears) Ontario Collegiate Drama Festival was born.

In 1984 the number of competing schools rose to approximately 150 across the province. Like its community theatre counterpart, the quality of productions is often astounding. Not that this is a great surprise since many of our professionals started out on the stage with this festival. Once again there is a list of alumni which reads like a who's who of the Canadian theatre community: R.H. Thomson, Seana McKenna, Alison McLeod, Scott Denton, Stan Lesk, Diane Douglass, Urjo Kareda, John Jarvis, David Schatsky, Don Shipley, Susan Hogan, Helen Shaver, Anne Anglin, Giza Kovacs, Denis Simpson, and so on.

Because of its unfortunate classification as "high school theatre," little attention is paid by the rest of the theatre community to this dramatic activity. Yet these are the formative years in the development of artists, the beginnings which affect much of what comes later. The teachers who direct these students and choose to expose them to the world of live theatre are molding the next generation of professionals. And as in community theatre, it's not hard to find the best. Each year there are three stages to the Ontario festival, two of which are finals. The first takes place in four areas around the province and stages the 36 strongest contenders. The final showcase, made up of only nine productions (they are all one-act), takes place over three nights in one location.

Audiences have been treated, over recent years, to the excitement of dance drama, the grandeur of historical panoramas, and the high-flying pace of musical theatre. Throughout the province, teachers are working to stretch the notion of what high school drama is about. Brian Van Norman, a prolific playwright and teacher from Cambridge, Ontario, has consistently broken new ground with such excellent shows as *Flight* (a dance drama choreographed to the orchestral version of *Chariots of Fire*), and *Breath of the Wolf* (a searing look at Spain's Franco). Also working with historical material (even though he departed long enough last year to stage a zesty punk *Dracula*) is B.J. Castleman from Cedarbrae Collegiate in Scarborough. His ritual dramas, filled with music, dance and choral work, have documented everything from the Nuremberg Trials to the British invasion of Calais. Then there's David Daylor from Hamilton, whose consistently powerful entries are not usually based on original material, but whose quality of performance is staggering. He is flanked in strength by North Bay's Marty Southcott and Karen Tripp; their collective creations have often represented Canadian high schools in American Drama Festivals. And francophone Ontario has strong representation from Lise Loiselle and Hélène Gravel (Sudbury) and Norman LaFlamme (Cornwall), all three of whom are working collectively in developing new script material with their students.

While there is an unavoidable emphasis on festivals because of their visibility and accessibility, it must be noted that festivals make up only one part of the amateur scene. Theatre Ontario, for example, has a total of 215 group members (made up of approximately 1,300 individuals) most of which participate in festival activities but some of which do not. Most of the companies run full seasons, even selling subscriptions, since it is rare that a company produces less than three shows a year. Consequently a large part of the work takes place outside of festivals, without the sometimes controversial ingredient of competition. Some groups oppose competition so strongly they have formed their own, non-competitive, festivals.

Much of the contact with professionals takes place during the regular run of shows. Play polishers, guest directors, make-up consultants, playwrights, and, occasionally, actors, all work with groups from time to time in a paid capacity. Through Theatre Ontario's Talent Bank, which keeps resumés of professionals on file, any group may access such a resource person, simply by applying. So while the productions may be assigned the label "amateur," they are often assisted or even fully directed by professionals.

The ongoing blurring of categories has a long history and, thankfully, it shows no signs of changing. Overlapping of this sort can only strengthen the existing tenuous channels of communication and result in a more open, mutual recognition by both communities. A healthy theatre community has no room for snobbery. There is, after all, so much to share and hope for: a pride of common roots in a united theatre community where everyone contributes in whatever way they can.

Mira Friedlander

Notes

[1] Betty Lee, *Love and Whisky:* The Story of the Dominion Drama Festival and the Early Years of Theatre in Canada 1606-1972. Toronto, Simon & Pierre, 1982. p. 114.

[2] Ibid. p. 85.

[3] Ibid. p. 303.

Drama in Education

An understanding of the nature of drama as subject and drama as a teaching method is necessary in order to understand what is happening in Dramatic Arts in Canadian schools today. If one looks at drama as subject, one must examine the drama-theatre continuum. What drama teachers have been coming to grips with over the past two decades in particular has been the process versus product argument. Prior to 1970, there was general acceptance of the fact that Dramatic Arts (then called Theatre Arts in some provinces) was basically about putting on plays. There were those exceptional teachers who understood the dramatic process and incorporated it into their productions. Generally, however, all activities were geared to result (product). Administrators and parents could understand this because there were models within their own experience and in their communities. Also, that was what the Americans did. Theatre programs involved the training of children in "theatre" arts—acting in particular.

With the 1970s came the change in a big way. Previous to that time there had been tiny pockets in North America of those who espoused creative drama. But with British literature of the late 50s and the 60s (Peter Slade, Brian Way) taking hold and such new Canadian texts as *Nobody In The Cast* being published, Canadian teachers were offered an alternative. What these new works were saying in effect was "drama is process-centred learning. It takes learning into the personal realm. Children must organize, interpret their perceptions, and draw on their experience to translate this material into drama. In addition, dealing with fictional situations and problems is an activity that enables children to extend their HERE AND NOW—to broaden their perspectives."[1] The emphasis was placed on drama as teaching method to encourage child-based learning. During the years since, informed educators have worked hard to promote the incorporation of drama into the repertoire of all elementary teachers and to build awareness on the part of secondary school teachers of its value to them. In particular, dramatic art pedagogy is gradually being adopted by English and Social Studies teachers. Techniques such as role playing are being incorporated in subject areas like Family Studies and Business Education as well.

Certain theatre teacher pioneers, such as Frederic Wood, Ira Dilworth, and Tom Kerr in British Columbia, Florence James and Mary Ellen Burgess in Saskatchewan, Harold Turner in Manitoba, Herman Voaden and Charles Jollife in Ontario, Charles Rittenhouse in Quebec, and Don Wetmore in Nova Scotia, had developed exciting projects across Canada previous to this time. Such teachers had a significant impact upon the growth of theatre. Whereas these isolated programs existed from the first decade of the century to the 1960s, today such theatre-oriented projects exist within the senior grades of many secondary schools and as part of enrichment programs and extra-curricular activities. These programs provide students with very tightly focussed opportunities to work completely within the realm of theatre in all of its facets—creating original scripts, stage management, directing, performing, designing and so on. Many important faces and voices that we see and hear in our various performing and communications media at present began their careers in this way. Their love for the theatre was nurtured at an early stage.

Recently the Calouste Gulbenkian Foundation published the results of an enquiry into the place of the arts in the British school curriculum. It found that they were providing "vital contributions to children's education in six main areas:" developing the full variety of human intelligence; developing the ability for creative thought and action; the education of feeling and sensibility; the exploration of values; understanding cultural changes and differences; and developing physical and perceptual skills.[2]

British drama educators such as Peter Slade and Brian Way had influenced teaching to some extent in Canada prior to the late 60s, Slade through his book *Child Drama,* and Way through his two cross-country workshop tours which began spontaneous drama in Canadian schools. These tours were organized by the Canadian Child and Youth Drama Association (C.C.Y.D.A.) which subsequently brought other experts from abroad.

Yet it wasn't until Dramatic Arts started to receive official approval on a larger scale as a legitimate credit or subject in secondary schools, coinciding with the arrival of noted international drama educator Dorothy Heathcote, that the influence of British drama educators began to impact upon Canada. She gave her famous first summer session at the University of Toronto's Faculty of Education in 1971, the same year as the commencement of a Dramatic Arts Specialist Certificate. Teachers who participated in that first course with Heathcote were significantly influenced by her student and process-centred approach, and most profoundly by her teacher-in-role technique. Since that time Dorothy Heathcote has given sessions across Canada as have Gavin Bolton, Cecily O'Neill, Tony Goode and other important drama-in-education teachers from Britain.

As the British invasion was going on, there were local teachers of influence at work. Probably the three most important, in terms of their national impact, were (and are) Richard Courtney and David Booth in English-speaking Canada, and Gisèle Barret in Quebec. As well, Peter McWhir, who conducted workshops all over Alberta, the west and the north throughout the 70s, Joyce Wilkinson, who worked in Saskatchewan schools and recently moved to Lethbridge's Drama Teacher Education Program, and Juliana Saxton of the University of Victoria, have had a significant impact upon the country.

Most prolific in providing a theoretical base for drama in the Canadian education system has been Richard Courtney, a professor in the Curriculum Department at the Ontario Institute for Studies in Education (O.I.S.E.), where masters and doctoral degree programs are available. Courtney has also worked at the Universities of Victoria and Calgary, as well as at institutions in England and Australia. His *The Dramatic Curriculum,* published in 1980, has provided the framework for current planning, implementation and evaluation of drama programs across Canada and in other parts of the world. It is one of the most important books on the subject in print.

David Booth, the Head of Dramatic Arts at the Faculty of Education, University of Toronto, has given more drama and language arts workshops across Canada than any other individual. He is constantly in demand internationally as a speaker and workshop leader as well. His impact upon teachers, especially in elementary schools, has been profound. Booth has authored a myriad of classroom texts that illustrate the power of drama as a learning process.

As a teacher at the University of Montreal, Gisèle Barret has established a reputation of international importance as both practitioner and theorist in the area of drama education. Barret has been particularly influenced by Quebec's unique position as a francophone minority in North America. Unlike the rest of Canada, the development of drama in Quebec has been most strongly influenced by France[3] and, to a lesser degree, by the British and Americans.

All three of the above mentioned drama educators are involved with teacher training. Such training is crucial to the on-going growth of drama-in-education. Two pioneering universities, Victoria and Calgary, established continuous four year programs in 1968. Montreal and McGill followed suit shortly afterward. Since then, programs have developed across the country, despite the general lack of priority by Ministries of Education, for the arts. Because of this lack of commitment, the training provided for teachers is somewhat limited and varies from province to province.

Most teachers using drama in elementary schools are generalists. From Kindergarten to Grade 6, drama is integrated with the rest of the curriculum and is essentially part of the language arts program. Drama is also being incorporated more into social studies activities. In most provinces teachers of drama at the secondary level are required to have "appropriate" training. What is "appropriate" varies a great deal. It is possible for students to enter a Dramatic Arts course during their B.Ed. year without any related undergraduate courses. This means that instructors of the one year Dramatic Arts option may have to deal with students from completely different backgrounds—theatre, music, psychology, history, physical education, and occasionally mathematics and science.

The weakness with this approach to educating drama teachers is that expectations exist in schools for these new teachers to be actively involved extra-curricularly in directing the school play. This is a reasonable expectation. However, one can develop the skills needed for such work by taking specialized courses in addition to basic instruction provided during the teacher-training period. What is important is to maintain a healthy balance between drama and theatre. The advantage of different backgrounds is that the instructor can get straight to the concept of integration and teach how drama can be used effectively as a method of learning.

There is much diversity in terms of training programs offered across the country. In the fall of 1982, the University of Regina began an experimental program for arts specialists, Kindergarten to Grade 12, which provided each student teacher with training in visual arts, dance, drama, music and aesthetics. Graduates of this program qualify to teach the Provincial Aesthetic Education Program. Probably the most thorough training is received by those who enrol in Quebec's Bachelor of Education degree program. It requires that those training in the arts prepare for both elementary and secondary levels, and that teachers train as specialists in two subjects at the elementary level. In Ontario, the Faculty of Education at the University of Toronto has the only sequential post-training Dramatic Arts Specialist Certificate in Canada. To complete this certificate a teacher must have completed two years of classroom drama teaching. In some provinces, however, teachers of drama are not required to be specialists. This is the case in New Brunswick, Prince Edward Island and Newfoundland.

Acceptance of drama as both subject and method has been gradual and not without argument. *The Arts In Ontario Schools: A Discussion Paper,* recently published by the Ontario Ministry of Education, states categorically: "In recent years, drama in education has been completely redefined. Emphasis now is on learning through drama rather than on the teaching of drama." It also goes on to say that "theatre is a valuable adjunct to the exploration of issues and concepts with students. Theatrical experiences have much to offer, but a balance with goals of drama in education must also be struck. Good theatre grows out of good drama."

Other provinces are not quite sure about the matter. British Columbia's secondary school documents place a great emphasis upon theatre skills. They indicate a very strong bias toward performance as the ultimate goal or conclusion to a student's program. There are very definite differences of opinion depending upon whether one sees drama and theatre as a continuum or whether one tends to compartmentalize. Here, too, lies a philosophical difference between Ontario and British Columbia approaches to drama education. In its Grade 8 guide, the British Columbia Ministry of Education states, "after the students have worked in creative drama, and have achieved enough personal security and maturity, they are ready for the *shift* to theatre skills."[4] In Ontario the emphasis is upon constant interaction as the drama-theatre continuum grows in sophistication through the intermediate and senior divisions.

Any teacher in Canada who is committed to role playing as an essential, ongoing part of their drama program would be surprised to read in the same British Columbia Grade 8 guide that "dealing with a single topic in a period is possible, but spending a month solely on one topic would be lethal."[5] Many Grade 8 teachers spend long periods of time using one topic or theme developing all sorts of skills as they deepen the drama experience and work against stereotype. Consequently, across Canada there is great variation in terms of depth of experience. If drama is about students exploring social situations (such as immigration, peer pressure, fear of a nuclear holocaust, pollution) and developing group skills, rather than looking superficially at theatre skills, then time as such becomes irrelevant. Good drama comes from rich sources and the richest source is the young person's life experiences. Appropriate literature and other material selected in relation to student input and needs will encourage commitment and once that is given, an effective drama teacher can work with a concept indefinitely.

W ayne Fairhead shows Jan Pienkowski's *The Haunted House* to a Grade 3 class in Toronto in preparation for playmaking on the theme of haunted houses.

At present there is quite a lot of drama curriculum development taking place across the country. Alberta has just completed a new elementary optional drama program that can be taught as a separate subject or in an integrated fashion with other subjects. As well, a group of drama educators has begun to revise the secondary drama program which had originally been written in the late 60s and early 70s. In Saskatchewan, drama at the elementary level is embedded in language arts programs. At the secondary level, as is common across most of Canada, drama is an elective subject. No detailed guide for drama at this level exists in Saskatchewan. What is being developed, though, is an aesthetic education program (Grades K-9) which will include drama, music, art and dance. The Department of Education for Prince Edward Island has no special documents or policy guidelines for drama. However, as part of English courses (Grades 7-12), Canadian plays are being included more on courses of study. Recently published in British Columbia are *Directing and Scriptwriting* (Grade 12) and *Stagecraft* (Grades 11 and 12). *Elementary Fine Arts* has just been released for younger children. In New Brunswick, prescribed drama programs at any level in public schools are non-existent. However, at present a committee is developing a Grade 12 drama syllabus. New drama guidelines and supplementary documents are being developed in Nova Scotia for Grades 7-9. Development of folk-related programs in Newfoundland have been very successful and are constantly being extended. Also being developed across Canada are a smattering of schools for the arts and performing arts. At present, ministry of education policies for these establishments and their programs are unclear.

Drama-in-education in English-speaking Canada has been very much influenced by British thinking, in terms of being process oriented and focussing upon student development. The American influence has also been a factor, as can be seen with British Columbia's guidelines, where presentation (product) aspects are emphasized. Quebec is somewhat unique within the Canadian context because in addition to British and American influences there has also been the cross-fertilization from France ("jeu dramatique" and "théâtre école"). The American influence, unlike in other parts of Canada has been in such areas as the relationship of drama to psychology (drama as therapy). In Quebec today the emphasis in drama at the elementary level is on working in, through and for the group (the "collective" creation). At the secondary level it is to "make students likely to use dramatic language as a method of expression, communication, and creation as much on the individual level as on the collective."[6]

Now that many provinces have established drama curriculum guidelines and put support documents in place, local boards of education are developing "second generation" documents. These set out more specific plans for teachers, are often written by teams of practicing teachers, and take local conditions into consideration. This is especially important in making known the best sources for drama work. Such materials have been successfully developed in both urban and rural settings across Canada. Curriculum planners at the local board level need to take such aspects as multiculturalism and specific student needs into account when selecting literature and other written and media resources for inclusion in curriculum guidelines.

At present there are projects being developed, for example, in such areas as Integrated Studies and Integrated Arts where drama is part of a total program. In the City of York (Toronto) a Grade 9 Integrated Arts course is being piloted for the 1984-85 academic year.[7] Students earn one and a half credits within a structure that sees them working for fifty percent of their time in an integrated fashion, and for fifty percent of their time in each of dramatic arts, music and visual arts. During their Integrated Arts time they work on a common unit in all three areas. The overall criteria for such a program are to develop an appreciation of the interrelationship between the arts, to provide opportunities for students to develop skills that relate specifically to their present and future lives, to encourage growth of positive social attitudes and skills, and to expose students to new dimensions of learning.

As a result of these criteria, it is expected that students enrolled in the program will, in terms of artistic experience, develop an understanding of the dependence of the arts upon one another for total artistic expression; become active participants in the arts; become aware, sensitive and knowledgeable audiences in the future; develop their own individual artistic potential within a safe process-oriented, nurturing environment; and explore various forms of artistic communication. As well, it would be expected that each student come to understand the central role of drama due to the live person-to-person(s), person-to-environment, aspect; develop positive group dynamics; accept the cultural self of others, both personally and as source for meaningful dramatic experiences; and be assisted with regard to future choices in terms of curriculum, career, and interest (leisure time pursuits).

G rade 12 students in Toronto enact a scene from an original play created through exploration of stories relating to their arrival in Canada.

In addition to drama within the classroom, there is a great deal of extra-curricular work that occurs. This is almost exclusively presentational in form. Many teachers work in this area on a volunteer basis. Within the Canadian context, one of the historical reasons for drama being within the curriculum of most secondary schools has been the strength of extra-curricular activity. Prior to the late 1960s, there were very few drama electives in existence but there were strong drama clubs. For the most part these clubs did plays. In recent years, such work has been significantly affected by declining enrolments and teacher/board disputes over working conditions. As a result of declining enrolment, younger teachers have been let go and often, because of the aging nature of the teaching profession, the energy required for maintaining healthy and dynamic drama clubs has faltered.

Despite this fact, many schools across Canada produce exceptional theatre. The difference between today and twenty years ago, let alone back in 1945, is that a lot more original work is being developed by students and teachers. Schools are creating imaginative pieces that range from local-based docu-dramas in the tradition of *Ten Lost Years* and *The West Show* to adaptations of poignant social commentaries such as *For Colored Girls Who've Considered Suicide, When The Rainbow Is Enuf.*

Productions designed and developed by high school students for young children have become very popular. Much of this fresh work, and the production of Canadian scripts, is taking place at provincial drama festivals. In 1983 ninety-three schools participated in the Newfoundland Provincial Theatre Festival. 1984 saw about one hundred and fifty take part in the Sears Ontario Collegiate Drama Festival. And in the west in both British Columbia and Alberta, successful provincial festivals are also flourishing. The Manitoba Drama Educators' Association convene a festival annually as well. Often debated with regard to these festivals is the subject of competition. Certainly all of them tend to emphasize the prime importance of participation to learn. Student involvement with extra-curricular production, especially within an inter-school context, can promote and highlight the presentational aspect of the drama-theatre continuum. Such qualities as the encouragement of cross-grade interaction between students have set the scene for acceptance by administrators of the value that is inherent in the dramatic process.

Besides enrichment through participation in extra-curricular activities, students sometimes have the opportunity of working with professional artists in their classrooms. The artists are usually sponsored by boards of education, arts councils and, on occasion, provincial ministries. Individual teachers, when their budgets allow, also design their year's program in such a way as to integrate specific artists into the sequence of a particular course. Through such visits students and teachers are exposed to experts. Skills are taught and commitment to the arts is transmitted. Such involvement supplements the on-going work of the drama teacher. Projects can include playwrights-in-residence; mime, movement and mask artists; designers; and a wide variety of other drama-related artists.

During the past fifteen years in particular, theatre companies that develop theatre especially for young people have increased in number and improved in quality. These companies tour schools from September to June. They also perform during the summer, both outside of the educational structure and for summer school programs. As a result, children in remote, rural areas get to see and participate in high quality theatre experiences which, in the past, were not easily available. Students living in urban centres have the advantage of being able to attend live theatre on a regular basis if economics permit. What is exciting about some of the touring companies is that they are modelled very much upon the British Theatre-in-Education (T.I.E.) troupes.

Before a company such as Carousel Players (St. Catharines, Ontario) goes into a school, pre-activities material is sent to the teaching staff in order that they can prepare children for the play. Quite often the work is participatory in structure so that students learn about the content of the piece by "doing" and being involved actively in the action of the dramatic event. Sue and Ken Kramer's Globe Theatre in Regina pioneered this approach to children's theatre in the late 60s. When the actual drama-theatre experience is over, individual performers visit classrooms and lead discussions with the students and their teacher. Often they also involve the class in further dramatic activities. When the company leaves the school, they also leave post-activities with the staff so that the drama can be extended. As a result, the experience is much more than a quick forty-five minute performance.

Because of the traditional viewpoint of the arts being an educational "frill," drama educators in particular have had to battle tenaciously with often stubborn, ill-informed school officials. The battle seems to have paid off—up until this point.

What will happen as the country moves into a more conservative political era remains to be seen. Apart from a few enlightened individuals, what has influenced the progress of drama-in-education more than anything else has been the pressure exerted by such organizations as the Association of British Columbia Drama Educators, L'Association des Professeurs d'Expression Dramatique du Québec and the Council of Drama in Education (C.O.D.E.). Recently the Canadian Child and Youth Drama Association changed its name to CCYDA—Drama Canada Inc. in an effort to unify drama educators. Most recently a new organization was created, the Dramatic Arts Consultants' Association of Ontario, the first association of its kind in Canada.

The roots of drama-in-education, however, lie with the early pioneers who were in charge of school productions and who, on occasion, even taught elements of theatre within the curriculum. Today, drama is accepted as both subject and teaching method. In its present manifestations, it has the capability in the hands of good teachers to assist young Canadians in exploring their identity and place; to facilitate the development of self-confidence; to help bring about an understanding and acceptance of both the commonalities and cultural differences of others; to develop skills of speech, thought and written expression; to assist in the acquisition and understanding of symbols; to nurture a love for live theatre, an understanding of the drama process, and respect for the artists through whom our essential culture grows and blossoms; and to explore co-operatively and individually one's own talents and gifts. Through drama, students are being helped on their journey toward self-fulfillment and, as such, it is of prime importance to the learning process.

Wayne Fairhead

Notes

[1] Robert Barton (Co-ordinating Editor) and David Booth (Writer), *Drama in the Formative Years: Curriculum Ideas For Teachers.* Toronto, Ontario Ministry of Education. 1984. p. 3.

[2] Peter Brinson (Chairman), *The Arts In Schools: Principles, Practice and Provision.* London, Calouste Gulbenkian Foundation, 1982. p. 10.

[3] Gisèle Barret, *Expression dramatique et pedagogie: essaie comparatif France-Québec-Canada.* Montreal, 1982. (Unpublished).

[4] Laurie Lynds (Chairperson); Peter Ajello; Diana Cruchley; Keith Simpson; *Prologue: Drama 8.* Victoria, British Columbia Ministry of Education. 1980. p. 7.

[5] Idem.

[6] *Programme d'études secondaire art dramatique.* Québec, Gouvernement du Québec, Ministère de l'Éducation. 1983. p. 9. Most provincial Departments of Education have their own dramatic arts curriculum documents. These are available from their curriculum departments.

[7] Wayne Fairhead (Co-ordinating Writer); Evelyne Crozier; Kathleen McCabe; Sally Spofforth; *Integrated Arts Grade 9.* Toronto, Board of Education for the City of York, 1984.

That "Other" Theatre: Children's Theatre in Quebec

Children's theatre, that is to say theatre which adult professionals create and perform for young audiences between the ages of five and twelve,[1] has been developing at an impressive pace in Quebec since 1973-74. From that point until 1984, the production of scripts and performances has consistently increased; the companies whose work is concentrated exclusively or in large part on this form of theatre have continued to grow as independent entities; an annual festival, meetings, and colloquia have been organized regularly. Slowly but surely, this sector has begun to stake out its territory, and has developed special and original forms of writing, staging and audience building uniquely adapted to the young.[2] Indeed, children's theatre is "another theatre," a genre still being created. While children's theatre is closely linked to the general art of the stage, it none the less has its own characteristics. It is at one and the same time conceived specifically for its young audience and yet attuned to the most rigorous demands of general dramatic writing. Its most successful creations show a high degree of creativity.[3]

A Fascinating History

In Quebec, children's theatre first developed within the administrative structures and according to the artistic policies established and pursued by adult theatre companies.[4] The choice of scripts, the budgetary projections, the production of plays were all undertaken by managers, actors and directors who were also staging plays for adults. Thus from 1950 to 1965, children's theatre was an integral part of the movement aiming to establish a theatre grounded on classical and modern texts, which sought to build regular audiences in the two large urban centres, Montreal and Quebec City.

The first children's theatres were incorporated into the regular seasons of Les Compagnons de Saint-Laurent (from 1949 to 1951), Le Théâtre-Club (from 1958 to 1962) and Les Apprentis-Sorciers (from 1961 to 1967). Young audiences grew so large that these companies had to double the number of performances—and still had to turn people away.

Later, two other established theatre companies integrated the production of children's plays into their previous adult-oriented administrative and artistic structures: Le Théâtre du Rideau Vert (Montreal) and Le Théâtre du Trident (Quebec City). The former committed itself to children's plays with exemplary enthusiasm and openness from 1967 to 1978. The Rideau Vert revived certain television scripts which their authors had adapted for the stage, offered puppet shows by Nicole Lapointe and Pierre Régimbald, and produced scripts by André Gailloux, all as part of its regular programming. Supernatural and magical elements were present in each production, and were determining artistic factors in the choice of plays. The Trident proved itself incapable of a lasting commitment to young audiences in spite of all the efforts of author-director François Depatie, who took responsibility for this activity in 1974. This company abandoned all productions for the young in 1976, five years after its founding. In order for children's theatre to develop in earnest, it became necessary for companies to devote themselves to this genre almost exclusively.

The first company solely to produce children's plays was the Théâtre pour Enfants de Québec (TEQ), started in 1965 in Quebec City by Pauline Geoffrion. Beginning as a division of the Estoc, a small experimental theatre, the TEQ set out on its own to produce plays and invited puppeteer Pierre Régimbald and mime artist Marc Doré to join it. In January 1966, the TEQ produced a puppet play by Monique Corriveau, a well-known children's writer. As early as the next season, Pauline Geoffrion named Marc Legault artistic director of the company and set a policy which TEQ would follow faithfully. This policy favoured the promotion of Québécois scripts and entrusted their staging to Quebec City artists.

In its first season as an independent theatre company, TEQ produced four plays, two of which were written by Monique Corriveau; in 1968-69, TEQ staged four plays, two of them being big hits in Quebec City and on tour: *Tournebire et le Malin Frigo* by Pierre Morency,[5] and *Faby au Far-West* by Patrick Mainville.[6] Yet in spite of a very sound financial situation, strong management and a most successful artistic policy, TEQ's subsidy was not renewed by the Ministry of Cultural Affairs in 1969. Pauline Geoffrion refused to compromise and TEQ closed its doors with a final production, the bitterly and evocatively titled *Jean de la voile, le bec à l'eau,* by Jean Royer.

The history of TEQ is enlightening. Born in the bosom of an adult company, it asserted its artistic and administrative independence very quickly and found its wings with rare speed, thus proving its vitality and necessity. Under the direction of Pauline Geoffrion, TEQ always maintained its policy of creating new plays as the only way to encourage authors and actors. But the Ministry of Cultural Affairs and the Ministry of Education did not know what to do with it. Should they subsidize the company? Open the schools to it? TEQ came too soon, as it were. Its experience, however, was not to be wasted. From 1973 on, companies and theatre collectives would opt more and more for scripts and performances specifically aimed at young audiences.

The most significant development in children's theatre in Quebec started to take shape around 1973-74. Quebec society was then in the midst of turmoil. After the 1970 October Crisis and its aftermath, the Parti Québécois picked up steam, and its goals of political and cultural independence provided an unquestionable stimulus to young artists. The "jeune théâtre" movement[7] was spurred on by creative passion, theatrical experimentation and original scripts. And children's theatre was part of it. Several consecutive events contributed towards bringing together its most active builders: the organizing of writing workshops by Monique Rioux and the Théâtre de la Marmaille where authors, actors and children worked together; the launching in 1973 of an annual festival which included performances, critical discussions and workshops; and the founding, in 1976, of a children's committee as an autonomous section of the Association québécoise du jeune théâtre.

The new children's theatre movement which began then did not develop as a continuation of its predecessors. Rather, it broke with the past. The essence of this break was to be found in the choice of themes, characters and story lines. Most of the new stage innovators considered children to be complete human beings who should not be confined in a protected ghetto of a gilded childhood. They believed that theatre could offer children something other than light and superficial entertainment. The characteristics of this new theatre can be summarized as follows: it stressed experimentation and creativity; it was innovative with regard to scripts and methods of staging; it focussed its critical attention on the thematic content of its plays, with a view to making them progressive and liberating; its main concern was its young audiences, whom it considered its most important critics and from whom the artists would seek the knowledge and inspiration needed for their writing; and it brought its plays to a variety of locales.

A Theatre of Complicity

The writing of plays and shows for children has most often been linked to the conditions of their production and performance. It took a long time for artists and theatre producers to accept that children's audiences were normal, regular ones with their own tastes, preferences and indeed, needs—in short, audiences which knew how to recognize and appreciate what suits them. The fact is that stage artists at first created a theatre for children without asking themselves essential questions about the nature of the relations which children could establish—or refuse to establish—with that genre.

The theatre that was offered children in the first place—that is, from 1949 to 1965—had its main *raison d'être* in its entertainment value. Theatre artists wished to amuse young audiences by making them laugh and introducing them to the "magic" of the stage: the magic of masks, costumes, stories; the magic of magicians, clowns and fairies. They adapted the tales of Perrault, the Grimm brothers and Andersen, and made use of legends drawn from Quebec and international folklore. *Blue Beard, Pinocchio* and *Puss in Boots* were regularly revived in adaptations which always lightened their content, often distorted them and emphasized their humorous and fabulous details.

Theatrical writing for children during the 1960s was also marked by television. Roland Lepage, for example, adapted for the stage three episodes from his popular TV program, *la Ribouldingue,* and children derived great pleasure from recognizing on stage characters they already knew, played by the same actors. Certain authors, with varying degrees of success, even tried to create stage versions of television series or serials, centering their scripts on main characters who would be put in diverse situations and experience a variety of adventures. These attempts proved less successful on stage, however, and authors soon came to the conclusion that television was not a suitable model for their stage writing.

From 1968 to 1975, participatory theatre enjoyed considerable vogue. *Tournebire et le Malin Frigo* was one of the first scripts to be crafted in such a way as to deliberately seek children's participation. "The better the children react to the stimuli coming from the stage, the better the play," was how the thinking went. But since such "encouragement" was, more often than not, emotional manipulation, authors gradually dropped this approach. Suzanne Lebeau and Le Théâtre du Carrousel tried, instead, to orient actor-audience relations towards what they called "complicity." In *Ti-Jean voudrait ben s'marier, mais...* (1974), they invited children to take part in the performance in roles and tasks of their own choosing. More recently, in *Une lune entre deux maisons* (1979),[8] the actors invited the audience to be a witness to the growing friendship that develops between the characters. Children did not participate physically in the action, but they were accomplices in it. The concept of complicity has a place in children's theatre because the young want to feel involved in what's happening on stage, but in a way which respects their individuality.

Clearly, theatrical writing for children must first and foremost have meaning for the young. When such material is produced in a school environment, the school often demands that the play should underline, reinforce, continue or act as a substitute for the regular curriculum. From 1974-75 on, when theatre companies began to tour the province, the schools welcomed their shows about reading, geography, nutrition and sexuality. They even commissioned plays on sexism, the metric system, vandalism and pollution. It is doubtful, however, whether dramatic writing which is subordinated to the school program has produced any important scripts whose impact extended beyond the moment of their staging. Besides, the schools have yet to find a way of becoming partners in theatrical productions. They have accepted or refused and even censored individual performances, but still haven't found the means to establish a creative dialogue with theatre artists.

The best Quebec children's scripts were written specifically for children and were primarily intended for them. They express the creative desires of their authors and deal with contemporary concerns through forms attuned to contemporary artistic practice. Whether in the form of realism, fantasy, protest or exposition, whether in a poetic mode or one stressing social commitment, these plays centre on themes of interest to children, namely identity, power, fear, friendship, emotion, and relations between children and adults. Their dramatic structures, their characters, and their language have an unquestionable theatrical quality. These plays derive their individuality from the fact that they have been written *for* a particular audience, yet not a limited or exclusive one, which is the usual practice.

The following is a list of the very best: *Une ligne blanche au jambon* (1970) by Marie-Francine Hébert[9] is a fantasy about identity with plays on words and literal meanings (the highwayman steals...a highway, but he is Sheriff Rif's double, and the two characters exist only in Petit Pois' dreams); *Cé tellement "cute" des enfants* (1975), by the same author,[10] is a play of gritty and scathing realism and a landmark work which helped transform dramatic writing for children; *Sers-toi d'tes antennes* (1976) by Michel Garneau is a poetic and political fable about politics; *le Grand Jour* (1976) by François Depatie is a drama about collective and individual commitment whose fragmented structure echoes the complete differentiation between acting and set design. The writing here is eminently theatrical and fuses all the scenic elements to create a production the internal dynamic of which is the search for unity.

L'Âge de Pierre (1978), staged by the Théâtre de la Marmaille, dramatizes the fears and apprehensions of the young. A visual spectacle stressing gestures and

François Camirand in the 1982 Théâtre de la Marmaille production of *l'Umiak*, directed by Monique Rioux. Photo: Paul-Emile Rioux.

movement over speech, this play had an unsettling effect on critics, despite its obvious qualities and clarity of purpose. A multi-media show using to advantage music, juggling and circus techniques, mime and gesticulation, it was ahead of its time. *Un jeu d'enfants* (1980), produced by the Théâtre de Quartier,[11] treats the place of children in our society, specifically in an urban setting. Because it denounced certain practices (parked cars in school playgrounds, for instance), it was censored by the Catholic School Board of Montreal, thus jeopardizing its school performances. Because of its interesting dramatic structure and its clear and stimulating statement, it remains a model. Its invention of child characters and its use of theatre in the round are also to be noted. *Pleurer pour rire* (1981) by Marcel Sabourin[12] underlines the value of expressing one's feelings confidently and freely. Finally, *Je regarde le soleil en face* (1982), by the Théâtre de Carton, deals with ecology and our relations with nature through a script in which the present and the past intertwine with legends and history.

The quality of these texts is such that each deserves a separate lengthy analysis. The authors of these works, be they individuals or collectives, have, since 1973, achieved a mastery of writing styles. Several of them have even moved on to the task of producing a substantial corpus. François Depatie, Marie-Francine Hébert, Suzanne Lebeau, and Louis-Dominique Lavigne must henceforth be considered established authors, and thus their plays merit close study.

Monique Rioux, Claude Poissant and Lorraine Pintal are in the process of defining

Denis Roy, Lucie Routhier, Louise Bombardier and Benoît Lagrandeur in the 1984 Théâtre Petit à Petit production of *Sortie de secours,* directed by Claude Poissant and René-Richard Cyr. Photo: Martin L'Abbé.

the specifics of directing plays for children, while Daniel Castonguay and Michel Robidoux are doing the same for the areas of set design and stage music, respectively. It's from this perspective that I offer the following definition of children's theatre, that "other" theatre:

> This form of theatre poses questions about what children know and recognize, what speaks to them and how it speaks to them, what they delight in and what upsets them. [...It] proposes a significant development of themes and content which can make the young audience feel involved. It arouses in them certain vibrations and allows them to experience situations, places, characters and themes which, while familiar, evoke in them undiscovered realities and point them towards uncharted explorations. Starting from signifying elements of dramatic language, children's theatre addresses itself to young people through themes, fables and characters to which they can relate, and to which they can tune in.[13]

In 1985, children's theatre finds itself in an ambiguous situation in Quebec. It has evolved in an exemplary way. Its founders and builders have given it the autonomy it needed to flourish by providing it with adequate administrative structures and personnel to carry out its tasks; it continues to hold annual festivals (the eleventh, in August 1984, was one of the most exciting); its productions are subsidized and find a home in schools and auditoriums. The Maison Théâtre (Maison québécoise de théâtre pour l'enfance et la jeunesse) finally opened its temporary headquarters in October, 1984. Yet this form of theatre still runs up against the lack of a clear policy on ways to bring art to children. The Quebec Ministry of Education, as well as the school boards of the province, have been asked to define such a policy but have not as yet come up with clear and satisfactory responses. Should children be exposed to the arts? In 1985, it is still the artists who stand out as the most ardent defenders of the democratization of artistic activity and its appreciation.

Hélène Beauchamp
Translated by Elliot Shek

Notes

[1]Theatre for adolescents is in a category of its own, and thus requires a different kind of analysis. Together with Chantale Cusson, the author edited "Jeunesse en jeu," a special issue of the theatre journal *Jeu,* on theatre for adolescents (No. 30, 1984.2). She is presently engaged in further major research in this area.

[2]Children's theatre, within its specific characteristics, remains accessible at all times to any interested theatre-goer.

[3]On the subject of children's theatre in Quebec, see *Le Théâtre à la p'tite école* by Hélène Beauchamp and le Groupe de recherche en théâtre pour enfants, published by the ministère des Affaires culturelles du Québec, 1978, enlarged second edition, 1981 and *Le Théâtre pour enfants au Québec de 1950 à 1980—histoire et conditions de son développement,* by Hélène Beauchamp, to be published by Hurtubise HMH, Montreal, in September, 1985. See also "Theatre for Children in Quebec: Complicity, Achievement and Adventure", *Canadian Theatre Review,* No. 41, Winter 1984.

[4]Exceptions are La Roulotte and Le Vagabond, mobile theatres financed by the city of Montreal, whose activities are linked with those of the parks and playgrounds during the summer season.

[5]Pierre Morency, *Tournebire et le Malin Frigo* followed by *Les Ecoles de Bon Bazou*. Montreal, Leméac, coll. "Théâtre pour enfants", 1978.

[6]Most of the unpublished texts are available at the Centre d'essai des auteurs dramatiques. See the *Bibliographie annotée sur le théâtre québécois pour l'enfance et la jeunesse, 1970-1983,* edited by Hélène Beauchamp, Université du Québec à Montréal, 1984, and the bibliography in the work of the same author to be published by Hurtubise HMH (See note 3).

[7]On the most important events in Quebec theatre since 1969, see the articles of the journal *Jeu* and Jean-Cléo Godin and Laurent Mailhot, *Théâtre québécois I,* Montreal, Hurtubise HMH, 1970 and *Théâtre québécois II,* Montreal, Hurtubise HMH, 1980.

[8]Suzanne Lebeau, *Une lune entre deux maisons*. Montreal, Québec/Amérique, coll. "Jeunes Publics", 1980.

[9]Marie-Francine Hébert, *Une ligne blanche au jambon*. Montreal, Leméac, coll. "Théâtre pour enfants", 1974.

[10]Marie-Francine Hébert, *Cé tellement "cute" des enfants*. Montreal, Québec/Amérique, coll. "Jeunes Publics", 1980.

[11]Théâtre de Quartier, *Un jeu d'enfants*. Montreal, Québec/Amérique, coll. "Jeunes publics", 1980.

[12]Marcel Sabourin, *Pleurer pour rire*. Montreal, VLB éditeur, 1984.

[13]Hélène Beauchamp, *Les Enfants et le jeu dramatique, Apprivoiser le théâtre*. Bruxelles, A. de Boeck, coll. "Univers des sciences humaines", 1984. p. 15.

Theatre for Young Audiences in English Canada

Theatre for Young Audiences (TYA) in English Canada has grown consistently stronger over the last ten years. But the genre still suffers from an unfortunate stigma that delegates artists working in the form to second-class citizen status. The stereotypes ironically parallel many adults' preconceptions about children generally, who are perceived as irrelevant, irritating, and trivial. Given that sad state of affairs, it is no wonder that artists who work for children are held in low esteem.

But in the last decade a new progressive movement has emerged in Canada that has made great strides in overcoming many of the problems that have plagued theatre that is aimed at children and youth. I simply refer to it as "Theatre for Young People" in contrast to what is normally called "Children's Theatre."

To me, Children's Theatre sets out with the objective to entertain—with the hope of developing future theatre audiences. The plays presented tend to be adaptations of classic children's stories and fairytales or original works that place an emphasis on spectacle, music, fantasy or adventure. At its best, Children's Theatre can be stunningly theatrical; at its worst, this approach becomes condescending, facile and silly.

Theatre for Young People sets out with the objective to reflect the concerns and reality of its audience with the hope that the play will give the spectators some tools to better cope with a complex and confusing world. The development of future audiences is not a concern because the present young audience is considered to be a valid, important entity in itself—whether or not they choose to go to the theatre when they grow up is up to them. The plays presented are often (though not always) realistic and contemporary with an emphasis on topical social issues addressed from the child's perspective. At its best, Theatre for Young People can be illuminating, moving and exciting; at its worst, this approach can also become didactic, simplistic and tedious.

As time has gone on, these two forms have become less and less segregated, due in no small part to the influence of Québécois TYA. Winnipeg's Actors'

Showcase, Saskatoon's Persephone Youtheatre and Toronto's Young People's Theatre have all enjoyed great success with the plays of Quebec's La Marmaille and Le Carrousel, which blend fantastical situations with issues of great topical concern.

In the end, the issue Theatre for Young Audiences finds itself confronting is content versus fluff. In the past, adults attempted to protect children from the world's rather depressing realities. Serious TYA artists believe that children already know about divorce and the threat of nuclear war and have a need and the right to participate in the dialogue. After all, they aren't just future audiences—they are the future.

School Touring

Apart from a few important exceptions, the majority of TYA is performed on tour in school gymnasiums. A large amount of theatre does take place in theatres (the largest of these being Toronto's Young People's Theatre) but a number of factors are responsible for the advent of "school touring."

1. Logistics: The population of Canada is distributed over such a large geographical area, touring is the only way to bring theatre to isolated communities. Edmonton's Citadel-on-Wheels/Wings covers tens of thousands of miles by land and air serving not just Alberta but the Northwest Territories and performing for native people in the Arctic.

2. Economics: It is much less expensive to take small productions directly to the school than to bus audiences to theatres. One case in point is Regina's Globe Theatre which has used touring as the primary means of bringing theatre to the people and developing a regional voice. Rex Deverell, their resident writer since 1972, has written dozens of plays for the young that uniquely reflect the political and social realities of Saskatchewan. For the Globe, touring is not just an economic choice but a political and artistic necessity.

3. Non-Elitism: Many believe that TYA is the only true form of populist theatre in Canada. School touring allows theatres to take their work to an audience that is truly a cross-section of the population, encompassing all socio-economic groups and geographic areas. Toronto's Theatre Direct Canada has been touring to audiences reaching 100,000 annually for nearly a decade, with plays (such as Robert Morgan's *How I Wonder*) that closely examine the experience of young people.

The Mechanics of School Touring

The typical school tour will include three to six actors and a stage manager, who travel with the set, props and costumes in a passenger van. A tour will last three to nine months with one to four shows in the repertory. Calgary's Stage Coach Players will often carry one play for five to seven year olds, one for eight to twelves, another for high schools—and a fourth that is performed for the community at large on evenings and weekends.

There are a number of constraints on school tours that have influenced the kind of plays and styles of production that have been evolving over the years:

Touring and Production Elements: Two different venues each day, five days a week means that a fast breakdown and set-up is essential. Most school tours use minimal sets, props and costumes; little or no lighting and sound. However, as quality designers become more interested in this genre, standards of design have also risen dramatically and major breakthroughs and discoveries have been made in tour design. Nova Scotia's Mermaid Theatre has long flourished under the evocative designs of Tom Miller. While much of their early reputation was based on their treatments of Micmac legends and Miller's marvelous mask and puppet work, in past years the company has, with Miller's designs, used historical regional material with success.

The Venues: Gymnasiums are large and have poor acoustics. Tight school budgets have swollen audience sizes with three to five hundred not at all uncommon. Because this audience sits on the floor, sightlines can become a problem unless the stage movement is carefully thought out. A number of important scripts have emerged that beautifully overcome these obstacles. John Lazarus' *Schoolyard Games* explores playground violence with the play set on climbing bars—a situation that not only complements the gymnasium, but often takes place in that very room.

Time Limits: School schedules and the economic necessity of two performances per day, tend to limit plays' running time to less than one hour. The fact that most school touring productions are one-act plays is a mixed blessing. This shorter form is certainly easier for writers to handle technically—and with the dearth of outlets for the one-act play, TYA companies have become one of the few venues for playwrights to work in the form. Certainly these plays tend to be less complex than longer pieces; but at their best they are succinct, passionate and energetic—qualities all too often lacking on our mainstages. My own play, *New Canadian Kid,* is perhaps one of the country's most performed TYA scripts. The play is anything but subtle, broadly examining the problems of immigrants by reversing the languages: the Canadians speak gibberish, the immigrants English. The play is almost two dimensional but the humor and emotion seem to touch a basic reality that connects with people in a compelling way, and within a forty-five minute time span.

TYA Today

Because of the length of the tours, the isolation and the lack of major subsidy, the typical school touring company of the past was made up of very young actors, often just out of theatre school. Work with a school touring company was viewed as a necessary evil in the training of young professionals, who also used the experience to earn their Equity card—the key to getting work on adult mainstages. Because the tours were isolated and the audiences largely captive, overall production values suffered—as did the reputation of TYA. However, the last ten years has seen a different movement begin, due in part to the rise of "Theatre for Young People," whose serious objectives opened the doors for higher quality work.

Because many of the artists began to see TYA as a viable and important opportunity in itself and not merely as a stepping stone to bigger and better things, talented professionals with a long-range commitment to the form began to raise the standards enormously. These artists saw a number of major advantages that TYA had over mainstream theatre:

1. Artistic Freedom: Most adult stages in Canada are artistically handicapped by the pressures of the box office. TYA has direct connections to children through the schools and thus has tremendous opportunities for experimentation and development. Elizabeth Gorrie, artistic director of Victoria's Kaleidoscope Theatre, has built her international reputation on a continuing interest in integrating visual imagery with theatre. Her work frequently eschews plot and character, focussing on an interplay of music, dance and dialogue to illuminate the specific theme. Few practitioners of Performance Art have the breadth of audiences to draw on that Gorrie has been able to test her work upon for the last decade.

2. Social Responsibility: Many TYA artists view their work as an opportunity to really reach out and touch their audiences in a meaningful way. Children will soon be inheriting the institutions adults now control: if their political consciousness can be raised, there may be a chance for a more humanitarian world when they take over the reins of power. Companies like Edmonton's Catalyst Theatre have made that social objective their raison d'être. Using theatre-in-education techniques to interact with their audiences, pieces such as *Project Immigration* force the audience to confront their own attitudes about race by letting them collectively decide who may immigrate and who may not. Throughout the country, actors are becoming frustrated working on adult mainstages where they are often forced to perform meaningless plays for middle-class audiences. Many of these artists turn to TYA as an alternative.

3. Isolation: The relative obscurity of TYA both because of society's attitudes and the far-flung touring activity offers TYA artists the rare chance to experiment and perfect pieces of theatre without the often negative and artificial pressures much theatre work is exposed to, which often destroy productions (and particularly new plays) before they have had a chance to develop in performance. At Green Thumb Theatre, plays are kept in the repertory for a number of years and the playwrights continue to make revisions and adjustments to the text over this long gestation period.

This is not to say that TYA is not subject to criticism. In fact, because many TYA companies participate in International Festivals, they undergo relentless scrutiny by peers in the field. Given the reality that many theatre critics ignore TYA completely, this kind of feedback is essential—and is an advantage that most adult theatre in Canada lacks. There is such an obvious dearth of serious theatre criticism in this country that most adult companies are rarely subjected to any kind of penetrating analysis. It can safely be said that the opportunities for exchange and artistic growth in TYA far surpass that available to other theatre genres.

I have touched on the work of just a few TYA companies, although there are many that have built strong national and international followings throughout the country. The two companies I know best are Green Thumb Theatre of Vancouver (I was co-founder and am currently artistic director) and Toronto's Young People's Theatre (I recently served as playwright-in-residence). A closer look at these two organizations might be instructive because their examples embody many of the problems and directions Canadian TYA faces.

Young People's Theatre

Young People's Theatre was founded in 1966 by Susan Rubes, who built it into Canada's largest theatre for the young and spearheaded the conversion of an historic building into Canada's first major performing arts facility for children. YPT now has a first class mainstage theatre with 468 seats, a 175-seat studio theatre, and an extensive school tour.

Artistic director Peter Moss began his term in 1979, overseeing the company's transition into the new space. He inherited a whopping deficit that was incurred in YPT's move into a permanent theatre and the consequences of that change in direction. Moss quickly renovated the brand-new auditorium in order to radically increase the audience capacity, thereby making the operation financially viable. He also developed the programming strategies that ensured the company's artistic and financial security—a move that was necessary for survival but problematic for the company on a number of levels.

Sam Moses, William Colgate, Albert Schwartz, Keram Malicki-Sanchez, Alicia Jeffery and Denise Kennedy in Peter Moss' 1984-85 Young People's Theatre production of Mordecai Richler's *Jacob Two Two Meets the Hooded Fang,* designed by Astrid Janson.

Box office pressures ensure that the mainstage is dominated by "Children's Theatre" fare. Classics like *A Christmas Carol* (and Canadian classics such as *Jacob Two Two Meets the Hooded Fang*) tend to be solid audience draws. But YPT's spectators tend to be allergic to more challenging fare. When Moss decided to stage John and Joa Lazarus' *Dreaming and Duelling,* a provocative new play that dealt frankly with teenage sexual conflict, a storm was created within and without the theatre that still resonates today. Subsequent seasons have pragmatically avoided such controversial fare, sticking to modern classics (*Of Mice and Men, Look Back in Anger*), an annual Shakespeare for youth audiences, and well-known chestnuts for the younger set.

This compromise in content has not meant a compromise in quality. YPT productions set a standard of excellence that few theatres in the country can rival. Canada's finest directors, designers and actors are brought to YPT mainstage productions, creating works of consistent technical accomplishment.

YPT's school touring shows have, on the other hand, retained a strong content orientation. Productions of *Drink the Mercury* (From England's M-6 Theatre in Education), Joel Greenberg's *Nuclear Power Show,* and Susan Zeder's *Doors* are issue oriented plays (environmental waste, nuclear power, divorce) that schools are more receptive to than general audiences.

The dilemma facing TYA in Canada is that we perform for children who are brought to the theatre by adults. Children are engrossed by plays that come out of their own experience. But their caretakers are attracted by recognizable titles—and a desire to protect their offspring from unpleasant or traumatic experiences. Teachers have learned that plays that are not just fluff are worthwhile discussion vehicles for the school. Parents have yet to catch on to the fact that plays that address real life issues are of interest and value to their families—and quite often far more entertaining than fairy tales, which are, as Bruno Bettelheim so aptly points out in *The Uses of Enchantment,* better read than seen. The future task for Young People's Theatre—and TYA in general—is to find ways to attract family audiences to plays that are relevant to their lives.

Green Thumb Theatre

Since its founding in 1975, Green Thumb has established a solid international reputation with tours of England, West Germany, Sweden, the United States, Australia, Singapore and Hong Kong.

While certainly only one of many Canadian TYA companies to travel abroad, a brief look at the company's development is instructive because Green Thumb is very much part of the national and international movement that I have been describing as Theatre for Young People. Grips Theater Berlin calls it "Emancipatory Theatre" for the young; it has links with the "Free" Theatres in some Scandanavian countries, has much in common with Theatre-in-Education in England and has ties with similar-thinking artists throughout the rest of Europe and South America.

But it is interesting to note that Green Thumb began in a vacuum, with little or no knowledge of what was taking place elsewhere in the world. As the company evolved, it gradually became aware of other groups developing similar work—in fact, far advanced work—in other parts of the world. What set the groundwork for this discovery was the company's artistic mandate—to develop and produce new Canadian plays for young people. This concern with creating serious scripts for the young was perhaps unique in its stubborn singlemindedness which has produced dozens of new scripts that have been staged extensively by other theatres across Canada.

Green Thumb's early work leaned more in traditional directions with plays that drew from fantastical, historical and mythological sources. The difference was that the themes tended to take themselves seriously. During this phase, perhaps *Shadowdance* (1977) was the most distinctive piece. A collective creation directed by Yurek Bogajewicz (of the Polish Theatre Lab) and written by Sheldon Rosen, the play was almost operatic in conception with over half the text being sung, using daring theatrical transformations and bizarre physical imagery to evoke a medieval story of a fool's dance with Death. *Shadowdance* borrowed the safe classic children's images and exploded them, startling many and offending some: several communities banned the show, declaring it satanic and anti-Christ.

My play *The Windigo* (1977) examined cannibalism among the Ojibway people; Irene N. Watts' *A Chain of Words* (1978), was a collection of very resonant Japanese folk tales; John Carroll's *The Nose Returns* (1977) used a fantastic space age detective to explore the moral issues surrounding biological cloning.

In 1979, the production of Joe Wiesenfeld's *Hilary's Birthday* began Green Thumb's second phase. This realistic play about a nine year old girl's problems with her mother's new boy friend was an honest, earnest, kitchen-sink play for

T he 1980 Green Thumb Theatre production of *Juve,* compiled and directed by Campbell Smith. Photo: David Cooper.

kids, one of the first of its kind in Canada. The children found the piece captivating and were sensitive to the play's subtlest nuances. Clearly, the time had come to create a body of work that reflected the child's concerns.

Subsequent works included Campbell Smith's *Juve,* based on interviews with youth in crisis and performed by youth; John Lazarus' *Schoolyard Games* and his *Not So Dumb* (on learning disabilities); Peggy Thompson's *The Bittersweet Kid*(on diabetes); Colin Thomas' *One Thousand Cranes* (on children's fear of Nuclear War), and *Feeling Yes, Feeling No,* a child sexual-abuse prevention program.

The company has found a remarkable acceptance, particularly from the educational community, in spite of the highly controversial nature of the work. This is due in part to the high production values but mainly to a long-term commitment to community development. Adults are the wall separating us from our audience: children. In order to be able to reach our audiences, we nurture communication with the educational community, making sure they understand and hopefully support our objectives. In this way we have been able to take chances—and from time to time break new ground. It must be stated though that some schools still manage to surprise us with a prickly over-sensitivity to the tamest of themes and language. While these obstacles can be overcome, it does require enormous patience and empathy on the part of both the educators and the theatre company; a trust that takes a long time to develop—and that must be nurtured.

The International Children's Festivals

No overview of Theatre for the Young in Canada would be complete without a look at the Festivals. First conceived by Elizabeth and Colin Gorrie of Kaleidoscope Theatre, spearheaded by producer Ernie Fladell, and given its shape by the first artistic director Chris Wootten, the Vancouver Children's Festival was born in 1978.

The setting is, without doubt, exceptional. Set on Vancouver's picture-postcard-perfect bay surrounded by mountains, the festival site has few rivals in the world. The performances take place in specialized tents that are erected strategically throughout the park. On-site performers provide constant free entertainment, and a wide range of activities (from face-painting to kite-flying) is constantly available to the children.

The remarkable success of this week-long event (some 80,000 spectators buy tickets) has led to the implementation of sibling festivals in several other Canadian cities. There is now a circuit of children's festivals crossing most of the country every May.

The programming is eclectic, leaning to the musical and visual. Canada's premier troubador, Raffi, built his career at the festival, as did Sharon, Lois and Bram. Brilliant clowns such as Felipe Petit have stunned audiences; Australia's Fruit Fly Circus has been a box office smash; Japan's Kaze-No-Ko has made a number of visits providing top flight entertainment, particularly for younger children. The festivals have also spawned some very important theatre projects, such as the Green Thumb-Grips Theater Berlin co-production of *Trummi Kaput,* and the hosting of major TYA companies from around the world, including Portugal's O'Bando, England's Ludus Dance-in-Education, Italy's Teatro Briccioli—to name a few.

While there have been some concerns about the festivals' relationship to local theatres, and the festivals' tendency to program rather lightweight fare without regard to the importance of artistic exchange—the overwhelming consensus is that the events are a magical celebration of the family whose emphasis is on entertainment.

Theatrical exchange and artistic communication are still byproducts of these events and some enormously important contacts have been made between international artists because of the festivals. And it seems quite clear that the rise in Canadian TYA companies' tours abroad has been in large part due to the fact that the festivals provide an important showcase.

TYA—The Future

Although TYA is quite separate from theatre in general, it is still affected by many of the same factors that face Canadian theatre as a whole. Clearly, the artistic and financial crisis that has in many ways paralyzed artistic growth has also hurt TYA badly. The form is already underfunded and undervalued, and with everyone else suffering it is difficult to be at the bottom rung of the ladder. Corporate sponsors are reticent to fund a form of theatre that has such a low profile—and an audience that does not control the purse strings. Funding agencies do their best to help but government restraint has hit them hard. The result? Almost no new TYA companies have come up in the last ten years. Less new work has been developed, fewer committed professionals are willing to dedicate their careers to the form. Television and film pay designers, actors and directors ten times the amount theatre offers. With theatre in an artistically conservative trend that has given it the vitality of a brontosaurus, it is not much of an artistic compromise to play an extra in a Tom Selleck movie instead of a role in a badly directed and ill-conceived Shakespeare. Both are painful, but one buys groceries.

Although many difficulties face TYA, there have been some encouraging developments nationally. Exchange between anglophone and francophone theatres has increased significantly, due in part to the fact that ASSITEJ Canada (the International Association of Theatres for Children and Youth) has struggled to remain a bilingual organization. Ironically, severe funding cuts have jeopardized the national body's existence and to survive may require it to create separate anglo-francophone associations. But in the meantime, crucial links have been established between theatres working in the two official languages. The plays of Suzanne Lebeau and those developed by La Marmaille have seen numerous productions in English Canada. It was particularly exciting to have l'Association québécoise du jeune théâtre host a three day colloquium on the Green Thumb/Grips Theater's co-production of *Trummi Kaput* in Montreal. In the spring of 1984, Young People's Theatre had its first intensive script development workshop, a three week project that included a Québécois component. The fact that both sides are beginning to recognize and value the other's unique contributions can only help to strengthen TYA and create new possibilities for innovation and growth. It will be very interesting to see what the next ten years have in store for our distinctively invisible genre.

Dennis Foon

The Growth of
Dance in Canada

A remarkable expansion of dance activity has occurred world-wide during the last twenty years and Canada has shared in this phenomenon. At the onset of this general growth in the art, only three professional dance companies existed in the country. Today, the number and variety of companies in all the major cities is surprising.

In common with many other countries, Canadian ballet and modern dance were originally imported art forms. They have become part of Canadian culture as Canadian choreographers and dancers have adapted and used them as vehicles for self-expression.

This assimilation occurred in a relatively short time. It wasn't until the third decade of this century that visitors performed here with sufficient frequency to inspire emulation. Canada benefitted from its proximity to the two most artistically active regions in the United States. North American tours by foreign artists easily accommodated visits to either Vancouver from California or eastern Canada from New York City and Chicago. Anna Pavlova performed in Vancouver as early as 1910 and continued to visit both east and west Canada in subsequent years. Nijinsky danced with the Diaghilev Ballet in Vancouver in 1917 and the Fokine Ballet appeared in Toronto in 1921. Visits by other dancers occurred from time to time, increasing in frequency during the late 1930s and early 40s as young companies forming in the United States also began to tour. A major stimulus to ballet activity in North America at this time came from the post-Diaghilev Ballets Russes companies; the Ballets Russes de Monte Carlo and their rivals, the Original Ballet Russe. Glamorous and volatile, these companies sparkled with talent presented in a wide range of excellent ballets. They drew new audiences for the ballet and inspired some to be part of it.

This could not happen without access to high quality training. There were few established teachers in Canada who offered training in the classic technique and none who specialized in the modern dance forms of Germany or America. Outstanding among the few were two Russian emigrants: Esak Ruvenoff who joined Canadian-born Maurice Morenoff (né Lacasse) in Montreal in 1925 and Boris Volkoff, settled in Toronto since 1929. As the 1930s progressed, more teachers arrived to make a new life in Canada. They brought their knowledge and stylistic heritage and'set about imparting it with energy and drive. An early arrival was June Roper, a Texan trained in California who opened a school in Vancouver in 1935. During the next six years until her retirement, she produced at least ten dancers who were accepted into the Ballets Russes and other first-rate companies and many more who entered other branches of the profession. Gwen Osborne, later joined by Nesta Toumine in Ottawa, completes the handful of pioneer teachers who produced Canada's first home-grown professional dancers.

It was the beginning. Canadians were successfully competing in international companies, increasing numbers of teachers established schools and the need for performance opportunities within Canada became pressing.

By the end of World War II, several amateur dance companies had emerged. Teachers formed them from the senior students of their schools and they gave occasional performances in their home communities. Gweneth Lloyd and Betty Farrally, immigrant teachers from England, followed the same pattern. They opened their school in Winnipeg in 1938 and formed a ballet club to give performances in 1939. Although still amateur in status, it became the Winnipeg Ballet in 1943. As the group strengthened, Lloyd felt that a great deal could be gained from interaction with similar groups elsewhere. Positive responses to the idea came from the Volkoff Canadian Ballet in Toronto, the Ballets Ruth Sorel in Montreal and the Vancouver Ballet Society. The result was the first Canadian Ballet Festival, held in Winnipeg in 1948. Unfortunately, the Vancouver group could not reach Winnipeg due to heavy floods. Nevertheless, the event was successful enough to prompt the formation of the Canadian Ballet Association to ensure that the festival became an annual event.

The 1949 festival in Toronto included ten companies, and subsequent festivals, rotating between Montreal, Ottawa and Toronto, included many others. The festivals ceased after 1954 but their value had been inestimable. Young dancers benefitted from the experience of performing before large audiences and works created by previously unknown choreographers were reviewed by Canadian and American critics, some receiving praise for their quality and originality.

The Winnipeg Ballet, first to suggest the festivals, was also first to become a professional company. They declared themselves as such in 1949 and upon receiving a charter from the Queen in 1953, became the Royal Winnipeg Ballet.

Lloyd's early ballets showed real choreographic talent, great taste and above all, an ability to communicate to Winnipeg audiences that ballet was not elitist and somewhat removed from reality. Lloyd's artistic policies established the principle of accessibility to varied audience tastes, and it worked. The Royal Winnipeg ballet became and has always remained very much part of its home community. Extensive touring has been a necessity since Winnipeg is still a relatively small city. A varied repertoire has been productive for this also, since the company can meet the desires of small towns and sophisticated cities alike. A complement of 25 dancers is sufficient for mounting their works but at the same time is not unwieldly to tour.

There were some difficulties in making the transition to a new artistic director when Lloyd left the company in 1950, but continuity in philosophy was regained when Arnold Spohr, a Winnipegger trained by Lloyd and Farrally and for several years a soloist with the company, took the reins in 1958. Spohr has consolidated the image of the Royal Winnipeg Ballet. He has broadened the stylistic range of guest choreographers, hired dancers from elsewhere when necessary, but at the same time fostered Canadian talent through the company school. The company

E velyn Hart in the 1983 Royal Winnipeg Ballet production of *Romeo and Juliet.* Photo: David Cooper.

has received several international awards over the years. The most satisfying were probably the gold medal and certificate of outstanding artistic achievement received by Evelyn Hart in the Varna competition of 1980. Hart is a product of the Royal Winnipeg Ballet School and is an outstanding example of the quality now entering the company. Usually labelled as "young and fresh," the Royal Winnipeg is one of the three major ballet companies in Canada.

The founding of the National Ballet of Canada resulted from a decision by a small group of citizens that Toronto should have its own classical company. Boris Volkoff had been producing professional dancers and running an amateur group in Toronto since the 1930s, but was not asked to form the new company. Instead, the group of citizens, impressed by a Toronto visit of the Sadler's Wells Ballet in 1949, looked to England for advice. Dame Ninette de Valois recommended Celia Franca, an experienced performer highly respected for her dramatic portrayals who also had experience in production, staging and choreography. Franca accepted the invitation to come to Canada and at least review the talent available. She attended the 1950 Ballet Festival in Montreal and was not impressed, yet agreed to return the following year to further search for talent. There was some resentment within the dance community in Toronto and elsewhere at the deliberate importation of an outsider to form a "real" ballet company, especially when it was labelled national. But Franca took up the challenge. From a summer school in Toronto and an auditioning tour across the country, she selected a small group of dancers to begin performances in November of 1951.

The founding of the National Ballet came quickly and it has for some years enjoyed an international reputation as a large (65 dancers), high quality classical company. This status was not easily achieved, however, in a country still pioneering in the establishment of professional dance.

When Franca accepted her position in 1951, she was faced with responsibility for the finances of the company, which were miserably small, and no school through which to train her dancers. Franca's goals were based on her previous experience with major companies in England. She demanded, pushed and inspired the talent she had found into ever-increasing standards of performance. Society ladies, through the National Ballet Guild, helped raise funds for the ballet and in 1959 a school was formed to provide dancers with the style and quality required to build a company of international standards.

Franca gradually acquired a repertoire on which the company could grow. She knew that the great classical ballets would provide a measure and a training ground for the development of her dancers. She also used repertoire from the Royal Ballet in England which gave the company a much criticized hand-me-down look. This has been diluted in recent years, however, with the addition of works from other sources. Through productive guest artists such as Nureyev and Erik Bruhn in the past, award-winning television productions and international acclaim of their own dancers, the National Ballet achieved recognition as a world-class company.

Erik Bruhn's appointment as artistic director in 1983 suggests that the classical base within the repertoire will remain but with new ideas on what should complement it. He has already requested works from three Canadian modern dance choreographers, adding new interest to the National's short programs. Danny Grossman was the first surprising choice in 1984, followed by Robert Desrosiers and David Earle in 1985. Desrosiers began his career as a dancer with the National

Ballet but later turned to modern dance. He creatively draws upon elaborate props, make-up, costumes, characterization and dance to make a surrealistic but integrated fantasy. Bruhn hopes to persuade audiences who habitually gravitate to the standard classics also to try the bizarre delights of Desrosiers' *Blue Snake* and other excellent Canadian works.

The National Ballet School, directed since its inception by Betty Oliphant, also enjoys a world-wide reputation. Since the retirement of the National Ballet's first principal dancers, Lois Smith, David Adams and Earl Kraul, the independently operated school has provided the company with internationally acclaimed performers. Karen Kain and Veronica Tennant are superb examples of the school's methods and philosophy.

The beginnings of Les Grands Ballets Canadiens in Montreal were totally in reverse of the other two companies. It did not emerge from integration with its community, nor was there a plan by Montrealers for a major company in Quebec. It did not even come into existence via performances in a theatre.

Ludmilla Chiriaeff arrived in Montreal in the winter of 1952 as an immigrant with her husband and two children. Almost penniless, she began to teach as soon as she was able. Her artistic pedigree was impeccable. Born in Riga, she had trained and danced in Berlin, danced briefly with Col. de Basil's Ballets Russes and then taught and danced in Switzerland. The Second World War had disrupted and scattered her family and she chose to come to Canada because she felt it offered a stable future for her children.

Chiriaeff's self-appointed task of building a company for French Canada was monumental in the atmosphere of the 1950s. She was regarded as an outsider and during the early years of the company, the mixed collection of dancers frequently gallicized their names for greater audience acceptance. The founding of the CBC French Television network in 1952 gave Chiriaeff her first opportunity to find work for the more advanced students in her school. Contracted to produce one dance program each week for *Concert Hour,* Les Ballets Chiriaeff first existed as a television ballet group. From 1952 to 1955, Chiriaeff created at least 400 works for television.

When the desire for dance on television waned, Chiriaeff knew it was imperative for her young company to transfer to the stage. After an appearance by the group at a Montreal festival in 1956, the Mayor of Montreal suggested she officially charter the company in order to receive public subsidy. This she did and in 1958, the company was re-named Les Grands Ballets Canadiens. The grandiose name brought derision from some but Chiriaeff was determined to give French Canadians a company of their own.

Today, an amazing network of ballet classes for younger children exists in Quebec. These in turn feed talent to L'École Supérieure of Les Grands Ballets. The company itself has also consolidated in strength, quality and acceptance within Quebec. For several years it was little known to the rest of Canada, concentrating on integration with the Quebec culture and developing a repertoire which was educational and relevant to audience taste. To retain and expand audiences, the company repertoire swung with popular demand. Heavily criticized for their continual performances of the rock ballet *Tommy* in 1970-71, Chiriaeff pragmatically pointed out that it saved them from financial collapse. The repertoire has continued to be eclectic, containing classical, popular and more avant-garde works. There has always been a strong effort to utilize French-Canadian talent among dancers, choreographers and composers. There have been changes in the position of artistic director but Chiriaeff has never actually left the company. She remains the power behind the throne and receives the recognition she deserves, together with Gweneth Lloyd, Betty Farrally and Celia Franca, as one of the four great ladies of Canadian dance.

Although dominated by the three major companies, smaller ballet groups exist in other cities. The Theatre Ballet of Canada was formed in Ottawa in 1980 by fusing artistic and administrative elements from two expiring companies, Ballet-Ys in Toronto and Entre Six of Montreal. Lawrence Gradus, appointed artistic director of the new company, had joined Les Grands Ballets Canadiens from American Ballet Theatre in 1968 and then formed Entre Six in 1974. Theatre Ballet of Canada is a concert group of nine dancers and its repertoire is based on Gradus' choreography, which is a smooth melding of ballet and contemporary dance. After a splashy beginning showing much promise as another major force in Canadian dance, the company has moved into a fallow period. Gradus is admired by many as a genuine creative talent. A return to his former creative energy could achieve a valid position for Theatre Ballet as an alternative viewing experience to the three larger companies.

The Alberta Ballet, based in Edmonton, emerged from more conventional beginnings. It grew out of a school established by Ruth Carse, a former student of Boris Volkoff. The image of the company is traditional with a mixed repertoire from choreographers of various styles. The present artistic director is Brydon Paige, a Canadian whose training and career has been focussed within Canada. Although the company is needed and appreciated within Alberta, it has not yet achieved a national profile.

In harmony with Les Grands Ballets Canadiens' philosophy of promoting French-Canadian ballet, La Compagnie Eddy Toussaint in Montreal is developing works to interest younger audiences in the art. Toussaint has created a repertoire that is geared to popular taste, well performed by award-winning principals Anik Bissonette and Louis Robitaille and the other young company members.

The companies just described by no means constitute all the ballet activity in Canada. They are representative, however, of the art as it exists at a professional level. Many amateur and semi-professional groups are active but the bulk of other stimulation lies within the many schools which exist everywhere. Large and small, varying in offerings and quality of teaching, they are essential to the continuance of the art. Quite apart from the value of the training to the clientele, they provide a means to search for potential artists and, just as important, contribute to audience growth. The Royal Academy of Dancing and the Cecchetti Society, both based in England, have reached into Canada via their international network of examinations. Their highly structured systems of classical training have had the intended effect of improving teaching standards everywhere.

No comparable system exists for modern dance. Its origins and philosophy as an alternative to ballet diametrically oppose any universal method of training. Good movement technique is a necessity but the form that it takes is dependent upon the creative needs of a choreographer or company. In Canada, there are few teachers offering classes outside company schools and all the activity occurs in the larger population centres. It seems surprising, then, that there are so many modern dance companies and individual artists here. The interest lies in the flexibility and creative possibilities of modern dance as a means for expression.

Difficult to define, modern dance can be identified when it is seen as concert dance which is not obviously ballet. The modern dance community in Canada pursues just about every creative possibility that the definition provides. From independent artists to larger established companies, the form exhibits works that are comic, serious, personal, universal, easily understood, obscure and sometimes disturbing. It is a world of individualists, necessarily opinionated and tenacious. Some are defiant of the dance establishment, even sometimes of their audience. Most are seeking to move beyond entertainment, to awaken and provoke their audiences into paying attention to their statements.

Whether the statement is demanding reconsideration of established aesthetics of form and content, attempting new perceptions of social problems or demonstrating that other ways of moving can be just as pleasing as ballet, depends entirely on the individual creator. For all of them, established or new, survival is an ongoing struggle. Some teeter on the brink of being wholly professional, supplementing their income with teaching or other work. Many small groups have not survived.

The earliest teachers in Canada were from the European modern dance movement. During the 1940s, Ruth Sorel and Elizabeth Leese settled to teach in Montreal. Sorel's background was with Mary Wigman in Germany and her students participated in the Ballet Festivals. Leese had a varied background and worked flexibly between the European modern dance and ballet. She is probably best remembered for the ballets she created—*Lady from the Sea* entered the early repertoire of the National Ballet—but she was influential in the rooting of modern dance in Toronto and Montreal as well. During the 1950s other teachers arrived from Europe and Canadian students sought to extend their experience by studying abroad. Some of the finest modern dancers in the world visited Canada, so it was inevitable that, in such proximity to America, the developing modern dance movement from that country should gradually intermingle with the European movement in Canada. Students returning from New York and Americans settling in Canada have, together with the pioneer teachers and choreographers, created a vital and varied scene which defies any generalization.

The Contemporary Dancers of Winnipeg (recently renamed Contemporary Dancers Canada) claim to be the oldest modern dance company in the country. The company was founded by Rachel Browne, an American dancer who joined the Royal Winnipeg Ballet in 1957. Tiring of ballet, she left in 1964 to pursue modern dance. She was not enamoured by a particular style or technique but rather by the freedom to express her ideas through whatever movement was most suitable. Nor did she build the company around her own work. Contemporary Dancers is a rarity in modern dance, a repertory company. The wide selection of works by Canadian and American choreographers are balanced but conservative choices, which give exactly that image to the company.

Close on the heels of the Winnipeg group came the Toronto Dance Theatre. Formed in 1968 by three choreographers, it could have floundered on the rocks of artistic tensions. In fact, the opposite occurred. Feeling the need for community in a city unused as yet to modern dance, Trish Beatty, David Earle and Peter Randazzo gave each other tremendous artistic and personal support. Starting with eight original pieces, the repertory expanded at a steady rate, yet still allowing each choreographer time to shape strong works. They possess distinctive personal styles which have given variety to the repertory over the years. Canadians Trish Beatty and David Earle both trained in New York. Beatty performed with the Earl Lang Company for five years before returning to Toronto to open a school and start her own company. Earle trained in the Martha Graham school and danced with the Limon Company for a year before joining the London Contemporary Dance Theatre. Randazzo, an American, danced as soloist with the Martha Graham Company. Graham was their common denominator and that has been the foundation for their school and company.

The image of the Toronto Dance Theatre is as close to establishment as modern dance can come. It was the first non-ballet company to receive grants from the Canada Council. Yet the early years were a struggle for audience understanding and financial difficulties almost overwhelmed them in the late 70s. Past policy of supporting potential choreographers among their dancers has produced a talent which enables the company to move into its second generation. Christopher House, winner of the Chalmers Award for Choreography in 1982, is now a resident choreographer. Beatty, Earle and Randazzo have recently announced their retirement as directors. Kenny Pearl, a former student of Beatty and Earle, has been appointed in their place. Pearl returns to Canada after thirteen years of experience with such prestigious companies as those of Martha Graham and Alvin Ailey.

Le Groupe de la Place Royale, whose name is misleading since its transplant from Montreal to Ottawa in 1977, is by far the most radical among Canada's well-established companies. It is persistently supported by the Canada Council despite severe audience reservations in most parts of Canada. The Council nevertheless believes that support should be given for exploration by creators of integrity.

Originally formed by Jeanne Renaud and Peter Boneham in 1966, Le Groupe is an extension of the early modern dance movement in Quebec. Taking Renaud's approach toward the integration of various art forms, subsequent co-directors, Boneham and Jean-Pierre Perrault, carried the philosophy further to the integration of the arts within the performer. Dancers sing and play musical instruments, sometimes vocalizing while moving, exchanging roles as the work evolves. Creative cooperation occurs between the contributing arts, extending the experiments to results which are never easy for audiences to fathom. Le Groupe is not unmindful of its audience, but is primarily concerned with extending the possibilities of dance within the context of all art.

The originality of Le Groupe's approach, initiated by Jeanne Renaud, is only one of several descents from pioneers of the modern dance movement in Quebec. Soon after the appearance of Ruth Sorel and Elizabeth Leese in Montreal, came Françoise Riopelle and Françoise Sullivan. Closely linked with other artists in Quebec, they advocated that art should reflect its time and society. Much of their creative work was based on a realization of the world within the artist, both personal and universal. Their intuitive, multi-disciplinary approach spawned two companies and subsequently several choreographers who are now causing Montreal to be considered as the "hot bed" of creativity in Canada.

Two years after Renaud formed Le Groupe de la Place Royale, another company was founded by Martine Epoque. Through Le Groupe Nouvelle Aire, Epoque intended not only to promote Quebec artists but to develop further a movement

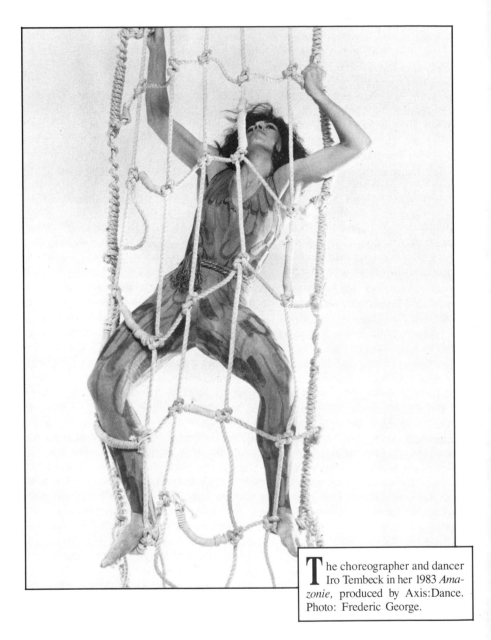

The choreographer and dancer Iro Tembeck in her 1983 *Amazonie*, produced by Axis:Dance. Photo: Frederic George.

technique which could be identified as Québécois. Le Groupe Nouvelle Aire was a transition to the new dance found in Quebec today. From the company emerged choreographers who left to form independent groups. Iro Tembeck was one of these. Now a highly respected choreographer/performer/historian, Tembeck has, perhaps, the keenest insight into the evolution and present activity of the new dance in Quebec.[1] She sees a recent trend in the depiction of the dark side of sexuality as a challenge to the barriers of audience passivity, the social etiquette of other performers and as a revolt against the Roman Catholic influence in Quebec society.

Other choreographers, including Tembeck, have turned to ritual for inspiration. Many use dramatic situations to convey their ideas. Whether sombre or joyous, innocent or perverted, the world of modern dance in Quebec assaults the senses with pique or dismay. The most well-known creators at the present time are Paul-André Fortier, Edouard Lock, Iro Tembeck, Linda Rabin and an independent creator/performer, Margie Gillis. Tembeck places the Quebec choreographers in one of two categories: those who explore content and those focussed in process. She forecasts a return to emotion as part of an historic cycle for modern dance in Quebec.

Despite Vancouver's early activity in ballet, no permanent professional ballet company was established there. The Anna Wyman Dance Theatre is the strongest company in the city, formed by Wyman in 1972. Born and trained in Austria where she danced in opera-ballet as a principal, Wyman then turned to modern dance for greater freedom. The company performs her works exclusively. Varied in theme and style, they are strong theatre pieces, some of which have successfully remained in the repertoire for many years.

Paula Ross is another Vancouver choreographer whose company is a reflection of her personal view of life. An intense, warm individual, her works also vary in theme and style, their quality bringing her the Chalmers Award in 1977.

Activity in Alberta is divided between Calgary and Edmonton. Theatrical dance has gained a toe-hold and even more than that in Edmonton. Here, the Alberta Ballet is only one side of the coin. The other side is stimulated by Grant MacEwan Community College where the Brian Webb Dance Company is company-in-residence. Sun-Ergos is a theatre and dance company located in Calgary. Based on the combined talents of Robert Greenwood and Dana Luebke, their works are visually striking and make strong emotional statements.

Ontario, containing the most intense concentration of population in Canada, also possesses the most eclectic activity. The Danny Grossman Dance Company in Toronto exhibits Grossman's choreography which audiences find entertaining and eccentrically his own. This company, together with the National Ballet and the Toronto Dance Theatre form the vanguard of dance in Ontario. Aside from the two companies already mentioned in Ottawa, there are many smaller companies, mostly in Toronto. Dancemakers is a repertory modern dance company which includes works by international choreographers as well as lesser known but solid local creators. T.I.D.E. (Toronto Independent Dance Enterprise) is a collaboration of four independent dancers who develop their works from contact improvisation. The listing could continue; those mentioned are but an arbitrary selection serving to illustrate the breadth of the Ontario scene.

Theatre dance has had much greater difficulty in establishing itself in the Maritime provinces on the east coast of Canada. Although there was early ballet activity in Halifax, the overwhelming interest of local people has been in social and ethnic dance. An umbrella organization, Dance Nova Scotia, includes all forms of dance in its supportive mandate, but theatre dance has been a small voice crying to be heard. Persistence is now bringing its reward, however, as Jeanne Robinson's Nova Dance Theatre becomes a professional company. Newfoundland is following a similar evolutionary path with the Newfoundland Dance Theatre.

Danny Grossman and Susan Macpherson in the 1982 première of *Portrait* by the Danny Grossman Dance Company. Photo: Arnold Mathews.

Although ballet and modern dance constitute the major portion of stage dance in Canada, there is extensive interest in ethnic dance forms, especially in Alberta, Saskatchewan and the Maritime provinces. Some of the performing groups appear in theatrical settings. Groups such as Shumka in Edmonton give spectacular and colourful performances of excellent quality. Other alternative theatre forms are provided by Les Ballets Jazz of Montreal and the National Tap Dance Company of Toronto. Both these companies are highly original in their approach to their respective forms, stretching beyond predictable jazz and tap routines to expressive works based on imaginative themes.

Amazingly, most of the members of Canada's dance community are well-known to each other. Spread across a thin strip of population stretching 3,000 miles, communication with audiences comes through frequent touring, and interaction with the profession occurs at the yearly Dance in Canada Association conferences. The conferences serve every layer of the profession from performer to creator, administrator, and educator. Marathon performances of single works by almost all companies except the largest ones, give delegates a fleeting view of the current year from coast to coast. Through choreographic awards each year, support and encouragement is given for quality and innovation. Several currently successful choreographers were given early recognition in this way.

It would be satisfying if, at this point, a final summary of Canadian dance could include a succinct statement on the national temperament and the style or styles that it produces. Impossible. Canada is a nation on paper, but even its constitution recognizes that it is a multi-cultural collection of peoples. Max Wyman, dance critic in Vancouver for many years, can perceive no national style and concludes that the diversity we possess may be better for the health of the art and its artists.[2]

Diversity also describes the related and even more recently established art of mime in this country. Within two decades, essentially since Claude St. Denis founded his Mime Workshop in Montreal, activity has multiplied so rapidly that mime is no longer a rare or specialized event. The flexibility of the art allows it to be experienced not only in traditional theatre settings but also in parks and streets. Artists work singly, in couples and in small companies. Some stay close to the technique developed by Etienne Decroux in France, others employ the wider-ranging philosophy of Parisian teacher Jacques Lecoq. Presentations may include masks, puppets, dialogue, dance, clowning or anything else that represents man's interactions with his world.

Most of the present mime companies were founded during the 1970s. Arete, one of the strongest, was formed by Randy Birch, Kevin McKendrick and Don Spino in Calgary in 1974. They tour extensively in western Canada and beyond. Theatre Beyond Words, based in Niagara-on-the-Lake, was formed in 1977 by Harro Masko, co-founder with Adrian Pecknold of the earlier Canadian Mime Theatre. This company has toured all over the world including Russia, Australia and Japan. Other well-established companies are Omnibus (Montreal), Moebius (Toronto) and Les Enfants du Paradis (Montreal). As with many dance companies, mime artists develop special programs for children which they perform in schools and other more informal settings.

If a national image cannot be presented to the world outside, quality certainly can. Most of the dance companies previously mentioned have toured internationally, collectively reaching into much of the world. Individuals have been invited to perform or create for foreign companies, the most successful of these being choreographer Brian Macdonald and dancer Karen Kain. Macdonald in particular has become an international man of the theatre through his work with dance, opera and musicals at home and abroad.

Such integration with the larger dance world after so short an adolescence attests to the vigor and vitality of dance in Canada.

Jillian Officer

Notes

[1] See Iro Tembeck, "New Dance in Quebec", *Dance in Canada*, No. 40, Summer 1984.

[2] See Max Wyman, "Who Needs Canadian Dance?", *Dance in Canada*, No. 38, Winter 1983/84.

Developing Opera
and Musical Theatre

The year was 1958, the book was called *The Arts in Canada* and in it, Boyd Neel, Dean of the Royal Conservatory of Toronto, voiced the opinion that "it will be an exciting day when a completely Canadian opera is sung by a completely Canadian cast in a new Canadian opera house."[1] Little did the transplanted English physician-conductor realize that within a decade, his wish would be granted, if not to the last t's crossing, at least in a general sense. For it was on the 23rd of September, 1967, in Toronto's O'Keefe Centre, that the curtain went up on *Louis Riel.*

Before looking at that signal event in Canadian operatic history in greater detail, it may be useful to examine some of the conditions that gave birth to Boyd Neel's wish-fulfilling prophecy. We have to remember, to begin with, what Colin Sabiston and Pearl McCarthy told their readers three years earlier, in a survey volume called *Music in Canada.* "Once in Canada," they wrote in 1955, "every county town had an opera house, but no opera. Now we have opera, but no opera houses."[2]

In point of fact, Canada has had opera since the late 18th century. The earliest available evidence, a report in the *Quebec Gazette* of February 13, 1783, indicates that "On Monday evening last was presented at the Thespian Theatre, a part of the Tragedy of *Venice Preserv'd,* with the Comic Opera of the *Padlock,* Singing, Music &c."[3]

By examining similar newspaper reports of the period, the historian Helmut Kallmann has estimated that by 1810 as many as 100 opera performances may have taken place in Canada.[4] During subsequent decades, travelling companies, chiefly from the United States, paid regular visits to the major cities and towns of the central and eastern provinces, while major European opera stars such as Jenny Lind, Adelina Patti and Henriette Sontag took their sheafs of arias even further afield.

To say that these visitors supplied the years surrounding Confederation with a regular operatic life would be stretching the point. But to record that a city such as Montreal witnessed a local production of *The Flying Dutchman,* by that controversial modernist Richard Wagner, as early as 1871, is to acknowledge a substantial level of sophistication. Torontonians witnessed a fully staged *Norma* as early as 1853 and like Montrealers were able to depend on almost annual visits by travelling troupes well before the century's end. Though nothing comparable was happening in this period in western Canada, the opening of the CPR's Vancouver Opera House in 1891, with a production of *Lohengrin* by the Emma Juch English Opera from south of the border, marked the arrival of grand opera on the west coast in grand style.

The Vancouver Opera House could actually accommodate Wagner, albeit without the elaborate sets and large orchestras and choruses we expect today. But it would be wrong to deduce from Colin Sabiston's and Pearl McCarthy's remark that the so-called opera houses that subsequently dotted the landscape from Nelson, British Columbia to Yarmouth, Nova Scotia actually lived up to their name. They were town halls in most cases, adaptable for political rallies, minstrel shows and the occasional locally mounted operetta, rather than lyric theatres with full stage facilities and the aspiration to produce art.

Even in the larger centres able to undertake operatic production, the historical record through into the early decades of the 20th century indicates the difficulty in sustaining ongoing activity. In Montreal alone, the names of such enterprises as the Société canadienne d'opérette, the Canadian Opera Company (which mounted all of one production) and the Variétés lyriques appear and disappear through the 20s, 30s and 40s, without giving birth to a permanent company. No wonder Canada continued to be recognized, as it was in the days of Emma Albani and Edward Johnson, as an exporter of operatic talent.

As recently as 1958, the *Encyclopedia Canadiana* took its literary gloves off and told its readers: "To put the matter bluntly, there is not enough money to support singers, stage and musical directors and designers of sets and costumes. Also, without a professional national lyric theatre, Canadian composers have no incentive to write operatic music, however much they might like to develop Canadian themes for performance by Canadians."[5]

Although the *Encyclopedia Canadiana* overstated the case—the history of Canadian operatic composition stretches all the way back to Joseph Quesnel's *Colas et Colinette* of 1790 and includes such early landmarks as the light operas of Calixa Lavallée and such later works as CBC Radio's first operatic commission, Healey Willan's *Transit Through Fire* (1942)—the absence of permanent institutions, regularly devoted to production, has restricted operatic growth to this very day.

As for the absence of a professional national lyric theatre, a Canadian counterpart to the Vienna State Opera, say, or the Paris Opera, this has been the probably inevitable consequence of the very nature of Canada as a nation, with its population centres widely spread apart and its strong sense of regional identity. Save for the Metropolitan Opera radio and later television broadcasts, which are American in origin in any case, Canada's most nearly national operatic institutions have been the CBC Opera Company (1948-1955), with its access to the nation's airwaves, and the Canadian Opera Company, with its continent-wide tours.

An outgrowth of the Royal Conservatory Opera School during 1946-1950, the Canadian Opera Company began extensive touring in 1958 and has been responsible for the first operatic performances seen not only in the Yukon and North West Territories but in many more southerly Canadian centres. Initially accompanied by piano and later by a small orchestra, these tours paved the way for the development of indigenous companies in Vancouver, Calgary, Edmonton, Winnipeg, Hamilton, Montreal and Quebec City during the 1960s and 1970s.

These companies would likely not have arisen but for a boom in post-war theatre construction which, within the short span of a decade and a half, beginning with the construction of the Jubilee Auditoria in Calgary and Edmonton (1955-57), produced more than a dozen large, multi-purpose auditoria in cities from Vancouver to Charlottetown. These facilities not only made possible the presentation of opera, they required, by virtue of their considerable dimensions, a kind of production more elaborate than almost anything seen during the earlier days of railroad, coach, and bus and truck touring.

Not that Canada now has the opera houses whose absence Colin Sabiston and Pearl McCarthy lamented back in 1955. When Boyd Neel wrote in 1958 that "in two years' time, Toronto will possess one of the best opera houses in the world,"[6] he was anticipating the opening of O'Keefe Centre, a building which turned out to be a house rather than a home for the Canadian Opera Company. Like most of its sister auditoria built at this time, the O'Keefe suffered from the lack of an extensive background of on-site production to guide its design. As the largest opera company in the country, with a budget of $11 million and a schedule of more than 200 performances a year, the Canadian Opera still mounts only seven main stage productions annually. Its drive to give Toronto a real opera house is tied up with its desire to give at least one Canadian city a real opera season.

The Canadian pattern over the past quarter century has generally involved intermittent production, usually of one opera at a time for a run of a few performances. And while there have been repertory innovations, witness the Vancouver Opera Association's productions of Massenet's *Le Roi de Lahore* (1977) and Donizetti's *Lucrezia Borgia* (1972), both starring Joan Sutherland, there has been a pervasive conservatism in programming by virtually all the civic companies.

In Quebec City, the Théâtre lyrique de Nouvelle-France (later the Théâtre lyrique du Québec) achieved perhaps the most distinctive repertoire during the decade of the 1960s by mounting such flavourfully French works as *Lakmé, Les Pêcheurs de perles, Monsieur Beaucaire* and *Ciboulette*. But it was the 19th century Italian literature, from Rossini through Puccini, that most often held the boards in such centres as Calgary, Edmonton, Winnipeg and even Montreal, despite the latter city's titular championship of French musical culture.

For four seasons, 1971-1975, some of the country's most elaborate productions appeared in Montreal and Quebec City under the auspices of the Opéra du Québec, culminating in a lavish and financially ruinous *Tristan und Isolde* (1975), starring Jon Vickers. Opera in Montreal seems to run in cycles of boom and bust. Opera in the west, on the other hand, has grown more slowly and steadily, with one man, the Montreal-born director Irving Guttman, responsible for laying the foundations of no fewer than three companies: the Vancouver Opera Association (launched with *Carmen* in 1960), the Edmonton Opera Association (whose pre-Guttman debut as the Edmonton Professional Opera Association took place in 1963 with a production of *Madama Butterfly,* equally responsible for launching the career of Ermanno Mauro) and the Manitoba Opera Association (whose first staged production, in 1973, was also *Madama Butterfly*).

Because he was active at home and abroad, Guttman applied his gift for spotting voices to the task of giving all these companies balanced casts without having to resort to high-priced international stars. This had the twin effect in the west of developing audiences for opera rather than for names and of developing the talents of young singers (whether the imported likes of Marilyn Horne and Placido Domingo or the domestic likes of Judith Forst and Alan Monk) before they starred at the Met.

The training of young singers in Canada has been made difficult by the infrequency of actual production. While such companies as the Vancouver Opera Association, the Opéra de Montréal and the Canadian Opera Company have all established resident ensembles, with access to special coaching and workshop opportunities, and while institutions of higher learning such as McGill University, the University of British Columbia and most importantly of all, the University of Toronto, offer advanced training in the many facets of opera, there is no teacher like a year-round opera season. And if that is true for singers, it is equally true for composers, who can hardly lead our civic companies along paths of innovation when their role models have to be a handful of dead Italians.

The Canadian Opera Company's 1967 production of Harry Somers' *Louis Riel,* directed by Leon Major, set design by Murray Laufer.

Much of the most innovative work has depended either on festival sponsorship or the enterprise of those few operatic counterparts to the alternative theatre movement. It was the Stratford Festival's Third Stage that introduced such native works as R. Murray Schafer's *Patria II: Requiems for the Party Girl* (1972) and Raymond Pannell's *Exiles* (1973) and it was the National Arts Centre that commissioned Gabriel Charpentier's *Orphée* for its opening festival in 1969.

Because of the infrequency of production opportunities, few Canadian composers have been able to hone their craft and thereby develop dependable theatre skills. Before undertaking a Canadian Opera Centennial commission to produce the three-act, bilingual *Louis Riel,* with librettists Mavor Moore and Jacques Languirand, Harry Somers could claim as the sum total of his previous experience a one-act chamber opera, *The Fool,* written more than a decade earlier. Among Somers' colleagues, only Charles Wilson enjoyed regular stage exposure for his operatic output during the 1960s and 1970s, including the Canadian Opera's mounting, in 1973, of his full-length *Héloise and Abelard* and the Guelph Spring Festival's mounting, in 1978, of that expressionist psychological study, *Psycho Red.*

In order to combat this problem, two Toronto-based organizations sprang up, almost in tandem. Both Co-Opera Theatre, founded by Raymond Pannell, and Comus Music Theatre, founded by a group which included Michael Bawtree, Maureen Forrester and Gabriel Charpentier, set up shop in 1975 to explore the development of a Canadian musical theatre able to exist outside the expensive and convention-bound framework established by the nation's traditional opera companies.

"We were convinced that audiences for music-theatre would arise from the theatre audience, with crossovers from dance, classical music, opera, new music, jazz and even rock," Pannell wrote in the *Canadian Theatre Review,* in what amounted to an obituary for his eight year experiment. "Thus we sought co-production partnership with existing theatres."[7] Although Co-Opera Theatre eventually succumbed to financial and administrative problems and what one board member described as the failure of consumers to be "sufficiently excited by the idea of multidisciplinary Canadian-written opera,"[8] it did leave behind a legacy that included such ambitious undertakings as Harry Somers' ancient Babylonian mini-epic, *Death of Enkidu, Part I* (1977), co-produced with Toronto Free Theatre, and Pannell's own *Refugees* (1979), co-produced with Toronto Workshop Productions.

Comus Music Theatre survived Co-Opera Theatre, in part by being more commercial in its approach, producing popular musical theatre (the Harry Warren-inspired musical, *Harry's Back in Town* of 1976) as well as the Canadian Electronic Ensemble's musical journey into the world of James Joyce's *Ulysses,* titled *Nightbloom* (1984). But even its efforts have thus far contributed nothing that has come close to achieving standard repertory status or even significant subsequent exposure. While nothing could be more quintessentially Canadian than *The Shivaree* (1982), John Beckwith's celebration of the marriage rites of southwestern Ontario, with a libretto by James Reaney, even this lively opus awaits a second professional staging.

Perhaps what has been missing in the efforts of organizations such as Co-Opera Theatre and Comus Music Theatre is what has been missing internationally: the evolution of a new musical language as communicative to audiences of our day as the traditional tonal language of opera has been to audiences of the past. While composers can rejoice in a stylistic freedom greater than that enjoyed by any of their predecessors, the very enjoyment of that freedom seems to have turned many of them into experimentors rather than craftsmen.

Some of these experimentors, such as R. Murray Schafer, have earned their laboratory rights. Schafer's *Loving* (1966) demonstrated how the techniques of television can bypass a dependence on plot and his ancient Egyptian night piece, *Ra* (1983), re-cast the theatre-going experience into a dusk-to-dawn ritual.

But so far, at least, it is Schafer's colleague Harry Somers who has emerged victorious on the field of operatic battle with a work widely and repeatedly acclaimed. Dealing as it does with one of the most charismatic figures in Canadian history, *Louis Riel* struck a responsive chord (not to mention a fair number of tone clusters) in the Canadian psyche. Premièred by the Canadian Opera Company in 1967, repeated the next year, televised in 1969 and revived again in 1975, when it was taken to Ottawa and Washington, Somers' operatic magnum opus was described by Wendell Margrave in the pages of the *Washington Star* as "one of the most imaginative and powerful scores to have been written in this century."[9]

To find parallels to this magnitude of recognition we have to turn to the lighter forms of musical theatre, whose Canadian tradition stems from Marc Lescarbot's *The Theatre of Neptune in New France*(1606), a masque performed in the harbour of Port Royal, Nova Scotia, in honor of the return of Samuel de Champlain and Jean de Biencourt de Poutrincourt from coastal explorations.

The 1983 Comus Music Theatre production of R. Murray Schafer's *Ra*, directed by Thom Sokolowski at the Ontario Science Centre. Photo: Nancy Halpin.

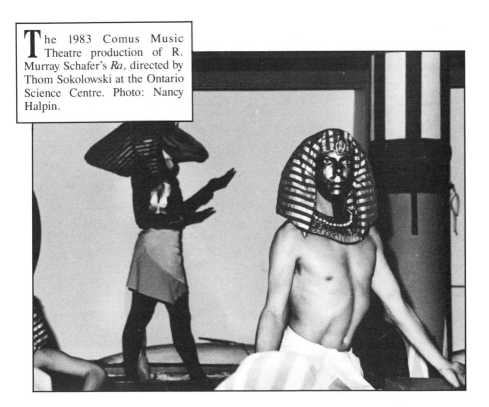

The Theatre of Neptune was performed only once. *Leo, the Royal Cadet,* on the other hand, was performed more than 150 times in various Ontario towns during the decades following its Kingston première in 1889. Oscar Telgmann's so-called "military opera" may well have been the most popular piece of Canadian musical theatre to precede the melodizing of Lucy Maud Montgomery's *Anne of Green Gables.*

The path from *Leo* to *Anne* is strewn with a succession of operettas, ballad operas, burlesques, reviews and musicals, attesting to Ross Stuart's claim that "musical theatre has been the single most popular form of Canadian theatre."[10] While much of this activity owed its origins to the same spirit of amateur enterprise that has given Canada its flourishing choral tradition, one can find among the countless amateur Gilbert and Sullivan societies the professional likes of Vancouver's Theatre Under the Stars (1940-1963), Winnipeg's Rainbow Stage (1954 to the present) and most influentially of all, the Charlottetown Festival, which opened in 1965 with the stage première of Norman Campbell and Don Harron's *Anne of Green Gables.*

I say most influentially in the case of the Charlottetown Festival because it is in the soil of Prince Edward Island that the Canadian musical has taken deepest root. Here at last was an institution with a specific mandate to present original Canadian musical theatre, something Rainbow Stage never attempted and Theatre Under the Stars attempted only once, in the case of *Timber!!,* Doris Claman's 1952 musical about romance in the British Columbia woods. Granted, none of Charlottetown's subsequent productions has matched the ongoing popularity of *Anne,* whose sentimental tale of orphan spunk has charmed the citizens of London, New York and Osaka as well as Anne Shirley's fellow Canadians. The very existence of the Festival's proscenium stage nevertheless has given a focus to a previously haphazard tradition of production.

Prior to the Festival's advent, the strongest production traditions belonged to two uniquely Canadian institutions, The Dumbells, Merton Plunkett and Jack McLaren's all-male World War I revue, which enjoyed a number of reincarnations (including one on Broadway) long after the silencing of the Guns of August, and *Spring Thaw,* which began its life in 1948, under Mavor Moore's direction, as a replacement production for Toronto's New Play Society. It became something approximating a Canadian inevitability for close to a quarter of a century—a record of longevity unmatched in the annals of the Canadian musical theatre.

Spring Thaw turned out to be both a prototype and a proving ground. In addition to Mavor Moore himself, who has been aptly described as the "father of the modern Canadian musical theatre,"[11] the satirical revue employed a who's who of Canadian writers, directors and performers. It inspired such successors as *My Fur Lady,* the 1957 McGill University spoof that helped in turn to launch the careers of choreographer Brian Macdonald, composer Galt MacDermot and some of the most distinguished future mandarins in the corridors of cultural power.

The congeniality of the revues format to the Canadian scene is readily understandable, given the habit of self-deprecation that Canadians evidently develop during the early stages of their toilet training. Moreover, the appetite for topical satire crosses linguistic boundaries. The *Fridolinons!* produced annually by Gratien Gélinas in Montreal between 1938 and 1946 (with revivals in 1956 and 1964) enjoyed just as much popularity in French Canada as comparable revues did in English

Canada. Louis Negin's *Love and Maple Syrup* managed, during the late 1960s, to poke bilingual fun at both language groups.

It has been harder, until recent years, to detect a comparable vein of distinctiveness in the Canadian musical. Despite the pioneering efforts of Mavor Moore, with *Sunshine Town* (1957), his affectionate tribute to Stephen Leacock, and *The Optimist* (1956), an adaptation of Voltaire's *Candide,* the notion of the indigenous musical was slow to take hold. Even today, the giant image of Broadway casts its shadow over Charlottetown's Confederation Centre, influencing the style and content of the shows. But alongside the Charlottetown likes of *Kronborg: 1582,* the Cliff Jones rock version of *Hamlet* that actually made a disastrous trip to the Great White Way, there has developed a newer, more informally structured genre of musical theatre responsive to Canadian reality.

It has taken several forms. In works such as George Ryga's *The Ecstasy of Rita Joe* (1967) and *Grass and Wild Strawberries* (1969), the dramatic structure of a straight play was loosened to accommodate an enlivening musical commentary. In a work such as *Cruel Tears* (1975), bluegrass music, supplied by Saskatchewan's Humphrey and the Dumptrucks, became the very basis for transforming Ken Mitchell's truck driver's *Othello* into a "country opera."

Other works have exhibited the beauty of the small. The free-wheeling format of cabaret produced a range of intimate entertainments addressing themselves to subjects as diverse as women's liberation (in the case of the Sandra O'Neill-Barbara Hamilton show, *Sweet Reason*) and René Lévesque, the separatist Premier of Quebec (in the case of Guy Moreau's 1976 romp, *Mon cher René, c'est à ton tour*), with the record for sustained popularity clearly going to John Gray's *Billy Bishop Goes to War* (1978), which crossed both the country and the Atlantic Ocean, only to be shot down in New York.

It would be difficult to imagine a John Gray in an earlier generation, but the proliferation of small theatre spaces and the increasing willingness of Canadians to sing and laugh about themselves has finally made writing musicals and revues a full-time career option. Gray's success with *Rock and Roll* (1981), a nostalgic look at small town Canadian culture, Cedric Smith's success in adapting musically Barry Broadfoot's Depression saga, *Ten Lost Years* (1974), and David Warrack's and Jim Betts' string of 1970s and 80s cabaret excursions all point to a creative self-confidence few would have predicted when the long-running *Justine* (1970) emerged from the grimy precincts of Robert and Elizabeth Swerdlow's Global Village in downtown Toronto.

There appears to be little concern in any of these newer works either with emulating external models or trying, self-consciously, to produce Canadian archetypes. Their variety reflects Canada's variety; their differences in subject and structure are responses to local conditions. But if universal truths can be said to reside in Walden Pond, there is every reason to believe that the truer Canada's musical theatre is to its immediate circumstances, the greater will be its chance to speak not only to a local audience but to the international community. Considered from this point of view, the trend of recent years toward looking inward may in the long run produce the clearest vision.

William Littler

Notes

[1]Boyd Neel, "Opera" in *The Arts in Canada: A Stock-taking at Mid-century,* ed. Malcolm Ross. Toronto, MacMillan, 1958, pp. 65-66.

[2]Colin Sabiston and Pearl McCarthy, "Opera and Ballet" in *Music in Canada,* ed. Sir Ernest MacMillan. Toronto, University of Toronto Press, 1955. p. 95.

[3]James B. McPherson, Helmut Kallmann, Gilles Potvin, "Opera Performance" in *Encyclopedia of Music in Canada,* eds. Helmut Kallmann, Gilles Potvin, Kenneth Winters. Toronto, University of Toronto Press, 1981. p. 695.

[4]Idem.

[5]Colin Sabiston, "Opera" in *Encyclopedia Canadiana,* Vol. 8. Ottawa, Grolier Society of Canada, 1958. p. 56.

[6]Boyd Neel, op. cit. p. 63.

[7]Raymond Pannell, "Goodnight Co-Opera, Sweet Dreams", *Canadian Theatre Review,* No. 40, Fall 1984. p. 24.

[8]David A. Rubin, "A View from the Board", *Canadian Theatre Review,* No. 40, Fall 1984. p. 30.

[9]*Encyclopedia of Music in Canada,* op. cit. p. 563.

[10]Ross Stuart, "Song in a Minor Key: Canada's Musical Theatre", *Canadian Theatre Review,* No. 15, Summer 1977. p. 50.

[11]Ross Stuart, "Musical Theatre" in *Encyclopedia of Music in Canada,* op. cit. p. 657.

PART FIVE

The Emergence of The Theatre Professional

Training the Theatre Professional

In Eastern Europe, actors are trained by the state and upon reaching a certain level of expertise they are licensed. With their licenses, they are guaranteed careers, salaries and possibilities of advancement within what becomes a reasonably stable and socially acceptable profession. Given such controls on the quality and number of actors being turned out each year, unemployment is virtually non-existent.

In Canada, on the other hand, actors study wherever and with whomever they can, using private teachers, colleges and universities, or, if they are extraordinarily talented and a bit lucky, a conservatory. Such studies guarantee neither a career in theatre nor even professional status. Many of those thus trained will therefore quickly find themselves unemployed. Some, on the other hand, may find themselves working, but in non-union theatres at wage levels below the poverty line. Still others will wind up apprenticing at a professional theatre either for free or, at best, for minimum wage.

The most talented of these young people may remain in the profession and a few might even manage to make a living wage if they are seen by the "right" people and if they are willing to split their stage time with film and television. A few more might even make a great deal of money and achieve some fame. But the odds against such success are truly enormous.

Yet despite this rather depressing state of affairs, the numbers of those wishing to study at theatre schools in Canada continues to increase, to the amazement of just about everyone in the profession.

Is the situation any better in other fields of theatrical endeavour? Hardly. For directors, there are even fewer opportunities than there are for actors. Combine that with the fact that virtually no one in Canada can really say for sure how a director should be trained, and one has just a small insight into why there is such a lack of qualified young directors in the country. For those considering careers in playwriting, courses exist at several levels, but the odds against any particular playwright ever being professionally produced are staggering. And the possibilities of production seem to decrease with each passing, politically conservative year. For those considering careers in design or theatre criticism, the possibilities are only slightly less daunting.

About the only area of the profession where need generally exceeds availability is in technical skills, where well-trained administrators, stage managers, lighting people, carpenters, builders and painters can find work almost anywhere in the country. But even these people generally receive wages far below what they could probably command in other related fields of endeavour.

Yet young people continue to demand entry to theatres and to theatre schools throughout North America. The fact is, theatre training across the continent has become big business. In Canada alone, 109 training institutions were listed in the *Canadian Theatre Review*'s 1982-83 *Directory of Canadian Theatre Schools.* These included four conservatories and nine graduate-level university programs offering generally high levels of professional training in areas such as acting, design, criticism and arts administration; 30 three- and four-year undergraduate university programs offering students degree opportunities in a wide range of theatre studies; 17 two-year community colleges (CEGEPs in Quebec) offering everything from Introduction to Theatre to Stage Singing and Make-up; and 49 private schools ranging from individual acting coaches to group work in scene study and mime.

The result is that almost anyone with a real desire to study theatre in Canada is able to do so as long as that person is willing to search long enough, pay high enough, and bear the social slings, artistic arrows and venal vagaries of an unplanned professional career. To someone from Eastern Europe, the variety and the waste must seem bewildering. To Canadians it is simply the norm.

The Black Report

About ten years ago, the Canada Council suggested a national study in the field of professional theatre training, and in 1976, a formal inquiry was begun under the general direction of Malcolm Black, a respected stage director and a theatre teacher at various points in his professional career. Black had, in fact, only recently resigned from York University where he had served as chairman of its Department of Theatre for two years. Also named to the Committee were University of Alberta theatre professor Gordon Peacock, designer Cameron Porteous, actor-director-teacher Gilles Marsolais and director-teacher Jean-Pierre Ronfard. Within twelve months, the *Report of the Committee of Inquiry into Theatre Training in Canada* was completed.

For reasons still unclear, the Canada Council withheld release of what came to be known as the Black Report for nearly a year. Officially, the Council claimed translation problems. Unofficially, it was suggested that the Council was not satisfied with the report's methodology and conclusions, particularly as they related to anglophone schools.

Whatever the reason for its delay, the Black Report certainly caused some stir in Canadian training circles when it finally did become public. And while one could argue with its apparently hit-or-miss methodology (particularly on the anglophone side), its anecdotal style and its lack of hard information, its overall point of view was indisputable: "theatre training has become an industry in our country—an industry that has grown without any realistic appraisal of the actual needs within the profession."[1]

Going further, the Committee recommended the setting up of a regulatory board to assess and report on professional theatre schools on an ongoing basis. "This body," the Committee argued, "would be responsible for granting recognition to training schools, recommending those for public subsidy, and ensuring that the profession is adequately represented in the training process." At the very least, there should be an annual meeting among theatre schools "to discuss philosophies and methods." The idea of a National Association of Theatre Schools was also mentioned.[2]

What this study ultimately did was to make clear the distinctions that do exist among the various types of theatre schools in Canada—the conservatories, the university theatre departments and the community colleges /CEGEPs. Unfortunately, for all its useful suggestions, little was done after its publication and today the Black Report merely gathers dust on library shelves.

The National Theatre School

At the heart of the Black Report—and still at the heart of professional theatre training in Canada—is the National Theatre School, the major conservatory in the field and the only *officially* bilingual theatre training institution in the country. Located on Montreal's rue St. Denis—the francophone heart of the city—the National Theatre School's roots are themselves essentially francophone (even today, the School's greatest strength is to be found in its French-language section which can be traced back to the Théâtre du Nouveau Monde's first acting school, opened shortly after TNM itself was formed in the city in 1951).

> "The teachers were almost all members of the troupe, and the troupe recruited its actors among the students of the school. After several years of operation the school of the Théâtre du Nouveau Monde had to close down for financial reasons. But it had established the *idea* of a school which, like the Old Vic Theatre School in London and the Strasbourg School, would combine in one autonomous organization the teaching of all the disciplines necessary to the practice of the dramatic arts (acting, production techniques, stage design) and the training of young stage performers. This idea, taken up, reworked, enlarged and adapted to the scale and specific conditions of the country, was submitted to a committee of English-speaking and French-speaking theatre professionals, and finally materialized in 1960 with the creation of the National Theatre School of Canada."[3]

In the early years, close links were maintained between NTS and professional companies—the Théâtre du Nouveau Monde on the French side and the Stratford Festival on the English side. Through the years attempts were made to link the school's two linguistic groupings but only in design and technical theatre did this have any practical impact. And as befits its national designation, NTS was very early on subsidized heavily by the Canada Council, the federal government and both the Quebec and Ontario governments. Other provinces made—and continue to make—contributions to the school on a less formal basis.

Criticism of NTS through the years has revolved around two areas—subsidy and location. The Canada Council subsidy has been particularly criticized because it comes from the same funds used to subsidize professional companies. It has seemed to many theatres—even those who are enthusiastic about the school—that in a weak economy, this represents unfair competition. From time to time, the School itself is also criticized for not serving its English-speaking students well. At the heart of that argument is the school's Montreal location and the natural problems facing anglophone students in North America's largest francophone city. Often suggested is a splitting of the school into two separate training centres; the francophone wing remaining in Montreal with an anglophone wing moving to Toronto. Though the idea does have much to recommend it, economic and political considerations make the idea difficult to realize. It is highly unlikely therefore that any basic change will take place at NTS in the foreseeable future, either in the nature of its funding or its location.

In terms of numbers, the school has a core faculty of about 15 which is supplemented regularly by visits from major figures in the profession—actors, directors, designers and technicians. In recent years, the school has also begun a playwriting program, but it is far too new to make any judgements about. Both the acting and the playwriting students attend the school for three years with design and technical students attending for only two years. In 1984-85, the school had a total enrollment of 150, almost evenly divided between French- and English-speaking students, and an overall budget of some $2 million. Eighty per cent of those attending were receiving either partial or full scholarships.

Training at NTS follows a fairly standard international model including voice, movement, improvisation and scene study. The two theatrical names most frequently invoked in discussions of pedagogy are Russian director Konstantin Stanislavski and French director Jacques Copeau. Students spend about thirty hours each week in class and another twenty or so in rehearsals. Performances—some public, some for invited guests only, and some private—go on from September to May.

Jean-Louis Roux, long-time artistic director of the Théâtre du Nouveau Monde and now head of the National Theatre School, says that "there is no *official* style at NTS. Theatre training is theatre training the world over basically. Our goal is to make students ready to work in the profession and that includes classical theatre, modern theatre and even experimental theatre. Because there is such a wide range, we invite a steady stream of professional guests each offering his or her own individual way of working."

As for the bilingual nature of the school, Roux points out that "for many anglophone students, this is the first time—perhaps the only time—they will be exposed to francophone culture. There are also a number of theatre visits each year for both groups to see English theatre at such places as Shaw and Stratford. In the beginning there was this wonderful idea to develop a national theatre school with a national theatre style based on the concept of co-lingualism. I still think it's a wonderful notion, a utopia to keep always in mind. I'm afraid though that the reality will remain more or less as it is now. Utopias require utopian conditions and essential to that is much more money than seems possible at the moment. Until that time comes, we will continue to keep our standard high (12 to 15 acting students per year in each wing, for example) and we will continue to try and hold out the best models of theatre we can find for our students."[4]

Conservatories

Between the establishment of Théâtre du Nouveau Monde's original school in 1951 and formal establishment of the National Theatre School in 1960 came the creation of the oldest purely francophone conservatory in the country, the Conservatoire d'art dramatique de Montréal. In the beginning, this conservatoire followed Paris theatre traditions almost slavishly, emphasizing a "heightened sense of the dignity and rigor of the dramatic art, a profound respect for tradition, an appreciation of the set ways of the theatre, a primacy of correct diction and a systematic rejection of local theatre." So said the Black Report. Appropriate to such a vision, its students for many years did almost nothing but French classics. It was the creation of the National Theatre School, with its goal of focussing on Canadian needs, which profoundly affected the Conservatoire de Montréal's own outlook. Interestingly, by the mid-1960s, there were few real differences in approach between the two schools

From these schools, it should also be pointed out, grew a number of innovative Quebec companies, a phenomenon not occurring to the same extent among theatre schools in English Canada. Among Quebec groups which can be traced to the two schools are the Théâtre populaire du Québec, Grand Cirque Ordinaire, Jeunes

Barry Yzereef and Alison Smiley in Leon Major's 1985 York University production of *La Ronde,* designed by Maxine Graham.

Comédiens, Théâtre du Même Nom (a play on the initials of Théâtre du Nouveau Monde), Enfants de Chenier, Rallonge, Voyagements, Manufacture and Théâtre en l'Air.

A second exclusively francophone conservatory—this one located in Quebec City—is the Conservatoire d'art dramatique de Québec, originally an offshoot of the Montreal Conservatory but now independent. Set up in 1958, the Quebec Conservatory originally shared with Montreal the same director, the same teachers and the same Paris-based methodology. In the last decade or so, the Quebec Conservatory has freed itself from its Montreal parent and has moved in its own direction. It too has spawned a number of troupes in the Quebec City area—Théâtre Euh!, Théâtre Parminou and the Théâtre du Vieux Québec.

One additional anglophone conservatory of note was opened in Vancouver in 1975, when the Vancouver Playhouse decided to establish its own school. Since that time, the Playhouse Acting School has been making a strong contribution to the west coast theatre scene despite minimal funding and less than optimal facilities. A two-year program run exclusively for actors, a third year is offered to some of the best students in which they work closely with the Playhouse and often appear in its productions.

University Programs

As for the various university *graduate* programs offering conservatory-style training across the country, most involve two years of study leading to a master's degree either in Arts or Fine Arts. Students usually do at least eighty per cent professional coursework. In performance studies, the University of Alberta and Toronto's York University stand out—Alberta for its work in directing, design and playwriting; York for its intense acting program built around a producing ensemble. Between 1980 and 1983, the York program was jointly run by David Smukler, one of the theatre world's leading voice coaches, and Michèle Collison George, one of the original members of Peter Brook's Theatre Research Centre in Paris. Students were offered the unique vision of these two major coaches, intense training and contact with some of the world's leading theatre practitioners. In 1984, Smukler and George both stepped down from their graduate company to devote themselves more intensely to voice work, research, acting and directing. A new program—but one essentially following the established model—was too early in its development for assessment at the time of writing.

Among other graduate programs of repute are those at the University of British Columbia (performance and technical theatre particularly), and at the Universities of Calgary and Victoria (directing and technical theatre). In 1970, York University introduced Canada's only graduate level program in Arts Administration.

As for the nearly fifty undergraduate university, community college and CEGEP programs across the country, it is interesting to note that only five were in existence before 1960. Thirty-three departments of theatre came into being between 1965 and 1974, a staggering figure but one fully understandable in light of the parallel growth of theatre activity itself across the country at this same time.

Are there differences between these programs? Few worth talking about save for the actual length of time required for degrees. Community Colleges and CEGEPs tend to offer two-year vocational programs in theatre while the three and four-year university programs tend to offer a mix of specialized training (acting,

The 1978 University of British Columbia production of Euripides' *The Bacchae* at the Frederic Wood Theatre. Photo: Guy Palmer.

design, technical, management, directing, playwriting and theatre history and theory) along with courses in subjects such as literature, social science, humanities and natural science. In theory, it's the universities which turn out the more intelligent and aware theatre specialists. In practice, it doesn't always work out quite that neatly.

A few schools in each region do stand out for the quality of students who make it into the profession. Among these—the Universities of British Columbia and Victoria in the west; the Universities of Alberta and Calgary in the prairies; York and Ryerson in Ontario; Concordia (English-language) and UQAM (Université du Québec à Montréal—French-language) in Quebec; and Dalhousie in the Maritimes. Each has made a commitment to serious theatre training within an academic context and, though the term "professional" might more accurately be "pre-professional," these schools do attempt to provide a strong theatre background for their students.

Private Training Programs

Of the private training programs, most are run by individual teachers interested in either creative/developmental drama for children or as introductions to the profession for young, would-be actors. Three are notable, however, all located in Toronto. These include Equity Showcase Theatre, the Centre for Actor's Study in Toronto (CAST), and the Maggie Bassett Studio. All are devoted to in-service training, that is, the maintenance and further development of skills for those already working in the profession, a recent phenomenon in the Canadian theatre.

Equity Showcase actually has two programs—a producing wing run in association with Canadian Actor's Equity Association, and a professional development wing offering ongoing training opportunities to Equity members. In its 25 years of formal existence, Showcase has produced more than a hundred shows, fifty in the last five years alone while under the direction of Tim Leary. In this program, actors and directors suggest performance projects, plays which will showcase those involved and which will reach as wide a public as possible. If chosen, the participants are given a theatre, a budget and publicity. No one in the company, however, is paid for his or her work. All do it simply for the experience and the opportunity to be seen.

It was Leary who created the professional development program of Showcase, a series of classes organized primarily for members of Equity. Ranging from Alexander technique on the one hand to voice and scene study on the other, at any given moment these classes have a combined enrollment of 150. Equity gives some subsidy to the classes with additional support coming from the Canada Council and various provincial and municipal agencies. Growing from this program have also been several national and international training congresses bringing to Toronto major teachers from Canada and abroad for periods of up to six weeks. In 1985, some of Equity Showcase's progams will also take place outside of Toronto.

"For a number of years now," explained Leary, "we have wanted to do work in other cities. But it has simply made no economic sense to get classes up outside of Toronto. You have to have a large concentration of actors to offer high-level professional classes and for English-speaking Canada that concentration happens to be in Toronto. Having one large centre like that may not be what the government wants, and it may be totally contrary to the way the country as a whole is run, but it is a cultural fact of life. Two-thirds of the professional actors in Canada happen to live in and around Toronto."

The Centre for Actor's Study in Toronto, another private school, is the brainchild of director Kurt Reis and operates as Reis gives time and energy to it. Again focussing on training for those *already* working in the profession, CAST has a small core of teachers (all working actors or directors) and a loose membership of professionals wanting to work with Reis and his studio. And studio is the key word. Reis is basically a Stanislavski-oriented director/teacher and his model is New York's Actor's Studio. The work at CAST therefore tends to focus on modern plays, particularly those with a naturalistic bent. CAST's success is in its modest programs, its tight focus and the quality of its part-time faculty. When Reis is around and free, a lot happens. When Reis is working, CAST tends to close up shop.

Still another interesting program is the Maggie Bassett Studio connected to Toronto's Tarragon Theatre. Operating programs of up to six weeks in length and utilizing theatre professionals as teachers, the Bassett Studio has offered a wide range of classes since its creation in 1980. These have included everything from children's theatre to stage fighting. It's an active and still growing school and one that has continued to offer something of value to those seeking non-institutionalized, professionally-oriented training opportunities.

Conclusion

Is there a Canadian training style, then? Can one generalize about the state and level of training in Canada? Perhaps the one thing that can be said is that there are clear points of commonality among the various training schools despite their varied mandates. Almost all would admit to a strong Stanislavski-bias in their training, even those that have been touched directly or indirectly by the ideas and techniques of Jerzy Grotowski (a frequent visitor to Canada), Eugenio Barba (an occasional visitor) and Richard Schechner (in Canada so often that he almost deserves citizenship).

Design training across the country has been influenced most directly by technological advances in the United States and by the frequent visits to Canada of international masters such as Josef Svoboda. Canadian-trained administrators have the touch and often the look of American regional theatres. Jon Jory, the guiding light of the Actor's Theatre in Louisville and one of the founders of the Long Wharf Theatre in New Haven, has spoken many times in Canada; and Danny Newman's aggressive subscription and management methods have been taught to Canadian managers from coast-to-coast. All these things tend to militate against the establishment of a uniquely Canadian work method. Yet, there are differences—in speech, in colour, in style. These are subtle differences to be sure, but differences nonetheless.

Whatever these differences are, though, one thing is abundantly clear: Canadians no longer lack opportunities to study at home as they once did. If there is now perhaps too much choice, if standards at Canada's theatre schools are just a bit too loose, if the whole situation is just a bit too expansive, the fact is that professional theatre training of a respectable international calibre does now exist in a land where just a few decades ago the whole idea of professional theatre was still considered an illusory dream. Such growth—indeed, such cultural maturity—speaks well of Canada's theatrical development since the 1960s. More than that, it goes far toward insuring that the professional theatre in Canada will continue to mature in the decades to come through the work of these young people so eager to *learn* their art.

Don Rubin

Notes

[1] *Report of the Committee of Inquiry into Theatre Training in Canada.* Ottawa, Canada Council. Published in March 1978. p. 11.

[2] Ibid. pp. 92, 131, 28.

[3] Ibid. p. 98.

[4] Interview with Jean-Louis Roux, Montreal, September 1984.

Standing in the Slipstream: Acting in English Canada

The place was England, and I was in my final term at the London Academy of Music and Dramatic Art—LAMDA. The panic was on. Britain had entered the Common Market. Canadians, who used to have free access to UK jobs and markets, now had only months to get their British Equity cards before immigration gates would close. What's more, it looked as if my friend at Central had already got her first job—and the important card. A Bristol theatre was beckoning. She had had her teeth capped and her Canadian accent taken out at the same time. She was making it!

I paced my West Hampstead bedsitter—2½ paces each way—and thought, "What about me? Robert Thomson from Richmond Hill, Ontario, Canada?" Should I rush out my glossy 8x10s with their blank resumés to all the British regionals I could find addresses to? Better still, why not apply for that 9 pound a week ASM job in Dundee, Scotland? Then a curious thought struck: I'm not English. What did I want to act in Britain for? Shouldn't I be acting in Canada? It seemed to my young thespian heart that to act was to be an expression of your own people, people you shared a country with and perhaps understood.

I had never been really comfortable with the sentiment that "true" theatre served a version of international art—meaning some other country's art. However, I set idealism aside for the moment. I'm really a very cautious fellow with an inquiring mind. You see, I'd taken a Bachelor in Science at the University of Toronto just in case a theatre career didn't pan out. I thought, "Is there a Canadian theatre, I mean, really?" First off, of course, Stratford, Ontario, came to mind. But on second thought, that was Shakespeare. I had meant *Canadian* theatre. After some mental work, I remembered a production of *Red Emma* that I had seen in an old gasworks called the Toronto Free Theatre. Sitting on the bleachers there had been a little barren, but the actors had sounded absolutely Canadian. Also, there was a pioneering energy that had made the production rough-hewn, yet quite exciting. The play was neither Anouilh nor Pinter, it was patchy. I was excited most by the communal conviction in that gasworks. I'd never seen anything quite like it before, not even the old Living Theatre. I decided I had my answer. I flew home. Maurice Podbrey offered me a job doing an American play at Centaur Theatre. I started.

Now forgive me for the past ramble, the associations to follow, and all the generalities therein, but these were headstrong times I describe. Expo 67 and Centennial year had focussed our country on our own nationhood. I had begun to notice Canada in a novel way through the eyes of the American draft resisters who kept arriving in the university dining hall. True, they were primarily leaving America, but they were also coming *to* somewhere. To my undergraduate mind, it implied that Canada was worth coming to for some reason. Jane Jacobs had written *Death and Life of Great American Cities* and came to live in Toronto herself.

Canadians were about to realize that they wanted to hear stories about themselves. We also realized the urgency to catch our history before it crumbled either under the wrecker's ball or under the onslaught of American culture pouring over the border. More and more we perceived justice through *Perry Mason,* living through *Life* magazine, and the world through *Time.* Theatrically, after sixty years of valiant attempts, the first complete lap of indigenous Canadian theatre was about to get underway. People in our theatre wanted "to hold as t'were a mirror up to nature," and they wanted it to be *our* nature. Just as 1967 acknowledged that Canada had been a political entity for one hundred years, so Canadians wanted our new plays and novels to affirm that we had a social entity as well—whatever that might be.

For myself, despite all this rampant nationalism, I still found the back of my head saying that I should really be making it in New York and London. I thought perhaps that I was just playing at theatre, perhaps I was deluding myself that I was really a professional. After all, I had left my Canadian training at the National Theatre School in Montreal to train in England. Proof and validation could only come from abroad, from our English and American cultural parents—or from those critics who represented them.

Now, after a dozen years of work, those voices are almost quiet (and ironically I now have agents in New York and Los Angeles). I attribute their faintness to two factors. First, as we were learning our craft, the pioneering began to bear fruit. Year by year standards and expectations slowly rose. It was a truly startling moment for me in New York in 1978 when, after seeing a string of plays, the mists of adoration (or the fog of inferiority) lifted and I actually perceived what was before me on stage. Oh yes, some good work here and there, plenty of skill and lots of money, yet by and large their success and failure ratio seemed no better than ours. Over the years I was even able to compare productions of the same play. Sometimes they were both fine, sometimes ours were just inadequate, and sometimes as with *Comedians* at the Bastion Theatre in Victoria in 1978 and *Cloud Nine* recently produced in Toronto, they were better. I thought the values and balances within the plays were given much clearer readings and the casting had fewer rough edges. Through these comparisons, I began to see the different sensibilities that we bring to our theatre.

The same happened earlier to me in England. Since I was seven, I'd wanted to be an actor—why, is really beyond me to say. Everyone knew the best actors were English, so it was there I should train. I tried many times to gain admission to English schools. Finally my dream came true with LAMDA. Euphoric, I moved to Great Britain. I devoured English theatre from September to Christmas! However, for the rest of my year I went to concerts instead. I didn't realize it, but it was the gloss of the English theatre that I'd worn through. It was wonderful: for 40 p. ($1.00) you could stretch out on the upper tier of the Royal Albert Hall and the

R.H. Thomson and Gerard Parkes in the 1979 Theatre New Brunswick production of *Waiting for Godot,* directed by Malcolm Black. Photo: Don Johnson.

music wafted up. Don't misunderstand me, the Brits do some extraordinary theatre. All the same, I've had many a doze at Stratford-on-Avon. It was a big step for me to realize that the Brits have their own deadly kind of mediocrity. Peter Brook wrote a book about it.

The second factor in the quietening of my voices, really has to do with the low Canadian dollar. The dear CBC aside, it is the arrival and proliferation of American Pay TV, made for TV and just TV productions, that allow us to place our work directly beside that of a cultural giant.

Personally, I'm surprised by the comparison and sometimes I'm proud. What's more, the comparison has made many of us realize that given the nature of satellites, microwaves and Peoples Express fares, access to a large market does not necessarily entail leaving Toronto. The watershed has not yet been reached where a Canadian actor can live in Toronto and work in North America, but many of us are determined to give it a shot. In a way, that is really contradicting our entire history.

We've always been a nation of import/export. We import finished goods and solutions. We export raw materials. For years now we've exported the raw Pickfords, Plummers, Reids and Jewisons. For years now, whether it was the Loew's vaudeville circuit during the early century or Stratford in the 70s, we imported the finished goods, the directors and actors to solve our problems. Admittedly, for decades the import/export circuit was absolutely necessary. As with Sir Tyrone Guthrie, our imports were for a long time our only teachers. It was not until the 1960s and 70s that Canada could offer any real training and hope of a career to its raw talents.

Just as there was much howling from the multi-other-nationals when our national energy policy was introduced, so was there much protestation through our ten headstrong years of artistic nationalism. But the results are such that we now own and control much more of our energy resources and we now have a nationwide community of Canadian theatres producing Canadian plays for Canadian audiences. This could reverse itself with the present Conservative government. Given the time-frame, the first lap of solid theatrical inhabiting of our nation's soul has been accomplished remarkably swiftly—ten to fifteen years depending how you count it. I find that astonishing. What's more, it has been very exciting to have been part of it. What an opportunity to contribute to a beginning! To be part of establishing directions and raising standards!

North and south of the 49th parallel, "making it" has by and large two different meanings. South of the 49th it means breaking through a hundred thousand hopefuls to tap the horn of wealth and worldly recognition. North of the 49th, it means what it says. If you are making it in Canada now, you are helping to make the culture. I find that reason enough to stay. It is a curious fact, but in every interview I'm asked "Why do you stay?" When the question is no longer asked, I'll know that we will have definitely succeeded.

What is most astonishing of all, is that we have a first generation of Canadian artists that have mostly stayed. We stayed because we could. We stayed because we had a collective purpose large enough to generate a critical mass to build a nation's theatre. We stayed because it was exciting. It was in a bar in New York with a group of my compatriots, that I finally realized how strongly I felt about my country. It was there that we realized that our passions (nordic and subdued as they are) were to nurture and articulate our northern nature.

You see, it's really a question of the culture and the egg. If you don't have a culture, there's nothing for the articulators to work with or stay for. If you don't have the articulators—the writers, painters, actors, critics *and* audiences—the embryo culture has nothing to emerge with. To my mind our whole emergence has been slowed by the kind of patriotism we enjoy in English Canada. When things get rough, Canadians seem to turn up caring about their country and caring about who they are. At other times, our patriotism disappears into the woodwork. This is not exactly the energy necessary to fuel a vibrant and articulate culture, especially when we are constantly being blown about in the powerful slipstream of the United States. American patriotism is much closer to the sleeve. It is active. It is a patriotism that often feeds on itself and often impairs its own vision. The American coverage of the 1984 Olympics bore testament to that.

I think there is a core in Canada that is deeply patriotic. But apart from wartime, we are not sure how to let it be known. Ours is a *re*active patriotism—we will react to a stimulus. We can't really do it like the Americans yet we keep trying. Our award shows I find annually embarrassing. Our electronic and print media—with the blessed exception of the CBC—seem to know no other option. Only rarely does someone like Terry Fox spark us to some sort of national feeling and the unique expressions that spring from it. And Terry Fox aside, when was the last time we erected a statue to a Canadian? As always, it's so difficult for a young and tentative expression to stay on its feet given the power of the culture blowing in from the south looking for yet more revenue. It is so easy to sit back and be carried by the "successful" and "desirable" cultural winds of *Hill Street Blues* and *Dallas*. It takes determination and a persevering grit to turn it off and produce your own. It takes a determined individuality to hoist yourself from the armchair of the cultural intravenous. I feel that that determination and individuality have become part of our indigenous style.

Clare Coulter and Eric Peterson, among so many that I would like to acknowledge here, are wonderful actors. That individuality is part of their quality. They have had to struggle, but not for the jobs and auditions as is so habitual in the United States. They have had to struggle to remain themselves while working in that enormous cultural slipstream. They and their like are one of the delights of the Canadian theatre for me. The people who are rising to the top are the stickers and the stayers. They, by and large, have been the determined pioneers. They would probably be accepted as character performers in New York or Los Angeles, yet here they are leading actors. That is style.

Pam Brighton, an English director, commented recently on the lack of energy she found in English actors when compared to their Canadian counterparts. "Status quo Preserved" is too often the quality of the English acting style. Here, we have no status quo but are constantly establishing one, breaking it and trying to improve it in a new direction. I saw four of the recent BBC TV productions of Shakespeare. With the notable exception of John Cleese as Petruchio, I thought the complacency amongst the performers was quite shocking. The determination that we possess and the energy that comes with it, is style. It is not a smooth or glossy style. Gloss comes only with a finer and finer buffing of a set technique. Our style produces edges and angularity as it probes and searches new ground. While the ride may be bumpy, the risk and freshness with which the digging is undertaken often reveal distinctive riches. I think of Eric Peterson in *Billy Bishop Goes to War* and Clare Coulter in almost anything.

The style of our acting is also the result of the rewards offered. There is satisfaction in the doing, but little fame, less money and no unemployment insurance. This not only discourages the actors who are not in it for the struggle, but it also helps keep the vision in the tele and the play in the theatre. These qualities are often lost to formula, market research and the T.V.Q. where there's the lure of real money to be made. (T.V.Q. is the rating of television performers in the United States. A "personality's" marketability is determined and catalogued. It is used as a casting consideration.)

Lastly, our acting style includes a certain collective vulnerability. I often think that our country, surrounded on the world stage by so many powerful voices, has had to listen—a kind of vulnerability—since our fate is so affected by other states. More powerful countries often do not feel they have to listen and share with others for their survival. My final stylistic observation is that, generally, Canadian actors are more self-directed, self-generating than others. I'm sure it originates from our formative years which involved working on so many new scripts. Actors were expected to have opinions and input on the development of scenes and characters.

K ate Trotter, Robin Craig and Clare Coulter in the 1984 Tarragon Theatre production of Caryl Churchill's *Top Girls,* directed by Jean Roberts. Photo: Andrew Oxenham.

Workshops entailed much discussion, and often actor improvisations contributed heavily to the writing.

It is fascinating and frustrating to observe what I think is a similar first lap in Canadian film. What's more, because of the enormous amounts of money required for each project, the seeding of authors, actors and audiences is more sporadic and progress haphazard. Often I feel this is because assembling large amounts of money attracts those whose interests are not necessarily film.

It is almost impossible, as an actor, to make any creative impression in the Los Angeles franchised productions with cloned sensibilities. But in some of the smaller films (with, of course, the director's nod) it is possible to screen some of the particular strengths of the Canadian actor's contribution. I'm thinking of the films *Grey Fox, Who Has Seen the Wind* and *Ticket To Heaven.* On the other hand, the film of Margaret Atwood's novel *Surfacing* suffered from a plainly inadequate script (not Atwood's) yet might have had a chance of turning out respectably had casting been different in the two major roles. However, the producer bowed to the import/export syndrome, importing actors who would solve the initial financing problems. It was also assumed that their presence would solve the future marketing of the film—they didn't. Basically they lacked the ability—which many of their Canadian counterparts had—to dig deeper than the script and to flesh out the half-formed. The film did not live up to Atwood's work and failed. Again, don't misunderstand. I don't claim that all Canadian actors are gifted script revisionists, I just want to state that at the heart of my generation's formative years lay the expected ability to contribute to a script's development.

In 1973, when I packed my bags and left England for the newer lands, I had little idea how remarkable these dozen years would be in Canada. Nor was I entirely sure that I wasn't turning my back on any chance of a "legitimate" career. Opportunities looked very slim in Canada. There was much indifference, disagreement and animosity to overcome. Yet what a dozen years it has been. Our first lap has been well run. While the baton is being tossed to a younger generation, I sense that mine must now turn to the classics with all the same grit, determination and individuality of style. Having initially rejected Shakespeare—in the Stratford, Ontario, context—as not being "Canadian," twelve years later I accept that it is within the works of this magnificent playwright that my generation can define the next facet of our Canadian theatricality.

R.H. Thomson

Directing in Quebec

The role of the director has only recently received much attention in Quebec. While it appears that the public is more or less aware of the job and functions they perform, crowds do not flock to see a director's work—more often they are attracted by the playwright, the actors or the reputation of the company.

No matter how the director's task is defined, his presence in the theatre itself cannot be ignored. He can, as the need arises, play the roles of either privileged reader or fundamental creator—the "very soul" of the production. On the other hand, he can function as the "critical eye," observing and giving advice. Or, on a less exalted plane, he can simply conduct rehearsals, in effect leading exercises which are then performed in public. It is also significant that when there is no director, his very absence indicates a conscious decision to modify and orient the production towards a certain interpretaton.

The lack of detailed, factual studies on directing leaves all conclusions on the subject open to debate. We have to make the most of the information that has filtered down here and there throughout the history of Quebec theatre or which has slipped into dramatic texts themselves. By reading between the lines and drawing inferences from certain hypotheses, we can begin to document the work of Quebec's directors.

> An emphasis on directing—indicating a resurgence in theatrical presentation throughout Europe—has not yet found any counterpart in Canada.[1]

The defining characteristic of the period 1940 to 1960 was the close indentification of major directors with the birth of new theatre companies. In almost all cases, the actual founders of these companies were directors who had trained as actors and frequently played major roles in their company's productions.

The concept of directing at that time easily fitted the definition provided by Patrice Pavis in his *Dictionnaire du Théâtre:* "The stage manager or occasionally the lead actor was in charge of pouring the production into a prefabricated mold. Directing was limited to the basic principles of blocking."[2] Even though such a notion reduces and restricts the director's role, it does open up possibilities: as the individual responsible for the production and the company, the theatrical representation will depend on the quality of the training and ideas which the director has received, and which he may then pass on to others.

The history of Father Emile Legault and the company which he founded in 1937, Les Compagnons de Saint-Laurent, provides a concrete example of this process. Thanks to his company, changes slowly but surely began to take place in the restricted world of "French-Canadian" culture. Although some consider Father Legault primarily as a good animateur rather than as a director, that does not lessen his contribution in streamlining modern stage practices. Having received a Quebec government grant to study theatre, Legault went to Paris to learn the latest theatrical techniques. There he observed the experiments of the Cartel (Jouvet, Dullin, Baty, Barrault) and studied the works of Gordon Craig and Jacques Copeau. The knowledge he acquired provided a healthy stimulus to the growth of theatre in Quebec.

The style of the Compagnons de Saint-Laurent was marked by simple staging, stylized set design and costumes and by a clear, innovative delivery: "Real theatre will only exist when the audience and the actors speak with one voice and one heart" (Jacques Copeau).[3] Such a statement does not imply a pale imitation of reality—quite the contrary. For Legault, theatre must interpret reality, re-create it in some way so that it acquires a new dimension—the dimension of poetry. His goal was to raise theatre to an artistic level far beyond that of photographic realism.

Legault's ideas on theatre, which were certainly radical in his time, are remarkable in that he recognized the importance of all the elements in staging and what each one meant: "The ideal work vigorously unfolds from a design in which each stroke is necessary, compelled and compelling, and everything is of a piece.... Theatre must first of all 'make known,' not just 'be heard'."[4] Hence Legault gives dramatic action pride of place followed by dialogue, which serves dramatic action but cannot substitute for it. Influenced by Copeau's philosophy of dramatic art, he gives a very contemporary definition of the actor: "The actor must be an appealing speaker, but primarily he is an acrobat, a dancer and a mime with a complete mastery of the instrument that comprises his entire being: head, shoulders, trunk, arms, legs and feet."[5] In contrast to the theatrical traditions in Quebec at this time, which tended mainly towards the pseudo-realistic style of the popular boulevard plays, Legault and his Compagnons introduced a new and refreshing concept of theatre.

In 1943, a new company appeared—L'Equipe, founded and directed by Pierre Dagenais. It is generally agreed that Dagenais was the first director of "Canadian" theatre in the 1940s. Dagenais drew most attention for *A Midsummer Night's Dream*, which he staged outdoors in August 1945, in the gardens of the Ermitage. "The setting was natural: the stage was 85 feet wide and 100 feet high, with rocks, trees, elves and fairies appearing everywhere in the forest."[6] Another praiseworthy and audacious project was *No Exit* by Jean-Paul Sartre, who was then virtually unknown in Quebec. The play excited young intellectuals in the audience: "The production revealed a simplicity, an intelligence and a clarity rarely achieved on the Montreal stage. Pierre Dagenais has created a bewitching atmosphere that leaves a stunning impression on the audience."[7]

When Sartre came to Montreal to give a lecture, he asked L'Equipe to play *No Exit* for him since he had never seen it performed. Sartre was obviously pleased and asked the actors to play the piece again in its entirety, which they did gladly. Jean Béraud lauded Dagenais' direction in these terms: "This performance by L'Equipe is...one of the most memorable in the history of our theatre...Pierre Dagenais' direction deserves praise first of all for successfully translating one hour and forty minutes of dramatic progressions into a series of masterfully paced crescendos and decrescendos. The blocking of the actors, especially in the sequences where they close in on one another, is the work of a great director."[8]

In talking about his work, Dagenais claims affinity with a kind of realism derived from American theatre which pays close attention to detail. He does not believe in adapting the classics, which he feels should be played just as they were written with no changes in the text, design, costumes or style as revealed in the writing. Only one modification is permitted, and that is in delivery—"style parlé," or language as it is naturally spoken. Dagenais cites Louis Jouvet who, instead of end-stopping alexandrines, delivered them as if they were spoken dialogue. For Dagenais, the context, time and place were ultimately all artificial—only the *basics* mattered and endured. Form and style were unimportant since theatre was fundamentally the depiction of man for man. Judging by his productions and his ideas derived from these principles, one might conclude that Dagenais' strength lay in directing actors, especially in *No Exit*. On the other hand, his staging of *A Midsummer Night's Dream* and the use of a specific location with natural elements also made an enormous impression. Both productions were in any event enthusiastically received by the critics and the public.

With the founding of the Théâtre du Nouveau Monde (TNM), direction began to play a greater role in the mounting of productions. This company brought together a core of actors trained by Emile Legault at the Compagnons de Saint-Laurent: Jean Gascon, Jean-Louis Roux and Georges Groulx. After leaving the Compagnons, they all studied and worked in France.

Jean Gascon has directed most of the productions at the TNM, including almost all the plays of Molière. Outstanding features of TNM productions include style and decorum, but they are distinguished most of all by their professionalism. Jean Gascon defined the company's style through his directing of Molière's plays: "Consistent tone, uniformity of style in all aspects of staging, restraint rather than indulgence in burlesque passages, straightforward projection of the text so that the comedy is forceful and fills the theatre, natural delivery of the verse halfway between the pomp of classical tradition and the mincemeat of more modern readings."[9] As well as synthesizing various influences drawn from the dramatic arts, TNM productions have a definite "French-Canadian" flavour so that TNM has even been criticized for "canadianizing" the classics.

In his many productions, Gascon seems equally at home directing a Molière comedy or a Shakespearean drama, a realistic work by Marcel Dubé (*le Temps des lilas*) or a boulevard comedy by Sacha Guitry (*Mon père avait raison*) or even a poetic drama by Paul Claudel. Among Gascon's most acclaimed productions was Claudel's *l'Echange,* presented in 1956. Gascon's demanding interpretation married the rhythms inherent in Claudel's phrasing to a sharply defined visual style combining gesture and attitude. That combination lent a sculpted quality to the work, whose action at first glance might seem static.

Gascon's staging in fact added a new dimension to *l'Echange:* the text was lifted off the page and transfigured in flesh and spirit. The acting and direction were closely and forcefully linked: the staging did not involve mere blocking but a carefully planned placement of the actors in patterns which fit into the overall flow orchestrated by the director. The painter Jean-Paul Mousseau built an impressive collection of abstract shapes and objects to create a setting which allowed the text to stand out in all its nakedness, while Solange Legendre's costumes could not be pinned down to a particular time and place.

Gascon has also directed musical comedies such as *The Threepenny Opera* and *Irma la douce.* TNM presented *Threepenny Opera* on its tenth anniversary in 1961 as a musical comedy that was more a social event than an act of political awareness. The play's anarchistic aspects were somewhat overshadowed by the grandiose staging but Gascon's direction was bold and full of irony.

Considering the large number of classical plays Gascon has directed, his belief that "the great classics are always relevant" is not surprising. Speaking in terms that recall Pierre Dagenais' thoughts on the same subject, Gascon feels that "great plays depict man's struggles with destiny, duty, love, passion and political hatred. Man does not change, the problems remain the same." At the same time, he states enigmatically that "ideally, there should be no place for directors in the theatre." Unless Gascon has fallen victim to the occupational hazard of overstating his case, this apparently means that, for Gascon, the director's function should first of all be to guide the actors: "If a play could be rehearsed for six months, the director would become much less important. He is there to bring together the craftsmen so that they can work on a play and mount it in the allotted time."[10]

Another of TNM's co-founders, Jean-Louis Roux, has also directed. He tends to be tighter and more cerebral than Gascon, and has brought an exemplary rigor and unadorned style to the company's productions.

The overall style of the TNM reveals a strong post-war French influence. Although that approach did well at the box office, after ten years it ran out of steam. But in May of 1961, an experimental work may have stimulated TNM to seek new directions. This rejuvenating shot in the arm was administered by a highly controversial production of Aeschylus' *The Libation Bearers,* entitled *Oreste,* adapted and directed by Jean-Pierre Ronfard. The staging united elements of theatre, music and dance, and was very badly received by the press. Above all, the critics attacked the excessive gesticulation, the grimacing masks and the staccato rhythmic patterns which obscured Aeschylus' text: "Grotesque and monumental unawareness...infantile translation...dime-novel trash...Orestes wears a costume which makes him look like a professional cyclist inexplicably returning from an underwater fishing expedition.... And to top it all off, there's the diction, ranging from whispers to bellows to various noises emanating from a set of kitchen utensils undoubtedly activated by a breeze from Olympus."[11]

Although the reviews seemed to predict a short, disastrous career for the young director Jean-Pierre Ronfard, history proved the critics wrong and made them seem a bit ludicrous on at least two counts. First, Ronfard's career eventually led him back to the TNM to direct two plays by Claude Gauvreau—*Les oranges sont vertes* in 1972 and *la Charge de l'orignal épormyable* in 1974. Later he sinned again by adapting Shakespeare (*Lear* in 1977), then drew heavily on the classics and theatre

history to create *Vie et mort du Roi Boiteux* (1981-82). Secondly, in these caustic, apocalyptic descriptions of how *Oreste* was staged, it is still easy to recognize today the unique style of Jean-Pierre Ronfard.

As the TNM rose to prominence in Montreal theatre, another company made its debut—the Théâtre-Club, led by actors Jacques Létourneau and Monique Lepage. Despite Létourneau's solid work as a director, the Théâtre-Club's reputation rested chiefly on the productions of Jan Doat. Doat was a French director who had resided briefly in Montreal before he began working from time to time at the Théâtre-Club. His first production was Musset's *le Chandelier* in 1955. The experiment was a success: the production was judged to be sincere, refined, brilliant and full of emotion. Doat's treatment of the play's romanticism was restrained but fervent and always elegant. In 1956, Doat and the Théâtre-Club collaborated again on *Twelfth Night*. The director transformed the auditorium into a travelling theatre with a proscenium that moved towards the audience and changed the theatre into a circus ring roughly similar to an Elizabethan stage. There was a minimum of sets, all portable; among them was a clever device conceived by Jacques Pelletier: the curtains for the back-drop slid on rods to evoke the required atmosphere for each change of scenery. The brilliant, heavily stylized costumes were by Regor and Vladar. The staging, comprising a language of gestures compiled by the actors and played in symbolic, contrasting attitudes, was a great success.

Jacques Létourneau was also bold enough to direct Dumas' *The Three*

Musketeers. Mounting the play at all was already a gamble because of the problems involved in presenting simultaneous action in a number of settings. "The production sparkles with youthful ardour: hell-bent for leather with rattling sabres, crossed swords and gestures of bravado, it makes up for some imperfectly executed details and weak performances."[12] Létourneau revived Dumas' creaky melodrama by staging it straight without a hint of parody; in fact, he was criticized for being a little too serious. Nevertheless, the production was a big hit with the public. Audiberti's *le Mal court*, produced in 1959, matched the high standards set by *Twelfth Night*: Létourneau's direction was brisk, while Jean-Claude Rinfret's sets and costumes contributed to an excellent visual presentation.

The Théâtre du Rideau Vert has specialized in a playing style suitable for boulevard plays and light comedy. Still, its dedicated, painstaking approach to boulevard pieces has contributed to the growth of theatrical presentation in Montreal. Another distinguishing feature of this company is its record of hiring directors who were trained in television (since 1952) but who have been actors in the theatre. It is also noteworthy that the company has presented not only Parisian boulevard plays but also works which have little in common with the facile treatment of themes usually associated with popular comedy. In 1956, for example, Florent Forget directed Lorca's *Dona Rosita*. In 1957-58, the Rideau Vert revived Sartre's *No Exit*, originally produced by Pierre Dagenais and L'Equipe starring Rideau Vert's artistic director Yvette Brind'Amour as Inès. In the revival, Brind'Amour played the same role and also directed, but the solid production could not erase the memory of L'Equipe's triumph.

To celebrate the company's tenth anniversary, Brind'Amour decided to produce Montherlant's *la Reine morte*. The choice was problematic and the execution arduous. Paul Gury's direction lacked control: details were weak, and the style was erratic. But Robert Prévost's sets and costumes were very seductive, an indispensable quality for any production attempting to do justice to the high standards the play sets itself. Overall, even though Rideau Vert's interpretation was not a complete success, *la Reine morte* is considered one of its best productions. The company also produced *le Dialogue des Carmélites*, but the production was a failure because of Jean Dalmain's slipshod and imprecise direction.

Rideau Vert has not been especially interested in well-known directors and their work, but the company is unique in having produced plays full of challenges with a limited appeal to the public at large. The theatre's contribution to the repertoire in this regard certainly deserves praise.

In 1956, the Festival d'art dramatique allowed the amateur Théâtre de Quat'Sous, founded by Paul Buissoneau, to enter *Orion le tueur* which drew considerable attention to the company. This burlesque farce by Jean-Pierre Grenier and Maurice Fombeurre was directed by Buissoneau in a fresh style which drew on music hall, literary cabaret and serious drama in a presentation full of movement, colour and comic relief. In 1957, Buissoneau produced Guillaume Hanoteau's *la Tour Eiffel qui tue*, which presents many opportunities to create visual poetry. In 1965, he established the Théâtre de Quat'Sous as his own professional theatre where he produced *Peuple à genoux, l'Osstidcho, Faut jeter la vieille* and revived *la Tour Eiffel qui tue* with considerable success. Buissoneau developed an acting style based on comic strips and silent movies, and his productions were triumphs of imaginative entertainment.

In the 1950s and 1960s, it was the new amateur and semi-professional companies who constantly presented new work. Among them were the Apprentis-Sorciers, founded by Jean-Guy Sabourin in 1955, and les Saltimbanques, established by Rodrig Mathieu in 1962. The desire to do avant-garde plays naturally led to experiments in design and new definitions of theatre. Among the productions in this period were Beckett's *Endgame*, several works by Ionesco (*The Chairs, The Bald Soprano, Jack or the Submission, The Future Is in Eggs*), Chekhov, Ghelderode, Synge, Lorca, Kleist, Ugo Betti, Marcel Achard, Claudel and Brecht. Despite poor delivery, variable standards of acting and clumsy staging, these performances were full of invention and totally dedicated to the spirit of exciting experimentation.

The Egrégore, founded in 1959 by Françoise Berd, intended to establish itself as the leading professional theatre of the avant-garde. Roland Laroche made his directing debut there with *Une femme douce*, adapted from the works of Dostoyevski, and the experiment was judged an outstanding success. The painter Mousseau tried out some new design techniques for the play involving multi-coloured clear vinyl panels. Unfortunately, other productions by L'Egregore never matched the standards set by *Une femme douce*.

In the 1960s, the main focus of theatre development was perfecting the art of the actor. Not coincidentally, perhaps, numerous institutions were established in this period. Amateur theatres united to form the ACTA (Association canadienne du théâtre d'amateurs), which in 1972 became the AQJT (Association québécoise du jeune théâtre). The Conservatoire d'art dramatique was placed under the responsibility of the Ministry for Cultural Affairs and operated through the Centre dramatique which in 1966 became the Théâtre populaire du Québec. In 1960, Jean Gascon founded the National Theatre School to train actors, set and costume designers and stage technicians.

The decade also witnessed an upsurge in Quebec drama which reflected a need to define the Quebec identity. Young playwrights formed the Centre d'essai des auteurs dramatiques to encourage the growth of dramatic literature in Quebec. It was not surprising that the discovery of a new Quebec dramatist, Michel Tremblay, also revealed a new director, André Brassard. Both had made their debuts in 1964-65 when Brassard directed les Saltimbanques in *Messe*, a collage of Tremblay's fantasy fiction.

In 1968, their work together on *les Belles-Soeurs* at the Rideau Vert was a revelation: "I cannot say what struck me most—the author's play or the director's staging."[13] After *les Belles-Soeurs*, "Directing in Quebec changed—being dull was no longer acceptable. The musical dialogue between the chorus and the characters indirectly recalled Greek tragedy as we might have wished—or guessed—it to be."[14] Brassard's talent continued to grow and diversify thanks to the variety of his productions: *Double-Jeu* (Comédie-Canadienne, 1969), *Waiting for Godot* (Nouvelle Compagnie Théâtrale, 1971), *À toi, pour toujours, ta Marie-Lou* (1971), *Andromaque* (Théâtre de Quat'Sous, 1974), *le Balcon* (Théâtre du Nouveau Monde, 1977), *Bonjour, là, bonjour* (TNM, 1980).

The appearance of new Quebec writers had an important influence on the evolution of theatrical presentation. The new form of writing in particular affected directing and, more specifically, how professionals thought of their own work. Le Centre du Théâtre d'Aujourd'hui, founded by Pierre Collin and Jean-Pierre Saulnier in

306

Nicole Leblanc in the 1971 Théâtre d'Aujourd'hui production of Jean-Claude Germain's *Si les Sanssoucis s'en soucient,* directed by the author. Photo: Daniel Kieffer.

1969, gave rise to companies such as Jean-Claude Germain's Les Enfants de Chénier du Théâtre du Même Nom.

Germain's writing is based on story outlines and improvisations worked out by the actors. The company uses only the essentials: a bare stage and a minimum of sets and props. All of this determines a special mode of theatrical presentation. The stage is an empty space, an "open possibility," since there aren't any external constraints. Everything must arise from the text, from the actors, and from the use of language. Space is filled only with these elements. The dramatic presentation is kept at a distance and seen for what it is—a place to play. The audience too must re-examine its traditional concepts of theatrical space, reinforced by a long history of stage conventions. This purified space rapidly transforms itself into all possible spaces through the medium of the text and the actors' interpretations:

> My approach implies great respect for the actors. In effect, the way I work
> depends to the highest degree on the actors' intelligence as well as their physical

presence—but it is intelligence that determines those physical aspects. My directing proceeds in a geometric fashion—in other words, the actors know its principles of operation. I never waste time on detail—that's up to the actors. Our experiments strive to create a style of dramatic writing which operates on an 'economic' as well as a symbolic level.[15]

During these years (1969-71), the Grand Cirque Ordinaire explored the same staging techniques, the only difference being that there was no single individual author. A piece would grow through improvisation to collective creation. According to this concept of drama, theatrical space exists to be populated, to be conquered by the spirits of play and celebration. The space becomes a circus ring, a circus of life, a place where anything can happen, anything can be created or said—but because life can be mundane as well, it is a place where one can say or do nothing too.

In new experiments such as these, the work of the director takes a subordinate role to the performances of the actors and leaves few traces. In a sense, the playwright is also absent for a while to let the actor or individual speak. "In 1973, these young companies discovered that the essence of theatre no longer lay in representation but in communication and self-realization using an adaptable instrument which could be perfected."[16]

This change encouraged a deconsecration of theatre as "pure art" and provided an entry for social and political issues. But there were inherent dangers as well: universal access to theatrical techniques frequently led to personal therapy and voyages of self-discovery. These abuses of collective creation quickly plunged Quebec theatre into lethargy and stagnation. They may also have contributed to perpetuating and reinforcing the sacrosanct myth of the star performer—the actor/martyr whom one admires and identifies with and who supposedly speaks to and for all his people.

Several years passed before playwriting in Quebec got its second wind and authors, then directors, returned to their rightful places in the theatre. The recovery of Quebec playwriting also raised new questions about directing. Several observations in a study of directing in Quebec by Lorraine Camerlain merit discussion.[17] First of all, many directors still get most of their training as actors. The majority of productions involve new work, a situation which seems normal and healthy for Quebec drama. But it is interesting to note how Quebec directors treat these plays: generally speaking, they remain very faithful to the text, striving to articulate its implicit and explicit nuances while showing great respect for the author. At first glance, this attitude seems full of admirable intentions, but it also reveals symptoms of something else: directors seem particularly afraid of misreading or misunderstanding the text and being blamed in case of disaster. In short, they are afraid of misdirecting a good text and doing it considerable damage. They also seldom participate in the process of writing a play.

As far as the established canon of Quebec theatre is concerned, the lack of revivals is unsettling. Once the text has proven its worth, surely then opportunities arise for directors to clearly and openly practice their art. Quite the opposite appears to be the case and remounts are often disappointing: "Take, for example, the undeviating fidelity of the revival of *Tit-Coq* at the Nouvelle Compagnie Théâtrale in 1981 with staging virtually identical to the original by the same director and virtually the same sets. In my opinion, this reduces the work to the status of a museum piece (dead, carved in stone) instead of allowing a re-examination of the work and the society in which it was born and still lives."[18]

The problem suggests another equally disturbing question for Quebec playwrights: perhaps many of these plays are too dull to merit repetition and might fail on stage in a second production. Individual examples of brilliant directing do exist, however—works whose success is eloquent testimony to their willingness to explore and experiment. These productions resist classification since they are the work of individuals and companies outside the established theatres operating under difficult material constraints.

Directions and trends in these performances vary widely, from unique experiments complete in themselves to series of explorations undertaken in a specified context of theatrical research. Among them are both remounts and adaptations such as Roger Blay's production of *Macbeth* in 1978 and Alexandre Hausvater's productions of both dramatic and literary classics like *le Décaméron, Hamlet, les Frères Karamazov* in 1982 and *Mahagonny* in 1984.

Strongly influenced by Grotowski's theatrical experiments, Le groupe de La Veillée is known for its "paroxystic" kind of acting. Recently this company staged productions based on literary texts, novels and fragments of a journal. Théo Spychalsky directed *Till l'Espiègle* (1982) and *The Idiot* (1983), while Gabriel Archand did Jean Genet's *le Miracle de la Rose* in 1984. Other experimental theatres include Jacques Crête's L'Eskabel and Pierre-A. Larocque's Opéra-Fête. These companies stand out for their use of space, creation of environmental designs through the use of special audio-visual techniques, and a slow, disjointed, strange playing style which lends a dream-like atmosphere to their productions.

Les Enfants du Paradis—later renamed Carbone 14—under Gilles Maheu, and Les Mimes Omnibus, directed by Jean Asselin, explore a wealth of possibilities for mime in their productions. Gone forever is the misconception that a mime is nothing more than a pale, ghost-like face. The evolution of the body in space and its movements create a highly complex language complete in itself and capable of simultaneously expressing harmony and imbalance, stasis and movement, beauty and horror. The art of mime is no longer confined to only one level of interpretation.

Each of these productions deserves an in-depth analysis, and recent experiments confirm that growth and appreciable changes are evident in the staging of theatre in Quebec. One can only hope that these experiments will continue and awaken in theatre professionals a desire to make directing a recognizable art. Along with that recognition should come an awareness of its importance so that directing no longer occupies the paradoxical status of a missing link in the process of theatrical presentation.

Diane Cotnoir
Translated by Mark Czarnecki

Notes

[1]Jean Hamelin, *Le Renouveau du théâtre au Canada français.* Montreal, Editions du Jour, 1962. p. 7.

[2]Patrice Pavis, *Dictionnaire du Théâtre.* Paris, Editions Sociales, 1980. p. 254.

[3]Cited by Emile Legault. *Le Théâtre canadien-français.* Vol. 5, Archives des lettres canadiennes. Montreal, Fides, 1976. p. 818.

[4]Ibid. p. 819.

[5]Ibid. p. 820.

[6]Pierre Dagenais. *Le Théâtre canadien-français.* p. 823.

[7]Jean Hamelin. op. cit. p. 35.

[8]Jean Béraud, *350 ans de théâtre au Canada français.* Montreal, Le Cercle du livre de France, 1958. p. 257.

[9]Jean Hamelin. op. cit. p. 80 regarding Jean Gascon's direction of *Tartuffe* for the 1952-53 TNM season.

[10]Jean Gascon. *Le Théâtre canadien-français.* pp. 826, 827.

[11]Yerri Kempf, *Les Trois Coups à Montréal: chroniques dramatiques 1959-1964.* Montreal, Déom, 1965. pp. 89-90.

[12]Jean Hamelin. op. cit. p. 99.

[13]Verbal commentary by Adrien Gruslin, spring 1982.

[14]Verbal commentary by Martial Dassylva, spring 1982.

[15]Jean-Claude Germain, "Quelques articles du credo théâtral de Jean-Claude Germain", *La Presse,* May 6, 1972.

[16]Hélène Beauchamp-Rank, "La Vie théâtrale à Montréal de 1950 à 1970". *Le Théâtre canadien-français.* p. 290.

[17]Lorraine Camerlain, "Echos d'une enquête actuelle", *Jeu,* No. 25, 1982.4. pp. 41-82.

[18]Ibid. p. 49, fn. 17. Gratien Gélinas directed the revival.

Directing in
English Canada

Theatre directing in Canada is as large a topic as theatre itself, since Canadian theatre is primarily a director's theatre. No actors' theatre in the *commedia dell'arte* tradition, no actor-manager in the British tradition, has seriously threatened his place.

But this does not tell us much because, once given his inevitability, his role fragments in a dozen directions. Is he the perfunctory creator of dinner theatre entertainments, the intellectual coaxing an original script to life, or the freelancer who pretends to be equally at home with Ibsen and *Charley's Aunt*?

And there is the fragmentation of background. Is he, like Robin Phillips, an indifferent actor with a knack for drawing from others that which he cannot find in himself? Or, like Walter Learning or Richard Ouzounian, a producer compelled by the structure of Canadian theatre to direct as well? A former stage manager or administrator? Or even a director from the start?

It is widely felt that directing is the weak link in Canadian theatre. High standards for acting have been set by the National Theatre School. Professional designers, technicians and stage managers are the norm in Equity houses from coast to coast, in a country which two decades ago scarcely possessed a professional theatre.

But in directing, the banner of amateurism continues to fly. This is not purely from neglect. A strong body of opinion contends that directing is an apprentice skill. What school, it is argued, can provide student directors with a professional cast, a theatre and a production budget for the mastering of their craft?

Hence the ubiquitous assistant director, who after amassing experience in other people's shadows suddenly proclaims himself a director. Immediate contacts win his first assignments and then, if able, he goes on the freelance circuit. After virtually starving there he may, with bravado and luck, become an artistic director. With less of either he may retreat to the CBC or academe, peeping out every so often to remind us that he once was a professional director; and that, were it not for the pitiable state of Canadian theatre, still would be.

This summation is tongue-in-cheek, but it is nonetheless true that the theatre industry can not yet offer many directors a width and depth of experience to compare favorably with that of their colleagues elsewhere.

Consider a freelance director. In an average season he may arrange a half-dozen assignments, each involving about four weeks work if one includes research and casting. Even assuming he finds lower paid summer theatre work, he is still idle much of the time.

According to agreements negotiated on his behalf by Actors' Equity, he will be paid from $1,800 in the smallest G class theatre to $6,500 in the largest A class theatre. The average assignment will pay three to four thousand dollars.

Here a painful paradox emerges. A gross income of $24,000 for six productions is meagre, considering that several of them will be out-of-town, with attendant expenses. And even six productions, major ones, is optimistic. The director will be forced to supplement stage work with teaching or radio and TV directing, none of which is more than superficially related to the skills he needs in order to excel on the stage.

From the theatres' standpoint, however, these Equity minimums are generous. In most cases they become the standard salary. This means that there is no financial advantage for theatres in hiring young and aspiring directors. They can, for the same price, hire veterans; and do.

The conclusion? First, that there is virtually no training, except half-heartedly in one or two university theatre facilities. Secondly, there is little opportunity to break into the field.

The image one ought to hold in mind is of a director in his mid- to late-thirties, living in a one-bedroom apartment and supplementing his income teaching a couple of university courses. If he/she wishes to raise a family, serious compromises of professional dedication are almost inevitable.

The Director As Exotic Creature

To continue in the best tradition of cliffhangers and of theatre polemics *à la* Bernard Shaw, we will now cast our hypothetical director into the theatre he will work in.

Canadian theatre lacks both a top and bottom. At bottom, there is no working-class tradition of popular theatre of the music-hall variety. At top, there is nothing like the European notion that theatre can be a forum or vent for seething anxieties over great public issues.

What remains is a middle theatre for the middle-class; a middle-class accustomed historically to touring shows from London and New York and which, today, is still reluctant to create an agenda of issues it would like to see addressed in the arts. One consequence is that theatre boards of directors are amply supplied with people who consider quite risqué the idea that theatre may actually be about *them*— with predictable consequences for original plays.

The advent of film and, later, television—largely unopposed by an indigenous theatre tradition—has led to a situation where even among serious artists the American model, in which theatre takes second place to the electronic dramatizers, is dominant. This is no England, where an R.S.C. director may pride him/herself on never having worked in television. Here there is a faint but real aura of eccentricity which attaches itself to those who commit themselves to legitimate theatre.

The Structure: Small Theatres

The "alternate" theatres were created in the late 1960s and early 70s to show the mainstream theatres that original plays could be popular, and to aid in the development of a vital, rather than a museum and bourgeois theatre.

But the failure of many of these theatres to enlarge their audiences and to rival the mainstream has led to stagnation and to a posture of creative defensiveness. Directors who, in more integrated theatre cultures, would have worked their way easily from smaller to larger theatres and achieved public esteem have remained in the small theatre circuit or abandoned directing altogether.

Among the latter are names like Jean Roberts (one of the few women directors in the country) and Martin Kinch, a co-founder of Toronto Free Theatre, who have just recently left the CBC; both worked primarily in television. Bill Lane, one of the Free Theatre's most promising directors, is now in radio. Others have gone to New York or London, where an integrated theatre culture has allowed them access to greater resources. Des MacAnuff is the best-known among them.

Those who have remained in the small theatre circuit often, however, do so of their own free will. The reluctance of this maturing generation of directors to assume their rightful place at the helm of Canadian theatre is part of a complex phenomenon. Many of them entered theatre at the end of the 60s, an era of distrust toward authority. In theatre this manifested itself in the many movements toward destructuring of theatre and, particularly, de-middle-classing it.

These directors clustered around the small theatres and there, making a virtue of necessity, identified themselves romantically as outsiders. This is not to say that they did not work assiduously to develop an audience for new work and for the more challenging foreign works that could not be seen in the larger theatres. But they were content to polish this small gem rather than move on to vitalize and reform the mainstream theatres.

Examples include George Luscombe, whose Toronto Workshop Productions has for nearly three decades represented one man and one point of view; his talent for presentational theatre has rarely graced larger stages. Of the 60s generation, Ken Gass (Factory Lab), Clarke Rogers (Theatre Passe Muraille), Pam Hawthorne (New Play Centre) and Paul Thompson (Passe Muraille founder) have shown an aggressive disinclination to work in large theatres. Bill Glassco, founder of Tarragon Theatre, and Guy Sprung of Toronto Free Theatre have worked only intermittently in larger theatres.

For many of these directors, artistic independence, in the guise of controlling a small theatre, has become an affectation. The artistic in theatre is held to be antagonistic to mainstream theatre and its audience. In some cases, such as the Free Theatre under Sprung, this policy has led to continued vitality and relevance. But more often it leads to the situation best represented by the Tarragon under Urjo Kareda: careful, intellectual, but unexciting. In extreme cases, such as Passe Muraille under Clarke Rogers, it leads to artistic temper tantrums and facile revolutionary rhetoric. Neither extreme is likely to capture the imagination of the broad public.

The positive side of the alternative theatres has been the emergence of a director-specialist who might be called the "new work director." Because many Canadian playwrights are young and relatively few have seen their works produced, these directors are often very nearly the co-writers of new plays.

H ardee T. Lineham and Jo Ann McIntyre in the 1982 Centaur Theatre production of Judith Thompson's *The Crackwalker,* directed by Clarke Rogers. Photo: Raymond Poitras.

This skill, in itself valuable and in fact essential in a country where the creation of a canon of plays is theatre's most important task, is highly developed in the theatres just mentioned. What is lamentable is that many of these directors have prided themselves on failing to prepare to work on larger stages and with a wide variety of plays from the repertoire. Unlike the typical director of an original play in London or New York whose resumé will also include many classical productions, these directors are not likely to stretch new writers to create larger or more complexly structured scripts.

And the new work director, who both because of his 60s background and the fancied similarity of his converted warehouse to Artaud's *atelier,* prides himself on freedom from "bourgeois" attitudes, is working in a country that is in fact mostly bourgeois. And it is this largely bourgeois audience that stands most in need of self-expression. The new work director who continues to choose plays about minorities and the alienated, ironically serves the bias of the middle-class, Royal Alexandra-going audience that original plays are irrelevant. This in turn reinforces his marginal status, and his romantic self-definition.

The Large Theatres

The large theatres, it is important to remember, are still young theatres, dating from the 1960s. Most of the smaller professional companies were founded at the beginning of the 1970s. With the exception of the Manitoba Theatre Centre, earlier professional companies of the 1950s largely disappeared. MTC, by first defining itself as a "regional" theatre deserving of government and community support, created the successful model that has been emulated.

Because of the high operating costs of these theatres, their artistic directors are often chosen from the ranks of stage directors who (it is assumed) can defray at least one expense by directing several productions themselves.

Although there has been some to-and-fro-ing between large and small theatres (Passe Muraille's Clarke Rogers, for example, briefly ran Theatre Calgary in the early 70s), the boards of directors of many large theatres have preferred to choose foreign candidates, usually British, or British immigrants even if these had little prior background in theatre (Christopher Newton and Edward Gilbert being two who come to mind).

The carpetbagging foreign artistic director, who uses a Canadian theatre as an employment centre for actors from his homeland, is actually a rare creature (Peter Coe when he was at Edmonton's Citadel, for example) but he has created a stereotype that is often in the minds of Canadian directors and actors.

The subtler problem of having major theatres run largely by people who arrived in Canada as adults is that their taste and priorities were set elsewhere. That is why even such supportive figures as John Neville and Edward Gilbert seem curiously maladroit when trying to produce original plays. In spite of themselves, they help perpetuate the rift between the large theatres and the small, raucously nationalistic ones.

The preponderance of British-born artistic directors influences the national playbill enormously. Shakespeare is often produced; likewise Shaw, Ayckbourn and Coward. Molière, Giraudoux, and Goldoni are hardly heard from. Only the rare non-British but European artistic director, such as Marion André (Theatre Plus) or Tibor Feheregyhazi (Persephone Theatre) has made any serious attempts to explore playwrights from those other traditions that represent so large a proportion of Canada's population.

The balance of plays in a regional theatre season are given to guest directors. These are often other artistic directors, or former artistic directors, so that a great horse-trading system has developed among a.d.s. The true freelancer, such as Brian Rintoul or Stephen Katz, who has never run a major theatre, is a relatively exotic and infrequent bird of passage.

The dominance of large theatres by *arrivistes* who consider foreign plays the norm, together with an audience having a colonial mind-set, leads to situations that are bizarre, to say the least. Only rarely is a translation of Ibsen or Chekhov into the Canadian vernacular undertaken. Audiences go with great docility to hear their Russians, circa 1890, bellowing "By Jove!" and "Preposterous!" in whatever dated British translation is at hand, and notice nothing out of order.

This creates an awkward situation for a young director who wants to work the large stages. If he has worked in small theatres, he will have done original work, exotic foreign plays, and popular classics in vernacular adaptations by John Murrell or David French; or at least is familiar with them. The large theatre will seem out-of-date and claustrophobic. If he wishes to change the situation, he must strive to become an artistic director himself. At this point he will encounter the foreign bias and timidity that characterizes most search committees of major theatres.

It is important to note the exceptions to this situation. The Vancouver Playhouse in the late 60s produced original works as seminal as *The Ecstasy of Rita Joe.* Montreal's Centaur and Theatre Calgary have nourished original playwrights, while Regina's Globe has been political, provocative and international in its playbill.

But there is still a *perceived* image among small-theatres directors that the large theatres are unfriendly to innovation. And the perception, despite exceptions, is often true. Malcolm Black, the incoming director of Toronto's Theatre Plus, recently programmed *A Taste of Honey* and *Privates on Parade*—very good for cultural self-awareness in Nottinghamshire. Meanwhile, fifteen years after its première, Toronto has never seen a major revival of *Ecstasy of Rita Joe*—or many other important Canadian scripts, for that matter.

The Large Theatres—Working Conditions

Because of the triumph of the subscription system, large theatres are locked into a system of rehearsing plays for three weeks or so and then running them from four to six weeks, depending on the size of the city and the subscription list. They are also committed to a "variety" of programming, especially in cities (the majority) where there is only one major theatre.

The playbill is set by the artistic director, who may or may not collaborate with guest directors in choosing plays. The typical situation is that the guest director is offered a show without being asked what he personally has a passion to do at that moment. In the course of a season he may direct Shakespeare, Ibsen and *Charley's Aunt,* without much regard for his own qualifications or preference.

Even the artistic director is hamstrung. He must program according to the theory of the lowest common denominator in the audience rather than by his own temperament. The consequences of this may be seen by looking at one of the rare exceptions to it. John Wood, one of the few indigenous Canadian directors who has demonstrated anything that one might call "temperament," in his tenure at the National Arts Centre created some interesting programming. In the same season, for example, he staged both Chekhov's *Uncle Vanya* and *The Wood Demon*—the latter a virtually unperformed early draft of the former—solely out of theatrical curiosity. Likewise a production of *Henry V* into which he freely introduced, as a dream sequence, a scene from *Henry IV.*

By contrast with this *Henry V,* which was interesting in that it demanded more sophistication from the audience, one can look at Richard Ouzounian's *Taming of the Shrew* at the Manitoba Theatre Centre, which was staged in modern dress as a "new wave" send-up of Shakespeare. This may be seen as an example of making Shakespeare "accessible"—which is to say, assuming that the audience is unsophisticated and needs pandering.

By and large, regional theatre productions have taken the Ouzounian approach: to be accessible and entertaining rather than challenging. (This is not, by the way, a comment on the *quality* of the productions: the MTC *Shrew* was a very accomplished production, as much as the *Henry V.*)

In five years of seeing regional productions (about fifteen per year), only a very few bore the imprint of a director being mated with a play for which he had, and

Audra Lindley, Wally McSween, James Whitmore, Allan Royal and Ron White in the 1984 Citadel Theatre production of *Death of a Salesman*, directed by Len Cariou. Photo: Ed Ellis.

realized, a passion. There was Peter Froehlich's *Endgame* at the Neptune in Halifax, Des McAnuff's *A Mad World, My Masters* at CentreStage in Toronto, and Clarke Rogers' *The Crackwalker* at the Centaur in Montreal. Of course, there were by reputation others—Cedric Smith's *Threepenny Opera* at Magnus in Thunder Bay, Len Cariou's *Death of a Salesman* at the Citadel—but the total is small, especially from the viewpoint of a theatregoer in any one of those cities.

Partly this is because of the youthfulness of the profession. It is difficult to do a provocative production of *She Stoops to Conquer* when one is too busy learning for the first time the style of movement and language necessary for such a play—and likely coaching several of the actors in it, as well. There has simply not been the density of theatre activity that would give both directors *and audiences* the sophistication to excel in the exotic. Michael Langham, a veteran of British and American theatre, was doing his sixth *Love's Labour's Lost* at Stratford two years ago. In the Canadian theatre system, most directors would be thankful to be doing their first.

In sum, then, a director working in a large regional theatre is typically in this situation: He is directing a play not chosen by himself, in a style he is likely unfamiliar with, in a rehearsal period which is too short and fixed without regard for the size or complexity of the production. Even the artistic director is likely not a friend of the play in question, having chosen it for ulterior reasons ("time to do an Ibsen;" "time to do an American classic; heads it's Miller, tails it's Williams; I like Odets, but who'd come to see it?").

The winds of change, however, have finally blown high enough to begin to affect the large theatres. Since the battle over the importation of yet another foreign artistic director for Stratford five years ago, most large theatres have diplomatically restricted their searches to candidates already working in Canada (with the charmingly obtuse exception, as always, of the Citadel in Edmonton). People trained in the alternate theatres, such as Don Shipley, Keith Digby, Janet Amos, James Roy, Martin Kinch and Bill Glassco have recently taken over regional theatres. The balance of regionals continue to shuffle the ever-diminishing deck of existing artistic directors, whose wanderings from theatre to theatre are positively Moses-like in scale and duration.

Younger artistic directors, such as Richard Ouzounian during his year at CentreStage, are committed to the inclusion of original work in every season, and have begun to use Canadian translations of classics. Such changes augur well for the atmosphere in which guest directors will work in the years to come.

And, most significantly, artistic directors are increasingly being hired as producers without obligation to direct plays. Apart from creating more work for freelancers, this eliminates the problem of professional jealousy that occurs when an a.d. is faced with hiring a brilliant director whose production may outshine his own. A producer-artistic director, one hopes, may be more clearly committed to excellence in every production.

The Intangibles

The notion of "director" comes to us from nineteenth century Germany and reflects the hierarchical notions of the time. But the "regisseur," with his echoes of regal authority and the terrorizing of actors, is not very welcome in the twentieth century; especially in a country as little given to dictatorial behavior in any area of its life as Canada. Many small theatres reject the notion altogether in favor of collectivist approaches.

Even in large theatres, where the traditional notion supposedly still holds, the atmosphere in the rehearsal hall is more often collaborative than executive. Directors defer to the views of playwrights, designers and actors to an extent which would be surprising in Europe and even the United States.

This no doubt reflects a national disposition. But it also means that playwrights are not ordered to re-write what needs re-writing, or designers to re-shape what is difficult to work with. Instead, the argument is made that specialists know their business, and that the deferential approach produces more good work in the long run. But it remains true that our theatre is inherited from models which depended on the final arbitration of the director.

The softening of this role in Canadian theatre means there is nobody left to demand, however disagreeably, artistic excellence. The result is much mediocre work over which nobody's feelings are hurt because nobody is ultimately responsible for it.

Sitting through an indifferent *Sweet Bird of Youth* at the Arts Club in Vancouver, or a respectful disinterring of *Death of a Salesman* at the Vancouver Playhouse, a shouted, rattletrap *Three Musketeers* at Manitoba Theatre Centre, or a soggily acted *Lesson From Aloes* at Montreal's Centaur, one is confronted with the question not so much of an artist's reach exceeding his grasp, but of an indifference to reaching in the first place.

One suspects, especially when hearing the actor's common cry for directors who will actually give direction, that the lack of push often arises from the director's lack of commitment to the play in question, and to the lack of a sufficiently high standard of excellence demanded of his profession.

Certainly part of the problem is that we lack the competitive system that exists in countries where theatre arouses public interest and scrutiny, and directors held thus accountable develop an intellectual aggressiveness that is lacking here.

But much that is excellent in Canadian theatre has been created despite the lack of prior public demand (the taste, once created, hopefully perpetuates itself). It is difficult to see why the same may not be done with directing.

Ray Conlogue

The Canadian
Theatre Designer

In the world of theatre design, there is no showcase more prestigious, internationally, than the Quadrennial Expositions held in Prague, Czechoslovakia. In 1975, Canada submitted to the Prague Quadrennial for the first time. It was a small exhibit, yet received unexpected acclaim. As a result, the Canadian government was prompted to offer assistance, and the task of assembling future shows was entrusted to the Associated Designers of Canada. In 1979, the Canadian submission to the Quadrennial was granted an award of special merit for excellence. In 1983, Canada again submitted and was again given a special merit award; in addition one individual designer, Roy Robitschek, was awarded a special commendation. The exhibit was then shown in London and, after that, in Paris. Canadian theatre design was considered the equal of any in the world.

The term "theatre design" includes the design of settings, costumes and lighting for live performance. (Recently, the importance of sound design and special effects has begun to be recognized in program credits, but the recognition is not yet general.) Since the 1950s, Canada has gradually begun to generate a family of theatre designers producing work with a high level of craftsmanship, inventiveness and imagination. I can remember, myself, that when I arrived in Toronto from Boston, only twenty years ago, the general theatre design that audiences were used to was—more often than not—crude, uninformed and unpolished.

Sets were mostly put together with canvas-skinned flats, painted, and with no realistic trim or detail. Those in charge of the designs seemed to have little exposure to, or understanding of, visual concepts like Surrealism, Constructivism, Impressionism or Minimalism. There was no expression of electronic or photographic media. Designers had hardly any experience with symbolic or graphic conceptualization in terms of design, and sets usually ended up as box-like spaces with decoration inside of them. As a matter of fact, theatre design as a profession really did not exist; one could hardly expect to rely upon it for a livelihood, and most of the designing was being done by people who depended on other kinds of work for a living.

The changes in Canadian theatre design over the last thirty years took place imperceptibly, but, by the mid-80s, audiences across the country have come to expect, as the norm, an extremely refined design sensibility. While most countries may have a few main centres of theatrical activity, Canada has twenty or thirty from coast to coast (some of the larger cities even containing two or three), and this gradual transformation was happening in every one of them. In 1985, the kind of theatre design being done in Canada is occasionally brilliant, frequently provocative, and often of the first rank. Some examples will follow. Surprisingly, the history of this artistic development is one that goes back only about forty years.

Prior to World War II, professional theatre in Canada consisted mostly of American touring companies featuring "Broadway" productions. The plays, the actors, the designs were packaged together primarily in New York and presented in the larger Canadian cities, particularly Montreal, Toronto and Vancouver. In the U.S.A., the components of a theatrical profession had been in existence since the nineteenth century, and designers had been prominent by name since at least the 1920s. Certainly, there were men and women of talent in Canada, but Canadians who had aspirations to a career in theatre ordinarily found it necessary to leave the country.

There was one small exception in Toronto. In 1919, a building called Hart House was built at the University of Toronto, as a bequest from the Massey family for student recreational activity. It contained an ideal 450-seat Little Theatre and a long succession of plays were produced there under directors such as Roy Mitchell, Bertram Forsythe, Carroll Aikins, Edgar Stone, Nancy Pyper and Robert Gill. The first people enlisted to design stage settings at Hart House were some of the prominent easel painters of the time—Arthur Lismer, Lawren Harris, A.Y. Jackson and J.E.H. Macdonald.

For the generation between the mid-20s and mid-40s, a tradition persisted that individuals who were to design for the theatre would train originally in the Fine Arts. Among the leading recognized Canadian painters of today, Graham Coughtry, William Ronald and Harold Town all contributed to design and graphics for theatre and for the early television productions of the CBC. The first home-grown pre-war practitioners of theatre design art—Marie Day, Murray Laufer, Martha Mann, Suzanne Mess among others—trained originally in the Fine Arts. The Ontario College of Art had an important role in the development of many of them.

In 1946, the New Play Society was founded by Dora Mavor Moore in Toronto, and this is generally considered to be one of the cornerstones of indigenous professional theatre in Canada. Three years later, in 1949, the Canadian Repertory Theatre was founded in Ottawa. These companies, as well as the soon-to-follow Crest Theatre and Canadian Players, in Toronto, paved the way for higher standards in Canadian theatre.

Then came in 1950, the Canadian Opera Company; in 1951, the National Ballet of Canada; and in 1953, the Stratford Festival. These three companies became pre-eminent in providing a major spawning-ground for Canadian design talent. The size and scope of their productions was large, and the classical repertoire created an atmosphere of quality and an audience that has developed steadily ever since. Some of the noteworthy designers who had their first exposure at that time were Rudi Dorn, Bill Lord, Brian Jackson, Les Lawrence, Mark Negin and

321

Lawrence Schafer. Non-Canadians who played a large part in helping to shape many of these talents include Kay Ambrose, Desmond Heeley, Leslie Hurry and Jurgen Rose.

A large expression of indebtedness must also be made to Tanya Moiseiwitsch, who came from her native England to be one of the founding members of the Stratford company. She championed the thrust stage at Stratford which has had enormous influence on the form of North American theatre ever since. Moiseiwitsch's uncompromising craftsmanship, exuberant imagination, and unerring good taste established levels for Canadian theatre design that all of us have recognized as exemplars ever since.

I believe that it was as a result of Moiseiwitsch's kind of vision that Canadian theatre designers began to move away from the consideration of design as decor, or decoration, and toward an art form more three-dimensional, more plastic and more intrinsic to a theatrical interpretation of the text. The thrust stage at Stratford asserts its influence here. In one stroke, it drew the audience into a more intimate and closer physical relationship with the actors, and put a new emphasis on the spatial considerations of staging. Costume and lighting became the elements of highest visibility, and greater attention had to be applied to detail, authenticity and nuance. If scenic painters working previously within the framework of a proscenium could employ bold strokes to achieve an acceptable imitation of reality, now colours, materials and methods of construction had to aspire to a level of naturalism more common to film or television. The young Stratford apprentices and designers of the 50s, trained to this perception, carried the message to their successors across the nation.

Regretfully, a similar kind of development did not happen within the opera or ballet companies. Owing to their nature as organizations whose most immediate concern is for touring and international esteem, neither was able to establish a domestic production facility, and both have felt most strongly mandated to commission design contributions from more internationally recognized designers.

This problem is universal. As the cost of mounting opera and ballet production has escalated, companies internationally have discovered the virtue of renting sets and costumes from one another, and native construction has dwindled. Recently, young Canadians have been able to receive from the Metropolitan Opera in New York the kind of practical work experience that they cannot find here.

In the 60s, the mood of Canadian theatre was one of expansion. Major companies were formed in the regions. To celebrate the centennial of Canadian confederation in 1967, a number of new playhouses were built across the country with fly galleries and state-of-the-art machinery. In 1960, the National Theatre School was founded in Montreal, and began offering courses in theatre design, instructed originally by Robert Prevost and François Barbeau.

The first graduates of that course, including designers such as Michael Eagan, John Ferguson and Phillip Silver, began to enter the profession during the 60s. These were the first to have been educated and trained exclusively in Canada, specifically for theatre design, and they are some of the most well-rounded in our working world. Their training familiarized them with the broadest expressions of architecture, history, painting, sculpture, and the performing arts, and the regional theatres now had physical facilities and technicians capable of realizing their most imaginative concepts. Moreover, these designers had fluency in the design of sets, lighting and costumes, as have those who followed. It has become the norm that designers usually do not limit themselves to only one discipline.

In the 70s, another group of young people received training at the Wimbledon School of Art in England, and returned to practice in Canada. They included Maxine Graham, Judith Lee and Cameron Porteous, and they came back fortified by the long tradition of British theatre design. Our designers were more aware of design creativity in Poland, Czechoslovakia, Germany and the rest of Europe. Stratford began a tutorial system first instituted by Daphne Dare and later sustained by Susan Benson. This was the first time that a resident designer was appointed, with full design responsibility, or final approval for all designs, and direct on-the-job guidance for young designers.

By the mid-1970s, there was an increase in the numbers of schools offering theatre design training, and a proliferation of theatres in the major cities doing productions of varying scale on a range of budgets from generous to miniscule. If there were a dilemma in this, it was that emerging talented designers would find it more difficult to find work in the larger companies; so, the tutorial systems at Stratford did help to bridge a major gap. However, no other such training grounds have yet emerged for lesser experienced designers to obtain exposure to large-scale production.

Now, midway into the 80s, we can look back over a forty-year history of professional theatre in Canada, and identify some of the more influential factors and trends. High on the list would be the remarkably large amount of government subsidization; Canada has been, for the past twenty or thirty years, exceptionally generous in its support of the arts. In theatre, this has meant that the more established companies have been financially able to mount the kinds of productions that speak of high quality and mature taste.

However, this kind of financial responsiveness has created drawbacks as well as benefits. Government funding has been balanced in favour of the producing companies, as opposed to individual artists. Although this does not mean government influence over artistic choices of material and presentation, it has tended to put some measure of a damper over risk-taking by the larger companies. Thus, the more experimental or contentious plays have tended to be presented by the alternate theatre groups, among whom financial means are low—and design must necessarily rely heavily on ingenuity. To our benefit, this has resulted in a proliferation of adventurous companies, and some highly innovative designs.

One such example is the design by Astrid Janson for *The Master Builder,* produced by Tarragon Theatre in 1983. Janson is one of our designers who finds new expression in the most incongruous of materials. In this production, she brilliantly managed to evoke, by the use of hanging polyethylene packing materials, more of the mood of icy atmosphere and frozen emotions than would have been created by a more durable, Scandinavian, authentic, "master-built" traditional set. The lighting design by Harry Frehner was sensitive to this interpretation and almost subliminally underscored it. The Tarragon, after ten years, has graduated from the fringe theatre category, but still has a concentrated playing space, and still draws immensely from its roots in daring presentation.

Because government subsidies can be relied upon from year to year, some theatre companies have found it possible to engage the services of a resident designer who has then the major advantage of working with the same technicians, assistants and fellow designers on a number of productions over the space of several years.

Clare Coulter, William Needles, Linda Griffiths and John Blackwood in Bill Glassco's 1983 Tarragon Theatre production of *The Master Builder,* designed by Astrid Janson. Photo: Nir Baraket.

In this way, it can be possible to stretch the potential of all parties involved, and accomplish unexpected new dimensions of design.

Cameron Porteous has enjoyed such a working relationship at both the Vancouver Playhouse and at the Shaw Festival. Cameron has stated that, without this kind of special collaboration with lighting designers, properties makers, etc., he would never have been able to succeed in properly developing and realizing his designs for *Caesar and Cleopatra* at Shaw in 1984. The scale and complexity of this Egyptian design was vast, and the teamwork organization allowed Cameron the freedom of time and effort to keep the design elements fresh and unhackneyed.

In the past five years, there has been increasing activity among independent producers creating privately financed "commercial" productions. In these packages, many of which tour nationally, the run is open-ended, and the production plays as long as there is an audience. The difference to the designer—and this is now reflected in contracts—is that the design fee may now contain residual payments in addition to the original contract amount. It is still difficult to make a reasonable living at theatre design in Canada. With the rise of a new commercial theatre, designers may have an opportunity for more reliable and continuous sources of income as more work will be going to independent scenic production companies.

Are there specific characteristics of Canadian theatre design which differ from the design in other countries, and are there even differences in approach between designers in English-speaking and French-speaking Canada? I would have to conclude that differences are probably minimal. We don't really see the expression of any major movements or trends or political philosophies. There don't seem to be any significant differences in design across the country that reflect regional differences in culture or geography. Certainly there are various individuals and schools which have helped to shape our talents, but the most distinctive differences seem to be the ones in the styles of individual designers themselves.

Canadians generally accept themselves with a sense of humour, so there is not a great attitude of self-consciousness or turgidity about our designing. There is a readily available pool of talented scenic artists here so that our designers have the luxury of being able to employ painted scenery—which may not be the case in other parts of the world. In fact, there are numbers of excellent craftspeople

S usan Benson's costume design for Avo Kittask as the Mikado in the 1983 Stratford Festival production of *The Mikado*. Photo: Robert C. Ragsdale.

busy in our theatre world—carpenters, modellers, jewellers, haberdashers, milliners, and makers of props, wigs and boots—giving the designer especially wide latitude to explore materials and detailing.

On the other hand, because the costs of materials and equipment have become so high, not many of us have been able to experiment much with projection or photographic techniques in theatrical design. Our colleagues in film and television have found these techniques more readily available, and there has, lately, been more cross-fertilization among the disciplines. Hopefully, there will be more.

I would like to mention several more recent designs that seem—to me, at least—to best illustrate the great diversity of design talent in Canada. At the Stratford Festival, over three seasons, Susan Benson contributed designs for a series of Gilbert and Sullivan operettas—*The Mikado, The Gondoliers* and *Iolanthe*—that were models of a muted and tasteful, but benignly wicked parody of, respectively, Japanese scroll paintings, *commedia dell'arte* and British music hall. Phillip Silver, also at Stratford, brought high levels of interpretation to *Virginia* and *Translations;* the one an introspective, almost oriental arrangement of translucent screens and shadowed branches echoing the delicacy and persona of Virginia Woolf, the other a dank, earthy, mossy summoning-up of nineteenth century Ireland.

Two other designers—Mary Kerr and Michael Levine—employ a strong vibrancy of colour. Kerr's designs for *In the Jungle of Cities* at Toronto Free Theatre used an overvaulting scaffold construction. Levine employed a mounting series of cardboard-seeming flat surfaces in the fantastic designs for *The Skin of Our Teeth* at the Shaw Festival. These are some of the diverse elements of Canadian design— wit, insight, freshness of approach, historical authenticity, exploration of materials and spatial relationships.

It is as difficult to pin down Canadian theatre design as it is to define succinctly the Canadian national character, though most of us believe there is one. There is a sense of individualism here, and a strong sense of belonging to the North American continent, although we honour our roots in Europe and other parts of the world. There is intellectual curiosity and a fascination with exploration, adventure and the natural world. All of these things express themselves in our theatre design art, and we hope that we may be able to display this expression again, at the next Prague Quadrennial.

Tom Doherty

Theatre Criticism in Quebec 1945-1985

Theatre historians now agree that the "revival"[1] of dramatic art in Quebec began after the end of the Second World War. Since 1938, Gratien Gélinas had been delighting local audiences with his annual reviews known as the *Fridolinades*. With the production of his play, *Tit-Coq,* in 1948, he laid the cornerstone for this revival. Not long after, Marcel Dubé followed suit with the production of his drama *Zone.* These points of reference, useful as they may be, tend to classify any dramatic activity that occurred previously as formless and archaic. As history will surely demonstrate, this is a case of oversimplifying and making hasty judgments.

What can be said about dramatic writing also applies to acting and stage design. The early work of Father Legault and his Compagnons[2] is a prime example of this. Commentators are continually citing critics, historians and observers, from Jean Béraud to Jean-Claude Germain, or Michel Bélair to Jean-Cléo Godin, who claim that the Compagnons were the first company to stage quality productions. Once again, what had been done before was disparaged, set aside and given little further consideration. Jean-Claude Germain has stated, for example, that "there is no doubt that the Compagnons also brought a sense of form, of quality, of dramatic precision, that heretofore had hardly existed."[3]

The quick unanimity which greeted, from the beginning, the arrival of the Compagnons and the production of *Tit-Coq,* must be considered suspect. This unanimity illustrates, however, the attitudes of theatre critics of the last few decades.

The Era of Journalists and Enlightened Amateurs
In order to understand the nature and the function of theatre criticism since 1945, we must begin at the "Belle Epoque" (1900-1914). During this period the large daily newspapers[4] made permanent appointments of critics who dealt with the various branches of the arts. Before this, the manager, owner, or a staff member who happened to be free on the night of the performance, attended the play and gave his impressions in an article that was often slapdash and trite, and always

superficial. Theatre criticism at that time was more a question of public relations than of critical analysis or judgment of artistic work.

With the appearance of permanent journalists and of specialized arts coverage,[5] the situation changed rapidly. Although the reviews followed the same basic format, they were better written and gave an in-depth analysis of the plays—and they were published on a regular basis. At the same time, critics were developing a method of analysis and an aesthetic of theatre. Even though this first revolutionary step happened rather late, it may be compared with the burst of theatrical activity which occurred at the beginning of the twentieth century. It had its limits, however.

Many American companies[6] brought their plays on tour but local critics had no influence whatsoever on the repertoire or the kind of productions developed in New York. Nor did they have much influence on local audiences who, attracted by flashy, alluring advance publicity promising grand spectacles, purchased their tickets before opening night.

This situation of the relative ineffectiveness of critics continued unchanged after World War II. On the one hand, touring companies remained, proportionately, as numerous and impervious to criticism. The publicity which preceded their productions, the cautious attitude of newspaper publishers worried about losing their major advertisers, and the frequency of performances (one new show a week per theatre) made the work of theatre critics particularly thankless. They had little influence on the kind and quality of productions.

On the other hand, on the local scene, there were theatrical troupes of undetermined status and the unpaid amateurs. Under-equipped and with virtually no financial backing, they had to work within a political and religious environment that did not encourage the growth of the arts. In order to survive and establish themselves, they attempted to please everyone by playing it safe and avoiding innovations. In this context, it is easy to understand why the Compagnons, with their concept of theatre aesthetics and the principle of anonymity,[7] were hailed by critics and their work considered a revolution in the development of the art of dramatic expression. But this was a revolution that could be accommodated, a controlled "New Wave." Their innovative approach, and that of Pierre Dagenais and his Equipe (established in 1943), at a time when uniformity was the order of the day, marked the beginnings of a new concept of theatre. At the time, critics could have become involved in a heated debate over aesthetics, newly imported concepts, repertoire and ethics. They could have revived the conflict over *le Cid,* angrily taking sides, making suggestions and passing judgment. But nothing happened. Critics, as a group, were unanimous in their praise.

There were, of course, a few dissenters who pointed out weaknesses in the performances of actors and shortcomings of productions. Father Legault sometimes found that critics were severe about the work of the Compagnons: "Certainly we had our bad days. And the critics did not make any bones about telling us what they thought."[8]

Jean Béraud, theatre critic at *La Presse* from 1931 to 1965, let fly with a few slings and arrows,[9] as did Jean Desprez of Radio-Monde: "The Compagnons are back on the right track, according to Béraud.... Guy Hoffman and Denise Pelletier are in the process of helping a company, whose exhaustion was becoming alarming, get back on its feet again."[10]

But nothing too vehement was said. No one dealt with the basic issue. All that took place were a few small critical skirmishes. It would be easy to infer from the state of affairs that there was some degree of complicity between critics and producers. Jean Béraud suggested: "We should be doing something about making things easier for actors to earn a living, so that they will not be faced with the prospect of running after any kind of work they can get. Then we could afford to be more critical."[11]

This firm defense of actors applies to directors as well, and goes far beyond defending any particular individual. Articles written by columnists of the time reflect the same concern and hopes that had been expressed for Father Legault, Pierre Dagenais, Gratien Gélinas and Marcel Dubé.[12] Their ultimate objective, an obsession if you like, was to create and develop a national theatre.

Basically, the problem can be reduced to the following: from 1945 until the Quiet Revolution in the early 1960s, theatre criticism was subjected to demands unrelated to the theatre but which formed a basis for critical scrutiny. Local critics and the French-speaking theatre community presented a united front, all the more so because of the alluring threat of foreign theatre, which relegated genuinely relevant critical disagreements unworthy of consideration. The preoccupation with nationalism tended to make them concentrate on the bits and trifles of dramatic activity. Yerri Kempf may well claim, after the fashion of Jean Barbeau,[13] that Gélinas is not a great dramatist ("...when compared to a Hamlet or a Misanthrope, Gélinas' characters do not carry much weight..."), if on the other hand, he recognizes that Gélinas "...has opened a new door on the future...."[14]

It was to be a future that would see the creation and development of a national theatre. No longer would it be necessary to restrict activities to "bold projects, suggestions, prophecies and bitter complaints because we have lost hope."[15] One is well aware of the limitations imposed on criticism in circumstances such as these. The critic will describe, relate, contradict and occasionally question. Sometimes he will find fault with a specific aspect of a production. But his critical evaluations can never completely disregard other considerations. Harsh criticism of a newly-established national theatre would destroy it in its infancy and encourage domination by the foreign (American and French) stage. Critics were aware that the struggle to establish an indigenous theatre was essentially a national and collective one. So they did everything in their power to avoid internal dissension or arouse the anger of the authorities.

This was not a difficult task because critics were sincere in their defense of the dogmas of the time. Most columnists had spent their formative years in classical colleges, or had at least been exposed to them, so they were products of the same environment as the local amateurs, writers and actors. They all shared the same conception of theatre: middle-class, conventional, correct, well-spoken and, preferably, beautiful. Above all else, they venerated the classics.

Michel Bélair, describing theatre producers of the 50s, exaggerates only slightly when he maintains: "Above all, they believed that the theatre was a means of attaining culture, a kind of *force de frappe* which, if properly deployed, would allow popular culture to reach the higher realms of universal culture."[16] This explains why they had such a poor opinion of burlesque, which they considered cheap and vulgar.

Finally, and this is by no means the least consideration, these critics from the print media found themselves limited by journalistic constraints. Columns in a daily newspaper or a few pages in a magazine appearing on an irregular basis did not lend themselves readily to serious debate. Nor did they allow for a more detached look at the plays. These spontaneous, emotional day-to-day reviews did not allow the critics time to undertake a long and thorough analysis of the theatre or of their own work.

Writers Have Their Say

From 1955 on, theatre in Quebec evolved rapidly and made great strides. Established companies (Théâtre du Nouveau Monde and Rideau Vert) and semi-professional ones (Egrégore and Théâtre-Club) increased in number. At the same time, their repertoire diversified. Even if it was not yet obvious that a national theatre was being created, it was well on its way. These various elements, to which must be added the return of touring companies from France and increased support from government agencies (the Canada Council and municipal arts councils), partly liberated critics from the task they had previously set themselves. Now that there were fewer constraints, it was possible to devote more of their time to their real responsibility—that of being critics.

Yet they encountered difficulties since they were disconcerted by the dynamism exhibited by the local theatre and the unexpected perspectives it offered. Critics were completely comfortable with the popular success of Edwige Feuillère's interpretation of the role of *Phèdre* (April 30, 1957) since they were still attached to the classics. Maurice Huot called it "A perfect, unforgettable evening of which the critic can express no reservations."[17] Jean Vallerand was similarly lavish with his praise: "Itwas a profoundly moving event such as one experiences only three or four times in one's lifetime."[18] More philosophically, Jean Béraud expressed his pleasure that *Phèdre* attracted a larger audience than *la Dame aux Camélias*. Tongue in cheek, Jean Vallerand queried elsewhere, "Are there still people out there who want to see *la Dame aux Camélias*?"[19]

With the classics, things were going well. The triumph of the great French actress as Racine's heroine was "yet another opportunity to observe how Canadian audiences have developed good taste."[20] Somewhat earlier, the Barrault-Renaud company had offered another occasion for the affirmation of critical doctrines. But the group, concerned with its "modern" image, had put on a play by Claudel. Obviously, Claudel is not Racine. But all the same, it is "grand" theatre. Jean Vallerand asserted: "This is a grandiose, moving play. How it affirms Claudel's genius!"[21]

Critical coverage deteriorated once companies began to move away from traditional theatre. Avant-garde writers, or those considered as such (Genêt, Ionesco, Beckett) were coldly received. Critics took a middle road, avoiding outright condemnation or overt praise, and most often expressed banal platitudes. When Jacques Languirand and his Théâtre de Dix Heures produced Genêt's *The Maids* in April of 1957, critics had difficulty concealing their confusion: "There is a bit too much boom and bombast, but the exaggeration ties in with the malevolent and vengeful theme...Jacques Languirand, you have taken on a tough assignment!"[22]

Jean Hamelin voiced his assessment of another avant-garde company, the Apprentis-Sorciers playing Ionesco's *The Chairs,* in the same prudent and paternalistic tone: "Their diction is often deficient when it is not poor; their staging is mediocre enough and their performances are clumsy. However, ...they do show signs of having made some interesting discoveries and of having an innovative spirit."[23]

Critics soon began to take a harder line, particularly when the writer of a new play happened to be from Quebec. Modernism lacking foreign critical approval was often rejected. "If our young theatre really wants to head in this direction, we might as well go back to the days of *Félix Poutré*."[24]

But when a foreign (French) critic was the first to belittle a local avant-garde writer, columnists were quick to follow suit. Victor Barbeau stated of Languirand's *Violons de l'automne:* "It is unfortunate that the author has written a play which is, as *Le Figaro* maintains, filthy, tedious and sterile." And as if this were not enough, he added: "Even with the best intentions in the world, it would be virtually impossible to pick out one scene that was not an affront to good taste and good sense."[25]

These criteria of good taste and good sense, cited so openly by Barbeau, influenced all critical commentary of the period. Strangely enough, it was neither the critics nor academics who would challenge these criteria. It was to be the authors themselves.

At the beginning of the Quiet Revolution, the language debate had already begun. The theatre got embroiled in the fray somewhat late in 1963. That year, a group of young writers founded the revue *Parti pris*. With both a political and cultural orientation, this *revue de combat* understood well how to disturb the established order. For the first time, literary and dramatic criticism, which existed only in the print media, would be systematically attacked: "Literary criticism in Quebec is ignorant of what literature really is. [It is] party to a literature of evasion, a literature which is an accessory to the established order."[26]

Reduced to the level of "creeps" and "mercenaries of the status quo," "our critics are dilettantes fascinated by publications by Seghers while important work is published right under their noses,"[27] *Parti pris* asserted. Besides being pro-French, criticism in Quebec was thus perceived as bourgeois and colonial. This first charge was followed by a second, more fundamental one: "We hope that artists will have the courage to write, to paint or to film works of art which cry out almost unbearably. In so doing, they will affirm their true vocation, which does not exactly happen to be that of reassuring the Madam President of the Friends of Art!"[28]

This desire for purification led the *Parti pris* group to opt for "joual" and the sordid aspects of day-to-day life which, according to them, were an accurate reflection of Quebec society in 1963. Traditional critics were shaken and, incensed, reacted vigorously. The fight was on and continued until 1970.

It is difficult to explain all that took place during this epic battle, but one thing is certain: writers were not about to accept the judgments of critics they did not respect. On the attack, authors became critics themselves. Traditional critics responded impetuously and clumsily. They began by rejecting the idea of a "new" Quebec and "Québécitude." Yerri Kempf, theatre columnist for the revue *Cité libre* declared: "I would like to point out the aberration of these self-opinionated young people at *Parti pris* attacking the use of universal French and supporting the creation of a literature of pure joual. Blinded by an ill-conceived nationalism, they have not yet realized that the use of a deteriorating language, with its limited vocabulary and questionable syntax, is a barrier to social progress. It dooms to mediocrity the collectivity which clings stubbornly to its use."[29]

In response to this "creep" who had not understood the issue, André Brochu of *Parti pris* explained the necessity for, and value, of joual. It must be used "for an essentially critical function, for the purpose of revealing a state of disintegration of language analogous to the disintegration of society."[30]

At the same time as the battle over joual, a new front opened up, that of repertoire and models. Jean-Claude Germain, actor, playwright and director, fired broadsides at the so-called "collaborators." He rejected "Claudel's rubbishy metaphysics" and was "overjoyed at the failure of *Bérénice* at the T.N.M." "I am a violent Racinophobe," he declared.[31] Still more iconoclastically, he wrote a terse article with the eloquent title, "*L'Avare:* un osstidcho involontaire" ("*The Miser:* an Unwitting Dupe"): "[Molière] no longer has any vital significance. [His theatre] is without depth; [it is] a beautiful empty shell."[32]

The dispute continued unabated, coming to a climax in August of 1968, with the première of Michel Tremblay's *Belles-Soeurs*. The triumphant success of the play raised the ire of the traditionalists: "Those supporters of avant-garde theatre and followers of political autonomy for Quebec have hailed it as a masterpiece. Most sensible people consider it an aberration."[33]

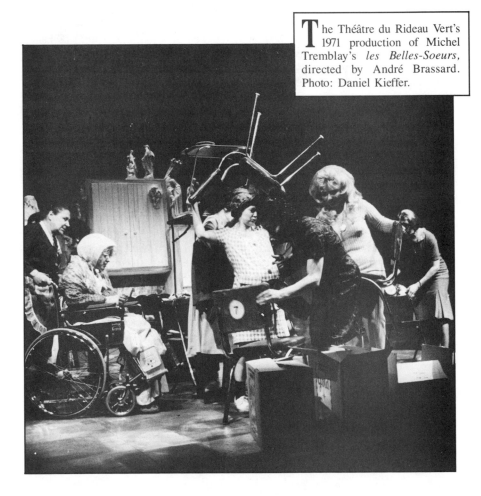

The Théâtre du Rideau Vert's 1971 production of Michel Tremblay's *les Belles-Soeurs,* directed by André Brassard. Photo: Daniel Kieffer.

The heated exchanges which followed, between Martial Dassylva, André Major, Roger Duhamel, Michel Bélair, Jean Basile and Jean-Claude Germain, to name only a few, constitute the greatest moments in the history of Quebec dramatic criticism. Martial Dassylva declared of *les Belles-Soeurs:* "In view of the coarseness and vulgarity of the text, I cannot help thinking that the directors of the Rideau Vert have perhaps done the author a great disservice by agreeing to produce his play... This is the first time in my life that I have heard so many curses, swear words and obscenities, and all in a single evening."[34]

André Major responded to Dassylva: "Let's try for a moment—which would be absurd—to have the sisters-in-law speak differently. Michel Tremblay would not be able to do it because he has talent, he is intelligent, and he loves the theatre."[35]

The question of the conflict already appeared settled despite several subsequent somersaults. The younger writers increasingly imposed their conception of theatre, leading traditional critics to abdicate. In 1973, a repentant Martial Dassylva provided the crowning conclusion with a resounding critique of his previous position: "When Michel Tremblay's *Belles-Soeurs* was first produced in 1968, I spoke out strongly against joual.... Having been brought up in an environment where the emphasis was on the French classics, I was unable to conceive, either physically or intellectually, that we would go as far!"[36]

It must be noted that between 1968 and 1973, an event occurred which was to have a profound effect on the theatre in Quebec: the university community became involved in dramatic criticism.

The University Community and *Jeu*

While the battle over the use of joual continued, producers organized themselves and captured all the available critical platforms. Most of the literary, social and cultural revues (*La Barre du Jour, Liberté, Cité libre*) and all the news magazines (*le Magazine Maclean, Châtelaine*) devoted whole pages and sometimes entire issues[37] to the subject of dramatic activity. On a number of occasions, groups founded their own magazines devoted solely to the theatre. This was the case with *Théâtre Vivant,* founded by the Centre d'essai des auteurs dramatiques in 1965, and with *Cahiers de l'ACTA* (Association canadienne du théâtre d'amateurs) which later became the revue *Jeune théâtre* of the AQJT (Association québécoise du jeune théâtre).

From an historical standpoint, the most significant publication of the period[38] was that of the Nouvelle Compagnie Théâtrale (NCT). Remaining firmly committed to their original objective, that of presenting classical works to students, the NCT began publishing manuals of literary analysis for classroom use in 1967. These were distributed by the Quebec Ministry of Education. Highly didactic in nature, the *Cahiers* offered the first introspective approach to critical analysis. Dramatic works were systematically analyzed, their authors interpreted and basic theatrical conventions explained to an increasingly numerous public. Moreover, after 1970, the *Cahiers* became available to everyone. Although often considered too scholarly, they announced and anticipated the beginning of academic dramatic criticism.

There are two reasons for the surprising failure of the universities to comment on the conflict over language.[39] First, they had always been reluctant to become

The Nouvelle Compagnie Théâtrale's 1976 production of Réjean Ducharme's *Inès Pérée et Inat Tendu*. Photo: André Le Coz.

actively involved in controversy. Second, there was an overriding preoccupation with assimilating the new French criticism that prevailed at the time. If the main object of the latter had been the poetics of theatre rather than the poetics of narrative, in all likelihood the universities would have been involved in analysis of drama long before. In a brief article published in 1975, Laurent Mailhot looked back and explained the reservations of academics: "There are—there were?—a number of reasons why critics in the academic community had reservations about French Canadian and Québécois theatre: There were no basic analytical tools; many texts were either unpublished or unavailable; sometimes it was impossible to locate related documents. And finally, there was a lack of knowledge about the socio-historical context, source materials, research techniques, staging and production methods and how the plays were received. But where they had the most difficulty was trying to discover how to develop a theory and methodology for an in-depth study of theatrical activity."[40]

Mailhot was right, of course. The first major critical works produced by the universities were textual analyses or historical overviews.[41] Considerations such as production methods, the sociology of the theatre, actual working conditions or performance symbolism were deemed too esoteric.

It took another few years to develop a more universal and systematic approach to the process of theatre criticism. Launched by young academics already practicing the new criticism, a new trend began in 1976. It was inspired by the earlier efforts of the Association québécoise du jeune théâtre.[42] In fact, some of its members were recruited from the ranks of the AQJT. Subsequently, two groups emerged. During the winter of 1976, the Cahiers de théâtre *Jeu* appeared for the first time. A year later la troupe de la Grande Réplique founded its own publication, the *Revue de la Grande Réplique,* which became *Pratiques théâtrales* in 1980, and then *Théâtralité.* The troupe was associated with the Université du Québéc à Montréal and favoured a Brechtian approach to the production of plays. Unfortunately, the revue's irregular publication and the changes in its editorial staff have limited the impact of its critical approach.

The periodical *Jeu,* in contrast, is fortunate in that it is backed by a strong organization. The editorial staff consists of seven to nine people supported by nearly one hundred contributors "managed" by a board of directors. A total of thirty-three issues have been published since 1976. *Jeu* has not strayed too far from the objectives it set itself at its inception. In the first issue, Gilbert David, the original founder and driving force behind the publication, explained the aims of the revue: "*Jeu* intends above all to inform, to describe, to (re)produce the practice-theory-practice process without accepting the dictates of a criticism which would subordinate all theatrical activity to an ideological orthodoxy and without, on the other hand, subscribing to an undiscerning or opportunistic pluralism."[43]

With such an aim, *Jeu* appealed for a "collective collaboration."[44] Anxious to avoid obscurantism and intellectualism, the publication actively recruits contributors from within the theatrical community—playwrights, actors and directors.

Three phases in the history of *Jeu* are discernable: from 1976 to 1978 it examined retrospectively theatrical activity between 1960 and 1975. Issues focussed on major companies and theatrical movements. In 1978, after Gilbert David and Lorraine Hébert returned from studies in France, the revue began to concentrate on current activity in the theatre. Productions were analyzed in a more profound and perceptive manner. The semiological approach was refined and more space set aside for professionals from the theatre, often in the form of interviews.

In 1980, *Jeu* took another step forward in its analysis by increasing the number of special issues discussing specific aspects of theatrical activity (sociological, historic, aesthetic or thematic). In the same manner, there were issues about women and the theatre, playwriting, directing, acting, and theatre and the young.

Since its inception, the influence of the publication has steadily increased. With a circulation of 1,200, it rallies today nearly all the active elements of the world of the theatre. Part popular review, part academic journal, *Jeu* exemplifies the evolution of dramatic criticism towards maturity, able to tackle the next crisis...

Jean-Marc Larrue
Translated by Audrey Camiré and Anton Wagner

Notes

[1]The term used by Jean Hamelin.

[2]The company was established in 1937 but did not become really active until 1940.

[3]Jean-Claude Germain, *Jeu,* No. 13, Fall 1979. p. 22.

[4]*The Gazette, Montreal Star, La Presse, La Patrie, Le Canada* and *Le Devoir* assigned their columns to freelancers.

[5]Usually one person was responsible for covering all dramatic entertainments.

[6] These companies were American but also European.

[7] Father Legault had patterned his concept of the theatre after the style of Copeau.

[8] Emile Legault, "Quelques notes sur les Compagnons". *Le Théâtre canadien-français*. Archives des lettres canadiennes, Vol. 5. Montreal, Fides, 1976. p. 259.

[9] Jean Béraud, *350 ans de théâtre au Canada français*. Montreal, Cercle du livre de France, 1958. p. 269.

[10] Idem.

[11] Jean Béraud, *Variations sur trois thèmes*. Montreal, Editions Fernand Pilon, 1946. pp. 105-106.

[12] The first two were directors. Gélinas wrote, acted, directed and produced. Dubé was a playwright.

[13] Quoted by Jean-Cléo Godin, *Le Théâtre québécois*. Montreal, Hurtubise HMH, 1970. p. 43.

[14] Yerri Kempf, *Les Trois Coups à Montréal*. Montreal, Déom, 1965. p. 37.

[15] Jean Béraud, *Variations sur trois thèmes*. op. cit., pp. 150-152.

[16] Michel Bélair, *Le Nouveau Théâtre québécois*. Montreal, Leméac, 1973. p. 22.

[17] *La Patrie,* April 30, 1957. p. 12.

[18] *Le Devoir,* May 1, 1957. p. 7.

[19] *Le Devoir,* April 27, 1957. p. 3.

[20] Jean Béraud, *350 ans de théâtre*. op. cit., p. 307.

[21] Jean Vallerand, "Claudel au Saint-Denis", *Le Devoir,* January 18, 1957, p. 8.

[22] Pierre Saucier, "La Pièce de Genêt", *La Patrie,* April 28, 1957. p. 71.

[23] Jean Hamelin, *Le Renouveau du théâtre au Canada français*. Montreal, Editions du Jour, 1962. p. 138.

[24] Quoted by Jean-Cléo Godin, op. cit., p. 174. Louis-Honoré Fréchette's patriotic melodrama was widely performed by amateur theatre companies for over half-a-century after its première in 1862.

[25] Ibid., p. 173.

[26] André Brochu, "L'Oeuvre littéraire et la critique", *Parti pris,* Vol. 1, No. 2, November 1963. p. 23.

[27] Laurent Girouard, "Notre littérature de colonie", *Parti pris,* Vol. 1, No. 3, December 1963. p. 36.

[28] Denys Arcand, "Les Divertissements 2", *Parti pris,* Vol. 1, No. 5, February 1964. p. 56.

[29] Yerri Kempf, op. cit., p. 31.

[30] André Brochu, "D'un faux dilemme", *Parti pris,* Vol. 2, No. 8, April 1965. p. 58.

[31] Quoted by Laurent Mailhot, "Jean-Claude Germain critique", *Jeu,* No. 13, Fall 1979. p. 93.

[32] Idem.

[33] *Dossier de presse (1966-1981) de Michel Tremblay.* Sherbrooke. Séminaire de Sherbrooke, 1981. p. 6.

[34] Martial Dassylva, "L'Amour du joual", *La Presse,* August 29, 1968. p. 64.

[35]André Major, "Un Exorcisme par le joual", *Le Devoir,* September 21, 1968. p. 14.

[36]Martial Dassylva, *Un Théâtre en effervescence.* Montreal, Editions La Presse, 1975. p. 19. In his self-critique, Dassylva referred to himself as a "native of the region of Menaud." Menaud was Félix Antoine Savard's hero in *Menaud, Maître-draveur* (1937). He was a patriotic French Canadian and spoke a "pure" French. The novel takes place in the Charlevoix area (Baie St.-Paul) where Dassylva was born.

[37]*La Barre du Jour,* Vol. 1, Nos. 3-5, Fall 1965.

[38]A bilingual magazine, *Theatre in Canada, (La Scène au Canada),* subsequently *Scène Canada,* appeared in Toronto during the same period (1965). It was published by the Canadian Theatre Centre (Centre canadien du théâtre) but had little impact.

[39]André Brochu, Gilles Marcotte, and a few others got embroiled in the conflict, but these were individual and isolated efforts.

[40]Laurent Mailhot. "Le théâtre québécois et la critique universitaire", *Canadian Drama,* Vol. 1, No. 2, 1975. p. 97.

[41]For example, Godin and Mailhot's study and *Le Théâtre canadien-français.*

[42]The AQJT published the revue *Jeune théâtre.*

[43]Gilbert David, "Enjeu", *Jeu,* No. 1, Winter 1976. p. 6.

[44]Ibid., p. 3.

Canadian Theatre Criticism

The position that the theatre critic plays in Canada can still be seen as a defensive one, as the 20th century moves into its final phase. Indeed, it is doubly defensive, maintaining the critic's accustomed responsibility of defending theatre itself against the indifference of a public which did not come to this country for cultural reasons, while at the same time defending his own right to establish critical standards. There have been some strong leaders in the past but the troops following them shift with discouraging frequency.

Before recording some of those leaders, to establish the critical position historically, let me rough in the prevailing situation of employment facing the profession today. This must be seen against a background of a newly burgeoning indigenous theatre—which must be put into perspective also.

Reflecting a country which, being sparsely populated, clung to colonial ways long after independence came with Confederation in 1867, our stages favored touring companies from outside for over a half-century. The fact that we have a theatre at all, in a century of electronic substitutes, is partly owed to the thousands of touring players who visited from Britain, France and the United States, countries whose activity easily over-shadowed our own.

Some of these visitors were of a distinction which plainly defied local competition, including as they did thespians from Edmund Kean to Henry Irving to John Gielgud and Ralph Richardson; from Sarah Bernhardt and Constant-Benoît Coquelin to Louis Jouvet; from Edwin Booth to Katharine Cornell and the Lunts.

Canada welcomed great artists but it also saw many lesser talents. (Some of them even settled down here, to play in stock companies or give lessons.) But a depression and rising freight rates reduced the circuits in 1929 and on, until the country was forced to depend on local talent, somewhat reluctantly. (Of the many touring stops, only Toronto remains receptive today, though far from dependent.)

Independent Canadians prefer to trace our stage back to more indigenous sources, to the garrison theatres and even further—to native peoples' rituals. But it wasn't until those depression years that a truly indigenous theatre organized itself, under the banner of the Dominion Drama Festival. This drew our performers in competition from across the country, from sea to sea.

Those competitive national festivals, leading up to a final "play-off" which moved around the dominion, attracted many talented Canadians who had no hope of making a living acting in their own country. Where the professionals elsewhere sharpened their techniques in long (if sporadic) runs, the amateurs in Canada did not have that advantage but they frequently did have much longer to rehearse.

Visiting adjudicators, often men of high distinction (Harley Granville-Barker, Robert Speaight, Michel St. Denis) had no trouble praising the results. Indeed, they agreed that the real shortage lay in directors, not players. When a director like Tyrone Guthrie arrived in 1952, he found no shortage of acting talent to back his imported stars, Alec Guinness and Irene Worth, when the Stratford Festival began production the following year. Nor did his successor, Michael Langham, lack for Canadian talent to assume leads thereafter.

Thus the Dominion Drama Festival, which lasted for three decades after being instituted in 1933 with the support of the Earl of Bessborough, then Governor-General, was the closest Canada came to a national theatre. Being non-professional, it could not survive in the face of the progress of which it was part. But it did give an outlet to much talent in the interim and brought about the National Theatre School. The introduction of radio and television, with their built-in commercialism, gave Canadian actors the right to call themselves just that on their income tax forms. Professionalism became fully established. By 1953, Guthrie's Stratford Festival convinced any still-doubting audiences that Canadians had the right to occupy the best of all possible stages.

This professionalism was accepted by the Canada Council as a requisite for subsidy. The Council followed the establishment of bodies such as the Stratford Festival, the Royal Winnipeg and National ballets and several symphony orchestras across the country, it must be noted. Before these it might have been said that the only real professionals in the arts in Canada were the musicians and critics, but that would not entirely hold water or reflect favourably on many dedicated people. Just let it be said that long before this official acceptance of the arts here, there were critics, some of whom achieved considerable distinction. Mind you, they had to work hard, being responsible for music, dance, film, painting and literature, as well as theatre. (If further called upon, or their ambition lay in these directions, they undertook reportorial and editorial tasks.)

Early in our history, cultural events were covered as general news of low priority. Editors took such matters lightly, on the whole, as being of modest public interest. Such assignments were given to members of the staff who had nothing more important to do, or were farmed out to outsiders with related interests. Often, since such assignments were regarded as entertainment only, they went to the reporter with the evening off. (That condition still lingers in some territories.)

In their efforts to convince management that the arts were important, and that criticism was a highly specialized form of writing, those who yearned to write criticism went beyond the call of duty to increase their coverage and to persuade editors to print their comments. When the growing number and awareness of his readers eventually encouraged an editor to print more cultural items, the critics worked their way into the fabric of a newspaper. American wire copy, however, still maintains its edge as entertainment coverage with many Canadian editors.

Eventually, by the mid-50s, there were enough working critics to band together to give out awards and to welcome guest speakers. This occurred first in Montreal, which could boast seven newspapers, in two languages. This Montreal Critics' Circle did not survive the decade, according to its president, Eric McLean, and Sydney Johnson (its treasurer), because of the conflict of members' work schedules falling between afternoon and evening papers. McLean, then with the *Montreal Star,* now with the *Gazette,* is a music critic, for this Montreal body embraced all the critical disciplines.

But it is just possible that the French-language critics at mid-century had other reasons for leaving a body originally headed by English-language colleagues. The days of the Quiet Revolution were upon them, and many Quebec critics sided with the artists who proclaimed it so vigorously. Any unification of critics became difficult.

In French Canada, then, the cause of nationalism often came first. In English Canada, the state of the art was still of prime concern. As suggested before, Canadian critics tend to be crusaders. Their very occupation here determines this.

Also there is always the problem of the critic's own individuality in a life observing the individuality of artists. He must deal in a fluctuating scene, so his commentary must ever be nimble to appreciate and deal with changing visions, new concepts. For many critics, unanimity of critical approval suggests a failure in their own individuality. No wonder that under such circumstances, there often is a tendency on the part of critics to take their own work more seriously than that of the artists who are the direct contributors.

This is particularly true in what can be termed "life's blood" criticism, that which reflects the day-to-day achievements or failures in current theatrical expression. The academic critic is allowed a more historical perspective, watching for the trends taken by that expression. While the daily working critic feels part of the daily creativity, clinging precariously to his objectivity, the periodical critics must look for overall developments, making note of similar trends in time and place.

This is not to denigrate the theatre journals for not getting "life's blood" on their hands. Their purpose has been more general and abstract. Such periodicals as the *Canadian Theatre Review, Canadian Drama, Performing Arts in Canada* and *Jeu* are certainly worthy extensions of theatre and drama commentary in Canada. The now-defunct *Scene Changes* also gave expression to many writers, especially young critics benefitting from Jeniva Berger's editorship. For a complete comprehension of this country's theatrical achievements and developments, many viewpoints are essential, the retrospective as well as the strictly contemporary. It is these perspectives which give the journal *Theatre History in Canada* its *raison d'être.* It produces critical finds from our past, uncovering personalities and projects which often have their parallels today. Thus it supplies the background to theatrical developments in a country which has largely been given a low mark in history.

In this regard, the latest plan for a series of Canadian Theatre Museums, largely initiated by the Association for Canadian Theatre History, should help further the country's consciousness that theatre has played a part in its past as importantly as it does today and will in the future.

Both "life's blood" and academic critics joined in Quebec's drive for its not-so-Quiet Revolution. They had been prepared, over a decade or more, for such crusading by observing the work of pioneers like Gratien Gélinas, Yvette Brind'Amour, Jean Gascon, Jean-Louis Roux, Pierre Dagenais and Marcel Dubé. As drama critic for the *Gazette,* I could bear witness to that growing excitement.

The Dominion Drama Festival, at its peak, gave a splendid example of this changing scene. Marcel Dubé had contributed a vigorous one-act play which won encouragement from Pierre Lefevre, the regional adjudicator, in 1952. Expanded to a full-length work, and retaining its vitality, *Zone* won the top Calvert Award in the D.D.F. finals in Victoria, British Columbia, where Lefevre was now serving as final adjudicator. The runner-up was Toronto's production of T.S. Eliot's *The Family Reunion.* That was in 1953, the year that the Stratford Festival made its successful appearance.

At that time, English-language actors still felt more at home in other nation's classics, whereas the French-language actors had found such new life in their own back-yards that many of their classically-trained talents had later to learn *joual* to survive.

Director Robert Rivard receiving the first Calvert Trophy from Governor General Vincent Massey for the best production in the 1953 Dominion Drama Festival, Marcel Dubé's *Zone,* performed by Montreal's La Jeune Scène.

Despite the long-time encouragement of the drama festivals, the urging of the critics, and such annual contests as the Ottawa Little Theatre One-Act Play Competition, English-language writers did not feel sufficiently confident to take to the stage in large numbers until the 1970s. There were some notable exceptions, notably those inspired by the New Play Society. By 1949 (when I arrived in Toronto), this pioneer body, valiantly led by Dora Mavor Moore, was able to offer a season of five original plays in balance with four classics. Among those produced by Mrs. Moore and her son, Mavor, was Morley Callaghan, the successful novelist. Callaghan responded twice, with *To Tell the Truth* (1949) and *Going Home* (1950). The Crest Theatre also kept on the look-out for new playwrights from its debut in 1954, and had some successes from Robertson Davies, Jack Gray and Mary Jukes, but against these we must put the whole canon of new and explosive work being done in Quebec at the same period.

As early as 1958, the *Globe and Mail* and the Stratford Festival held a joint playwriting competition. The winner was Donald Lamont Jack with his comedy *The Canvas Barricade*. Much publicized by the *Globe and Mail*, it was staged by the Festival in the 1961 season, with top performers such as Kate Reid, Peter

A nn Hayes, Peter Donat and Kate Reid in George McCowan's 1961 Stratford Festival production of Donald Lamont Jack's *The Canvas Barricade,* designed by Mark Negin.

Donat and Zoe Caldwell. But the author soon found other forms of expression more remunerative. Still, the campaign continued.

In 1972, Floyd Chalmers, a philanthropist with wide publishing experience, decided the time was ripe to honour the new playwrights. When the Toronto critics were approached to supply the jury, they decided to form another critics' organization. That was how the Toronto Drama Bench came into existence. Fortunately, plays eligible for the Chalmers Canadian Play Award have not been confined to Ontario dramatists. Given a growing exchange of scripts and touring productions, the Award (administered by the Ontario Arts Council) has become more representative of dramatic writing across the country. Past winners have included David Freeman, Roland Lepage, David Fennario (Quebec); W.O. Mitchell (Alberta); Charles Tidler, Anne Chislett, Sherman Snukal (British Columbia); and David French, James Reaney, John Herbert, Larry Fineberg, Rick Salutin, Erika Ritter, Allan Stratton and George Walker (Ontario). Their works have expressed different aspects of Canadian life shared by audiences across the country. But efforts to make the Chalmers Canadian Play Awards (there is also a separate annual Chalmers Children's Play Award) fully national have so far been unsuccessful.

The attempt to establish genuinely national play awards is a continuing concern of the Canadian Theatre Critics Association/Association des critiques de théâtre du Canada, founded in 1980 with the assistance of the Toronto Drama Bench. The CTCA has a far wider membership than the Drama Bench, in both founding languages, and has organized annual conferences in Toronto, Montreal and Quebec City. Any examination of Canadian theatre criticism today must include the national organization, though no common style or standards among its members may emerge. The Association has adopted several objectives pertinent to the field of criticism. Among these are the promotion of excellence in theatre criticism; the improvement of training opportunities and working conditions for critics; the dissemination of information on theatre on a national level, and promoting the development and awareness of Canadian theatre nationally and internationally.

While there is not one uniform set of critical standards applied across the country, it is apparent that the Canadian critic today has inherited the position of concern from Canada's critics of previous generations. Again one sees the tendency to side with the emergent theatre against its public. This has been, if anything, increased by the attitudes of government to culture, ambivalent to say the least. The celebrated "arms-length" relationship between the federal government and its own office of subsidy, the Canada Council, has been severely threatened. Only a stiff battle rescued the Council at the last minute, along with the Canadian Broadcasting Corporation, Telefilm Canada, and the National Arts Centre, from inclusion in a proposal before Parliament in 1984 (Bill C-24) to increase government control over Crown Corporations. The succeeding Conservative government under Prime Minister Brian Mulroney has instituted cuts in cultural subsidy, including a major threat to the public broadcasting of the CBC.

Canadian critics are inevitably drawn into such political involvement, affecting as they do the artists who come under their professional scrutiny. Such involvement has been deepened by the practice of having critics serve as "the reporter on the beat" of newspaper tradition. They are expected to handle all aspects of artistic activity, including government cuts in subsidy and resultant financial crises. A notable example occurred when the public, the artists and the critics all became deeply involved over a change of management at Stratford in 1979.

Today, not only is the change of directorship at Stratford top news, but that of every theatre centre across the country. Editors may not respond with interest to such vital news as the choice of plays or performers but they do show interest in the financial reports—the newspaper acting as guardian of the public purse.

And so the critic, more often than not, becomes involved with the personalities of the theatre he reviews. He becomes evaluator, announcer, publicist, bookkeeper, champion and father-confessor of our theatre. No wonder he tends to identify with the stage rather than the audience, or his newspaper, or broadcast station.

Nathan Cohen's fascination with the theatre led him to write a play (*Blue Is For Mourning*) and to appear on the CBC (*Fighting Words*) while he remained on the *Toronto Star.* Two of his successors have actually crossed the floor to cast their lot with the actors. Urjo Kareda, an eloquent voice in support of new playwrights, left first to serve as literary manager for Robin Phillips at the Stratford Festival, then took over Bill Glassco's crusade for new plays at Tarragon Theatre. His successor, the more acerbic Gina Mallet, left the *Star* with the intention of going into production, an even more startling reversal. Ray Conlogue, her opposite number on the *Globe and Mail,* was equally unprecedented when he received a sabbatical to work as an associate director. All three critics exemplify the strong involvement of the Canadian theatre critic with the profession.

Such involvement, I would like to point out, is part of the history of theatre criticism in this country. At the beginning, critics were anonymous, commenting on garrison productions when they "went public." Not always favourably, either. A Mr. Lambert, writing in 1806, protested sharply against the practice of men in women's roles. "It may be seen how despicably low the Canadian theatricals must be when boys are obliged to perform the female characters; the only actress being an old supernumary demi-rep." Such writers, and even the editors themselves, were inclined to be more favourable to touring thespians, being true Canadians.

The beginning of the 20th century saw theatre critics—or rather "the critics" because they could not afford to specialize at that time—earning their places on permanent staff and even emerging from the anonymity of earlier journalism. Many of them declared their interests firmly and stayed to become venerated. Retirement was not as much of a concern then, and age brought respect.

Certainly S. Morgan Powell of the *Montreal Daily Star* wrote until he reached his nineties. He'd had a career abroad and in Canada as a defender of the stage of Henry Irving, but gave the nod to indigenous theatre when it was encouraged by the Earl of Bessborough, Britain's Sir Barry Jackson and Canada's first major classic actress, Margaret Anglin. Tom Archer, his counterpart on the *Gazette,* also lent his support. Primarily a music critic, Archer relinquished his extra posts of theatre and film critic to this writer. I in turn relinquished my duties as film critic on the *Globe and Mail* to Alex Barris, and thus the *Globe* struck a blow for independence for theatre critics. That was in 1952.

In Montreal's French press, Jacques Laroche, writing in *La Presse* as Jean Béraud, was able much earlier to chronicle the important advances of Quebec's own theatre. He championed a far more exciting development than either of the English Montreal critics, or such Toronto colleagues as B.K. Sandwell of *Saturday Night;* Hector Charlesworth of the *Mail and Empire,* later the *Globe and Mail;* or Augustus Bridle of the *Toronto Star,* who helped launch the celebrated Arts and Letters Club, influential in founding the Canadian Arts Council. Critics had become influential. When Hector Charlesworth died, he was widely saluted for his "unflagging devotion to the arts."

In this commitment to the performing arts, Charlesworth was one with his contemporaries and successors across the country. Winnipeg's Frank Morris, and Roly Young (both moved east to Toronto) were deeply involved, Morris acting in Winnipeg and Young producing for Toronto's Civic Theatre while still in office. The *Globe and Mail's* Dr. Lawrence Mason espoused a chain of Canadian-owned theatres to maintain Canadian touring. Nathan Cohen, when he succeeded Jack Karr on the *Toronto Star,* took full advantage of that paper's wealth to extend national coverage. He was the most colourful of the critics since the Falstaffian Charlesworth, favouring a highly explosive style. "Is there a prescribed method of report?" he defended himself, and gave his own answer: "It depends on the critic's temperament." And so it always will.

To some extent Canadian theatre-writers have been influenced by outside critics, either from reading George Jean Nathan, James Agate or John Simon or, in person, by Harley Granville-Barker, Phillip Hope-Wallace and the other adjudicators of the Dominion Drama Festivals. But these outside critics did not share the Canadian burden of seeing that their homeland had a continuing theatre. They could take that for granted. We could not. Even today, the Canadian theatre critic must gird himself or herself to do battle for cultural survival, for the theatre's expansion and freedom.

With governments in danger of exerting undue influence on the arts they subsidize, the Canadian critic today feels more necessary than ever to the national scene. Politicians and committees of politicians are not given to long-range artistic overviews in their efforts to satisfy their constitutents' demands. The fight for high standards of appreciation becomes more important at such times as these. And gradually, the crusade to impress the media editors is being won. Greater national coverage is being achieved. Stephen Godfrey, for instance, has joined Jamie Portman, of the Southam chain, in covering a wider arts scene for the *Globe and Mail,* moving to Vancouver for that purpose. Portman had been alone in his great service to the country, letting one side of Canada know how the other side was expressing itself.

There is still a great problem in the ranks of the Canadian Theatre Critics Association in the constant turn-over of its members, as critics are transferred to other postings or even drop out of the field altogether. The new critics come from the universities, the news and sports departments. (Experience within the media still counts for more than special study or experience, in hiring staff for "the entertainment department.") But wherever they come from, the new Canadian critics soon actively enter into the cultural life they are covering. It is expected of them. And so they soon find themselves feeling as responsible as were their long-ago predecessors, and as necessary to the advance of Canada's theatre as are the directors, actors, designers and even those other concerned writers, the playwrights.

Herbert Whittaker

APPENDIX ONE

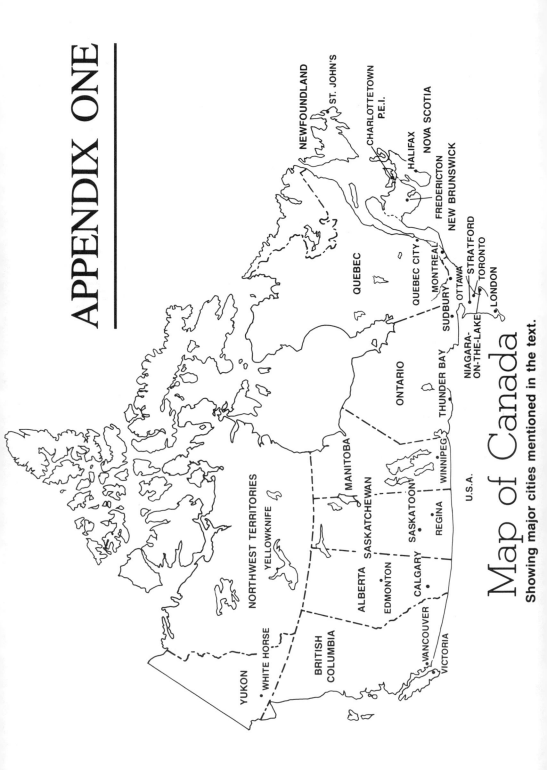

Map of Canada
Showing major cities mentioned in the text.

Population of Canada

October 1984 Census, Statistics Canada

Newfoundland	579,700
Prince Edward Island	135,900
Nova Scotia	874,100
New Brunswick	714,900
Quebec	6,562,400
Ontario	8,984,900
Manitoba	1,060,500
Saskatchewan	1,010,900
Alberta	2,344,700
British Columbia	2,882,800
Northwest Territories	49,900
Yukon	22,400
Total Population	25,223,100

APPENDIX TWO

Contributors

Marianne Ackerman is theatre critic for the *Montreal Gazette.* Born in rural Ontario, she graduated from Carleton University in 1976 with a B.A. in political science, and spent a year in Paris, studying French culture and language at the Sorbonne. After working as a reporter at the *Ottawa Journal* and *Sunday Post,* she took an M.A. at the University of Toronto's Graduate Centre for the Study of Drama in 1981, and promptly moved to Montreal upon graduation. Since then, she has specialized in cultural affairs as a freelance magazine, radio and newspaper journalist. She joined the *Gazette* in 1983.

Brian Arnott has been professionally active in Canadian theatre for over twenty years. For five years in the mid-1970s, he was a practicing critic writing under the pseudonym Brian Boru. He has been production manager for the Vancouver Festival and the cultural program of the XXI Olympiad. He has designed over 30 productions in Vancouver, Edmonton, Toronto, Ottawa and elsewhere and has written widely on theatrical subjects in most of the major North American theatre publications. Arnott has been a guest speaker at a number of international symposia. His consulting company, established in 1972, has worked for over 50 government agencies and arts organizations.

Audrey M. Ashley, born in Birmingham, England, managed the Midland Area office of the English Folk Dance and Song Society before coming to Canada in 1951. She first joined the staff of the *Ottawa Citizen* in 1952, and except for two years at the *San Francisco Chronicle,* her career in Canada has been spent at the *Citizen.* After almost 20 years of combining the job of theatre critic with that of editor of the music and drama department, she now devotes all her time to reviewing theatre and writing feature articles on theatre and music personalities, and making forays to Toronto, Montreal and New York to check on the theatre scene.

Hélène Beauchamp teaches in the Department of Theatre and Dance at the Université du Québec à Montréal. Her doctoral dissertation, *l'Histoire et les conditions du théâtre pour enfants au Québec 1950-1980,* is being published by Hurtubise HMH. She has collaborated in the work of several theatre companies, festivals and the Association québécoise du jeune théâtre and the Maison québécoise du théâtre pour l'enfance et la jeunesse.

Beauchamp has written for the cahiers de théâtre *Jeu* since 1976 and has contributed to numerous publications in Canada and Europe. She is the editor of the series Jeunes Publics for Editions Québec/Amérique in Montreal which has published a dozen plays for the young since 1981. Beauchamp is the author of *Le Théâtre à la p'tite école, Les Enfants et le jeu dramatique, Apprivoiser le théâtre,* and is a contributor to *Le Théâtre canadien-français* and *A Mirror of Our Dreams: Children and the Theatre in Canada.*

Jeniva Berger, born in Chicago, Illinois, moved to Toronto in 1958 after receiving her B.A. from the University of Toronto. In 1976 she received an M.A. from the Graduate Centre for the Study of Drama at the same university. A professional journalist and theatre critic since the late 1960s, she has been published in periodicals in Canada and Great Britain, served as theatre critic for the *Canadian Jewish News* and *Toronto Calendar Magazine,* and editor of the theatre magazine *Scene Changes* until 1982. Her writing credits also include books, films, radio and television. During her office as Chairman of the Toronto Drama Bench, Berger co-founded the Canadian Theatre Critics Association/Association des critiques de théâtre du Canada and has served as its President since 1980. Currently she is also Vice-Chairman of the Freelance Editors Association of Canada and the Toronto chapter of the Periodical Writers Association of Canada and is the Canadian representative on the executive of the International Association of Theatre Critics.

Brian Brennan, born in Dublin, Ireland, is a founding director and Vice-President of the Canadian Theatre Critics Association. Theatre critic of the *Calgary Herald* for the past 10 years, he is a frequent contributor to such publications as *Canada on Stage, Plays and Players, Variety, Canadian Theatre Review, TV Guide* and *Scene Changes.* He has lectured on theatre criticism at the University of Calgary and the Banff School of Fine Arts, and was a critic-fellow at the National Critics Institute, Eugene O'Neill Theatre Centre in New London, Connecticut, in 1981. An accomplished performer and musician, Brennan has contributed to numerous cabarets, television shows and theatrical productions in Canada, the U.S. and Great Britain.

Ray Conlogue has been the *Globe and Mail*'s theatre critic for five years, during which time he has had the opportunity to make an annual excursion to London's theatre district and more frequent ones to New York's, as well as travelling regularly across Canada. He took a degree in English Language and Literature at St. Michael's College, and went on to do a Master's degree at the Graduate Centre for the Study of Drama at the University of Toronto. At this time he acted in several Hart House Theatre productions, including a single leading role (in *Rosmersholm*) for which he was roundly panned. During the mid-70s, he reviewed theatre regularly for CBC Radio, and prepared several radio documentaries on aspects of drama.

Diane Cotnoir has contributed to the cahiers de théâtre *Jeu* since 1979. She studied at the Drama Department, Université du Québec à Montréal and is currently completing an M.A. thesis on directing in Quebec. She has taught at the Université de Sherbrooke and at the Université du Québec à Chicoutimi. Cotnoir's own directorial work includes Beckett's *Va et vient* (Montreal and Quebec City, 1979), Simone Benmussa's *la Vie singulière d'Albert Nobbs* (Montreal, 1981, Middlebury, Vermont, 1982), Louis Aragon's *la Chambre d'Elsa* (Montreal, 1982) and *le mot amour, ich sterbe, je meurs,* based on Verdi's *La Traviata* (Montreal, 1983, Quebec City, 1984).

Richard Courtney is Professor in charge of Arts and Education graduate programs at the Ontario Institute for Studies in Education, and is cross-appointed to the Graduate Centre for the Study of Drama, University of Toronto. He has previously taught at the Universities of Victoria and Calgary, and in London, England. He has been President of the Canadian Conference of the Arts, and the Canadian Child and Youth Drama Association-Drama Canada. He has lectured all over the world and in 1979 was Visiting Professor, Melbourne State College, Australia. Among his more than 100 publications, five of his books are in print: *Play, Drama and Thought;* two volumes of *Drama in Therapy* (with Gertrud Schattner); *The Dramatic Curriculum; Re-Play—Studies of Human Drama in Education;* and *Outline History of British Drama.*

Mark Czarnecki has been the theatre critic for the weekly newsmagazine *Maclean's* since 1980. Formerly a senior writer at *Maclean's,* he has written as a freelance journalist on theatre and cultural affairs for such magazines as *Banff Letters, Canadian Forum* and *This Magazine,* and has contributed to CBC Radio's arts program, *Stereo Morning.* A professional editor and translator, he has made Quebec culture a specialty. Among his published translations are André Major's novel *Inspector Therrien* and André Bourassa's critical study *Surrealism and Quebec Literature.* In 1982, he acted as performing arts consultant to the committee preparing the Applebaum-Hébert report on federal cultural policy. An ongoing interest in science has won him a Canadian Science Writers Award for a *Maclean's* feature on recombinant-DNA.

Tom Doherty was born in Boston where he designed his first stage set in 1952. He graduated as an architect from M.I.T., and worked both in theatre and architecture (in the office of Walter Gropius) until 1965, when he emigrated to Canada. Since then he has designed for theatres from Calgary to the Shaw Festival, to New Brunswick, was a project architect for the firm of Arthur Ericson, and acted as President of the Associated Designers of Canada (1976-1981). He has also served as a visiting design critic to the Ryerson Polytechnical Institute School of Architecture. Since 1979, Doherty has concentrated primarily on art direction for motion pictures.

Wayne Fairhead is Curriculum and Staff Development Consultant for the City of York in Metropolitan Toronto. Born in Australia, he has taught the Dramatic Arts Specialist/Honour Specialist Certificate at the Faculty of Education, University of Toronto, since 1980. At present he is teaching the B.Ed. Dramatic Arts elective. He is the immediate Past-President of the Council of Drama in Education, the founding member of the Dramatic Arts Consultants Association of Ontario, Executive Assistant for the Sears Ontario Collegiate Drama Festival, Chairperson of the Drama Advisory Committee for the Learning Enrichment Foundation, and is the newly elected President of the Canadian Child and Youth Drama Association-Drama Canada. He is also a freelance director, writer, editor and adjudicator. Fairhead is associate editor of *Look Both Ways: Theatre Experiences* and editor of *Spotlights on Australian Drama* and *Drama CONTACT!*

Howard Fink is a Professor of English at Concordia University, Montreal. He is the Director of the Concordia Radio Drama Project and former founding Director of the Concordia Centre for Broadcasting Studies. For the past 12 years the Project has been involved in the collecting, preserving, indexing and researching of Canadian radio drama scripts and background materials. Fink has published in the area of modern literature, and extensively in the history and analysis of Canadian radio drama. He is the author of *Canadian National Theatre on the Air 1925-1961. CBC-CRBC-CNR Radio Drama in English: A Descriptive Bibliography and Union List.*

Dennis Foon, originally from Detroit, received his B.A. from the University of Michigan, and his M.F.A. from the University of British Columbia, before co-founding Green Thumb Theatre for Young People in Vancouver in 1974. Since that time, Green Thumb has developed a reputation for demonstrating new excitement and potential for children's theatre through works which reflect the lives of young people today. Foon's own plays for the young include *The Windigo, Heracles, Raft Baby* and *New Canadian Kid*. His plays for adults include an adaptation of *The Hunchback of Notre Dame, Hotsy-Totsy* and *Children's Eyes*. Foon was playwright-in-residence at Young People's Theatre in Toronto during the 1983-84 season. He adapted and directed his plays *New Canadian Kid* and *Skin* for the Unicorn Theatre in London, England, and directed *One Thousand Cranes* and *New Canadian Kid* for Green Thumb's recent tour to Hong Kong, Singapore, Australia and New Zealand.

Mira Friedlander is a Toronto-based theatre critic and arts journalist. She contributes to the *Globe and Mail, Canadian Theatre Review, Performing Arts in Canada* and *Plays* (England). She also adjudicates and has worked for both community and high school theatre festivals in Ontario and out of province. As well as acting, Friedlander has directed for her own theatre company, The Women's Drama Collective.

Terry Goldie, Associate Professor of English at Memorial University, St. John's, Newfoundland, has published a number of articles on West Indian, African, Australian and Canadian literatures, as well as *Violence in the Canadian Novel Since 1960* (with Virginia Harger-Grinling). For a number of years, he was the theatre critic for the CBC Radio morning show in St. John's and has written on Newfoundland theatre for national radio, for the *Canadian Theatre Review*, and for the Toronto *Globe and Mail*. He has also written on contemporary Australian theatre for Canadian publications and on contemporary Canadian theatre for Australian ones.

Jack Gray is a cultural activist and a writer of plays for the stage, radio and television. He was assistant editor of *Maclean's Magazine* (1953-57) and wrote plays for the BBC, Grenada and ATV in England (1960-1970). He was Secretary-General of the Canadian Theatre Centre (1971-72), Chairman of the Council of Canadian Filmmakers (1977), National President of ACTRA (1978-1982), and a consultant for the Department of Communications on cultural policy, particularly broadcasting and film (1982-83). Gray is an executive member of the Canadian Conference of the Arts, President of the League for Canadian Communication, and President of the International Writers' Guild.

Richard Horenblas is a freelance theatre journalist in Toronto who has been writing about Canadian theatre and dance for the past decade. For the past 5 years, he has been reviewing theatre in *The Downtowner, The Uptowner,* and *Toronto Tonight*. Other publications include a variety of Canadian newspapers, magazines and periodicals. He has also worked as a script developer for both CBC Radio Drama and TV Drama and as a script consultant with Theatre Plus. Horenblas is currently conducting an oral history on the origins of the Stratford Festival.

Jean-Marc Larrue has been a Professor of literature at the Collège de Valleyfield in Quebec since 1974. Besides numerous articles on theatre in Quebec, he is the author of *Le Théâtre à Montréal à la fin du XIXième siècle*. He is presently completing a doctoral dissertation at the Université de Montréal on the organization and evolution of theatre in Montreal from 1880 to 1914.

Paul Lefebvre was born in Montreal. After studying at the Université de Montréal, he worked at the Théâtrothèque and taught contemporary Quebec drama. Since 1982 he has been an arts broadcaster for Radio-Canada, teaches playwriting to final year students in theatre at Collège Lionel Groulx, and is a drama critic for Montreal's daily *Le Devoir*. Lefebvre has been a member of the editorial board of the cahiers de théâtre *Jeu* since 1981 and is on the first executive of the Association québécoise des critiques de théâtre.

Solange Lévesque, born in Quebec City, graduated from the Ecole des Beaux-Arts and subsequently completed her M.A. in the humanities. For several years, she taught French as a second language and has taught at the Université du Québec à Montréal. Since 1979 Lévesque has devoted herself primarily to writing. The author of a novel and a collection of short stories, she contributes to the cahiers de théâtre *Jeu* and other literary periodicals.

William Littler was born in Vancouver where he graduated from the University of British Columbia. He held the post of music and dance critic of the *Vancouver Sun* between 1963 and 1966 when he became music critic (later dance critic as well) of the *Toronto Star*. A Vice-President of the Music Critics Association, Littler participated in the Association's first across-the-border exchange, becoming summer music critic of the *Houston Post* in 1973. He also directed the first Critics Institute in Canadian Music in Toronto, Ottawa and Montreal in 1975 and was elected founding Chairman of the Dance Critics Association of North America in New York in 1974. A frequent broadcaster and lecturer, he has taught courses in music and dance at York University, McMaster University and the University of Waterloo. He was the 1980 winner of the National Newspaper Award for Critical Writing. Littler is currently at work on a history of the National Ballet School of Canada.

Mary Jane Miller is Associate Professor of dramatic literature in the Department of Fine Arts, Brock University, St. Catharines, Ontario. She is one of the founders of the Association for the Study of Canadian Radio and Television, was book review editor for *Theatre History in Canada*, wrote annual reviews of television drama for *Books in Canada*, and has published articles on Canadian theatre history, Pinter's radio dramas, self-reflexive masks, and Canadian television drama.

Boyd Neil is a Toronto-based theatre critic. His feature articles and reviews have appeared in many Canadian and British magazines, including *Maclean's, Toronto Life, Quest,* the *Globe and Mail*, the *Toronto Star, Canadian Forum, Canadian Theatre Review,* and *Plays and Players*. He is theatre columnist for Toronto's *Avenue* magazine, and a graduate (M.A.) of the Graduate Centre for the Study of Drama, University of Toronto. He is co-editor, with Ronald Bryden, of the forthcoming book *Whittaker's Theatre: Herbert Whittaker and Theatre in Canada 1944-1975.*

Jillian Officer, born and trained in England, is holder of the Royal Academy of Dancing Advanced Teacher's Certificate. She emigrated to Canada in 1956, and joined the University of Waterloo in 1969 where she is Assistant Professor in the Dance Department, teaching history of ballet, technique and choreography. Her research interest is in Canadian dance history. Since 1981, Officer has been compiling a Dictionary of Canadian Theatre Dance.

Malcolm Page has been a Professor of English at Simon Fraser University, Burnaby, British Columbia, since 1966. A former President of the Association for Canadian Theatre History (1981-83), he is a member of the editorial boards of *Canadian Drama* and *Theatre History in Canada*, and B.C. editor for the forthcoming bibliography of Canadian theatre history. He is a frequent contributor to the *Canadian Theatre Review, Plays and Players, Twentieth Century Literature, West Coast Review, Canadian Children's Literature, True North/Down Under, Commentator* and *Scene Changes*. Page has also studied radio and television drama, and British, West Indian and Nigerian drama. Author of *John Arden*, he is now completing a compilation on Tom Stoppard and a book on *Richard II.*

Linda M. Peake is completing her studies at the Graduate Centre for the Study of Drama, University of Toronto, where she is writing a doctoral dissertation, *Theatre in Prince Edward Island: 1800-1920.* She has taught theatre arts at Seneca College, Toronto, and has directed and stage managed a large number of Canadian plays and works from the international repertoire.

Richard Perkyns, born in Newport, Isle of Wight, England, is Associate Professor and drama specialist in the English Department at Saint Mary's University, Halifax, where he has been teaching since 1969. He has worked extensively in Halifax community theatre, directing and/or performing in plays for S.M.U. Drama Society, Theatre Arts Guild and Pier One Theatre. He was artistic director of the Theatre Arts Guild in 1974 and a founder member of Halifax Independent Theatre. He has published articles in several journals, including *Canadian Drama* and *Theatre History in Canada*, and is co-editor of *Introduction to Literature: British, American, Canadian*. Perkyns is editor of *Major Plays of the Canadian Theatre 1934-1984*, a collection of twelve full-length Canadian plays.

Don Rubin is a founding member and former Chairman of the York University Department of Theatre. He is also founding editor of the *Canadian Theatre Review* (1974-1982) and was general editor of its book publishing program. Rubin is currently executive editor of the *World Encyclopedia of Contemporary Theatre*, a joint project of several international theatre organizations with the support of UNESCO. He is Chairman of the International Theatre Institute's Permanent Committee on Theatre Publishing and Vice-President of the ITI's Permanent Committee on Theatre Training.

Mary Elizabeth Smith is Professor of English and Chairman of the Division of Humanities and Languages at the University of New Brunswick in Saint John. She is the author of *Love Kindling Fire: A Study of Christopher Marlowe's The Tragedy of Dido, Queen of Carthage*, of *Too Soon the Curtain Fell: A History of Theatre in Saint John 1789-1900*, as well as of various articles on Elizabethan and Canadian theatre.

R.H. Thomson is a prominent English-Canadian actor on stage, television and film. He took a degree in Science at the University of Toronto in 1969, before studying two years at the National Theatre School in Montreal, and one year at LAMDA in England. He has performed in Canada, England and the United States. Recently in Canada he has acted in *The Jail Diary of Albie Sachs* at Toronto Workshop Productions, in *The Changeling* at Toronto Free Theatre, and *Ashes* for the Belfry Theatre in Victoria. His film credits include *Ticket to Heaven, If You Could See What I Hear, Les Beaux Souvenirs, Samuel Lount* and *Surfacing!* He was seen most recently as Charlie Grant in the CBC's historical film *Charlie Grant's War*. Thomson's directing credits include *A Midsummer Night's Dream* in High Park for Toronto Free Theatre.

Renate Usmiani, born in Vienna, Austria, is a Professor in the Department of English, Mount St. Vincent University, and is artistic director of The Mount Playhouse, a summer dinner theatre and cabaret. Her field of specialization is comparative literature, with a special focus on drama and theatre. She worked as a freelance reporter in the U.S. before moving to Canada and academic life. Having "discovered" Canadian theatre in the 1970s, she has since made it a major area of study. The result are three books: *Gratien Gélinas, Michel Tremblay* and *Second Stage: The Alternative Theatre Movement in Canada*. She has dealt with Canadian drama in a large number of articles and discussed the subject at international congresses in Canada, the United States and Europe.

Michel Vaïs is heard regularly as a theatre critic on Radio-Canada FM's *l'Art aujourd'hui*. He completed his doctoral studies in theatre at the Université de Paris and has taught theatre at McGill University, l'Université de Québec à Montréal and the Université de Montréal. A member of the editorial committee of the cahiers de théâtre *Jeu* since 1978, he has also contributed to numerous Canadian and European publications. Vaïs was a co-director of the théâtre des Saltimbanques (1964-69) and worked in the theatre as an actor, writer (television and radio) and as a director.

Anton Wagner was born in Wels, Austria, and emigrated to Canada from the U.S. in 1969. He served as dramaturge of the Playwrights Co-op in Toronto (1975-77) and was a founding executive member of the Association for Canadian Theatre History (1976-1984). Besides numerous articles on Canadian theatre and drama, he is general editor of John Ball and Richard Plant's *A Bibliography of Canadian Theatre History 1583-1975,* of *The Brock Bibliography of Published Canadian Plays in English 1766-1978,* and of the four volume Canada's Lost Plays series: *Colonial Quebec, The Nineteenth Century* (with Richard Plant), *Women Pioneers,* and *The Developing Mosaic.* Wagner wrote his doctoral dissertation, *Herman Voaden's Symphonic Expressionism,* at the Graduate Centre for the Study of Drama, University of Toronto. He is the Secretary of the Canadian Centre of the International Theatre Institute (English-language).

Robert Wallace is an Associate Professor of English at York University's Glendon College where he teaches modern drama, Canadian theatre and media studies, and co-ordinates the bilingual program in drama for which he annually directs a production. A writer for radio and television since the mid-1960s, he has scripted over 30 television programs and has written, produced and narrated, numerous radio projects including 8 one-hour documentaries on the arts, which were broadcast on CBC's *Ideas.* As a critic, he has contributed to *Modern Drama, Canadian Literature, The Oxford Companion to Canadian Literature, Open Letter, Profiles in Canadian Literature, Canadian Drama* and the *Canadian Theatre Review,* which he has edited since 1982. He has written 5 stage plays including *No Deposit No Return,* produced off-off Broadway in 1976 starring Saul Rubineck. Wallace is co-author of *The Work: Conversations With English-Canadian Playwrights* and drama editor for The Coach House Press.

Herbert Whittaker, first National Chairman of the Canadian Theatre Critics Association and founding Chairman of the Toronto Drama Bench, is drama critic emeritus of the *Globe and Mail.* He entered theatrical life in Montreal, his birthplace, as a stage designer after studying at the Ecole des Beaux Arts. Turning director (Montreal Repertory Theatre, 16-30 Club, Y.M.H.A., Brae Manor Summer Theatre, etc.), he was appointed to the executive of the Dominion Drama Festival. He has also designed and directed for the Montreal Festivals, the Shakespeare Society of Montreal, Jupiter Theatre and Crest Theatre, Toronto, Canadian Players and Alumni Theatre. Whittaker became radio editor, then theatre, film and dance critic for the *Montreal Gazette* by 1945. Invited to the same posts by the *Globe and Mail,* Toronto, in 1949, he was able to concentrate on theatre by 1952 until his retirement in 1975. Abroad he covered theatre for the *Globe and Mail* in Russia, Greece, Israel, France, China and Australia as well as the New York and London theatre seasons. Author of *Canada's National Ballet,* he has written for the *New York Times, Encyclopedia Americana, Stage* (London), and *Hemisphere* (Canberra).

Selected
Bibliography

Bibliographies and Research Guides

Ball, John, and Plant, Richard. *A Bibliography of Canadian Theatre History 1583-1975.* Anton Wagner, gen. ed. Toronto: Playwrights Co-op, 1976. John Ball and Richard Plant, eds. *The Bibliography of Canadian Theatre History Supplement 1975-1976.* Toronto: Playwrights Co-op, 1979.

Buller, Edward. *Indigenous Performing and Ceremonial Arts in Canada: A Bibliography.* An Annotated Bibliography of Canadian Indian Rituals and Ceremonies (up to 1976). Toronto: Association for Native Development in the Performing and Visual Arts, 1981.

Canadian Plays for Young Audiences. Toronto: Playwrights Union of Canada, 1984.

David, Gilbert, with Cusson, Chantale. *Répertoire théâtral du Québec 1984.* Montréal: Cahiers de théâtre Jeu, 1984.

Guilmette, Pierre. *Bibliographie de la danse théâtrale au Canada.* Ottawa: Bibliothèque nationale du Canada, 1970. *Supplément,* 1979.

Hare, John E. "Bibliographie du théâtre canadien-français (des origines à 1973)" in *Le Théâtre canadien-français.* Montréal: Fides, 1976.

Kallmann, Helmut, Potvin, Gilles, and Winters, Kenneth, eds. *Encyclopedia of Music in Canada.* Toronto: University of Toronto Press, 1981.

Lavoie, Pierre. *Pour suivre le théâtre au Québec: les ressources documentaires.* Québec: Institut québécois de recherche sur la culture, coll. "Documents de recherche," no 4, 1985.

Lemire, Maurice, et al. *Dictionnaire des oeuvres littéraires du Québec.* 4 vols. Montréal: Fides, 1980, 1982, 1984.

Playwrights Union of Canada Catalogue of Canadian Plays. Toronto: Playwrights Union of Canada, 1985.

Pontaut, Alain. *Dictionnaire critique du théâtre québécois.* Montréal: Leméac, 1972.

Rinfret, Gabriel-Edouard. *Le Théâtre canadien d'expression française:* répertoire analytique des origines à nos jours. 4 vols. Montréal: Leméac, 1975-1978.

Rubin, Don, ed. *Canada On Stage: Canadian Theatre Review Yearbook.* 8 vols. Downsview, Ont.: CTR Publications, 1974-1982.

Saint-Pierre, Annette. "Bibliographie du théâtre français au Manitoba," *Bulletin du Centre d'études franco-canadiennes de l'Ouest,* No. 5, May 1980.

Toye, William, gen. ed. *The Oxford Companion to Canadian Literature.* Toronto: Oxford University Press, 1983.

Tudor, Dean, gen. ed., et. al. *Canadian Book Review Annual.* III Literature and Language, Section 4, Drama. Volumes annually 1975-1984. Toronto: PMA, 1976-1979; Toronto: Simon & Pierre, 1981-1985.

Wagner, Anton, ed. *The Brock Bibliography of Published Canadian Plays in English 1766-1978.* Toronto: Playwrights Press, 1980.

General Surveys

Béraud, Jean. *350 ans de théâtre au Canada français.* Montréal: Le Cercle du livre de France, 1958.

Brooker, Bertram, ed. *Yearbook of the Arts in Canada 1928-1929* and *Yearbook of the Arts in Canada 1936.* Toronto: Macmillan, 1929 and 1936.

Conolly, L.W., ed. *Theatrical Touring and Founding in North America.* Westport, Connecticut: Greenwood Press, 1982.

Doucette, Leonard E. *Theatre in French Canada:* Laying the Foundations 1606-1867. Toronto: University of Toronto Press, 1984.

Edwards, Murray D. *A Stage in Our Past.* English-language theatre in Eastern Canada from the 1790's to 1914. Toronto: University of Toronto Press, 1968.

Evans, Chad. *Frontier Theatre:* A History of Nineteenth-Century Theatrical Entertainment in the Canadian Far West and Alaska. Victoria: Sono Nis, 1983.

Godin, Jean-Cléo and Mailhot, Laurent. *Le Théâtre québécois:* Introduction à dix dramaturges contemporains. Montréal: Hurtubise HMH, 1970.

—. *Le Théâtre québécoise II:* Nouveaux auteurs, autres spectacles. Montréal: Hurtubise HMH, 1980.

Lee, Betty. *Love and Whisky:* The Story of the Dominion Drama Festival and the Early Years of Theatre in Canada 1606-1972. Toronto: McClelland and Stewart, 1973 and Toronto: Simon & Pierre, 1982.

Orrell, John. *Fallen Empires:* Lost Theatres of Edmonton 1881-1914. Edmonton: NeWest Press, 1981.

Ryan, Toby Gordon. *Stage Left:* Canadian Theatre in the Thirties. Toronto: CTR Publications, 1981 and Toronto: Simon & Pierre, 1985.

Saint-Pierre, Annette. *Le Rideau se lève au Manitoba.* Saint-Boniface: Editions des Plaines, 1980.

Smith, Mary Elizabeth. *Too Soon the Curtain Fell:* A History of Theatre in Saint John 1789-1900. Fredericton: Brunswick Press, 1981.

Stuart, Ross. *The History of Prairie Theatre:* The Development of Theatre in Alberta, Manitoba and Saskatchewan 1833-1982. Toronto: Simon & Pierre, 1984.

Le Théâtre canadien-français: Evolution, témoignages, bibliographie. Archives des Lettres canadiennes, Vol. 5. Montréal: Fides, 1976.

The Performing Arts and Government Policy

Access Survey Research Corporation. *The Perceptions, Attitudes and Behaviour of Ontario Residents Toward the Arts in the Province: 1983.* Toronto: Special Committee for the Arts, Ministry of Citizenship and Culture, Government of Ontario, October 1983.

Anthony, Brian, ed. *Who Does What:* A Guide to National Art Associations, Service Organizations and Unions. Ottawa: Canadian Conference of the Arts, 1984.

—. *Who's Who:* A Guide to Federal and Provincial Departments and Agencies, Their Funding Programs and the People Who Head Them. Ottawa: Canadian Conference of the Arts, 1984.

Applebaum, Louis. "Speaking of Culture," *Opera Canada,* Vol. 22, No. 2, Summer 1981.

An Assessment of the Impact of Selected Large Performing Companies Upon the Canadian Economy. Ottawa: Canada Council, 1974.

Audley, Paul. *Canada's Cultural Industries:* Broadcasting, Publishing, Records and Film. Toronto: James Lorimer, 1983.

Bailey, Robert. *Rapport: The Arts, People, and Municipalities.* Ottawa: Canadian Conference of the Arts, 1978.

Book, S.H., Globerman, S., and The National Research Centre for the Arts. *The Audience for the Performing Arts.* Toronto: Ontario Arts Council, 1975.

Chartrand, Harry. *The Arts: Their Impact and Their Audience.* Ottawa: Canada Council, 1984.

— *An Economic Impact Assessment of the Fine Arts.* Ottawa: Canada Council, 1984.

Colbert, François. *Le Marché québécois du théâtre.* Québec, Institut québécois de recherche sur la culture, coll. "Culture Savante," No. 1, 1982.

A Cultural Development Policy for Quebec. 2 vols. Québec: Ministère d'Etat du Développement Culturel, 1978.

Culture as a Growth Sector in Canadian Development. Ottawa: Canadian Conference of the Arts, 1982.

des Landes, Claude, and Learning, Walter. "The Canada Council and the Theatre: The Past 25 Years and Tomorrow," *Theatre History in Canada,* Vol. 3, No. 2, Fall 1982.

Fulford, Robert. "The Canada Council at Twenty-Five," *Saturday Night,* Vol. 97, March 1982.

Gruslin, Adrien. *Le Théâtre et l'État au Québec.* Montréal: VLB éditeur, 1981.

Hay, Peter. "Cultural Politics," *Canadian Theatre Review,* No. 2, Spring 1974.

Hendry, Tom. *Cultural Capital: The Care and Feeding of Toronto's Artistic Assets.* Toronto: Toronto Arts Council, 1985.

—. "The Masseys and the Masses," *Canadian Theatre Review,* No. 3, Summer 1974.

How Government Works. Ottawa: Canadian Conference of the Arts, 1983.

Lamonde, Claude. *Rapport de la consultation du ministre des Affaires culturelles du Québec.* Québec: Ministère des Affaires culturelles, 1982.

Laporte, Pierre. *Livre blanc.* Québec: Ministère des Affaires culturelles, 1965.

Laurin, Camille. *La Politique québécoise du développement culturel.* 2 vols. Québec: Editeur officiel, 1978.

A Little Applebert. Ottawa: Canadian Conference of the Arts, 1983.

Lyman, Peter. *Canada's Video Revolution:* Pay-TV, Home Video and Beyond. Toronto: James Lorimer, 1983.

MacSkimming, Roy. *For Arts' Sake:* A History of the Ontario Arts Council 1963-1983. Toronto: Ontario Arts Council, 1983.

Mailhot, Laurent, and Melançon, Benoît. *Le Conseil des arts du Canada 1957-1982.* Montréal: Leméac, 1982.

Milliken, Paul. "PACT: Networking the National Community," *Canadian Theatre Review,* No. 37, Spring 1983.

"Un ministère de la culture?...Questions sur une question," *Liberté,* No. 50, March-April 1967.

More Strategy for Culture: More Proposals for a Federal Policy for the Arts and the Cultural Industries in Canada. Ottawa: Canadian Conference of the Arts, 1981.

Ostry, Bernard. *The Cultural Connection.* An Essay on Culture and Government Policy in Canada. Toronto: McClelland and Stewart, 1978.

Pasquill, Frank T. "Cultural Senility: Funding Patterns," *Canadian Theatre Review,* No. 2, Spring 1974.

—. *Subsidy Patterns for the Performing Arts in Canada.* Ottawa: Canada Council Information Services, 1973.

Pay TV and the Regulatory Requirements of the CRTC. Ottawa: Canadian Conference of the Arts, 1983.

La Politique du théâtre au Québec. Québec: Ministère des Affaires culturelles, 1984.

Report of the Canada Royal Commission on Radio Broadcasting. Ottawa: King's Printer, 1927.

Report of the Federal Cultural Policy Review Committee. Ottawa: Information Services, Department of Communications, Government of Canada, 1982.

Rioux, Marcel et al. "Rapport du Tribunal de la Culture," *Liberté,* No. 101, September-October 1975.

Royal Commission on National Development in the Arts, Letters and Sciences 1949-1951. *Report.* Ottawa: King's Printer, 1951.

Schafer, Paul. "Developing Our Culture," *Opera Canada,* Vol. 24, No. 1, March 1983.

—. "The Great Canadian Debate: Arts and culture vs political and economic interests," *Opera Canada,* Vol. 25, No. 3, Fall 1984.

Session 1944 House of Commons Special Committee on Reconstruction and Re-establishment, Wednesday, June 21, 1944. *Minutes of Proceedings and Evidence No. 10.* Ottawa: Edmond Cloutier, 1944.

The Special Committee for the Arts. *Report to the Honourable Susan Fish, The Minister of Citizenship and Culture* (The Macaulay Report). Toronto: Special Committee for the Arts, Ministry of Citizenship and Culture, Government of Ontario, Spring 1984.

A Strategy for Culture: Proposals for a Federal Policy for the Arts and the Cultural Industries in Canada. Ottawa: Canadian Conference of the Arts, 1980.

The Third Strategy. Ottawa: Canadian Conference of the Arts, 1984.

Woodcock, George. *Strange Bedfellows: The State of the Arts in Canada.* Vancouver: Douglas & McIntyre, 1985.

The Regional Theatre System

Annual CBAC Survey of Performing Arts Organisations. Toronto: Council for Business and the Arts in Canada, January 1985.

Dafoe, Christopher. "MTC: Past and Present," *Canadian Theatre Review,* No. 4, Fall 1974.

Gustafson, David Axel. *The Canadian Regional Theatre Movement.* Ph.D. Thesis, Michigan State University, 1971.

Kesten, Myles. "The NAC and the National Mandate," *Canadian Theatre Review,* No. 28, Fall 1980.

Mallet, Gina. "The St. Lawrence Centre: Toronto's Persistent Problem," *Canadian Theatre Review,* No. 38, Fall 1983.

Perkyns, Richard. "Two Decades of Neptune Theatre," *Theatre History in Canada,* Vol. 6, No. 1, Spring 1985.

The Alternate Theatre Movement

Friedlander, Mira. "Risk before security on the alternative stage," *Performing Arts in Canada,* Vol. 18, No. 4, Winter 1981.

—. "Survivor: George Luscombe at Toronto Workshop Productions," *Canadian Theatre Review,* No. 38, Fall 1983.

—. "A Vision Vanishes: Canadian Rep Theatre Can't Find a Home," *Performing Arts in Canada,* Vol. 21, No. 3, Winter 1984.

Gass, Ken. "Toronto's Alternates: Changing Realities," *Canadian Theatre Review,* No. 21, Winter 1979.

Neil, Boyd. "Toronto Free Theatre: Guy Sprung Keeps Those Theatrical Bangs Coming," *Avenue,* November 1984.

Quebec Underground 1962-1978. 3 vols. Montreal: Editions Mediart, 1973.

Smith, Patricia Keeney. "Living With Risk: Toronto's New Alternate Theatre," *Canadian Theatre Review,* No. 38, Fall 1983.

Usmiani, Renate. *Second Stage:* The Alternative Theatre Movement in Canada. Vancouver: University of British Columbia Press, 1983.

Playwriting in French Canada

Aubry, Suzanne. "En passant par l'acteur: table ronde avec des auteurs," *Jeu,* No. 33, 1984.4.

—. *Le Théâtre au Québec:* l'émergence d'une dramaturgie nationale. Montréal Centre québécois de l'Institut international du théâtre, 1983.

Camerlain, Lorraine. "Chronologie fragmentaire des créations québécoises depuis 1975," *Jeu,* No. 21, 1981.4.

David, Gilbert, des Landes, Claude, and des Landes, Marie-Francine. *Centre d'essai des auteurs dramatiques 1965-1975.* Montréal: C.E.A.D., 1975.

Gélinas, Gratien. "Jeune auteur, mon camarade," *Revue dominicaine,* Vol. 65, No. 2, November 1960.

—. "Pour un théâtre national et populaire," *Amérique française,* Vol. 7, No. 3, March 1949 and "A National and Popular Theatre" in Renate Usmiani. *Gratien Gélinas.* Toronto: Gage Educational Publishing, 1977.

Germain, Jean-Claude. "Le théâtre québécois contemporain et son langage," *Canadian Drama,* Vol. 1, No. 2, Fall 1975.

Gruslin, Adrien. "Dix ans de création collective: c'est singulier! entretien avec le Parminou," *Jeu,* No. 28, 1983.3.

LeBlanc, Alonzo. "The Question of Quebec Tragedy," *Essays on Canadian Writing,* No. 20, Winter 1980-1981.

Mailhot, Laurent. "Prolégomènes à une histoire du théâtre québécois," "Le Théâtre," No. 5 of the *Revue d'histoire littéraire du Québec et du Canada français.* Editions de l'Université d'Ottawa, Winter-Spring 1983.

Répertoire des textes du Centre d'essai des auteurs dramatiques. Montréal: C.E.A.D., 1981. *Annexe au répertoire.* Montréal: C.E.A.D., 1983.

Runte, Hans R. "L'Acadie s'engage: Le Théâtre de Laval Goupil," *Canadian Drama,* Vol. 4, No. 1, Spring 1978.

"Un théâtre qui s'écrit," *Jeu,* No. 21, 1981.4.

Usmiani, Renate. "The Playwright As Historiographer: New Views of the Past in Contemporary Quebecois Drama," *Canadian Drama,* Vol. 8, No. 2, 1982.

Playwriting in English Canada

Anthony, Geraldine, ed. *Stage Voices:* Twelve Canadian Playwrights Talk About Their Lives and Work. Toronto: Doubleday Canada, 1978.

Barlow, Curtis, Gibson, Shirley, eds. *Playwright's Guide to Canadian Non-Profit Professional Theatres.* Toronto: Professional Association of Canadian Theatres, 1984.

Berger, Jeniva. "Prized Possessions: Ontario's biggest playwriting awards are a showcase in themselves," *Scene Changes,* Vol. 7, No. 1, January-February 1979.

Bessai, Diane. "Documentary Theatre in Canada: An Investigation into Questions and Backgrounds," *Canadian Drama,* Vol. 6, No. 1, Spring 1980.

—. "The Regionalism of Canadian Drama," *Canadian Literature,* No. 85, Summer 1980.

Brissenden, Constance, ed. *Spotlight on Drama:* A Teaching Resource Guide to Canadian Plays. Toronto: Writers' Development Trust, 1981.

Filewod, Alan. "Collective Creation: Process, Politics and Poetics," *Canadian Theatre Review,* No. 34, Spring 1982.

Friedlander, Mira. "The new generation of Canadian playwrights," *Performing Arts in Canada,* Vol. 20, No. 3, November 1983.

Goldie, Terence W. "Political Drama between the Wars," *Canadian Drama,* Vol. 6, No. 2, Fall 1980.

Hollingsworth, Margaret. "Why We Don't Write," *Canadian Theatre Review,* No. 43, Summer 1985.

Nickson, Liz. "Canada: Bombing on Broadway," *Canadian Theatre Review,* No. 35, Summer 1982.

Noonan, James. "James Noonan on Playwrights Canada, the First Ten Years," *Theatre History in Canada,* Vol. 3, No. 2, Fall 1982.

Parker, Brian. "Is There a Canadian Drama?" in *The Canadian Imagination:* Dimensions of a Literary Culture. David Staines, ed. Cambridge: Harvard University Press, 1977.

Perkyns, Richard. "Introduction" to *Major Plays of the Canadian Theatre 1934-1984.* Richard Perkyns, ed. Toronto: Irwin Publishing, 1984.

Plant, Richard. "Introduction" to *Modern Canadian Drama.* Richard Plant, ed. Markham, Ont.: Penguin Books Canada, 1984.

Pollock, Sharon. "Canada's Playwrights: Finding Their Place," *Canadian Theatre Review,* No. 34, Spring 1982.

Rubin, Don, and Cranmer-Byng, Alison, eds. *Canada's Playwrights: A Biographical Guide.* Downsview, Ont.: CTR Publications, 1980.

Ryga, George. "Contemporary Theatre And Its Language," *Canadian Theatre Review,* No. 14, Spring 1977.

—. "The Need For A Mythology," *Canadian Theatre Review,* No. 16, Fall 1977.

Saddlemyer, Ann. "Circus feminus: 100 plays by English-Canadian women," *Room of One's Own,* Vol. 8, No. 2, 1983.

Voaden, Herman. "Introduction," *Six Canadian Plays.* Herman Voaden, ed. Toronto: Copp Clark, 1930.

Wallace, Robert. "Image and Label: Notes for a Sense of Self," *Canadian Theatre Review,* No. 12, Fall 1976.

—. and Zimmerman, Cynthia. *The Work:* Conversations with English-Canadian Playwrights. Toronto: Coach House Press, 1982.

Performing Arts Buildings

Arnott, Brian. "Architecture and the Artful Stage," *Canadian Theatre Review,* No. 6, Spring 1975.

—. "Technology & Design: A Point of View," *Canadian Theatre Review,* No. 33, Winter 1982.

—. "The World as Stage," *Canadian Architect,* Vol. 18, February 1973.

Brian Arnott Associates. *A Facility Development Workbook:* A Planning Guide for the Development of Buildings to Accommodate Non-Profit Arts Activities. Toronto: Ministry of Culture and Recreation, Government of Ontario, 1977.

Cook, Michael. "Trapped in Space," *Canadian Theatre Review,* No. 6, Spring 1975.

Currie Urwick Ltd. *An Assessment of Toronto's Cultural Facilities and Requirements:* A Report for the Toronto Arts Foundation. Toronto: 1964.

Davies, Robertson. "Robertson Davies on Architects and Architecture," Royal Architectural Institute of Canada, *Journal.* No. 37, August 1960.

Doherty, Tom. "Building the Magic Box," *Performing Arts in Canada,* Vol. 9, Nos. 2, 3, 4, Summer, Fall, Winter 1972 and Vol. 10, No. 3, Fall 1973.

Donat, Peter. "Theatre Architecture: An Actor's Point of View," *Architecture Canada,* August 1967.

Fairfield, Robert, et al. "The Playhouse" in *The Awkward Stage:* The Ontario Theatre Study Report. Toronto: Methuen, 1969.

Joliffe, Marlynn. "Victoria Playhouse Petrolia: The Building Burden," *Canadian Theatre Review,* No. 6, Spring 1975.

Joseph, Stephen, ed. *Actor and Architect.* Toronto: University of Toronto Press, 1964.

Kalman, Harold, Wagland, Keith, and Bailey, Robert. *Encore:* Recycling Public Buildings for the Arts. Don Mills, Ont.: Corpus, 1980.

Lebensold, D.F. "Form Follows Function," *Opera Canada,* Vol. 8, No. 3, September 1967.

—. "Theatre: A Need for Dialogue," *Canadian Architect,* Vol. 11, August 1966.

Lindsay, John C. *"Turn Out the Stars Before Leaving:"* The Story of Canada's Theatres. Erin, Ont.: Boston Mills Press, 1983.

Report on a Survey of Theatrical Facilities in Canada. 2 vols. Toronto: Canadian Theatre Centre, 1960-1962.

Roux, Jean-Louis. "Montreal Colloquium 67: The Design of Theatres," *World Theatre,* Vol. 16, 1967.

Seminar on Architectural Requirements for the Performing Arts in Canada. Ottawa: Centennial Commission, 1964.

Souchotte, Sandra. "Toronto's Baby Building Boom," *Canadian Theatre Review,* No. 21, Winter 1979.

Stuart, Ross. "A Circle Without a Centre: The Predicament of Toronto's Theatre Space," *Canadian Theatre Review,* No. 38, Fall 1983.

Theatre Passe Muraille, "Collective Conversation: The Space Show," *Canadian Theatre Review,* No. 6, Spring 1975.

Thom, R.J. "Shaw Festival Theatre, Niagara-on-the-Lake, Ontario: the Design Process," *Canadian Architect,* Vol. 19, January 1974.

Waisman, Allan H. "MTC: Building the Building," *Canadian Theatre Review,* No. 4, Fall 1974.

Wilcox, Richard Kent. "Environments" and "Notes to the Building Committee," *Canadian Theatre Review,* No. 6, Spring 1975.

Anglophone Theatre

Blackburn, R.D., et al. *Financial Management for Canadian Theatres.* Hamilton: Society of Management Accountants of Ontario, 1984.

Brown, J. Frederick. "The Charlottetown Festival in Review," *Canadian Drama,* Vol. 9, No. 2, 1983.

Carson, Neil. "Towards a Popular Theatre in English Canada," *Canadian Literature,* No. 85, Summer 1980.

Czarnecki, Mark. "Staging a Creative Rebirth," *Maclean's,* Vol. 98, March 18, 1985.

Davies, Robertson. "A Dialogue on the State of Theatre in Canada," *Royal Commission Studies*. A Selection of Essays Prepared for the Royal Commission on National Development in the Arts, Letters and Sciences. Ottawa: King's Printer, 1951 and *Canadian Theatre Review*, No. 5, Winter 1975.

Edinborough, Arnold, ed. *The Festivals of Canada*. Toronto: Lester & Orpen Dennys, 1980.

Fraticelli, Rina. "The Invisibility Factor—Status of Women in Canadian Theatre," *Fuse*, Vol. 6, No. 3, September 1982 and "La Condition des femmes dans le théâtre canadien," *Jeu*, No. 31, 1984.2.

—. and Lushington, Kate. "Fear of Feminism," *Canadian Theatre Review*, No. 43, Summer 1985.

Garebian, Keith. "English drama hits hard times in Quebec," *Performing Arts in Canada*, Vol. 19, No. 3, October 1982.

—. "Why is English theatre in Quebec becoming politically irrelevant?", *Performing Arts in Canada*, Vol. 15, No. 4, Winter 1978.

Gerson, Mark D. "Muriel Gold's English theatre is alive and well in Quebec—for now," *Performing Arts in Canada*, Vol. 15, No. 2, Summer 1978.

Goldie, Terry. "Newfoundland Theatre: The Proper Thing," *Canadian Theatre Review*, No. 34, Spring 1982.

Hoare, John Edward. "Community Theatre to Canadian Theatre," *Saturday Night*, Vol. 59, February 5, 1944.

Knelman, Martin. *A Stratford Tempest*. Toronto: McClelland and Stewart, 1982.

McCaughna, David. "The Big Sell: The Greening of Commercial Theatre," *Scene Changes*, Vol. 8, No. 2, April 1980.

Moore, Mavor. "An Approach to Our Beginnings: Transplant, Native Plant or Mutation?", *Canadian Theatre Review*, No. 25, Winter 1980.

—. "Cultural Myths and Realities," *Canadian Theatre Review*, No. 34, Spring 1982.

Noonan, James. "The National Arts Centre: Fifteen Years at Play," *Theatre History in Canada*, Vol. 6, No. 1, Spring 1985.

O'Neill, Paul. "These Our Actors" in his *The Oldest City, the Story of St. John's Newfoundland*. Erin, Ont.: Press Porcepic, 1975.

Page, Malcolm. "Change in Vancouver Theatre, 1963-80," *Theatre History in Canada*, Vol. 2, No. 1, Spring 1981.

—. "Vancouver in 1983: Summer Success and Winter Worries," *Canadian Theatre Review*, No. 39, Spring 1984.

Rittenhouse, Jonathan. "Festival Lennoxville: An All-Canadian Story," *Canadian Drama*, Vol. 10, No. 1, 1984.

Rubin, Don. "Celebrating the Nation: History and the Canadian Theatre," *Canadian Theatre Review*, No. 34, Spring 1982.

—. "Creeping Toward A Culture: The Theatre in English Canada Since 1945," *Canadian Theatre Review*, No. 1, Winter 1974.

—. "The Toronto Movement," *Canadian Theatre Review*, No. 38, Fall 1983.

Ryga, George. "Theatre in Canada: A Viewpoint On Its Development and Future," *Canadian Theatre Review*, No. 1, Winter 1974.

Saddlemyer, Ann. "Thoughts on National Drama and the Founding of Theatres," *Theatrical Touring and Founding in North America.* L.W. Conolly, ed. Westport, Connecticut: Greenwood Press, 1982.

Sawyer, Deborah. "Dinner Theatre," *Scene Changes,* Vol. 9, No. 5, July-August 1981.

Souchotte, Sandra. "Canada's Workers' Theatre," *Canadian Theatre Review,* No. 9, Winter 1976 and No. 10, Spring 1976.

"The Stratford Controversy," *Canadian Theatre Review,* No. 30, Spring 1981.

Stuart, Ross. "The Crest Controversy," *Canadian Theatre Review,* No. 7, Summer 1975.

—. "Theatre in Canada: An Historical Perspective," *Canadian Theatre Review,* No. 5, Winter 1975.

Tepper, Bill. "The Forties and Beyond: The New Play Society," *Canadian Theatre Review,* No. 28, Fall 1980.

"Theatre on the Prairies," *Canadian Theatre Review,* No. 42, Spring 1985.

Wallace, Robert. "Growing Pains: Toronto Theatre in the 70s," *Canadian Literature,* No. 85, Summer 1980.

—. "Holding the Focus: Paul Thompson at Theatre Passe Muraille Ten Years Later," *Canadian Drama,* Vol. 8, No. 1, 1982.

Wasserman, Jerry. "Vancouver: A Day in the Life," *Canadian Theatre Review,* No. 35, Summer 1982.

Whittaker, Herbert. "The Theatre" in *The Culture of Contemporary Canada.* Julian Park, ed. Toronto: Ryerson Press and Ithaca: Cornell University Press, 1957.

Francophone Theatre

Beaulne, Guy. "Un Demi-siècle de théâtre de langue française dans la région Ottawa-Hull," *Theatre History in Canada,* Vol. 4, No. 1, Spring 1983.

Bélair, Michel. *Le Nouveau Théâtre québécois.* Montréal: Leméac, 1973.

Béraud, Jean, Franque, Léon, and Valois, Marcel. *Variations sur trois thèmes.* Montréal: Editions Fernand Pilon, 1946.

Bolster, Charles. "New Directions for Theatrical Expression of the Modern Franco-Ontarian Culture," *Scene Changes,* Vol. 4, No. 8, December 1976 and Vol. 5, No. 1, January 1977.

Camerlain, Lorraine. "En de multiples scènes: l'expression des femmes au théâtre au Québec depuis 1974," *Canadian Theatre Review,* No. 43, Summer 1985.

"Dossier: Le théâtre acadien" in *Si Que 4.* Revue du Département des études françaises, Université de Moncton, Fall 1979.

Duplantie, Monique, Lefebvre, Paul and Vaïs, Michel. "L'Eskabel, dix ans de folie...ou presque," *Jeu,* No. 14, 1980.1.

Garebian, Keith. "Le Théâtre du P'tit Bonheur: French theatre at home in Toronto," *Performing Arts in Canada,* Vol. 21, No. 1, Spring-Summer 1984.

Germain, Jean-Claude. "Canada and Quebec: Beginning the Dialogue," *Canadian Theatre Review,* No. 34, Spring 1982.

—. "Théâtre Québécois or Théâtre Protestant?" *Canadian Theatre Review,* No. 11, Summer 1976.

Gobin, Pierre B. "Les années difficiles: crises et renaissances des théâtres à Montréal 1929-45: Problèmes de répertoires," *Theatre History in Canada,* Vol. 1, No. 2, Fall 1980.

"Le Grand Cirque Ordinaire," *Jeu,* No. 5, Spring 1977.

Gruslin, Adrien. "La Nouvelle Compagnie Théâtrale: une nécessité," *Jeu,* No. 30, 1984.1.

Hamelin, Jean. *Le Renouveau du théâtre au Canada français.* Montréal: Editions du Jour, 1962.

Hébert, Lorraine. "Pour une définition de la création collective," *Jeu,* No. 6, Summer-Fall 1977.

—. and David, Gilbert. "Le Théâtre Parminou: 'l'argent ça fait-y vot' bonheur?'," *Jeu,* No. 1, Winter 1976.

"Jean-Claude Germain," *Jeu,* No. 13, Fall 1979.

Joubert, Ingried. "Le théâtre franco-manitobain" in "Le Théâtre," No. 5 de la *Revue d'histoire littéraire du Québec et du Canada français.* Editions de l'Université d'Ottawa, Winter-Spring 1983.

Karch, Mariel O'Neill, and Karch, Pierre Paul. "Le théâtre québécois à Toronto" in "Le Théâtre," No. 5 de la *Revue d'histoire littéraire du Québec et du Canada français,* 1983.

Kieffer, Daniel. "Quebec Theatre: A Photographic Essay," *Canadian Theatre Review,* No. 11, Summer 1976.

Lapointe, Gilles. "*Vie et mort du Roi Boiteux* de Jean-Pierre Ronfard," *Canadian Drama,* Vol. 9, No. 2, 1983.

Lavoie, Laurent. "Le théâtre d'expression française en Acadie: situation de la recherche et publication" in "Le Theatre," No. 5 de la *Revue d'histoire littéraire du Québec et du Canada français,* 1983.

Lavoie, Pierre. "Québec/bilan tranquille d'une révolution théâtrale," *Jeu,* No. 6, Summer-Fall 1977.

—. et al. "*Vie et mort du roi Boiteux:* nouveau théâtre expérimental," *Jeu,* No. 27, 1983.2.

"Magnifique!: The Vibrancy of French Canadian Theatre," *Scene Changes,* Vol. 8, No. 9, January-February 1981.

Paratte, Henri-Dominique. "Acadie menacée, symbolique théâtrale et conscience d'autrui: Léonie Poirier et son théâtre dans le contexte néo-écossais," *Présence francophone,* No. 20, Spring 1980.

Roberts, Joy. "Eve Marie expands francophone culture in the west," *Performing Arts in Canada,* Vol. 15, No. 2, Summer 1978.

Rouyer, Philippe. "Théâtres au Canada" in *Théâtres au Canada.* Cahiers du CERT-CIRCE, No. 7. Bordeaux, 1980.

Sabbath, Lawrence. "Quebec: Coming Through the Storm," *Canadian Theatre Review,* No. 25, Winter 1980.

Sigouin, Gérald. *Théâtre en lutte: le Théâtre Euh!.* Montréal: VLB éditeur, 1982.

"Un théâtre 'intervenant': a.c.t.a./a.q.j.t. (1958-1980)," *Jeu,* No. 15, 1980.2.

"Théâtres—femmes," *Jeu,* No. 16, 1980.3.

Tourangeau, Rémi, and Laflamme, Jean. *L'Eglise et le théâtre au Québec.* Montréal: Fides, 1979.

Vaïs, Michel. "Les Saltimbanques (1962-1969)," *Jeu,* No. 2, Spring 1976.

Villemure, Fernand. "Aspects de la création collective au Québec," *Jeu,* No. 4, Winter 1977.

—. "Le Trident: au compte de dix," *Jeu,* No. 18, 1981.1.

21 ans de théâtre en français à Vancouver, 1946-1967: histoire de la Troupe Molière. Vancouver: Société historique franco-colombienne, 1982.

Weiss, Jonathan M. "Quebec Theatre of the 80's: the End of an Era," *American Review of Canadian Studies,* Vol. 13, 1983.

The Electronic Media

Allan, Andrew. *A Self-Portrait.* Harry Boyle, ed. Toronto: Macmillan, 1974.

Blanchard, Sharon. "Esse Ljungh and the *Stage* Series," *Canadian Theatre Review,* No. 36, Fall 1982.

Blouin, Louise. *Répertoire du théâtre français et étranger à la radio québécoise 1939-1949.* Mémoire de maitrise en lettres, U.Q.T.R., 1979.

Cook, Michael. "The Last Refuge of the Spoken Word," *Canadian Theatre Review,* No. 36, Fall 1982.

Corbeil, Carole. "Walking a Thin Line," *Canadian Theatre Review,* No. 36, Fall 1982.

Duchesnay, Lorraine. *Vingt-cinq ans de dramatiques à la télévision de Radio-Canada, 1952-1977.* Montréal: Société Radio-Canada, 1978.

Face to Face With Talent. 8th edition. Toronto: Alliance of Canadian Cinema, Television and Radio Artists, 1985.

Feldman, Seth. "The Electronic Fable: Aspects of the Docudrama in Canada," *Canadian Drama,* Vol. 9, No. 1, 1983.

Fink, Howard. "Beyond Naturalism: Tyrone Guthrie's Radio Theatre and the Stage Production of Shakespeare," *Theatre History in Canada,* Vol. 2, No. 1, Spring 1981.

—. "Canadian Radio Drama and the Radio Drama Project," *Canadian Theatre Review,* No. 36, Fall 1982.

—. and Jackson, John. "Radio Drama and Society, Homologies: an Analysis of Joseph Schull's *The Jinker,*" *Canadian Drama,* Vol. 9, No. 1, 1983.

—. with Morrison, Brian. *Canadian National Theatre on the Air 1925-1961. CBC-CRBC-CNR Radio Drama in English:* A Descriptive Bibliography and Union List. Toronto: University of Toronto Press, 1983.

Gonthier, Claude. "L'influence de Radio-Canada sur les dramaturges montréalais," *Critère,* No. 21, 1978.

Laurence, Gérard. "La rencontre du théâtre et de la télévision au Québec (1952-1957)," *Etudes Littéraires,* Vol. 14, No. 2, August 1981.

Lavoie, Pierre. "'Ici Radio-Canada'," *Jeu,* No. 12, Summer 1979.

Legris, Renée. *Propagande de guerre et nationalismes dans le radio-feuilleton (1939-1955).* Montréal: Fides, 1981.

—. and Pagé, Pierre, Allaire-Poirier, Suzanne, Blouin, Louise. *Dictionnaire des auteurs du radio-feuilleton québécois.* Montréal: Fides, 1981.

Miller, Mary Jane. "An Analysis of *The Paper People,"* *Canadian Drama,* Vol. 9, No. 1, 1983.

—. "Canadian Television Drama 1952-1970: Canada's National Theatre," *Theatre History in Canada,* Vol. 5, No. 1, Spring 1984.

—. "*Cariboo Country:* The Canadian Response to the American Television Western," *American Review of Canadian Studies,* Vol. 14, No. 3, Fall 1984.

—. "Radio's Children," *Canadian Theatre Review,* No. 36, Fall 1982.

Page, Malcolm. "From 'Stage' to 'Sunday Matinée:' Canadian Radio Drama in English, 1981-82," *Canadian Drama,* Vol. 9, No. 1, 1983.

—. 'Hirsch and the CBC," *Canadian Theatre Review,* No. 11, Summer 1976.

Pagé, Pierre, and Legris, Renée. *Le Comique et l'humour à la radio québécoise.* Aperçus historiques et textes choisis 1930-1970. Vol. 1. Montréal: La Presse, 1976. Vol. 2. Montréal: Fides, 1979.

—. *Répertoire des dramatiques québécoises à la télévision 1952-1977.* Archives québécoises de la radio et de la télévision, Vol. 3. Montréal: Fides, 1977.

—. and Blouin, Louise. *Répertoire des oeuvres de la littérature radiophonique québécoise, 1930-1970.* Archives québécoises de la radio et de la télévision, Vol. 1. Montréal: Fides, 1975.

Pavelich, Joan E. "*Nazaire et Barnabé:* Learning to Live in an Americanized World," *Canadian Drama,* Vol. 9, No. 1, 1983.

Peterson, Leonard. "With Freedom in Their Eye...," *Canadian Theatre Review,* No. 36, Fall 1982.

Ross, Line, and Tardif, Hélène. *Le Téléroman québécois, 1960-1971:* une analyse de contenu. Québec: Université Laval, Laboratoire recherches sociologiques, 1975.

Ryga, George. "Memories and Some Lessons Learned," *Canadian Theatre Review,* No. 36, Fall 1982.

Spoerly, Frederick. "Radio Drama at the CBC," *Canadian Theatre Review,* No. 13, Winter 1977.

Usmiani, Renate. "Canadian Radio Drama: Aspects of the Two Cultures," *Canadian Review of Comparative Literature,* Vol. 2, No. 1, Winter 1975.

Véronneau, Pierre. "Du théâtre au cinéma au Québec: bref historique," *Canadian Drama,* Vol. 5, No. 1, Spring 1979.

Westman, Karen. "Susan Rubes: guiding force of radio drama's renaissance," *Performing Arts in Canada,* Vol. 19, No. 3, October 1982.

Indian and Eskimo Ritual Drama

Barnett, Homer G. *The Coast Salish.* Eugene: University of Oregon Press, 1955.

Boas, Franz. *The Central Eskimo.* Lincoln: University of Nebraska Press, repr. 1964.

—. *The Social Organization and Secret Societies of the Kwakiutl Indians.* Washington, D.C.: U.S. National Museum, Report of 1895; 1897.

Clutesi, George. *Potlatch.* Sidney, B.C.: Gray, 1969.

Drucker, Philip. *The Northern and Central Nootkan Tribes.* Washington, D.C.: Bureau of American Ethnology, Bulletin No. 144, 1951.

Ernst, Alice H. *The Wolf Ritual of the Northwest Coast.* Eugene: University of Oregon Press, 1952.

Hofman, Charles. *Drum Dance.* Toronto: Gage, 1974.

Macnair, Peter L. "Kwakiutl Winter Dances: A Re-enactment," *Artscanada,* December 1973-January 1974.

—. "Potlatch at Alert Bay," *Artscanada,* December 1973-January 1974.

Patterson, Nancy-Lou. "Two Canadian Indian Masking Traditions," *Canadian Drama,* Vol. 3, No. 2, Fall 1977.

Ray, Dorothy Jean. *Eskimo Masks: Art and Ceremony.* Vancouver: J.J. Douglas, 1975.

Spradley, James P., ed. *Guests Never Leave Hungry: The Autobiography of James Sewid, a Kwakiutl Indian.* New Haven: Yale University Press, 1969.

Winnipeg Art Gallery. *The Coming and Going of the Shaman: Eskimo Shamanism and Art.* (Jean Blodgett, curator). Winnipeg: 1978.

Multicultural Theatre

Davis, Irene. "Ethnic Theatre in Canada Struggles for Recognition," *Performing Arts in Canada,* Vol. 21, No. 2, Fall 1984.

Gerson, Mark. "La Poudrière defends multi-cultural theatre from a powder magazine in Quebec," *Performing Arts in Canada,* Vol. 15, No. 4, Winter 1978.

Kertész, Sándor. *Curtain at Eight.* Toronto: Author, 1981.

Lister, Rota Herzberg. "Dramatizing Mennonite History: A Conversation with Urie Bender," *Canadian Drama,* Vol. 6, No. 2, Fall 1980.

"Multicultural Theatre," *Scene Changes,* Vol. 6, No. 9, November 1978.

Polyphony. The Bulletin of the Multicultural History Society of Ontario. (Special issue on multicultural theatre). Vol. 5, No. 2, Fall-Winter 1983.

Royal Commission on Bilingualism and Biculturalism. *Report.* Ottawa: Queen's Printer, 1967.

Sabbath, Lawrence. "Yiddish Renaissance," *Canadian Theatre Review,* No. 10, Spring 1976.

Drama-in-Education

Barton, Robert, Booth, David, Buckles, Agnes and Moore, William. *Nobody in the Cast.* Don Mills: Longmans Canada, 1969.

Bolton, Gavin. *Towards a Theory of Drama in Education.* London: Longman, 1979.

—. *Drama as Education,* London: Longman, 1984.

Booth, David, and Reynolds, Howard. *Arts: A Survey of Provincial Curricula at the Elementary and Secondary Levels.* Curriculum Committee of the Council of Ministers of Education, Canada, August 1983.

Booth, David W., and Lundy, Charles J. *Improvisation: Learning Through Drama.* Toronto: Academic Press Canada, 1985.

Courtney, Richard. *The Dramatic Curriculum.* London, Ont.: Faculty of Education, University of Western Ontario; New York: Drama Book Specialists and London: Heinemann Educational Books, 1980.

—. *Play, Drama and Thought: The Intellectual Background to Drama-in Education.* 3rd ed. New York: Drama Book Specialists, 1974.

Danby, Mark and Kemp, David. *Drama Through Storytelling:* A Practical Approach for the Teacher of Elementary Grades. Toronto: Simon & Pierre, 1982.

Deverell, Rita Shelton. "Drama-in-Education: Brian Way and the Alternate Catalogue," *Canadian Theatre Review,* No. 41, Winter 1984.

Friedlander, Mira. "Drama-in-Education: Schools After Fame," *Canadian Theatre Review,* No. 41, Winter 1984.

Johnson, Liz, and O'Neill, Cecily. eds. *Dorothy Heathcote: Collected Writings on Education and Drama.* London: Hutchinson, 1984.

Lundy, Charles J., and Booth, David W. *Interpretation: Working With Scripts.* Toronto: Academic Press Canada, 1983.

O'Neill, Cecily and Lambert, Alan. *Drama Structures:* A Practical Handbook for Teachers. London: Hutchinson, 1983.

Slade, Peter. *An Introduction to Child Drama.* London: University of London, 1958.

Tarlington, Carole, and Verriour, Patrick. *Off Stage: Elementary Education Through Drama.* Toronto: Oxford University Press, 1983.

Wagner, Betty Jane, and Heathcote, Dorothy. *Drama as a Learning Medium.* Washington, D.C.: National Education Association, 1976.

Way, Brian. *Development Through Drama.* London: Longman, 1967.

Theatre For Young Audiences

Baker, Jane Howard. *A Teacher's Guide to Theatre for the Young.* Vancouver: Talonbooks, 1978.

Beauchamp, Hélène. ed. *Bibliographie annotée sur le théâtre québécois pour l'enfance et la jeunesse, 1970-1983.* Montréal: Université du Québec à Montréal, 1984.

—. *Les Enfants et le jeu dramatique, Apprivoiser le théâtre.* Bruxelles: A. de Boeck, coll. "Univers des sciences humaines," 1984.

—. *Le Théâtre à la p'tite école.* Québec: Ministère des communications, 1981.

—. "Theatre for Children in Quebec: Complicity, Achievement and Adventure," *Canadian Theatre Review,* No. 41, Winter 1984.

—. *Le Théâtre pour enfants au Québec de 1950 à 1980 — histoire et conditions de son développement.* Montréal: Hurtubise HMH, 1985.

—. Filteau, Louise, and Lasnier, Marie. "Des marionnettes au Québec," *Jeu,* No. 19, 1981.2.

Berger, Jeniva. "Three for the Road," *Scene Changes,* Vol. 6, No. 2, March 1978.

Doolittle, Joyce. "The Child: A Place in the Life," *Canadian Theatre Review,* No. 35, Summer 1982.

—. "Theatre for the Young: A Canadian Perspective," *Canadian Theatre Review,* No. 10, Spring 1976.

—. "Theatre for the Young: Happy Un-birthday Words," *Canadian Theatre Review,* No. 18, Spring 1978.

—. "Theatre for Young Audiences: So Great a Need," *Canadian Theatre Review*, No. 41, Winter 1984.

—. Barnieh, Zina, with Beauchamp, Hélène. *A Mirror of Our Dreams*: Children and the Theatre in Canada. Vancouver: Talonbooks, 1979.

Fairhead, Wayne. "TYA Festivals: Keeping One Step Ahead," *Canadian Theatre Review*, No. 41, Winter 1984.

Foon, Dennis. "TYA Festivals: The Problems of Success," *Canadian Theatre Review*, No. 41, Winter 1984.

"Jeunesse en jeu," *Jeu*, No. 30, 1984.1.

Lewis, Sara Lee. "TYA on the Road: Canada's Intrepid Ambassadors," *Canadian Theatre Review*, No. 41, Winter 1984.

Redfern, Jon. "The Case For Children's Scripts," *Canadian Theatre Review*, No. 10, Spring 1976.

Rioux, Monique, Bilz, Diane, and Boisvert, Jean-Marie. *L'Enfant et l'expression dramatique*. Montréal: Editions de l'Aurore, 1976.

Smith, Patricia Keeney. "Toronto: The International Festival of Children's Theatre," *Canadian Theatre Review*, No. 36, Fall 1982.

Dance In Canada

Bell, Ken, and Franca, Celia. *The National Ballet of Canada*. Toronto: University of Toronto Press, 1978.

Citron, Paula. "The well-choreographed Montreal dance explosion," *Performing Arts in Canada*, Vol. 19, No. 2, Summer 1982.

—. "Women in Dance Part I: The Impact of the Feminine Consciousness" and "Women in Dance: Problems, Demands and Changes," *Dance in Canada*, No. 39, Spring 1984 and No. 42, Winter 1985.

Crabb, Michael. "The First Decade: Dance in Canada After 10 Years," *Dance in Canada*, No. 38, Winter 1983-84.

—. "Robert Desrosiers: Inside You There Is Always Something Trying to Pierce Through the Darkness," *Dance in Canada*, No. 21, Fall 1979.

—. ed. *Visions: Ballet and Its Future*. Essays from the International Dance Conference to Commemorate the 25th Anniversary of the National Ballet of Canada. Toronto: Simon & Pierre, 1978.

—. and Oxenham, Andrew. *Dance Today in Canada*. Toronto: Simon & Pierre, 1977.

Darling, Christopher and Fraser, John. *Kain and Augustyn*. Toronto: Macmillan Canada, 1977.

Geddes, Murray, Grundy, Pamela, Lyons, Sallie, and Parks, Grey. eds. *The Canadian Dancers' Survival Manual*. Toronto: Dancers' Forum of the Dance in Canada Association, 1980.

Hallgren, Chris. "The Mime Climate," *Scene Changes*, Vol. 6, No. 1, January-February 1978.

Hérbert, Lorraine. "Le mime corporel/un théâtre de l'épure: entretien avec Omnibus," *Jeu*, No. 18, 1981.1.

Jackson, Graham. *Dance as Dance*. Scarborough, Ont.: Catalyst, 1978.

Lefebvre, Paul, and Marleau, Denis. "Cet enfant incestueux: table ronde sur la danse-théâtre," *Jeu*, No. 32, 1984.3.

Lorrain, Roland. *Les Grands Ballets Canadiens*. Montréal: Editions du Jour, 1973.

Maguire, Terrill. "Choreography and Music," *Dance in Canada*, No. 9, Summer 1976.

Marleau, Denis. "La danse moderne au Québec: autour d'un témoignage de Jeanne Renaud," *Jeu*, No. 32, 1984.3.

Mason, David, and Street, David. *Karen Kain: Lady of Dance*. Toronto: McGraw Hill, 1978.

Naiman, Sandy. "*Cats* in Toronto: The Staging of a Musical," *Dance in Canada*, No. 43, Spring 1985.

Tembeck, Iro. "East and West and In Between: The Shape of Canadian Dance," *Dance in Canada*, No. 21, Fall 1979.

—. "New Dance in Quebec," *Dance in Canada*, No. 40, Summer 1984.

Weiss, William. "Le mime au Québec," *Jeu*, No. 6, Summer-Fall 1977.

Whittaker, Herbert. *Canada's National Ballet*. Toronto: McClelland and Stewart, 1967.

Windreich, Leland. "Points and Counterpoints at the First Canadian Dance Critics' Conference," *Performing Arts in Canada*, Vol. 22, No. 4, Winter 1983.

Wyman, Max. *The Royal Winnipeg Ballet*. Toronto: Doubleday Canada, 1978.

—. "Who Needs Canadian Dance?", *Dance in Canada*, No. 38, Winter 1983-84.

Opera And Musical Theatre

Baillie, Joan. *Look at the Record: An Album of Toronto's Lyric Theatres 1825-1984*. Oakville, Ont.: Mosaic Press, 1985.

—. "Looking for a Home: Toronto Deserves a Suitable Opera House," *Opera Canada*, Vol. 25, No. 4, Winter 1984.

Beaupré, Thérèse. "Allan Lund's vision: a chip off the old Broadway block," *Performing Arts in Canada*, Vol. 18, No. 1, Spring 1981.

Dyson, Peter, and Sirett, Mark. "Hope for the Future: Ensembles and training programs," *Opera Canada*, Vol. 23, No. 2, Summer 1982.

Freeman, Brian. "Co-opera Theatre: Toward a Canadian definition of Opera," *Scene Changes*, Vol. 6, No. 1, January-February 1978.

Gage, Patricia. "*Aberfan*: the first genuine television opera," *Performing Arts in Canada*, Vol. 14, No. 4, Winter 1977.

Garebian, Keith. "The dusk to dawn journey of *Ra*: Dangerous moments in the theatrical underworld," *Performing Arts in Canada*, Vol. 20, No. 2, August 1983.

Hamelin, Jean. "Pourquoi nos chanteurs d'opéra doivent-ils s'exiler?", *Chatelaine*, Vol. 35, January 1962.

Horenblas, Richard. "Spring Thaw: Everything Old Is New Again," *Scene Changes*, Vol. 8, No. 4, June 1980.

Joyce, Linda. "Come to the Cabaret!", *Performing Arts in Canada*, Vol. 16, No. 2, Summer 1979.

Kallman, Helmut, McPherson, James B., and Potvin, Gilles. "Opera Performance" in *Encyclopedia of Music in Canada*. Helmut Kallman, Gilles Potvin, Kenneth Winters, eds. Toronto: University of Toronto Press, 1981.

Morey, Carl. "25 Years: An *Opera Canada* Sampler," *Opera Canada*, Vol. 26, No. 1, Spring 1985.

Morley, Glenn. "Composing for the Theatre: Contemporary Directions," *Canadian Theatre Review*, No. 15, Summer 1977.

Pannell, Raymond. "Goodnight Co-opera, Sweet Dreams: Co-opera Theatre 1975-83," *Canadian Theatre Review*, No. 40, Fall 1984.

Rudel-Tessier, J. "The Theatre and Canadian Composers," *Canadian Composer*, No. 12, November 1966.

Stuart, Ross. "Musical Theatre" in *Encyclopedia of Music in Canada*. 1981.

—. "Song in a Minor Key: Canada's Musical Theatre," *Canadian Theatre Review*, No. 15, Summer 1977.

"They're Playing Our Song: How Canadian Is Our Musical Theatre?", *Scene Changes*, Vol. 8, No. 6, September-October 1980.

Theatre Training

André, Marion. "Theatre Training in Canada," *Canadian Theatre Review*, No. 17, Winter 1978.

Berger, Jeniva. "Focus on Theatre," *Teen Generation*, Vol. 42, No. 2, May-June 1982.

—. "The Hills Are Alive: The Banff School of Fine Arts," *Scene Changes*, Vol. 9, No. 1, March 1981.

Buck Douglas. "The Case for Management Education," *Canadian Theatre Review*, No. 40, Fall 1984.

Caldwell, Peter. "How to Get There From Here?", *Scene Changes*, Vol. 6, No. 10, December 1978 and Vol. 7, No. 1, January 1979.

Duligal, Susan, ed. *A Directory of Canadian Theatre Schools 1982-83*. Downsview, Ont.: CTR Publications, 1982.

Dupuis, Hervé. *L'Animateur de théâtre et sa formation*. Sherbrooke: Université de Sherbrooke, Option-Théâtre, 1979.

Gélinas, Aline. "Colloque sur la formation en art dramatique à l'U.Q.A.M.," *Jeu*, No.33, 1984.4.

Gruslin, Adrien. "L'enseignement du théâtre au cégep: une pédagogie active et signifiante," *Jeu*, No. 30, 1984.1.

Hébert, Lorraine. "Les écoles de théâtre au Québec: mûres pour une réforme? table ronde avec des formateurs," *Jeu*, No. 33, 1984.4.

Jeanes, Rosemary. "Equity Showcase Workshops: Revitalizing the Actor," *Canadian Theatre Review*, No. 28, Fall 1980.

McDonald, Joanne. ed. *Who Teaches What*. Ottawa: Canadian Conference of the Arts, 1984.

Report of the Committee of Inquiry into Theatre Training in Canada. Ottawa: Canada Council, 1978.

Saint-Denis, Michel. "The National Theatre School of Canada" in his *Training for the Theatre*. New York: Theatre Arts Books, 1982.

Warden, Joanna. "Schools for the performing arts: Of undefined value," *Performing Arts in Canada*, Vol. 20, No. 2, August 1983.

Acting In Canada

"The Canadian Actor at the Crossroads," *Scene Changes,* Vol. 5, No. 8, November 1977.

Dandurand, Anne, and Miljours, Diane. "Au premier plan: l'acteur; table ronde avec des acteurs," *Jeu*, No. 33, 1984.4.

Lapierre, Laurent, with Lagueux, Denis. "Le jeu et les hasards...la fortune et les nécessités," *Jeu*, No. 33, 1984.4.

Latham, David. "Let's Train the Actor, Let's Break the Rules," *Canadian Theatre Review*, No. 35, Summer 1982.

MacDonald, Dan. "Actors' Equity: A Commitment to Canada," *Canadian Theatre Review*, No. 19, Summer 1978.

Michaud, Ginette. "De psychanalyse et de théâtre: trois histoires de cas," *Jeu*, No. 33, 1984.4.

Pavlovic, Diane. "Pour une nouvelle approche du paradoxe du comédien: entretien avec des maîtres actuels," *Jeu*, No. 33, 1984.4.

Thomas, Powys, and Chadwick, Burnard. "On Being a Canadian Actor: Two Perspectives," *Canadian Theatre Review*, No. 1, Winter 1974.

Directing In Canada

Bond, Timothy. "Upstaged: A Canadian Director's Struggle in an Occupied Land," *Canadian Drama*, Vol. 4, No. 2, Fall 1978.

Brassard, André. "Discovering the Nuances," *Canadian Theatre Review*, No. 24, Fall 1979.

Camerlain, Lorraine. "Echos d'une enquête actuelle," *Jeu*, No. 25, 1982.4.

Fernie, Lynne. "Ms. Unseen: Svetlana Zylin, director," *Canadian Theatre Review*, No. 43, Summer 1985.

Gass, Ken. "On Directing Abroad," *Canadian Theatre Review*, No. 1, Winter 1974.

Hirsch, John. "On Directing in Canada," *Canadian Theatre Review*, No. 1, Winter 1974.

McCaughna, David. "Directors and their actors," *Scene Changes,* Vol. 7, No. 4, June 1979.

Ouzounian, Richard. "What's in a Name," *Canadian Theatre Review*, No. 40, Fall 1984.

"Questions de mise en scène," *Jeu*, No. 25, 1982.4.

Wallace, Robert, and Zimmerman, Cynthia. "The Audience and the Season: Four Artistic Directors in Search of a Community," *Canadian Theatre Review*, No. 37, Spring 1983.

Canadian Theatre Design

Acaster, Don. "Lighting Design," *Scene Changes,* Vol. 6, No. 4, 5, 6, May, June, July-August 1978.

Achard, Jan-Rok, and Pavlovic, Diane. "Donner (un) lieu à la complicité? table ronde avec des artisans de la scène," *Jeu*, No. 33, 1984.4.

Bains, Yashdip Singh. "Painted Scenery and Decorations in Canadian Theatres 1765-1825," *Theatre History in Canada*, Vol. 3, No. 2, Fall 1982.

Beaupré, Thérèse. "Susan Benson: Designing the Stratford Festival," *Scene Changes*, Vol. 9, No. 4, June 1981.

Benson, Susan. "Artists Not Craftspeople," *Canadian Theatre Review*, No. 33, Winter 1982.

Cabana, Laure. "Les Costumes au théâtre et leurs modèles dans la peinture," *Vie des Arts*, Vol. 7, Summer 1957.

Doherty, Tom. "Recognizing the Designer," *Canadian Theatre Review*, No. 33, Winter 1982.

Dolgoy, Sholem. "Lighting: Untapped Potential," *Canadian Theatre Review*, No. 33, Winter 1982.

Garebian, Keith. "Desmond Heeley: Premier Designer," *Performing Arts in Canada*, Vol. 21, No. 3, Winter 1984.

—. "Guido Tondino: a first-rate designer in a third world theatre," *Performing Arts in Canada*, Vol. 17, No. 4, Winter 1980.

—. "Vision and vitality in stage design," *Performing Arts in Canada*, Vol. 20, No. 1, April 1983.

Gurik, Renée Noiseux. "Dossier costume: à propos du métier de costumier au théâtre," *Jeu*, No. 31, 1984.2.

Hood, Hugh. "Murray Laufer and the Art of Scenic Design," *Artscanada*, Vol. 29, December 1972-January 1973.

Kerr, Mary. "*Mandragola*: A Designer's Portfolio," *Canadian Theatre Review*, No. 2, Spring 1974.

Laufer, Murray. "Designing at the Centre," *Canadian Theatre Review*, No. 3, Summer 1974.

Manning, Linda. "Gilding the Lilies," *Scene Changes,* Vol. 8, No. 8, December 1980.

Milliken, Paul. "Jim Plaxton brings a new visual innocence to the theatre without walls," *Performing Arts in Canada*, Vol. 19, No. 3, October 1982.

Neil, Boyd. "Set on Design," *Ontario Living,* Vol. 1, No. 2, May 1985.

Noiseux, Ginette. "Dossier costume: de quoi j'me mêle?", *Jeu*, No. 32, 1984.3.

"A la Quadriennale de scénographie de Prague," *Vie des Arts*, Vol. 21, Summer 1976.

Souchotte, Sandra. "Designing Women," *Scene Changes,* Vol. 8, No. 1, January-February 1980.

Strike, Maurice. "The Designer's Dilemma," *Canadian Theatre Review*, No. 1, Winter 1974.

Young, Richard. "Nicholas Cernovitch and the dynamics of light design," *Performing Arts in Canada*, Vol. 20, No. 1, April 1983.

Canadian Theatre Criticism

André, Marion. "Challenging the Critics," *Canadian Theatre Review*, No. 34, Spring 1982.

Arrell, Douglas. "'High Art They Called It': The Theatre Criticism of C.W. Handscomb of the *Manitoba Free Press*," *Canadian Drama*, Vol. 5, No. 2, Fall 1979.

Baldridge, Mary Humphrey. "Canada's Critical Dilemma," *Canadian Theatre Review*, No. 8, Fall 1975.

Selected Bibliography

Bryden, Ronald with Neil, Boyd, eds. *Whittaker's Theatre*. Herbert Whittaker and Theatre in Canada 1944-1975. Toronto: University of Toronto Press, 1985.

Dassylva, Martial. *Un Théâtre en effervescence: Critiques et chroniques 1965-1972*. Montréal: Editions La Presse, 1975.

Davies, Robertson. *The Well-Tempered Critic*: One Man's View of Theatre and Letters in Canada. Judith Skelton Grant, ed. Toronto: McClelland and Stewart, 1981.

Dossier de presse (1966-1981) de Michel Tremblay. Sherbrooke: Séminaire de Sherbrooke, 1981.

Edmonstone, Wayne. *Nathan Cohen. The Making of a Critic*. Toronto: Lester and Orpen, 1977.

Houlé, Léopold. "Notre théâtre et la critique," *Mémoires de la Société royale du Canada*, Vol. 35, May 1941.

Kempf, Yerri. *Les Trois Coups à Montréal: chroniques dramatiques 1959-1964*. Montréal: Déom, 1965.

Kozlinski, Wotjek. "Artists and Critics: Incompatible Yet Inseparable," *Canadian Theatre Review*, No. 33, Winter 1982.

Lavoie, Pierre. "Aimer se faire haïr ou haïr se faire aimer," *Jeu*, No. 31, 1984.2.

Lazarus, John. "Why are the Critics so Bad?", *Canadian Theatre Review*, No. 39, Spring 1984.

Lister, Rota. "The Study and Criticism of Canadian Drama in English," *Canadian Drama*, Vol. 1, No. 2, Fall 1975.

Mailhot, Laurent. "Jean-Claude Germain, critique," *Jeu*, No. 13, Fall 1979.

—. "Le théâtre québécois et la critique universitaire," *Canadian Drama*, Vol. 1, No. 2, Fall 1975.

Melançon, Robert. "Ne tirez pas sur la critique," *Liberté*, No. 134, March-April 1981.

Noonan, James. "The Critics Criticized: An Analysis of Reviews of James Reaney's *The Donnelly's* on National Tour," *Canadian Drama*, Vol. 3, No. 2, Fall 1977.

Piazza, François. "Le critique dans le théâtre," *La Barre du Jour*, Vol. 1, Nos. 3-5, Fall 1977.

Rubin, Don. "The Critical Response," *Canadian Theatre Review*, No. 8, Fall 1975.

Sawyer, Deborah C. "Herbert Whittaker: Insights of a drama critic," *Scene Changes*, Vol. 8, No. 1, March 1980.

Snowdon, Annette and Kelly, Mary. "Critics: The Last Word," *Scene Changes*, Vol. 8, No. 1, March 1980.

Wagner, Anton. "Dr. Lawrence Mason: Music and Drama Critic 1924-1939," *Theatre History in Canada*, Vol. 4, No. 1, Spring 1983.

—. "From Art to Theory: Canada's Critical Tools," *Canadian Theatre Review*, No. 34, Spring 1982.

Acknowledgements

The Canadian Theatre Critics Association/Association des Critiques de Théâtre du Canada is grateful for the generous assistance of many individuals, theatres and arts organizations which made the publication of *Contemporary Canadian Theatre: New World Visions* possible.

These include the board of directors of the Canadian Centre of the International Theatre Institute (English-language), particularly Curtis Barlow, Executive Director, Professional Association of Canadian Theatres; Steve Dymond, Executive Director, *Dance in Canada* and Jane Buss, Executive Director, Playwrights Union of Canada; Canadian Actors' Equity Association; Robert Wallace, Editor, *Canadian Theatre Review*; Michel Vaïs and the cahiers de théâtre *Jeu*, Ray Ellenwood and our translators, Mark Czarnecki, Audrey Camiré, Barbara A. Kerslake, Elliot Shek and Anton Wagner; Len Doucette, Roy Higgins, Ben Shek and Ross Stuart for their many valuable editorial suggestions; Allan Wells, Association of Community Theatres-Central Ontario; Jennifer Kasper, Fairview Library Theatre; and Richard Mortimer, Arts Branch, Wintario Programme, Ontario Ministry of Citizenship and Culture.

The CTCA would like particularly to thank Marian M. Wilson, Publisher and General Editor of Simon & Pierre for her unstinting support of this project and for publishing this comprehensive collection within an extremely short period of time.

The editor would like to express a personal note of thanks to the CTCA Editorial Advisory Committee, Jeniva Berger, Herbert Whittaker, Don Rubin, Mira Friedlander and Renate Usmiani, for their assistance and advice in editing *Contemporary Canadian Theatre*. The editor would also like to thank the Social Sciences and Humanities Research Council of Canada for its ongoing support of Canadian theatre and drama studies.

Anton Wagner, Editor

Photo Acknowledgements

The Canadian Theatre Critics Association is grateful to the following for use of photographs and illustrations

Canadian Theatre Review, pp. 52, 72, 76, 79, 98, 104, 108, 110, 115, 162, 164, 172, 259, 290;

Cahiers de théâtre *Jeu*, pp. 56, 63, 64, 66, 119, 123, 201, 202, 290, 304, 307, 332, 334;

CentreStage, p. 2;

University of Toronto Thomas Fisher Rare Book Library, p. 18;

Canadian Opera Company, pp. 12, 277;

National Ballet of Canada, p. 18;

Canadian Broadcasting Corporation and National Film, Television and Sound Archives, Public Archives of Canada, pp. 26, 179, 181;

Stratford Festival, pp. 31, 151, 325;

Centaur Theatre, pp. 38, 135, 314;

Citadel Theatre, pp. 43, 317;

Brigit Shim, Brian Arnott Associates, pp. 85-94;

Les Productions J.C. Lespérance, p. 129;

Carbone 14, p. 131;

National Arts Centre Archives, p. 139;

Factory Theatre, p. 145;

Shaw Festival, pp. 156;

Tamahnous Theatre, p. 168;

CBC TV, pp. 191, 193;

Richard Courtney, pp. 209, 211, 212;

Latvian D.V. Theatre, p. 221;

Black Theatre Canada, p. 224;

Theatre Ontario, p. 231;

Brampton Musical Society, p. 232;

Wayne Fairhead, pp. 240, 242;

Théâtre de la Marmaille, p. 249;

Théâtre Petit à Petit, p. 250;

Young People's Theatre, p. 257;

Royal Winnipeg Ballet, p. 264;

Axis: Dance, p. 270;

Danny Grossman Dance Company, p. 272;

Comus Music Theatre, p. 279;

Department of Theatre, York University, p. 288;

R.H. Thomson, p. 295;

Tarragon Theatre, pp. 298, 324;

Herbert Whittaker, pp. 341, 342.

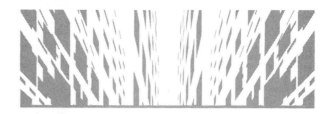

Index

SIMON & PIERRE WINS GOLD AWARD/FIFTH TRIENNIAL INTERNATIONAL EXHIBITION OF THEATRE BOOKS AND PERIODICALS. NOVI SAD, YUGOSLAVIA, 1979 — A FIRST FOR CANADA

Simon & Pierre received the Gold Award for the systematic fostering of theatre publications; the Silver Award went to Cambridge University Press. Other past Gold Award winners, in the same class, have included Gallimard, Paris; Editions du Seuil, Paris; Institute for Art History, Ministry of Culture, USSR; Guilio Einaudi, Turin, Italy. 2,000 books from 360 publishers in 70 countries competed.

Simon & Pierre displayed 50 titles in their Bastet Books, Canplay Series and Simon & Pierre lines. These included illustrated paperback and hardcover volumes. Titles ranged from musical comedy through drama and children's plays, to the history of dance in Canada.

Canadian Book Review Annual 1975-1984

New Canadian books in 18 subject areas are reviewed by specialists, within five basic categories: Reference Materials, Humanities and Applied Arts, Literature, Social Sciences, Science and Technology. CBRA's reviews are brief and include bibliographic information indexed by Subject, Author and Title. The performing arts are included in the Humanities and Applied Arts, and new Drama titles under Literature.

Established 1972

 Simon & Pierre Publishing Co. Ltd.
Les Editions Simon & Pierre Ltée

P.O. Box 280 Adelaide Street Postal Station
Toronto, Ontario, Canada M5C 2J4

Plays by Antonine Maillet, translated by Luis de Céspedes

La Sagouine
Evangeline Deusse
Gapi and Sullivan

Childrens Plays

Bastet Books — A Collection of Canadian Plays, Volume 4

Land of Magic Spell
Which Witch is Which?
The Clam Made a Face
Nuts & Bolts & Rusty Things
King Grumbletum & the Magic Pie
Professor Fuddle
Cyclone Jack
Billy Bishop & the Red Baron
Masque
Catalyst

Canplay Series

Put on the Spot
When Everybody Cares
Happy Holly
Christmas Cards
Let's Hear it for Christmas
The Naciwonki Cap
Robena's Rose-Colored Glasses
The Haunted Castle
Cat's Cradle
Twice Six Plus One

Audition Books

"And what are you going to do for us?"
Encore! Encore!

Theatre Books for the Classroom

Drama Through Story telling (K-10)
*Acting Techniques, Volume 1, Introductory Level
*Acting Techniques, Volume 2, Intermediate Level
*Acting Techniques, Volume 3, Senior Level
*Acting Techniques, Volume 4, Scene Study
*Teacher's Handbook, Volume 5, Includes all material from Volumes 1-4
*Publication 1986

Canadian Theatre History Series

Canadian Theatre History No. 1, Love & Whisky (1606-1972)
Canadian Theatre History No. 2, Prairie Theatre (1833-1982)
Canadian Theatre History No. 3, The Seats of the Mighty (1897)
Canadian Theatre History No. 4, Stage Left (1929-1940)

Canadian Dramatists Series

Canadian Dramatists No. 1, Politics and the Playwright — George Ryga

Dance Books

Dance Today in Canada
Visions: Ballet and Its Future

Other theatre and dance books by Simon & Pierre

Bastet Books

A Collection of Canadian Plays, Volumes 1-5

A Collection of Canadian Plays, Volume 1
Counsellor Extraordinary
Wu-feng
Love Mouse; Meyer's Room
Colour the Flesh the Colour of Dust
Exit Muttering

A Collection of Canadian Plays, Volume 2
Wedding in White
Three Women
The Devil's Instrument
The Pile; The Store; Inside Out
Westbound 12:01

A Collection of Canadian Plays, Volume 3
Marsh Hay
The Unreasonable Act of Julian Waterman
The Twisted Loaf; Soft Voices
Vicky
The Vice President

A Collection of Canadian Plays, Volume 4
Land of Magic Spell; Which Witch is Which?
The Clam Made a Face; Nuts & Bolts & Rusty Things
King Grumbletum & the Magic Pie; Professor Fuddle
Cyclone Jack; Billy Bishop & the Red Baron
Masque; Catalyst

A Collection of Canadian Plays, Volume 5
Four to Four
Greta, the Divine
Waiting for Gaudreault; A Little Bit Left
Dodo
Looking for a Job
Are You Afraid of Thieves?
Curriculum Comments (C.C.P. Volumes 1,2&3)
***Curriculum Comments (C.C.P. Volume 4)**

Each play is available in a single paperback.

Canplay Series

Popular Performance Plays of Canada, Volume 1
The Donnellys
A Wife in the Hand
Hoarse Muse
Put on the Spot; When Everybody Cares
What Glorious Times They Had—Nellie McClung

Popular Performance Plays of Canada, Volume 2
Mayonnaise
D'Arcy
Happy Holly; Christmas Cards
You'll Get Used to It!...The War Show

Each play is available in a single paperback.